THE
VIOLATE
MAN

THE VIOLATE MAN

MALE/MALE RAPE IN THE AMERICAN IMAGINATION

AARON C. THOMAS

VANDERBILT UNIVERSITY PRESS
Nashville, Tennessee

Copyright 2025 Vanderbilt University Press
All rights reserved
First printing 2025

Library of Congress Cataloging-in-Publication Data
Names: Thomas, Aaron C. author
Title: The violate man : male--male rape in the American imagination / Aaron C. Thomas.
Description: Nashville : Vanderbilt University Press, 2025. | Includes bibliographical references and index.
Identifiers: LCCN 2025007163 (print) | LCCN 2025007164 (ebook) | ISBN 9780826508140 paperback | ISBN 9780826508157 hardcover | ISBN 9780826508164 epub | ISBN 9780826508171 pdf
Subjects: LCSH: Male rape in popular culture | Popular culture--United States
Classification: LCC P96.R35 T46 2025 (print) | LCC P96.R35 (ebook) | DDC 362.883920973--dc23/eng/20250416
LC record available at https://lccn.loc.gov/2025007163
LC ebook record available at https://lccn.loc.gov/2025007164

Contents

Acknowledgments   vii
Introduction. The Violate Man   1

1 The New Prison Drama: Male/Male Rape on Stage   32

2 How to Make a Man: Male/Male Rape
   in Mid-Century Fiction   59

3 After the Production Code: Male/Male Rape
   in 1970s Cinema   96

4 Revenge Tarantino-Style: Male/Male Rape
   in 1990s Cinema   130

5 Testimony and Television: Male/Male Rape
   on Cable and Network TV   168

6 On Closure and Openness   207

Notes   219
Bibliography   251
Index   267

Acknowledgments

This book would not have happened without the advice, wisdom, and support of my editor at Vanderbilt, Gianna Mosser. A series of notes Gianna gave me at the annual meeting for the American Society for Theatre Research in 2023 considerably shifted the trajectory of this book and has strengthened it enormously. Working with the faith and support of a brilliant and insightful editor is one of the best gifts a writer can receive, and I have been privileged to have Gianna working with me on this book.

In 2017, I attended the National Endowment for the Humanities Summer Institute "Diverse Philosophical Approaches to Sexual Violence," led by Ann Cahill with faculty mentors including Susan Brison and Nicola Gavey. This summer institute impacted the book tremendously, shifting my thinking and forcing me to articulate the ways that a focus on male victims might ask us to interrogate many of the widely held principles in sexual violence studies. I cannot articulate how important the wisdom of, especially, Ann Cahill and Nicola Gavey has been for this research. At Elon University that summer I met many fellow travelers without whom I could not have written this book, especially Ashley Currier, who read and gave me feedback on the entire introduction, Angelique Szymanek, Amy King, Vicki Ketz, Sarah Fischer, Jamila Small, Michael Deckard, Gabriela Torres, Heather Hlavka, and Dianna Taylor.

The annual meeting of the American Society for Theatre Research has been my intellectual home for many years, and I am grateful for the support of my mentors and colleagues there, especially Brian Herrera, Nick Salvato, Patricia Ybarra, Henry Bial, Sarah Bay-Cheng, Pannill Camp, Noe Montez, Kate Bredeson, Donatella Galella, Kareem Khubchandani, Enzo Vasquez Toral, Paige McGinley, Donovan Sherman, Jacob Gallagher-Ross, John Muse, Miriam Felton-Dansky, David Calder, Tina Post, Joy Brooke Fairfield, Christine Mok, Gibson Cima, and the late Roger Bechtel. Thank you all for challenging my thinking and pushing my ideas in new directions.

I have been working on the research that would become *The Violate Man* since approximately 2007, when I began working on a literary analysis of the David Rudkin dramas *The Sons of Light*, *Afore Night Come*, and *The Triumph of Death*, which are not well known in the US but that influenced me a great deal. In graduate school at the School of Theatre at Florida State University, my closest mentor was Mary Karen Dahl, who wrote about violence and British drama, and it seemed almost a given that I would write about representations of violence and the ethics of those representations. Mary Karen taught me a great deal about how to write and how to read, and her influence is everywhere in these pages. In those early stages of working on research that would be incorporated into this book I would send long passages to Mark Lunsford, Michael Fatica, Michael Stablein, and Catie Humphreys so they could keep me honest about my writing goals, and I frequently still think of them as my readers when I write. My colleagues in graduate school have all influenced this book in one way or another, but Anne Towns, Ryan Clark, Julie Haverkate, Meghan Digneit, Joel Waage, Caleb Custer, and Enrico DiGiuseppe, in particular, have helped shaped the book's content.

The research for this book has been ongoing for a long time, and I've lived and worked in many places since it began. I am grateful for my friends and colleagues at Dartmouth College, especially Analola Santana, Irma Mayorga, Laura Edmondson, Dan Kotlowitz, Jamie Horton, David LaGuardia, Emily Kane, Keith Walker, Maral Yessayan, and Lucas Hollister, who read one of the earliest versions of Chapter 4. Special gratitude to the Société de Sandwich—yasser elhariry, Katie Hornstein, Viktor Witkowski, and Jonathan Mullins—for your wisdom, hilarity, and support. Thanks, too, to my friends and colleagues at the University of Central Florida, especially Julia Listengarten, David Reed, Chung Park, Vandy Wood, Cynthia White, Kody Grassett, Kate Ingram, Kristina Tollefson, and the late Mark Brotherton. At Florida State, I have been supported by colleagues and friends, especially Jason Tate, Meredith Lynn, Chari Arespacochaga, Jason Regnier, Greg Marcks, Tarik Doğru, Kellen Hoxworth, Hannah Schwadron, Dave Rodriguez, Malia Bruker, Jorge Hernández, Casey Sammarco, Christina Owens, Michael Franklin, Daniel Luedtke, Sukanya Chakrabarti, Lilian Garcia-Roig, Kris Salata, Allison Spence, Preston McLane, Yelena McLane, Brad Brock, Mona Bozorgi, Leah Hunter, Kate Gelabert, Colleen Muscha, Elliott Turley, Elizabeth Osborne, Yizhou Huang, Sarah Fahmy, Madeleine Martin, Jen Gillette, Leah Sherman, and Tony Gunn. You all have made my life endlessly richer, and I am so grateful.

I am thankful, as always, to my family and friends in California, too, especially Deborah, Sheila, Mia, Hannah, Julius, Dayne, Jordan, Ayana, Elizabeth, Justin, Ashley, Danny, Linda, Matt, Julie, Bobby, Sarah, Derek, John, and Tom.

Thank you, too, to my family in and around Endstation Theatre Company, Matt Silva, Walter and Jeanne Kmiec, Geoff and Ashley Kershner, Krista Franco and Drew Becker, Chris Martin, Joshua Mikel, Katie Cassidy and Nick Rabe, Jude Flannelly and Stephanie Spry, Chris Merlino, Chris Bailey, Stephanie and Patrick Earl, Bob and Kathy Chase, John Gregory and Carrie Brown, Makeda Payne, Kathy Clay, Deepsikha Chatterjee, Dan Gallagher and Angie Sweigart-Gallagher, John Kiselica, Kelly Dudley, Chris Evans, and George Carruth.

My most treasured sounding boards in this academic life continue to be Patrick McKelvey, Jessica Del Vecchio, Michelle Liu Carriger, Joe Cermatori, and Lindsay Brandon Hunter, who helpfully read the introduction at a very late stage. I don't have words for how much I appreciate your friendship, intelligence, and humor.

An early version of Chapter 1 was originally published in *Theatre Survey* under the editorial eye of Esther Kim Lee. See Aaron C. Thomas, "The Queen's Cell: *Fortune and Men's Eyes* and the New Prison Drama," *Theatre Survey* 55, no. 2 (2014), 165–84, © Cambridge University Press, reproduced with permission. I am also grateful for the work of David Bruin, who published my essay "Truth and Translation at the Heart of Violence," in which I worked out some of these ideas, in the journal *Theater*.

Introduction

The Violate Man

> You'll be sorry that you messed with the U-S-of-A
> 'Cause we'll put a boot in your ass; it's the American way.
> — TOBY KEITH, *Unleashed*

The Violate Man is about the discourse of male/male rape in US American culture since the mid-1960s. Male/male rape, we are told, is something about which people rarely speak and that is surrounded by codes of silence. Powerful cultural forces work to keep male rape victims quiet and keep serious discussion of male/male rape at a minimum.[1] But if male/male rape is a topic that we discuss infrequently (or at least one that we tell ourselves we discuss infrequently), the number of male/male rape narratives on television and in movies has increased exponentially since the 1960s, and for the last twenty years, news media have offered statistics and stories about incidents of male/male rape with increasing regularity. *The Baltimore Sun* reported in 2013 that a male sailor in the United States Navy who was raped by a fellow sailor was ordered by his commanders not to report the assault, triggering a hearing in the US Senate in order to investigate the way the military justice system deals with sexual violence.[2] A year later in 2014, the men's magazine *GQ* ran a damning story on sexual violence in the US military titled "Son, Men Don't Get Raped," that opened with the chilling sentences: "According to the Pentagon, thirty-eight military men are sexually assaulted every single day. These are the stories you never hear—because the culprits almost always go free, the survivors rarely speak, and no one in the military or Congress has done enough to stop it."[3] Most notably, in early 2010, David Kaiser and Lovisa Stannow of the organization

Just Detention International (formerly Stop Prisoner Rape) began a series of eight articles in *The New York Review of Books* reporting on the serious crisis of prison rape in US carceral systems, including in juvenile institutions and detention facilities administered by the Department of Homeland Security (now Immigration and Customs Enforcement or ICE). And although the federal Prison Rape Elimination Act was signed into law by President George W. Bush in 2003, twelve years later *The New York Times* noted that little had changed: several states have resisted complying with implementation of the law, and only minimal consequences are in place that might convince state governments to comply.[4]

News reports of male/male rape have not been restricted to describing assaults in prisons or in US military barracks. The Taguba Report, the Army's military inquiry into the Abu Ghraib prisoner abuse scandal in 2004, includes reports of rapes of teenage male detainees and the rape of an adult male detainee with "a phosphoric light."[5] And in 2011 a trio of volunteer firefighters in Piermont, New York, a wealthy, majority-white town of about 2,600 people, were accused of putting initiates through a ritual that included forcing a young recruit "to sodomize an existing firefighter."[6] If male/male rape, in other words, is a topic about which we do not often speak or that is surrounded by silence, it is also clear that we ought not to think of it as a mere *topic*. Data demonstrate and newsmedia reports substantiate that male/male rape is a lived reality in US American society, a health crisis in US American prisons, a rising epidemic in the US military, and a significant component of the problem of sexual assault on US college campuses.[7]

How we, as consumers of these news stories, are asked to think about male/male rape, however, is a subject that has been given very little academic consideration. This isn't to say that there is no work at all on same-sex sexual assault. To the contrary, scholars in the fields of criminology, sociology, and social work have all written serious inquiries into the phenomenon, but male/male rape has been understood perpetually as an *emergent* issue since the 1960s, as though we must always say—before discussing it—that it isn't something we normally discuss.[8] Further, because of cultural resistance to talking about male/male rape, our *thinking* about these acts of violence has remained unsophisticated, informed neither by academic studies about its causes, its frequency, or its prevention nor by educational programs that provide structured methods for considering the experience or effects of male/male rape. To the contrary, the way that we think about male/male rape draws primarily on artistic and informal discourse rather than sociological or criminological discourse about this violence: from rumors and innuendo circulated either casually or maliciously; from news stories that report such incidents in order to shock or sensationalize; from jokes that are often aimed at the expense of an imagined rape victim; and from fictional representations that are embedded within narrative structures such as films, television episodes, novels, commercials, plays, and other performances. This informal and artistic discourse—jokes, narrative representations, rumors, and short newsmedia segments—currently shapes our society's thinking about male/male rape. It is this discourse that *The Violate Man* addresses.

This book follows a history of male/male rape discourse in the United States, beginning in the 1960s. It charts the development of that discourse, describing the different ways that male/male rape narratives have asked us to think about sexual violence over the last sixty years. This discourse has been, and continues to be, productive of our thinking about the real world. *The Violate Man* finds that these narratives establish—and often maintain or reinforce—long-standing racialized and sexualized traditions about where male/male rape happens, who commits it, why it is committed, and which of us is vulnerable to its victimization. But, as Edward Said once said in his book on the discourse of the Orient, "The things to look at are style, figures of speech, setting, narrative devices, historical and social circumstances, *not* the correctness of the representation nor its fidelity to some great original."[9] What appear, in other words, to be "accurate" representations of male/male rape are produced by a long-established discourse *about* male/male rape. The most influential of these rape narratives also reinforce a complex series of masculinist assumptions that produce the male body as able-bodied, whole, and impenetrable, disallowing bodies broken by violence, sexual and otherwise, from the very category of male.

The title of this book is intended to illustrate linguistically some of the slippages and couplings that attend our cultural conceptions of male/male rape. The adjective *violate* in my title is an archaic usage that describes one who has been violated, one to whom violence has been done. *Violate* in this usage is also homophonous with the color *violet*, a shade often used to indicate queerness or gayness, and in this way my title rehearses or repeats the way that discussions of male/male rape refract around bodies: to speak about a man having been violated is to speak about him as *violate*, but one cannot help but also sense that he is *violet*. As this book will make clear, the act of rape, even the suggestion of rape, is often also a way of indicating or accusing a man of queerness. One can also easily hear the word *violent* lurking just below the word *violate/violet*: the two sound eerily similar, and although there is no natural link between queerness and violence, the two are often linked discursively, as we will see.[10] Implicit in my title, then, are the following connections and assumptions that I argue are already commonplace in US American culture: A body that has been violated—any violate body—is discursively or culturally transformed into a *violet* body, one that is feminized or homosexualized. And queer bodies—violate, violet bodies—are always already assumed to be *violent* bodies, that is bodies with the potential to commit predatory violence.

Narratively, the perpetrator of male/male sexual violence is nearly always represented as a queer figure—in many cases he stands in for queerness as such—and violence against this deviant, violent figure comes to be easily justified. But the standard narrative of the violate man, in fact, works in two directions. In many ways, representations of male/male rape barely differentiate between victims and perpetrators. *Both* become contaminated by the act of violence that one commits and another suffers. Discourse about male/male rape frequently sees both men as culpable, both as deviant, both as tainted. In these narratives, the violate man is homosexualized or queered by the violence committed against him, and this transforms him into someone with an allegedly inherent, deviant sexuality. This sexual deviance is, in turn, claimed to be violently predatory: his queerness transforms him into someone who can now be accused of possessing an essential urge to sexual violence. The perpetrator's erotic desire *for* the violate man is disavowed in this narrative because the violate man is himself presented as the one possessing deviant erotic desires and sexually violent urges. The rape victim is reimagined as a sexual predator. Violence *against* this violet/violent man can then be easily justified. In this ideological formulation, the violate man deserves to be further violated, incarcerated, or destroyed because he is a deviant sexual threat to society as a whole.

This particular ideological formulation ought to sound strikingly familiar because it has an obvious historical model: in the United States a very similar logic to this one produces the narrative of the Black male rapist.[11] In the standard lynching narrative propagated by white supremacy—one that has had enormous influence on the lives of Black men and boys in the United States—the Black man is transformed by the sexualized violence and erotic fantasies aimed at his violated body into someone who is himself accused of being sexually deviant, sexually violent, and aggressive.[12] These supposedly essential qualities of the Black man have historically justified his castration and lynching, and they are used at present to justify his surveillance, abuse, incarceration, and murder. As Carlyle Van Thompson argues, however, "the lynching of African Americans is not a simple ritual of racial hatred, but . . . also a ritual of intense sexual desire for the Black body. . . . Within the discourse of white supremacy, the Black body becomes defined as sexually undesirable, but, in a perverse manner, the ritual of lynching allows the white Americans involved as spectators and participants the freedom to express their often-sadistic sexual desires."[13] Here, too, it is the erotic desire *for* the violate man that this rape discourse disavows.[14]

I want to begin this book by describing two seemingly dissimilar narratives of male/male rape from the last decade. These two cases are linked by the fact that they both discuss male/male sexual violence, both have erotic and racialized dimensions, and both involve the criminal justice system, though they might seem otherwise unrelated. My goal, however, is to demonstrate links between discourses of male/male rape in newsmedia and discourses of male/male rape in popular media such as film, television, and fiction—to chart connections between the ways that narratives ask us to think about male/male rape and the real-world consequences of those narrative frames. This first brief section serves a secondary function as well: it is a reminder that if we say that we do not often speak about it, male/male rape nevertheless appears with frequency in the newsmedia that inform us and in the media that entertain us—as it does in the "patriotic" lyrics by Toby Keith that serve as the epigraph to this introduction. The two incidents below reflect ways that we are, in our culture, already choosing to speak about male/male rape, and that these discourses are accessible via media that large numbers of people already consume.

An Idaho Locker Room

In 2015, in a widely publicized incident, newsmedia reported that a group of white teenagers in Idaho, including a young man named John R. K. Howard, assaulted their mentally disabled Black teammate in a locker room by shoving a coat hanger up his rectum and then kicking the coat hanger. In a court hearing later that year, the young victim described the incident, saying, "Pain that I have never felt took over my body." The victim's family filed a civil suit against the school, alleging that the young man victimized by the assault had also been subjected to racist verbal attacks by his teammates for many months prior to the act of sexual violence.

In the criminal case against Howard in 2017, however, the judge sentenced the teenager responsible for the assault to a mere 300 hours of community service. Reporting on the sentence, the *Guardian*'s journalist could barely contain her outrage at this decision, stating that "In a series of extraordinary remarks, district judge Randy J. Stoker on Friday accused the press and the public for misrepresenting what happened in a rural Idaho high school locker room on 22 October 2015, lamenting 'people from the east coast have no idea what this case is about.'" Judge Stoker's statement is indeed astonishing. "This is not a rape case," he declared. "This is not a sex case. This started out as penetration with a foreign object. . . . Whatever happened in that locker room was not sexual. It wasn't appropriate. There's nothing in this record that supports anything close to the sexual allegation against this young man."[15] *Essence* magazine further quoted Idaho deputy attorney general Casey Hemmer as saying that "it's not our belief that this was a racially motivated crime. This was more of a vulnerable-victim motivated crime. I think it probably would have happened to anybody that was in the same kind of circumstances and mental state as the victim here."[16]

It is important to note that the testimony of the victim in this Idaho case has repeatedly been called into question, and the young man both changed his story and also asked specifically for the judge to be lenient to the assailants. The judge's reticence to sentence the assailant harshly might, therefore, have reasons other than the ones he stated in his remarks to the press. Still, what we can read quite clearly in Judge Stoker's remarks is a hostility toward the way the press reported the sexual assault: Stoker fundamentally disagreed with their way of framing this act of violence, referring to it as "not sexual," "not rape," "not sex." What happened in this Idaho locker room, however, was plainly a violent, penetrative assault in the rectum of one young man, and it was perpetrated by a group of other young men. It might, therefore, seem obvious to the *Guardian*'s journalist—and indeed to a majority of the newspaper's readers—that the violence committed by John Howard ought to be classified as rape or sexual assault.

But let us take Judge Stoker's conviction seriously and ask ourselves what the implications are when we refer to kicking a coat hanger that has been inserted into a young man's rectum as sex. In what way, actually, does it make sense to refer to this as a sexual act? What does it mean to talk about this as though it is rape? If we believe that such an act of violence *is* rape—and I do—what, then, does this designation mean, and how is an act of rape such as this related to acts of rape with which we are more familiar or acts of rape that (we believe) we understand better, such as date rape, stranger rape, prisoner rape, or marital rape?

Reading this assault as rape, here, prioritizes the experience of the violate man. Even if we assume that the assailant in this case did not experience an erotic charge, did not see what he was doing as sexual, does not usually penetrate his sexual partners in these ways—assumptions we cannot and should not make—it is highly likely that the experience of the victim will have been comparable in many ways to victims of other acts of rape. He certainly will have needed the types of medical and psychiatric care given to rape survivors in other contexts.

In Judge Stoker's formulation, however, an act of rape must be sex; for Stoker, the act of violence must also be (recognizable to him as) a *sexual* act in order for it to be rape. In other words, although it was a central premise of Susan Brownmiller's influential 1975 book *Against Her Will* that rape is an act of violence and not sex, Judge Stoker remained unconvinced of this argument in 2018.[17] Or rather, it is more accurate to say that Stoker's ruling is unable to envision the homoerotic, sexual, and gendered dynamics that might be involved in this violent, penetrative assault committed by a man on the body of another man. Judge Stoker's ruling further disregards what Black cultural critics as long ago as Frantz Fanon and James Baldwin have illuminated: that white men physically and sexually assault Black men precisely because of urges that are sexual.[18]

What is essential to appreciate about this event and the discourse surrounding it is that although there might be an understanding in the United States among a certain group of people (those Judge Stoker labels "people from the east coast") about the definition of rape, this understanding is not universally shared. And although, thanks to the work of second-wave feminists, we may now be able to articulate clearly our understandings about rape if a woman is the victim and a man is the perpetrator, our ideas about rape become confused, even inarticulable, when the victim of rape is a young man, especially when that young man is disabled and Black.

But although we might seem unable to make sense of the erotic, sexual, and gendered dynamics of sexual assault when a man is the victim, we nevertheless already possess a set of ideas about male victims and male perpetrators of rape, and these ideas have real-world consequences. What I am arguing, in other words, is that our ideas about rape and what rape *means*, inarticulable and inchoate though they may often be, derive directly from narrative discourses—in media reports, novels, movies, and television—that frame and make sense of male/male rape for us.

The consequences of these narratives are profound. It is these discourses that inform, in the first place, the actual violent assault that was committed by Howard and his teammates and, in the second place, Judge Stoker's interpretation of it. I want further to argue that the *only* way to begin to form an explanation for what Howard and his teammates did to their young male victim is to think about the dimensions of race, ability, sexuality, and eroticism that attended their violent act, even though these were precisely the dimensions that Judge Stoker's ruling disavowed.

A Punch Line

The tightly edited official trailer for David Palmer and Dax Shepard's movie *Hit & Run* promised its 2012 audience a particular brand of summer entertainment. The trailer is filled with action: gunfire, an assault with a golf club, Beau Bridges throwing an excellent punch, and numerous car-chase shots—tires spinning, dust rising, speed. The trailer also indicates that *Hit & Run* will be very funny. Kristin Chenoweth delivers a great joke early on about mixing Xanax with alcohol, and there is another, slightly more overused, bit in which a group of thirtysomethings accidentally walks into a motel room containing a group of scantily clad sexagenarians. In a later sequence Tom Arnold runs after his own minivan, firing his gun ineptly in the vehicle's direction. In short, the film promises to be both funny and exciting: "from the producer of *Wedding Crashers*," a new action-comedy aimed primarily at teenage and adult males.[19]

The tentpole joke of the trailer arrives at its end. Bradley Cooper, outfitted with bleach-blond dreadlocks, screams at Shepard that he is angry at his friend because he sent him to jail for eight months. Shepard's response is an acerbic bit of cleverness: "What? You didn't like the gym equipment?" The laugh, however, is cut short as we hear Cooper say "I got . . . in prison. Because of you." In the trailer, the ellipsis is replaced by the loud honk of a semi-trailer, and rather than focusing on the men in the conversation, the camera focuses on the face of the film's female star, Kristen Bell, who looks away from us, slightly horrified, a feeling the audience might presumably be supposed to share. The trailer takes a beat and then Shepard responds.

"I'm really, really sorry," he says. ". . . Was it a Black guy?"

In the film itself, Cooper and Shepard's exchange about prison rape is slightly more complex, but it is enough to note here, as we look at the trailer, that *Hit & Run* was promoted to its intended audience with a prison rape joke as its hook. In other words, the film's marketing team took the chance that a racialized joke about prison rape would appeal to its target audience, and they were correct. Perhaps even more interestingly, *Hit & Run*'s marketing team quite accurately assumed that the coded phrase "I got . . . in prison. Because of you" could be easily and immediately decoded by its audience. When Cooper says "I got . . . in prison," for some reason *we all know that what happened to him in prison is that he was raped.* He doesn't actually need to say so. In truth, however, it is neither obvious nor natural that we should assume that Cooper's character has been a victim of sexual violence. Mightn't he have been severely beaten in prison? Or stabbed? Or even tortured? Mightn't he have been forcibly initiated into a gang or otherwise humiliated? Indeed, once we have considered these possibilities, is not each of them, in fact, more likely to have occurred to Cooper's character than rape?

I draw three conclusions from this brief exchange. First, male/male rape has been encoded in our cultural imaginary in such a way that we can quite easily know and agree—within the time span of a very short television spot—that we are talking about rape even without anyone saying that rape is the topic under discussion. *Hit & Run*'s marketing team assumed precisely this. Second, prison has been linked epistemologically with sexual violence through our discourse, and if this linkage can easily be put to comedic uses, it can certainly be put to ideological, even political uses. Further, prison rape has become naturalized as something that simply makes sense to us. We have come to understand rape in prison as a normalized *fact* rather than say, a crisis, or something that horrifies us. Indeed, prison rape's facticity, here, is simply used as a joke. Third and finally, although male/male rape is often described as underreported, underexamined, or rare, many of us, at the same time, seem to believe that we know a good amount about "what goes on in prison." This "knowledge" is racialized in such a way that the standard image of the assailant of a prison rape is a Black man and that of his victim a handsome white man. In fact, we believe ourselves to know so much about the supposedly undiscussed phenomenon of male/male rape that a marketing team can reasonably expect a majority of people to laugh at the punch line *Was it a Black guy?*

The Power of Male/Male Rape Discourse

A trailer for a crime–heist comedy film with a reference to prison rape as its central joke might seem to have little to do with a group of young men sexually assaulting another young man with a coat hanger in an Idaho locker room three years later, but it is the argument of *The Violate Man* not only that these two events are linked but that linking them helps us to understand them both, that discourse about male/male rape has accrued and developed according to specific patterns over time, and that acts of male/male rape in the real world are not only interpreted according to these discourses, they are informed by them. Because, for example, we believe we know that male/male rape has become a fact of prison life, male/male rape comes to seem less plausible in other spaces such as locker rooms, military barracks, and apartments. Discourse about male/male rape frequently relegates such violence to the space of the prison, offering to us the idea that it is "prisoners" who rape other men and making it more difficult for us to believe that a man who is not a prisoner would commit violence of this sort. Further, because discourse about prison rape since the late 1960s has commonly identified Black men as rapists and white men as victims, a Black man becomes the obvious candidate as the rapist in the *Hit & Run* clip. The (discursive) appearance of the Black rapist is designed to get a laugh—at the expense of both the victim and the invisible Black "prisoner" whom the comedian conjures. And just as the Black man is invisible in the *Hit & Run* clip except as a fantasy of a rapist, he becomes illegible as a *victim* of rape in the Idaho case. Judge Stoker's denial of the sexual dynamics in the case works in concert with a denial of its racial dynamics. As Aliyyah Abdur-Rahman argues in *Against the Closet*, "it is within constructions of sexual perversions that we find the most searing, astute illustrations and indictments of race-based inequality in the United States."[20] Abdur-Rahman's argument prompts the question: Would the sexual aspect of the violence in the Idaho case have been legible to Judge Stoker if the case had aligned with the common discourse about male/male rape in the US—if, that is, the case had concerned a group of Black male aggressors and a white male victim?

It is important, too, that in both the *Hit & Run* trailer and the Idaho locker-room case, the victim of rape is feminized and humiliated by the rape, so much so that the discourse surrounding these victims takes pains to disrupt identification with the violate man. This refusal to identify is obvious in the trailer, in which Dax Shepard immediately makes a joke at the victim's expense and Kristen Bell turns away. But in the Idaho case, although Judge Stoker makes no jokes, he, too, refuses to identify with the violate man: If the violence is "not sexual," "not rape," "not sex," *that can only be from the perspective of the rapist/attacker.* It is unlikely, perhaps even impossible, that the victim would have experienced such a violation as "not sexual."

These are issues of interpretation, identification, mediation, and citation. What these two examples clarify is that male/male rape discourse in narratives and jokes fundamentally frames our thinking about incidents of male/male rape in the real world. This discourse not only teaches us how to make sense of male/male sexual violence, it also influences and informs the way we respond to men who have been violated. We are willing to speak about the victim of male/male rape, but we, like Judge Stoker, like Shepard's character in Hit & Run, are not willing to identify with him. Rather than a topic that is often avoided or silenced, discourse around male/male rape is something that is put to specific cultural uses, frequently and easily coded and decoded, and freighted with a complicated but widely shared set of cultural meanings, what I will call below a *poetics* of male/male rape.

This book argues that questions and analytical problems surrounding male/male sexual violence have much to teach us, not least about masculinity and power. Indeed, because masculinity and power are so embedded in the structural mechanisms of phallocentric society, an examination of representations of male/male sexual violence can illuminate society itself in unique ways. Male/male rape narratives in popular culture and media—as Jacinda Read argues in relation to feminism and the rape-revenge trope in Hollywood film—are not isolated to particular genres; they rather get mapped onto those genres and media where they are put to use.[21] It is my argument that male/male rape narratives are used by writers, filmmakers, and comedians in order to make sense of the changing landscape of US American masculinity, and that these narratives have shifted widely since the 1960s, reflecting masculinity's varying anxieties and concerns. Far from a topic that has been banished from discussion or that is spoken about only obliquely, representations of male/male rape are a rich subject for exploration, and such images have a great deal to say about how we think about sex, gender, sexuality, race, violence, power, ability, identity, and difference, as well as subjectivity itself and US American society as a whole.[22]

The Violate Man analyzes this US American poetics of male/male rape, one that uses narrative structure, metaphor, and other storytelling devices upon which we call to help us make sense of the news reports we hear, to help us vote, to help us think about rape on college campuses, and to modify our pornographic fantasies. Further, we need to examine male/male rape discourse carefully because these poetics also have a profound effect on how we deal with and study rape in the real world.[23] Our dependence on these narratives to explain real-world phenomena is evident even in some important sociological texts analyzing rape. Take, as only one example among several, the political scientist Amalendu Misra's *The Landscape of Silence: Sexual Violence against Men in War*, which attempts to explain male/male sexual violence in real combat zones by describing the motivations of *fictional* characters represented in films by Derek Jarman, Alan Parker, and Ōshima Nagisa.[24] Misra's analysis of wartime sexual violence includes reference to some of the texts I discuss in this book, most notably *The Shawshank Redemption*, but he treats these texts as evidence in support of his arguments about real-world situations rather than analyzing how these fictional narratives might instead be influencing his (and our) thinking as we try to make sense of sexual violence. To illuminate just one problem with this approach—although I think there are several—my analyses in Chapters 4 and 5 describe the ways many of these fictional narratives after the 1990s prioritize revenge, on the one hand, and confession or testimony, on the other, as the appropriate responses to victimization by rape. These narratives inscribe for us what "normal" responses to rape should look like, and if we identify with the character and his behaviors, we find ourselves treating real survivors of rape as responding abnormally or not doing "the right thing" that we "know" they need to do in order to facilitate a healing process that we believe we understand better than they do.

By attending to representations of sexual violence committed by men against men, *The Violate Man* also works to bring the act of rape more clearly into focus—apart from the gender binary with which it has so frequently been associated in academic study. The vast majority of studies of sexual violence understandably focus on rape as it affects female victims, and they are designed to address the pervasive problem of gender dominance in our society and the overwhelming "prevalence of sexual violence inflicted on women."[25] Most scholars of sexual violence developed their theories about rape based upon gender difference, that is, the rape of women by men.[26] It is my argument that because an attention to the discourse of male/male rape allows us to disaggregate the act of rape from the gender binary, such an analysis paradoxically clarifies the way all representations of sexually inflected violence function in our culture. Further, this book's specific focus on the discourse of male/male rape is an attempt to reflect and interrogate a cultural shift toward an increase in male/male rape narratives in theater, fiction, film, and television.

The topic of male/male sexual violence holds a central place in discussions of male/male violence and male/male sexuality. For both sexuality and violence, male/male rape is a limit, constituting the very edge on any continuum of relations between men. Accordingly, careful consideration of representations of male/male rape can illuminate myriad relationalities in US American society, opening various and numerous possibilities for analyses of

1. considerations of violence between men at the most quotidian level, including bullying, fraternal violence, and violence-inflected language, as well as violence on more national and global scales such as torture, war, and genocide;
2. considerations of sexuality such as the binary of heterosexuality/homosexuality, but also more nuanced sexual taxonomies related to desire, attraction, arousal, and pleasure;
3. considerations of gender identity such as masculinity and femininity and the related concepts of man and woman, as well as slippages across and away from these simple binaries;
4. considerations of sexualized power such as relationships between sexual dyads such as top/bottom and aggressor/receptor, but also ostensibly nonsexual social relationships such as winner/loser and topdog/underdog;
5. processes of racial formation and racism in the United States, whereby the Black male is consistently understood as sexually aggressive and the white male is understood as victimized or injured by him;
6. conceptualizations of difference along racialized axes such as the civilized and the barbaric or even the human and the inhuman, differences that are frequently used to justify violence, torture, police brutality, and war;
7. the spatial dimensions (inside/outside, over/under, behind/before) of bodies as they are penetrated or rendered permeable;
8. considerations of criminality, deviance, and vilification, as sexual violence is frequently rendered as the ultimate crime, and victimization by rape as the ultimate abasement;
9. discussions of shame and traumatic experience, as well as the silence, obfuscation, and desire for revenge that frequently accompany shame and the experience of trauma;

10. considerations of the intersections and interconnectedness of pleasure and pain, ecstasy and abjection that often accompany both sex and violence, but that are also linked to
11. questions of ability and debility, wholeness and dissolution, identity and subjectivity;
12. the capacities of theater, film, and other media to represent or perform pain, sex, aggression, and/or violation;
13. the identificatory practices of audiences as we witness representations or read descriptions of violence and are asked by cultural producers to identify or disidentify with either perpetrator or victim; and, finally,
14. the ethics of such representations.

As Eve Sedgwick demonstrates in *Tendencies* with the purported functions and ostensible meanings of the word *family*, disarticulating the factors that constitute and confer meaning onto our ideas about male/male rape is no easy task.[27] These components are consistently linked with one another and have come to appear natural to us. Almost all representations of rape, for example, are racialized in very specific ways—even those that disavow or appear to have nothing to do with race.[28] I also find it impossible to discuss the *gendering* of rape victims apart from a consideration of penetrative violence, and—though their discussions rarely consider representations of sexual violence as a topic—many theorists have discussed shame as linked to receptivity or loss and even as constitutive of subjectivity itself. These ideas are joined through narrative structures and metaphors that work ideologically to make their conjunction logical.

The use of rape as a metaphor is designed precisely to cover over these different ideas we associate with rape, naturalizing their links to one another and ideologically connecting, for example, shame to femininity, receptive sexuality to incarceration, wholeness to maleness, criminality to anality, whiteness to vulnerability, weakness to homosexuality, etc. My analysis here cannot hope to discuss fully every item listed here, but one of the central goals of this text is to disaggregate and address the "natural" connections to male/male rape that these ideas hold. *The Violate Man* works to analyze the power that rape—both real and metaphorized—possesses in our society. To do so is to begin to understand why talk about the raped male body is so ubiquitous, if frequently misrecognized as such.

Male/Male Rape and Gender Performativity: On Repetition and Citation

In *Rape and Representation*, Lynn Higgins and Brenda Silver argue that "rape and rapability are central to the very construction of gender identity and . . . our subjectivity and sense of ourselves as sexual beings are inextricably enmeshed in representations. Viewed from this perspective, rape exists as a context independent of its occurrence as a discrete event."[29] Higgins and Silver are making two arguments here, and I wish to describe each in turn, as both are important to thinking about how representations of rape work in our culture.

The first argument is that rape and penetrability are fundamental to the way we construct our gendered subjectivities. When Brownmiller said, in *Against Our Will*, that "Man's structural capacity to rape and woman's corresponding structural vulnerability are as basic to the physiology of both our sexes as the primal act of sex itself," she referred specifically to a female victim and a male perpetrator.[30] But let us modify Brownmiller's analysis slightly, for although *almost* any man has a structural capacity to rape that is basic to his physiology, it is clear that this same man, like the woman in Brownmiller's formulation, also has a structural capacity *to be the victim of rape*, and that this too is basic to his physiology. Simply put, men and boys are *violable* beings, and the common elision of this quite obvious fact is essential to the ideological power of the gender binary.

Catharine MacKinnon—who responded to Brownmiller by arguing that "to seek to define rape as violent not sexual is as understandable as it is futile"—also asks us to focus on gender as the key aspect of sexual violence.[31] MacKinnon describes her argument with Brownmiller this way: "Some feminists have reinterpreted rape as an act of violence, not sexuality, the threat of which intimidates all women. Others see rape, including its violence, as an expression of male sexuality, the social imperatives of which *define* as well as threaten all women."[32] MacKinnon here emphasizes that rape is definitional of male sexual practices, irrespective of sexuality (although she uses the word *sexuality*); what she means is that rape is *the way men have sex*: "Rape is not less sexual for being violent. To the extent that coercion has become integral to male sexuality, rape may even be sexual to the degree that, and because, it is violent."[33] In turn, as she notes in this passage, rape genders women, defining them and differentiating them from men. MacKinnon's argument helps us understand that acts of rape work to distance themselves from *categories of sexuality* through violent acts of gender differentiation.

As Ann Cahill responds to the differing positions of Brownmiller and MacKinnon, she argues that "if rape is socially constructed as a gender-specific method of supporting, producing, and enforcing a gender hierarchy, then that construction will be basic and essential to (although not necessarily exhaustive of) any one instance of rape."[34] In other words, acts of rape are intended to solidify gender positionalities—to emphasize the gender difference that claims that men are inviolable—through a violent reassertion of what it means to be "woman" and what it means to be "man." A man has the capability of asserting his position *as* male by an act of rape that, through its commission, explicitly genders him as male by simultaneously gendering the body of his victim as female.[35] The historian of violence Klaus Theweleit explains this gendering of men in the first volume of *Male Fantasies*, his influential study on fascism and misogyny:

> If male-female relations of production under patriarchy are relations of oppression, it is appropriate to understand the sexuality created by, and active within, those relations as a sexuality of the oppressor and the oppressed. If the social nature of such "gender-distinctions" isn't expressly emphasized, it seems grievously wrong to distinguish these sexualities according to the categories "male" and "female." The sexuality of the patriarch is less "male" than it is deadly, just as that of the subjected women is not so much "female" as suppressed, devivified.[36]

For Theweleit, the fascist male (re)asserts his maleness through acts of violence, and (re)asserts the woman's femaleness by actively suppressing her power and often killing her. Put more succinctly, for the men Theweleit describes, acts of violence *make* a man a man, and a woman is a woman because she is the victim of that violence.

In her analysis of slavery in the United States, Aliyyah Abdur-Rahman modifies Theweleit to argue that physical and sexual domination are "necessary for the master to experience both the separation (or differentiation) and the recognition that are so central to subjective development. The master's self—defined always against a separate, subjugated other—is formed, legitimated, and made autonomous *and powerful* through direct (physical and sexual) domination" of those he enslaved.[37] Or, as Thomas Foster succinctly puts it, "Black men were sexually violated and exploited because those actions served the racial hierarchy and subordination of black men under slavery."[38] This is a sexualized violence that simultaneously works to subjugate enslaved Black men and women and to provide white slavers a *gendered* experience of mastery, a legitimated, autonomous, powerful subjectivity.

Judith Butler has argued that "gender as substance, the viability of *man* and *woman* as nouns, is called into question by the dissonant play of attributes that fail to conform to sequential or causal modes of intelligibility."[39] Butler's argument is that gender exists through citation and repetition: "gender proves to be performative—that is, constituting the identity it is purported to be. In this sense, gender is always a doing, though not a doing by a subject who might be said to preexist the deed."[40] Gender, in other words, is always an activity; this means, not that gender is a *performance*, but rather that it constitutes itself through its own declaration.

Turning our attention to men and to rape—which I am arguing is an act of gender domination—we would do well to take Butler's Nietzschean note that there is no subject that preexists the deed. We can then say, *pace* Brownmiller, that men do not rape simply because they are men; rather, an act of rape is one means of *becoming* a man, of asserting one's maleness. Furthermore, an act of rape is a technique that places a subject *within a history of violent maleness, confirming one's membership in a category that exists prior to the subject himself.* A man does not, in other words, commit rape because of his maleness. On the contrary: an act of rape offers the opportunity for a man temporarily to achieve an always-contested maleness, a maleness that exits only relationally.[41]

In *Bodies That Matter*, Butler argued, following Foucault, that "there is no power, construed as a subject, that acts, but only . . . a reiterated acting that *is* power in its persistence and instability. This is less an 'act,' singular and deliberate, than a nexus of power and discourse that repeats or mimes the discursive gestures of power."[42] To modify Butler slightly, if the rapist uses the violence of his act of rape to create a power differential between himself and his victim, Butler suggests that this works "*through* the citation of the law" an act of rape itself performs.[43] Violence is often committed in order to confirm the feeling among its perpetrators that violence works to do what it says it can: as Butler says of the violence perpetrated at Abu Ghraib, the Iraqi detainees' "status as less than human is not only presupposed by the torture, but reinstituted by it."[44] The torturer cites the power of torture as he commits torture.[45] The rapist cites the power of rape as he commits rape, tapping into the already existent discourse of rape as an act of gender differentiation. He confirms the power of that act at the same time as he wields it as a method for attaining or maintaining power.

The work of Jasbir Puar makes visible, further, the racialized and xenophobic dimensions of penetrative domination. Addressing the sexualized torture at Abu Ghraib, Puar argues that central to the feminizing force of torture "is the fortification of the unenforceable boundaries between masculine and feminine, the rescripting of multiple and fluid gender performatives into petrified sites of masculine and feminine, the rendering of multiple genders into the oppressive binary scripts of masculine and feminine, and the interplay of it all within and through racial, imperial and economic matrices of power."[46] Sexualized torture such as that at Abu Ghraib is designed precisely as racialized gender dominance, sexualized domination that feminizes as it penetrates.[47]

Questions of penetration and penetrability relate to representations of male/male rape in fascinating ways because our gendered societies are already structured along the lines of penetration. Since antiquity, taboos have existed against males who have taken (or been violently placed in) the receptive position in penetrative anal sex between men. The classicist Kenneth Dover tells us that "Anthropological data indicate that human societies at many times and in many regions have subjected strangers, newcomers and trespassers to homosexual anal violation as a way of reminding them of their subordinate status."[48] Joshua Goldstein notes, further, that "The Aztec word for a powerful warrior translates as 'I make someone into a passive.'"[49] Dover's and Goldstein's analyses are focused on xenophobic divisions in which men differentiate between the enemy's (foreign) bodies and their own victorious, inviolate bodies through forced penetration. The man who is raped is a foreigner, and the rape is supposed both to designate his weakness as a member of an inferior racial group and performatively to destroy his sense of himself as a man, to violently remove him from the category of male. Ethnic difference as a motivation is also widely attested in the recent literature on male/male rape during military conflict.[50] Rape offers the opportunity, then, for a man also to gender himself as male through a racialized differentiation between bodies that attempts to mark some bodies as powerful and others as weak, foreign, less than human.

In "Is the Rectum a Grave?" Leo Bersani described a historical "structuring of sexual behavior in terms of activity and passivity, with a correlative rejection of the so-called passive role in sex." In a well-known passage, Bersani cites Foucault's study of ancient sexuality in the second volume of *The History of Sexuality*:

What the Athenians find hard to accept, Foucault writes, is the authority of a leader who as an adolescent was an "object of pleasure" for other men; there is a legal and moral incompatibility between sexual passivity and civic authority. The only "honorable" sexual behavior "consists in being active, in dominating, in penetrating, and in thereby exercising one's authority." In other words, the moral taboo on "passive" anal sex in ancient Athens is primarily formulated as a kind of hygienics of social power. *To be penetrated is to abdicate power.*[51]

Put another way, for the ancient Athenians, to be penetrated is to give up maleness.[52] And, as I am arguing, to penetrate another person regardless of gender is to assert oneself as male, to achieve maleness through the gendering of the penetrated person as female. This is an enduring system of discourse for understanding penetration, and penetrative acts of sexual violence not only display authority and perform power, they cite a history of discourse that renders a person who is penetrated as powerless, subjected, dominated, weak.

I want further to note the specifics of penetration when a man is raped. The mouth and anus can both be used for penetrative activities during consensual sexual contact between men and women—regardless of sexual orientation. The mouth and anus, then, must function as reminders of the similarities between bodies that are gendered differently. Michael Moon draws our attention to precisely this fact when he refers to "the generally enforced misrecognition of many men most of the time of the relation between their own ostensibly 'normal' male heterosexuality and their relation to the penetrable orifices of their own and other males' bodies; it is a sign of the 'scandal' of the liminal gendering—one might say the minimal gendering—of the mouth and anus."[53] The male body, of course, is neither impermeable nor impenetrable, and it need not be wounded or violently entered in order to be penetrated. (Even the simple, necessary act of eating, as Jane Bennett and others have noted, blurs the boundaries of the outside and the inside of the human body.)[54] As Butler says, "We can think about demarcating the human body through identifying its boundary, or in what form it is bound, but that is to miss the crucial fact that the body is, in certain ways and even inevitably, unbound—in its acting, in its receptivity, in its speech, desire, and mobility. It is outside itself, in the world of others, in a space and time it does not control."[55] This is true of human bodies in distress, bodies in extremis, or bodies at rest—irrespective of gender identification or gender performance.

The anus, however, is a special case. The anus has long been treated as though it possesses a unique power to describe the subjectivity of its owner. Guy Hocquenghem, for example, argues in *Homosexual Desire* that "whereas the phallus is essentially social, the anus is essentially private"; he even more definitively declares that "the anus has no social position except sublimation; the functions of this organ are truly private. They are the site of the formation of the person. The anus expresses privatisation itself."[56] As the anus is separated from the rest of the body as exceptional or particularly private, it comes to be the organ that makes each of us most individually separate from everyone else. Sedgwick and Moon elaborate on this analysis in a jointly written essay:

> Anyone interested in making anality a central concern of analysis must counter a pervasive epistemological bias in much psychoanalytic theory (as well of course as in the wider culture) in favor of the phallus and the phallic. On the conventional road map of the body that our culture handily provides us, the anus gets represented as always behind and below, well out of sight under most circumstances, its unquestioned stigmatization a fundamental guarantor of one's individual privacy and one's privately privatized individuality.[57]

What I want to underline here is Sedgwick and Moon's indication that the spatial relationship of the anus to the rest of the body ("behind and below") contributes to the power the anus possesses as a symbol or figure for the body's secrets, its privacy, its shame, and—most importantly for this discussion—the fantasy of the body's impenetrability. An act of rape has the particular ability to destroy this fantasy, conferring shame onto the body through exposure of the anus and penetration into a body that has been fantasized as impenetrable.

As Theweleit describes the violent practices of the fascist soldier-male in *Male Fantasies*, he pays particular attention to the fiction that a man is unbreakable, that his body is impenetrable, and that he commits rape and performs torture in an effort to break other bodies, repeating or reenacting for himself the fantasy of his own body's wholeness. "The key quality of the blow as an act of physical violence," Theweleit argues, "is its capacity to break and crack open, to smash to pieces. It produces the man as 'I,' not by 'switching him in' to some different reality, but by an eruption of muscular activity whose goal is to crush all existing distinction and to raise the man above the undifferentiated miasma."[58] An act of violent anal penetration, then, like an act of torture, produces a broken body; it is also a performative act in the Austinian sense, one that fashions the body of the violent man as whole, impenetrable, powerful. As Theweleit puts it, "what torture represents is an attempt by men *to maintain their own bodies*" through the breaking of bodies that are not their own.[59] This is a fantasy that "coercively requires that penetrability be located in the body of the tortured. In fact, forced penetration is a mode of 'assigning' that penetrability permanently elsewhere."[60]

It is important, also, that we explicitly link this fantasy of the body's wholeness and impenetrability to heterosexuality in particular. Robert McRuer has noted that "compulsory able-bodiedness and compulsory heterosexuality are interwoven," and this analysis allows us to understand—at least partially—how the breaking of a body through torture or rape has an attendant capacity to produce the body of the victim as a less-than-heterosexual, even homosexualized body, which in turn produces the rapist's body as simultaneously able-bodied and heterosexual.[61] If, as McRuer claims, "the subjective contraction and expansion of able-bodied heterosexuality . . . are actually contingent on compliant queer, disabled bodies," an act of rape actively produces a disabled, compliantly queer body, conferring power on the able-bodied, heterosexual subject–rapist.[62] Distributions and redistributions of power in male/male physical relationships that are dependent on violence, then, are also heavily dependent on the metaphorical power that we have historically attached to the anus and to penetrability, as well as to the association of the anus with brokenness and weakness.

These historical links between power, penetration, wholeness, and gender are what grant the words *screw* and *fuck* the meanings with which they are so often fraught, so that Jesse Sheidlower can describe the second definition of the verb *fuck* as "to harm irreparably; finish; victimize."[63] Certainly "to be penetrated is to abdicate power" in this use of the word, but even more importantly, the word serves as a persistent sexualization of power relationships in all contexts. When, for example, Philip J. Kaplan describes ruined businesses as *fucked*, as he does in his 2002 book *F'd Companies: Spectacular Dot-com Flameouts* and fuckedcompany.com, its accompanying website, or when Newt Gingrich tells a group of tobacco lobbyists that "You guys have screwed us," these men sexualize what are ostensibly nonsexual power relations.[64] Their uses of the words *fucked* and *screwed* both discursively highlight the erotics of these relations at the same time as they articulate and shore up a bias against any person who is penetrated in a sexual situation (with or without consent). These uses refashion the loser, the dominated, *as though he has been penetrated*. And the equation re-exerts its power on the original term; the sexually penetrated subject is re-inscribed as defeated, dominated, conquered.[65]

The common terms *fucked* and *screwed* draw attention to the sexualized dimensions of domination that already attend traditional masculinity. In *Extravagant Abjection*, Darieck Scott argues that considering rape as "not sexual" misses the erotic charge that always accompanies domination: "Indeed, to deemphasize the significance of 'sex urges' in the establishment and maintenance of [institutional rape during US American slavery] leads us to misunderstand a vital part of it. . . . Sex urges must play a part: sexuality that lies precisely in attraction and/or the enjoyment and expression of domination." Scott's analysis here echoes MacKinnon's: "We have not left the sex urge behind by identifying the political and economic determinants that make rape a virtual institution; we have instead identified part of what constitutes the sex urge."[66]

Representations of male/male rape function, then, as a component of a larger (that is, normative) cultural understanding of sex as a dynamic of power in which a subject differentiates himself from an object through penetrative dominance. This is one of the ways in which masculinity normally functions in our society. Discourse about male/male rape, however, works to hide the *normativity* of male/male rape, emphasizing instead its queerness (its abnormality) and conferring on its victims the criminality, shame, and secrecy so often already associated with queer life. In other words, although male/male rape is consistent with what we might describe as normal hydraulic sexuality in the United States, representations of male/male rape work to produce male/male rape as a fundamentally different type of act, creating a specter of queerness around this particular act of violence and conferring that queerness onto rape victims.[67]

To return briefly to Higgins and Silver's discussion in *Rape and Representation*, their second argument is that rape discourse helps us to make sense of our gendered subjectivities. Rape, they argue, is the context in which we understand ourselves as gendered, and that context is itself constructed through discourse about rape. The sexual violence scholar Susan Brison makes a similar point in *Aftermath*. When discussing the impossibility of forgetting the violence she experienced, Brison says that "given the stories of rape I'd grown up with and the ones I'd heard and read about again and again in adulthood, one might say I remembered the rape even before it happened, as a kind of postmemory, to adapt Marianne Hirsch's term, informing the way I lived in my body and moved about in the world."[68] The discourse of rape informed Brison's gendered sense of herself long before her own experience of violation.[69]

In *Just Sex?* Nicola Gavey articulates even more clearly the powerful heteronormative and masculinist discourse that affects women's psychological understandings of rape. She notes that this discourse—what Gavey calls "the cultural scaffolding of rape"—convinced many of the women she interviewed in her research to think of sexual acts they didn't want to have or sex into which they were coerced as *unpleasurable* or *uncomfortable* rather than violent. Gavey's book argues that although "it is possible that we more actively and self-consciously adopt positions in relation to oppositional discourses (such as feminism) and discourses which espouse new cultural ideals (such as the call to safer sex) . . . , the influence of more traditional cultural assumptions, patterns, and practices may be almost invisible."[70] The argument here is that these assumptions and patterns related to sexual violence are embedded in narratives, images, and other representations, and that they work to shape our subjectivities in ways that are nearly imperceptible. Similarly, discourses of male/male rape work ideologically to make sense of the confusing questions that attend masculinity and male subjectivity.

We might, quite fairly, ask questions like those Butler poses in *Frames of War*: Is a man who rapes a man a homosexual? How might he begin to square his actions with an understanding of his heterosexuality? How does a torturer who tortures using anal penetration maintain his masculinity and remove himself from the stain of homosexuality? Why is torture so often sexualized and sexualized queerly? Why is it so difficult for so many to imagine Black men as victims of sexual violence? Why do we persistently associate penetrability with femininity and wholeness with maleness? Why do we conceive of prison rape as violence committed by other prisoners rather than by prison staff? The answers to these questions can be found in the way that *fictional representations of rape* are offered to us for our interpretation. We must turn our attention to discourse.

If acts of rape are performative, as I have argued that they are, this means that they are also citational. To put this in the terms of prison abolitionists Mariame Kaba and Danielle Sered, "No one enters violence for the first time by committing it."[71] We can safely say, however, that for the majority of rape acts in the real world, particularly male/male rapes, what is being cited, re-performed, are not *real* acts of sexual violation that have been witnessed but those that have been seen on a screen or onstage, those that have been read about in books, acts of rape that have been discussed, joked about, or referred to using coded speech. US American society possesses a history of interpreting acts of male/male rape, a cultural poetics that has made sense of these acts of violation for us. An act of male/male rape today both situates itself within that history and, indeed, *uses* that history in order to make sense of it while it is happening. This is precisely how citation works. As Sharon Marcus says, "rape is not only scripted—it also scripts."[72]

The stakes for understanding male/male rape discourse are extremely high, and the readings in this book concern themselves with representations of male/male rape that have already been used—are currently being used—to make sense of this violation. To make an even bolder claim, it is my contention that representations of male/male rape—the discourse this book analyzes—are not only descriptive of violation, *it is precisely these representations that violent men cite when they commit new violations on violate bodies*.

Rape and Its Metaphorization

It is the argument of *The Violate Man* that, more often than not—because of racism, homophobia, misogyny, and other reasons—male/male rape and its meaning circulate within a symbolic economy where they are made to signify in ways that are vastly different from one another. Early in *Between Men*, Eve Sedgwick turns briefly to an analysis of *Gone with the Wind*. She describes how Margaret Mitchell's novel manages to figure a nonsexual attack by a Black man on a white woman as rape at the same time as it can describe violent, nonconsensual sex between white men and women as though it is not rape at all.[73] Sedgwick's argument is that for the white heterosexuals in the novel (and for its white intended audience), a description of actual sexual violence fails to denote rape, but an interracial assault that is not sexual reads as though it is rape because the man stealing something is Black and the woman from whom he is stealing is ostensibly white. Sedgwick argues that "We have here in this protofeminist novel, . . . a symbolic economy in which both the meaning of rape and rape itself are insistently circulated. Because of the racial fracture of the society, however, *rape and its meaning circulate in precisely opposite directions*."[74] Taking Sedgwick's work as her cue, Sabine Sielke reminds us "that talk about rape does not necessarily denote rape, just as talk about love hardly ever hits its target. Instead, transposed into discourse, rape turns into a rhetorical device, an insistent figure for other social, political, and economic concerns and conflicts."[75] The differences between what Sielke calls "the rhetoric of rape" and rape itself need to be emphasized: "rape narratives relate to real rape incidents in highly mediated ways only. They are first and foremost interpretations, readings of rape that, as they seem to make sense of socially deviant behavior, oftentimes limit our understanding of sexual violence."[76] Rape narratives and rape metaphors, in other words, often occlude real-world acts of rape, making rape itself more difficult to see, or rather, asking us to see rape in very particular ways.

Rape is commonly metaphorized in US American parlance, and this metaphorization is repeated equally insistently by television political commentators, print-media journalists, activists, and academics alike. It is the word *rape* as a metaphor that has allowed, for example, radio commentator Michael Savage to refer to the so-called gay agenda as a "giant propaganda machine" committing acts of "mental rape." Savage said in 2008, that "the children's minds are being raped by the homosexual mafia, that's my position. They're raping our children's minds."[77] Savage is hardly alone in his metaphorization of the term. The flexibility of the word *rape* as a signifier in US American culture has proved nearly inexhaustible. In an interview in 1994 promoting his film *Pulp Fiction*, for example, Quentin Tarantino discussed his collection of board games with *Rolling Stone*'s David Wild:

> "I've been collecting all this shit for years," says Tarantino, who is wearing a Racer X T-shirt today. "Then I finally decided I wanted to start collecting something new. At first I chose lunch boxes, but they really rape you on lunch boxes. They're just too fucking expensive. And as for dolls, well, you can't have much fun with them! You have to keep them in the box. So, I started with board games."[78]

Tarantino's usage here frames the high prices of collectible lunchboxes as though they are designed to injure a vulnerable and helpless victim (Tarantino and other collectors) and to demonize those selling the collectibles as sexually violent predators. More recently, and in the same vein, Donald Trump warned a rally in 2016 that "we can't continue to allow China to rape our country, and that's what they're doing."[79] Trump used the metaphor of rape as a way to get his supporters to, in the first place, see themselves as victims of injury, and in the second place, desire revenge for what he was then calling "the greatest theft in the history of the world." But in these metaphorizations the *idea* of rape is made to do ideological work. Each of these descriptions uses the image of rape in order to re-characterize the activity it purports to describe, managing, because of the incendiary imagery associated with rape, to confuse both sex and violence with very different (nonsexual, nonviolent) activities. The coupling of sex and violence with ideas that the speaker means to characterize as "bad"—antihomophobic propaganda, high prices, currency manipulation, theft—metaphorizes and metamorphoses the objects described so that audiences respond to them *as though they are* sexually violent.

In these instances, the use of rape as a metaphor covers over these fissures in logic. I wish to argue that the use of the discourse of rape is a specifically ideological project, at work even when the person using these discursive formations is unaware of their attendant political implications. It is crucial to understand that these discursive formations work to occlude actual incidents of rape. If the metaphors function correctly, we are directed away from consideration of rape in its reality and are instead asked to respond to something that manifestly *is not rape* as we would to an act of sexual violation. *Rape and its meaning circulate in precisely opposite directions.*

Additionally, because we in literary studies have a tendency to read things that are not rape as though they are rape—this happens, for example, whenever scholars refer to events that are not sexually violent as "symbolic rape"—it is important for this project to be very careful about its definition of rape. Because of this important distinction between rape and its representation, this book will be as specific as possible when it uses the term *rape*. For the sake of clarity *The Violate Man* will use the US Justice Department's definition of rape, a definition only recently broadened in 2012 to include male victims. The DOJ's new definition of rape refers to "penetration, no matter how slight, of the vagina or anus with any body part or object, or oral penetration by a sex organ of another person, without the consent of the victim."[80] This revised definition is notable for removing gender from consideration for either the victim or the perpetrator and for recognizing that rape need not involve genital contact on the part of the perpetrator of the violence. The Justice Department's old definition, in place since 1927, described rape as "the carnal knowledge of a female, forcibly and against her will." The old definition's extraordinary antiquation aside, it is vital to note here that in addition to the 2012 definition's recognition that men can also be rape victims and women can also be perpetrators of rape, the new definition also makes the careful switch from "forcibly and against her will" to "without the consent of the victim." This change reflects an important and widespread cultural shift in our society's definition of rape: most US Americans now understand rape as a crime defined not by the *presence of force* but by the *absence of consent*.

This shift in US American thinking about rape and consent is significant. In her history of legal responses to sexual violence, *Consent: Sexual Rights and the Transformation of Liberalism*, Pamela Haag notes not only how recent the concept of consent is to US understandings of sexual violation but also how foundational the concept is to American liberalism as such; the idea makes almost no appearance in US American jurisprudence until the postbellum period. As she puts it, "The opposition of consent to violence is a rich object for historical analysis because it is a concept that underwrites the three dominant social relations of liberal culture: it is relevant to the meaning of sexual freedom; it shapes ideas of citizenship as defined through consent to a 'social contract'; and in a market economy driven by ideologies of free contract it contributes centrally to the assumed legitimacy of a labor relation."[81] Although the issue of consent is seemingly ubiquitous in "he said, she said" narratives in which women are victimized by rape—where the veracity of their testimony is called into question or the women are accused of making themselves sexually available—questions of consent appear almost nowhere in representations of male/male rape. In the narratives I discuss in this book, male/male rape is almost uniformly violent, and questions of whether or not the victim might have consented almost never arise. Indeed, the absence of consent as a topic of discussion in male/male rape narratives is one of the key discoveries of this study, a marked difference from narratives in which women are the victims of rape. Because of this absence, the first chapter to examine the issue of consent in this book will be Chapter 5, as we look at male/male rape narratives from the early 2000s.

One final important reason that *The Violate Man* discusses rape separately from other sexual violence—such as castration, for example—is simply that the cultural *poetics* of rape are very different from those of castration or other sexual assaults.[82] Castration, male/female rape, and other types of sexual violence signify differently than male/male rape in the US American imaginary, and although they might deserve similar punishments in criminal courts or belong together in terms of classifying acts of violence in the real world, representations of these other acts of sexual and sexualized violence make meaning differently than representations of the violent, penetrative assaults this book describes.

This book confines itself to literature, film, and television made in the United States. The arguments in *The Violate Man* are tied to the way we speak about male/male rape in US American culture, but one could write a book about British male/male rape discourse that would differ significantly but necessarily chart many similarities. Images of male/male rape appear in E. M. Forster's short story "The Torque" (c. 1958), chapter 80 of T. E. Lawrence's *Seven Pillars of Wisdom* (1922) and its film version *Lawrence of Arabia* (1962), as well as the Alan Clarke film *Scum* (1979), the miniseries *The Jewel in the Crown* (1984), Ian McGuire's novel *The North Water* (2016), important and scandalous London theater such as Howard Brenton's *The Romans in Britain* (1980), and numerous plays comprising the New Brutalist movement such as Anthony Neilson's *Penetrator* (1994), Sarah Kane's *Blasted* (1995), and Mark Ravenhill's *Shopping and Fucking* (1996). This book references these cultural objects very little if at all.[83]

In fact, once one begins collecting references to male/male rape across various media, one finds rather a large number of them. It will not be possible to discuss them all, even restricting myself to those originating in the United States. This book has little to say, for example, about the male/male rapes in Kenneth Cook's novel *Wake in Fright* (1961), Diana Gabaldon's *Outlander* (1991), Dennis Cooper's *Frisk* (1991), or the rapes in the three-episode arc "Imaginationland" on the Comedy Central show *South Park* (2007).[84] Similarly, the documentary film *Turned Out* (2004), the Peter Yates film *An Innocent Man* (1989), Uri Barbash's *Beyond the Walls* (1984), Jean-Claude Lauzon's *Un Zoo la Nuit* (1987), Michael Rymer's *In Too Deep* (1999), Gregg Araki's *Mysterious Skin* (2004), Bruno Dumont's *Twentynine Palms* (2003), Justin Kurzel's *The Snowtown Murders* (2011), Stephen Dunn's *Closet Monster* (2015), Joel Edgerton's *Boy Erased* (2018), Uberto Pasolini's *The Return* (2024), and Brady Corbet's *The Brutalist* (2024) get no more than a mention in the following pages.

I list some of these films and novels here to give the reader an idea of the wide and widening range of this discourse. A comprehensive analytical history of male/male rape discourse in world literature and cinema is beyond the scope of this book, but the pieces I have chosen will clearly articulate the important patterns in this discourse, and they will chart a history of our changing thinking about male/male rape and the many ideological components that continue to subtend it. The pieces I've chosen to analyze in depth do not necessarily offer what I would consider the most humane, the most nuanced, the most careful or complex ways to think about male/male rape, but they have, for better or worse, taught us how to think about it and given us the language that we use to speak about it.

Mapping The Violate Man

Nearly each chapter of *The Violate Man* discusses a different medium: Chapter 1 is about theater, Chapter 2 fiction, Chapters 3 and 4 film, Chapter 5 television, and Chapter 6 performance poetry and sculpture. The chapters also move more or less chronologically, charting developments in this discursive history. I am not, however, making a claim that male/male rape discourse begins in the theater, moves to fiction, and then finally ends up on the big screen. I have chosen instead to focus on specific moments that are influential or powerful and, in each instance, I articulate the contemporary discourses that crystallized around these representations, specific ideas we can take from each of these historical moments.

Chapter 1 describes the foundational text of male/male rape in drama, Canadian playwright John Herbert's *Fortune and Men's Eyes*. I examine this play for the specific narrative traditions it establishes. Herbert's play is a prison drama, and it cemented the tradition of prison as a homosexualized space where power is exerted through sexual violence. This play is the first example of what I call the new prison drama; its descriptions of rape as a problem in American (both US and Canadian) prisons fundamentally change the way prisons will be subsequently represented. *Fortune* also links male/male rape in prisons specifically to homosexual desire, as well as cordoning off the danger of rape by locating it in prison. This chapter concludes with examinations of Miguel Piñero's *Short Eyes* and Rick Cluchey's *The Cage*, detailing how these stage dramas and their representations of incarceration and sexual violence were deeply influenced by Herbert's 1967 play.

Chapter 2 discusses four novels, all concerned fundamentally with masculinity, beginning with Gore Vidal's 1965 revised version of *The City and the Pillar*. I historicize Vidal's interpolation of a rape narrative into his 1948 novel, and I describe the way it adopts the traditional associations of male rape victims with disempowerment and brokenness. Next, I discuss James Dickey's novel *Deliverance*. I track the way Dickey connects male/male rape to masculinity, to nature, and to the American South. I argue that critical reception of the novel has conflated Dickey's work with the film adaptation of *Deliverance*, and I argue that the novel is neither misogynist nor homophobic but instead figures rape as an event in a ritual process of becoming, a violent, painful experience that enables one, if not all, of *Deliverance*'s characters to move closer toward a version of masculinity that differs profoundly from its dominant iteration in US American culture. Departing even further from the associations of the violate man with femininity,

I then analyze James Baldwin's novel *If Beale Street Could Talk*. I describe how Baldwin places responsibility for prison sexual violence with a white-supremacist police force that eroticizes and violates Black men, and I find Baldwin's refiguration of the violate man to be a challenge to the traditional readings of prison rape found in Chapter 1. This chapter closes by looking at Chester Himes's novel *Yesterday Will Make You Cry*. Himes wrote *Yesterday* while incarcerated in the 1930s, and although his novel wasn't published until after his death, his book is a startling text that reframes masculinity, prison, race, and homosexuality in ways that contrast sharply with received ideas about those topics in the mid-century US.

I move in Chapter 3 to New Hollywood cinema and three films from the period, all of which feature male/male rape. I describe the new world of film violence opened up by the dismantling of the Production Code and the new possibilities for what could be shown onscreen. The films in this chapter are John Schlesinger's *Midnight Cowboy*, John Boorman's *Deliverance*, and Jerry Schatzberg's *Scarecrow*. Each features a significant male/male rape onscreen, but the films have been remembered differently by audiences, and the chapter carefully examines the different techniques used by the three filmmakers to tell these stories in ways that have been memorable for some films and forgettable for others. I also discuss some of the central anxieties about the "buddy film" that male/male rape seemed, especially, to symbolize in the 1970s. This chapter closes with some ideas about rape jokes, about laughter as one way to distance ourselves from the vulnerability of the violate man.

Chapter 4 addresses the proliferation of images of male/male rape in US American cinema in the 1990s. The films *Pulp Fiction*, *The Shawshank Redemption*, *The Prince of Tides*, *American Me*, *Sleepers*, and *American History X* all feature male protagonists who are victimized by rape. I examine each film in turn, with a focus on the way that the films treat the affective experience of the victims' shame. This allows us to turn our attention to the processes of identification so central to the cinematic experience and to the way that shame works in the body of the viewer, as each of the films asks its audience to identify in different ways with the victim of rape. I pay special attention to *Pulp Fiction*, and I use Tarantino's film as a prime example of the tendency among these 1990s films to appear to raise awareness about the emotional experiences associated with rape, while at the same time they articulate violent revenge as the appropriate response to those experiences.

Moving from film to television, Chapter 5 charts a history of male/male rape discourse on TV by following the HBO series *Oz* and the second season of the ABC series *American Crime*. Because of television's ability to focus on characters for a long period of time (in the case of some shows this can be measured in years), the medium is particularly suited to examining the long-term effects of sexual violence on male victims, and the storylines on *Oz* and *American Crime* both exploit this ability. This chapter also argues that the medium of television itself favors the confession and that, as male/male rape moves from premium cable to broadcast TV, the narrative focus turns from staging the terror of being raped to staging the aftermath of having been raped, a dramaturgical shift that serves the demand of the confessional: that the victim must speak. The chapter closes with four recent examples of the confessional narrative, demonstrating this mode's continued hold on male/male rape discourse: two books—Garrard Conley's memoir *Boy Erased* and Jonathan Parks-Ramage's novel *Yes, Daddy*—and two recent television series, Michaela Coel's *I May Destroy You* and Richard Gadd's *Baby Reindeer*.

The book's last chapter addresses my own position as a scholar. I also describe two artists whose work departs in significant ways from typical representations of male/male rape in mainstream culture—the sculptor and performer Benjamin Peterson and the poet and actor Kevin Kantor. This final part of the book offers some possibilities for rethinking openness and closure and for attempting to think differently about the violate man—not as a figure who haunts masculinity but as a person who lives with and through brokenness and vulnerability.

As I close this introduction, I wish to explain what might appear to be a rather glaring omission from this book. Although pornographic films frequently stage scenes of nonconsensual sex, *The Violate Man* does not examine any gay male pornography. This book is, to be sure, about fantasies, many of which are erotic—the fantasy of inviolability attached to masculinity, fantasies of domination and submission, fantasies of shame and humiliation, fantasies of Black violence and white vulnerability, and fantasies related to the power of institutions such as schools, hospitals, police forces, psychiatric offices, churches, fraternities, and prisons that capture and discipline our bodies. The argument of this book, however, is that discourse about male/male rape *shapes* those fantasies. These fantasies of sexual violence have real-world effects that are not restricted to some discrete realm of the erotic but inform our everyday lives. If I do not analyze pornography directly in these pages, then, one of the premises of this book is that when we eroticize sexual violence—as pornography often does—we do so according to a cultural poetics informed by precisely the discourse that this book examines.

CHAPTER I

The New Prison Drama
Male/Male Rape on Stage

> Prisoners do not occupy a zone of exile outside the circle of juridical and philosophical humanity; the prison that holds them is one of the primary sites through which the very idea of modern humanity is imagined and contested.
>
> —CALEB SMITH, *The Prison and the American Imagination*

The December 1970 issue of the Canadian newsmagazine *Maclean's* features an article by film critic John Hofsess designed to promote the new movie-version of *Fortune and Men's Eyes* and to alert readers to that drama's importance to Canada as a nation. The piece is subtitled "A Report from the Set in a Quebec City Prison" and announces John Herbert's play of the same name as "the most famous Canadian drama of the last decade—it's been translated into eight languages and performed in 14 countries." Hofsess's first paragraph, however, does not contain *Fortune*'s list of accolades; instead, the author begins his piece with the following extraordinary narrative:

> Two years ago the CBS television program *Sixty Minutes* reported "a routine incident" in a Philadelphia jail. A white youth, arrested for possession of marijuana and jailed overnight, was gang-raped the next morning by six black convicts in the back of a paddy wagon en route to a courthouse. Police found the boy bleeding and in shock. Such incidents [are] commonly and mistakenly referred to as "the problem of homosexuality in our prisons," . . . yet, statistics indicate that more than 80% of sexual assaults in

American prisons are committed by blacks against whites and are motivated by a different lust, a hateful rage that knows no containment.[1]

This sensationally racialized paragraph, shockingly graphic for the opening of an article in a magazine's film-review section—particularly in a piece designed to promote a movie—betrays an enormous amount of anxiety. Hofsess makes a plea for public understanding of the "truth" of prison rape: it is the responsibility of "blacks," not "homosexuals"; it is motivated by uncontainable hatred and rage, not lust; "white youths" are its victims, "gangs" of "black convicts" its perpetrators.

Stranger still, Hofsess's article returns neither to the issue of gang rape in the Philadelphia prison system nor to his vehement racialization of this violence; the remainder of this piece in *Maclean's* features descriptions of the actors in *Fortune and Men's Eyes* and a laudatory interview with screenwriter-playwright John Herbert, displaying unabashed affection for all involved. This article was designed to promote a Canadian film about prison and prison sexual violence. The main actors in this film were all white—those who played the guards, the rapists, and the rape victims. Yet this same article anxiously attempts to cordon off prison rape so that it is the responsibility of incarcerated Black men and that its primary victims are innocent, young, white men. As Phillip Brian Harper argues, US American anxiety about Black masculinity "is so intense as to characterize even sites from which African-American men are notably *absent*."[2] As in the trailer for *Hit & Run* that I described in this book's introduction, Black men are conjured up and imported into this story about prison sexual violence where no Black men even appear; the author transforms a narrative apparently entirely about white men in order to reinforce widely held perceptions about the sexual insatiability of Black men.

If Hofsess was anxious about the content of *Fortune and Men's Eyes* in 1970, he was certainly not alone. From the play's opening in New York's West Village in 1967, to a London production a year later, to its Los Angeles premiere in 1969 followed by a second New York production in the same year, to the film version released in 1971, *Fortune and Men's Eyes* seemed to engender anxiety everywhere. Discussions of the play in print tended, paradoxically, to be both emotional and careful. Perhaps even more interestingly, although *Fortune* was the first American play to represent male/male rape *as* rape, critics discussing the play in the 1960s and 1970s appear to have had no notion that *Fortune* broke ground in any way. The reasons for this apparent historical oversight are related to changing ideas about homosexuality, sexual violence, race, and incarceration during this time period and, as we shall see, *Fortune* became a focal point for these new discursive formations.

Prison Rape Discourse and the 1960s Shift

Although *Fortune* was the first play to deal explicitly with male/male rape, it was certainly not the first document to discuss rape within American prison systems. In *The Prison Journal* in 2013, a group of authors including David and Cindy Struckman-Johnson preface an essay on prison-rape prevention with a historical note, relating that "Sexual abuse—the act of being pressured or forced to engage in sexual contact against one's will—has long been a toxic problem in US prisons. First exposed by [Joseph] Fishman's review of American prisons in 1934, sexual abuse was declared [by Alan J. Davis, writing in 1968] to be 'epidemic' among young inmates in the Philadelphia jails in the 1960s."[3] In order to discuss the twenty-first-century problem of sexual violence in prisons, the Struckman-Johnson piece draws a line of continuity and identity through three different historical moments: 1934, 1968, and 2013. Before discussing *Fortune and Men's Eyes* and its representation of rape in the late 1960s, I want briefly to disaggregate the moments in the Struckman-Johnsons' timeline, examining more closely how our current discourses about male/male sexual violence differ from those of even the recent past. Despite the historical continuity described by the Struckman-Johnsons, discourse around prison rape, in fact, differed widely in these three moments. It has a very particular, racialized history, it has shifted enormously over time, and as I will argue here, discourse in the 1960s saw a significant break with the past and issued in new ways of thinking and talking about rape in American prisons.[4]

Joseph Fishman's *Sex in Prison* (1934), the first important study of sexual activity in US carceral facilities, did not "expose" a problem called "sexual abuse" among incarcerated populations. That a phrase like *sexual abuse* forms no part of Fishman's lexicon is perhaps unsurprising, but Fishman also never uses the word *rape* in his exposé. Even more notable than Fishman's choice of descriptors for sexual violence is the almost total absence of such violence in his book. *Sex in Prison*, simply put, is not about rape. To the contrary, what Fishman aims to discuss is the "sex problem" in prison, by which he means homosexual sex and homosexuality.[5] Indeed, the chapter the Struckman-Johnsons construe to be about male/male rape in prisons is intriguingly titled "Homosexuals Who Are Formed in Prison."

Fishman's chapter is devoted primarily to three narratives. In one, a young man called simply C. S. is "debauched and made homosexua[l] for life."[6] Although the author describes his story as "tragic" and "depressing," C. S.'s sexual activity—at least as Fishman reports it—is entirely nonviolent, and the young man, in fact, reports experiencing a great deal of pleasure with his male sexual partners. Fishman's second story is quoted wholesale from Alexander Berkman's *Memoirs of a Prison Anarchist* (1912), and it concerns a prisoner named George who falls hopelessly in love with a younger man named Floyd.[7] Berkman calls George's love for Floyd "a wonderful thing," and this entire section of the *Memoirs* is an apology for the fantasy of a platonic homosocial desire similar to the one we find in the early chapters of E. M. Forster's *Maurice* (c. 1913).

The third story in "Homosexuals Who Are Formed in Prison" is about an unnamed prisoner who is most definitely sexually assaulted: the man's rapist threatens him with a stiletto if he doesn't comply and then violates him repeatedly for the next two years. But Fishman's response to this violence is a fascinating reflection of his own historical moment. "The prisoner," he says, "[insisted] that he had not become sympathetic to homosexuality, although he received some pleasure from it.... His attitude led me to believe that this was too shameful an admission for him to make even though he had indulged in homosexuality for two or three years."[8] Fishman's focus here is on the probability, even inevitability, of the *homosexuality of the victim* in this case, and his use of the word *indulged* is telling. The author's interpretive frame for genital contact in prison is one that understands such contact as related to pleasure, to homosexual desire, and to sensual indulgence. In this 1934 text, then, the topic under discussion was not rape at all, but was, as the title of Fishman's study makes clear, homosexual sex, even when the man had been violently raped.

Thirty-four years later, Alan Davis's report in *Trans-Action* would contrast starkly with Fishman's. His report is a shocking and terrific exposé that details five separate rape incidents in the Philadelphia prison system using the prisoners' own language. Davis's piece is stunning for several reasons. First, as the Struckman-Johnsons note, Davis claims that rape is epidemic in the Philadelphia prison system: his data show that these sexual assaults are not isolated incidents but are occurring on a widespread basis and have become, in fact, a part of the very structure of the Philadelphia carceral system. Second, Davis attempts to make a clear distinction between what he calls *consensual homosexuality* and rape. He claims, however, that "it was hard to separate consensual homosexuality from rape, since many continuing and isolated homosexual liaisons originated from a gang rape, or from the ever-present threat of gang rape."[9] If, in 1934, Fishman attributed nearly all genital contact in prison to "homosexuality," Davis's 1968 perspective is that anything that might be referred to as homosexuality in prison is, in effect, the result of violence, and he mistrusts officials who are "too quick to label such activities as 'consensual.'"[10] Further, Davis notes with surprise that "the typical sexual aggressor does not consider himself to be a homosexual, or even to have engaged in homosexual acts" but "defines as male whichever partner is aggressive and as homosexual whichever partner is passive."[11] Davis understands rape, then, as nonconsensual and the result of aggression, but he also sees it fundamentally as a sexual act: even in this blistering account he does not use terms equivalent to *assailant* or *victim* but describes *partners* and speaks of *passivity*.

We might explain this paradox by considering the most explosive element of Davis's report—the racial dynamics of the violence reported in *Trans-Action*. Of the incidents of sexual assault Davis studied, more than 84 percent were committed by Black men; 56 percent of assaults studied were committed by Black men on white victims. Davis attributed this disparity to the "fact that 80 percent of inmates" were Black, while positing that sexual assaults in general are "expressions of anger and aggression prompted by the same basic frustrations that exist in the community."[12] For Davis, the majority of rapes were committed by angry, disenfranchised, and disaffected Black men who took advantage of the opportunity afforded by their racial majority in prison to act out an anti-white aggression that their minority status outside the prison would not allow them to effect. Davis's report is intently and anxiously focused on racializing the sexual violence in these prisons. He sees race as the most salient factor in his analysis. But he still cannot help but understand sexual violence through the older lens of sexuality from the 1930s, conferring homosexuality on both the perpetrator of such violence and his victim.

Davis's analysis here would become typical of post-1960s responses to prison sexual violence. Sociologists reported collections of overwhelmingly racialized data but did little to make sense of the confusion that male/male rape creates vis-à-vis taxonomies of sexuality. In statistical analyses of prison rape, we see a similar insistent and anxious racialization in texts such as Anthony Scacco's *Rape in Prison* (1975), Daniel Lockwood's *Prison Sexual*

Violence (1980), and William F. Pinar's *The Gender of Racial Politics and Violence in America* (2001); this continues through the 2013 Struckman-Johnson piece in *The Prison Journal*, which states unequivocally that "it is well established in the literature that Caucasians are often sexually victimized by African Americans."[13] The racialization of male/male rape as the responsibility of Black men coincides precisely with the history charted by Michelle Alexander in *The New Jim Crow* (2012), in which politicians purposely and ideologically linked violent crime with the achievement of civil rights for Black folks. Rising crime rates in urban areas and "law and order" campaigns were mobilized as arguments against Black freedom.[14] This same discourse needed the prison rapist to become a Black man. "Even rape is predetermined," argues Tommy Curry, "because whether a Black man commits rape or not, he will always be seen, even in consensual sexual relations, to be a rapist. His mere presence intends a rape, and the prison is built to house this inevitable act."[15] What Curry helps us understand here is that as the images of the Black rapist are mobilized outside of the prison, and as mass incarceration rises in the 1960s, rape in prison is laid inevitably at his feet. Already the scapegoat for sexual deviance outside of the prison, he becomes the inevitable scapegoat for sexual deviance inside.

That Black male sexuality, for Alan Davis, is understood as fundamentally aggressive also works to cement the idea of white male vulnerability that will become typical of representations of prison rape at least through *Oz* in the early 2000s (see Chapters 4 and 5). For the historian Regina Kunzel, this anxiously repeated image of the (heterosexual) white man as the victim of a sexually violent Black man is a project that serves ideologically to reinforce heterosexuality by supplanting the possibility that sexual activity in prisons might be due to a desire for homosexual pleasure, explaining it instead by placing blame on Black men and their supposed aggressively deviant sexuality. "However alarmed the reports of prison sexual violence were in this period," Kunzel argues, "and however much they stoked fears and resentments about race, they worked paradoxically to ease concerns about the instability of sexual identity. The discomfiting fact of the participation of heterosexual men in homosexual sex was explained away by discourses of race."[16] We see this explicitly in the Hofsess piece with which this chapter opens: the problem is not "homosexuality" but "a different lust." This repetition in the literature, then, of an aggressive Black sexuality that victimizes white masculinity in prison, does important cultural work as it shores up the boundaries of heterosexuality by resuscitating racist images that have been used in US American culture since at least the nineteenth century. Further, because Davis—along with most other social scientists in the 1960s—is only able to understand rape as a kind of violent homosexuality, his report removes altogether the possibility of the Black man either as an object of sexual desire or as a possible victim of sexual violence.

According to Kunzel, Davis's report in *Trans-Action* "launched, in turn, an epidemic of investigations, sensationalistic journalistic exposés, prisoner autobiographies, and film and fictional representations of American prisons and jails, the primary focus of which was the alarming frequency and horror of rape among male inmates."[17] We might more accurately describe this rise in attention paid to prison rape as a shift in ways of thinking about sexual activity in prisons. This shift coincided with an important group of historic events all occurring between 1968 and 1971, the years of *Fortune and Men's Eyes*' greatest popularity. These include the decriminalization of consensual homosexual sex in England and Wales in 1967, the relaxation of theater censorship in Britain in 1968, the decriminalization of homosexuality in Canada in May of 1969, the Stonewall Riots in New York City that June, the killing of George Jackson in August of 1971, and the prison uprising in Attica, New York that September.[18] *Fortune and Men's Eyes* and male/male rape, then, became central to several larger transnational conversations in the late 1960s and early 1970s, and the popularity of discourse surrounding these topics emerged during a time of extreme upheaval, as interpretive paradigms for homosexual sex, prison violence, conditions of incarceration, and theatrical propriety all were shifting in the United Kingdom, Canada, and the United States.

Functioning as a public and very popular representation of this confluence of topics, John Herbert's play became a contested site for critics, activists, and audiences alike. The play, with its images of underrepresented populations (gay men, Black men, prisoners, rape victims), has from the first been an unstable quantity, a floating signifier hotly debated by both critics and audiences. This chapter traces *Fortune and Men's Eyes* as a representation of male/male rape in an American prison and explores the ways this violence was described by critics and understood by audiences. I am interested in how both groups anxiously negotiated the nexus of issues addressed by the drama. As the first play to portray male/male rape as rape, *Fortune* would also set a precedent for how male/male rape would be read in subsequent representations and would fundamentally shift representations of prison in popular culture. This Canadian play, which perhaps appears marginal to the history of American theater, ought to be considered, rather, as central to the history of representations of prison across all media, constructing the interpretive frame through which audiences would come to understand sex and violence in prisons in the United States, as well as Canada and the UK.

The New Prison Drama

Herbert's play concerns a group of four young men in what he calls "a Canadian reformatory," a prison for juveniles. The play is set in the boy's dormitory/cell, but "the whole upstage wall is barred" so that Herbert has designed the most dominating feature of the set to be a signifier for the boys' incarceration.[19] *Fortune* follows a young man named Smitty, a first-time offender who is taught the difficulties, horrors, and politics of prison life by his three cellmates, Queenie, Mona, and Rocky. As is typical in earlier prison dramas such as William Douglas Home's *"Now Barabbas..."* (1947) and Tennessee Williams's *Not about Nightingales* (1938), the young men in Herbert's play represent "a most bewildering variety of different types. Each man is distinct and completely different from each of the others."[20] Queenie, the most flamboyant of the play's characters, is a hardened and clever prison queen, adept at prison politics and expert in her manipulation of sexual power. Herbert describes Mona, on the other hand, as "hang[ing] suspended between the sexes, neither boy nor woman"; Mona is quiet and submissive, and the play always treats him as an honest, sensitive character who cannot quite take care of himself.[21] Both Queenie and Mona are trans-feminine figures, and although they are incarcerated in a juvenile institution for young men, Herbert represents their genders as more complex than the state's enforcement of the gender binary. This complexity is reflected in the way they gender themselves and one another. Queenie, for example, consistently refers to herself in the feminine, but although Queenie and Rocky both use female pronouns to describe Mona, he introduces himself using Jan, his male name, and seems to dislike both feminine pronouns and being called Mona. Rocky, by contrast, is brutal and mean, insulting everyone in the cell as often as possible and constantly attempting to differentiate himself from the two "queers" with whom he is forced to bunk.[22]

Before Herbert throws the naive everyman Smitty into this mix, he offers the audience a brief exchange of prison argot as the three young people try to figure out what's going on outside their cell:

MONA: It's the new arrivals.
ROCKY: Anybody ask you to open your mouth, fruity?

QUEENIE: Oh, lay off the Mona Lisa, for Christ sake, Rocky.
ROCKY: Always getting her jollies looking out that hole.
QUEENIE: Does Macy's bother Gimbel's?
ROCKY: They got their own corners.
QUEENIE: Well she ain't in yours, so dummy up!
ROCKY: Don't mess with the bull, Queenie!
QUEENIE: Your horn ain't long enough to reach me, Ferdinand.
ROCKY: You might feel it yet.
QUEENIE: Worst offer I've had today, but it's early.[23]

This rapid-fire dialogue immediately accomplishes a number of things for Herbert's dramaturgy. It disorients the play's audience by mobilizing unfamiliar language; it also demonstrates the power structure of the cell as Rocky bullies Mona and Queenie defends him. The struggle for dominance in this dormitory is, so far, not a violent one, but the terms of the fight are, even from these first few minutes of *Fortune*, intensely sexualized. It is important to note, as well, that the winner in this miniature verbal battle is Queenie. That is, Herbert sets up a convention, from the first minutes of the play, where Rocky's threats of violence are revealed as empty through the skill of Queenie's pointed humor. In this way, Queenie establishes her power as the cleverest, shrewdest character both in the cell onstage and with the audience in the theater.

Queenie's relationship with the audience depends, as well, on another mode of knowledge that she and the audience share. For if Herbert intends the prison argot to clarify the audience's distance from the world portrayed onstage in the play, not all of the language Queenie and Rocky use in these first few moments is particular to prison life. Take, for example:

ROCKY: Look at the queer watchin' the fish! See anything you can catch, Rosie?
QUEENIE: How's the new stock, Mona? Anything worth shakin' it for?
MONA: They're all so young.
QUEENIE: That'll suit Rocky. If he could coop a new chicken in his yard, he might not be so salty.[24]

This dialogue is not simply the occasionally inscrutable argot of prisoners; it is also a conversation filled with language specific to and shared by gay men and trans women in 1960s New York. As historian George Chauncey has noted, much gay argot "derived from the slang of female prostitutes" and was adopted by feminine men such as Queenie long before such language became commonplace for a majority of gay people. That this exchange with Rocky is highly inflected with gay male camp reflects camp's status as both "a cultural *style* and a cultural *strategy*."[25] Such analysis helps us to understand how Queenie's ability to make the audience laugh and verbally trounce Rocky is, in fact, heavily dependent on her ability to communicate in code to a gay and trans audience already familiar with the conventions of camp. As David Halperin has argued, "camp is about cutting everyone down to size. . . . Camp is about deflating pretension, dismantling hierarchy, and remembering that all queers are stigmatized and that no one deserves the kind of dignity that comes at the expense of someone else's shame." Herbert crafts Queenie in a style typical of gay camp; each of her witty retorts to Rocky's threats "both presumes and produces community" with her audience.[26]

As soon as Smitty enters the scene, the three young men begin to school him in the workings of the reformatory. Talk turns immediately to violence as Queenie and Rocky describe a young Iroquois man who was severely beaten by three of the guards. They also describe the politics of the prison, which, in *Fortune and Men's Eyes*, circulate around sex. Queenie, Rocky, and Mona each play particular sexual roles. The dialogue remains campy, but it is not at all frivolous. Sexual positions indicate positions of power, even as the young men squabble:

QUEENIE: You've got a one-track mind, and it's all dirt.
ROCKY: My shovel's clean.
QUEENIE: I don't know how. Every time you get in a shower, you've got it in somebody's ditch.
ROCKY: Don't be jealous. I'll get around to shoveling it in yours.[27]

Queenie describes Rocky as a top, but a bit later, as the two tell Smitty how best to survive among the other prisoners, Rocky describes submitting sexually to older prisoners: "You'll have to serve a little keester to the politicians who wanna put you in the barn," he says. Smitty quickly informs the three homosexually active young men that he's "not . . . queer" and that he has a girlfriend, but Mona informs him that "life inside is different."[28] According to the young men in *Fortune*, there is no such thing as a prisoner who is not sexually attached to someone else for protection or political gain. At no point does Herbert's play diverge from this sexualized representation of the hierarchies of carceral life, and as the inmates describe it, the punishment for aspiring to independence from this sexual economy is rape.

In the play's first scene, Queenie, attempting to convince Smitty to get himself an "old man," describes a time when Mona was repeatedly raped. "One day in the gym," Queenie tells us, "a bunch of hippos con her into the storeroom to get something for the game, and teach her another one instead. They make up the team, but she's the only basket. They all took a whack, now she's public property. . . . [D]on't wait until they give you a gang splash in the storeroom. Mona had to hold on to the wall to walk for a week."[29] Queenie's description of Mona's rape is brutal, and the idea of being gang-raped so terrifies Smitty that he agrees when Rocky offers to be his old man. Apparently, however, Smitty hasn't quite understood the arrangement, and his confusion prompts the first scene of the play to end with the following terrifying sequence:

> ROCKY: Get movin' . . . into that shower room.
> [. . .]
> SMITTY: No! I changed my mind. I don't want an old man.
> ROCKY: You got a old man, an' that's better than the storeroom, buddy boy!
> SMITTY: I'll take a chance.
> ROCKY: I'll make sure it's no chance. It's me or a gang splash. Now move your ass fast. I'm not used to punks tellin' me what they want.
> *He grabs Smitty's arm, twisting it behind the boy's back.* SMITTY *gives a small cry of pain, but* ROCKY *throws a hand over his mouth, pushing him toward the shower room.* SMITTY *pulls his face free.*
> SMITTY: Rocky . . . please . . . if you like me . . .
> ROCKY: I like you . . . an' you're gonna like me![30]

The stage goes to black. Herbert does not dramatize Rocky's rape of Smitty. Rape here remains unspoken as rape, and Herbert metonymically substitutes the visual of rape with the violence described in the stage direction—arm-twisting and forced silence.

Act 1 of *Fortune* continues with Smitty rebelling against Rocky at Queenie's urging. She tells Smitty that he needs to be "nobody's punk" and convinces him to get out from under Rocky by beating him up. Smitty agrees, and Queenie offers herself sexually to him. To the offer of sex Smitty responds with an unenthusiastic but assenting "It'd be a change, anyway."[31] Act 1 ends with Smitty severely beating Rocky in the shower room, and this sequence of violence, like the rape in the scene previous, takes place offstage, the particulars of the beating left to the audience's imagination.

Whether or not there is a sexually violent component to Smitty's revenge as he assaults Rocky, Herbert never makes explicit in the play's text.

Fortune's second act begins with a shift as we find Queenie rehearsing her routine for the prison Christmas show. She does a fan dance in drag "looking like a combination of Gorgeous George, Sophie Tucker and Mae West"; Queenie sings a camp version of the Tucker tune "A Good Man Is Hard to Find" but, in a Mae West flourish, she has twisted the lyrics to "A hard man is good to find."[32] Smitty, Rocky, and a prison guard are all sexually aroused by the dance, and in contrast to Smitty's lack of enthusiasm at sex with Queenie at the end of act 1, he now says "you look sexy as hell" and tells her to "sing it for Daddy, and don't forget I like the wiggle accompaniment."[33]

Smitty has, over the course of the play, become a hardened convict, and Herbert makes clear that the prison system is responsible for this transformation. After Queenie, Rocky, and the guard leave for the Christmas show, Smitty tells Mona how much he likes him and that he wants to be Mona's "old man." Mona reveals that he is in jail on a sex charge—he was robbed and beaten by a gang of men and then accused of "making a pass" at them—but Mona refuses to have sex with Smitty.[34] He is in love with Smitty and doesn't want him to be a part of his real life, a life of constant sexual abuse at the hands of other prisoners and guards; "I—separate!" he tells Smitty, "I separate things in order to live with others and myself. What my body does and feels is one thing, and what I think and feel apart from that is something else.... It's to the world I dream in you belong."[35] The two reconcile and are laughing together when Rocky and Queenie enter and (apparently out of jealousy) cause a fight. The guard breaks up the brawl and blames Mona for it. He is accused, as he was in court, of "making a pass," and the guard hauls him offstage to be beaten. Smitty threatens Rocky and Queenie; he then listens as Mona is beaten—again Herbert asks us to imagine the offstage action. Smitty returns to center stage a changed man. "His face now seems to be carved of stone," Herbert declares; "the mouth narrow, cruel and grim, the eyes corresponding slits of hatred. He speaks in a hoarse, ugly whisper.... Looking coolly out to the audience with a slight, twisted smile that is somehow cold, sadistic and menacing." The play ends with Smitty directly threatening the audience with revenge for the violence against Mona to which he has just been listening: "I'm going to pay them back. I'll pay you all back."[36]

On paper, *Fortune and Men's Eyes* is a complex, slightly awkward combination of social critique, gay romance, and campy humor. David Rothenberg, moved by the story and the fact that it was based on the author's own experiences in a Canadian prison, produced the play's original theatrical run using his own life savings when he couldn't find anyone else to fund it.[37] Rothenberg intended his production of *Fortune* as a critique of the prison system in the United States. This critique contained an awareness of the racial makeup of US prisons that is not in the play's original text: the producers cast gay Black actor Robert Christian as Mona, a role ostensibly written for a white actor and played by a white actor in most subsequent productions of *Fortune*.[38] Christian's casting reflected the producers' awareness of the increasing number of Black men incarcerated in the United States and the vehemently racialized discourse surrounding prison rape in the late 1960s. Christian's appearance as Mona was important, not least because *Fortune*'s only apparent awareness of incarcerated men of color is the mention of the Iroquois prisoner whom we hear the guards beat in scene 1. Further, Christian's casting moves us away from the typical racialized portrayal of male rape victims in the literature: both Mona and Smitty are attacked in *Fortune*, and so the play in this original production described both a young feminine Black man and a young masculine white man as vulnerable to sexual violence.

This first production's intended social critique was made still clearer through weekly discussions following shows. "Tuesday nights became discussion night at the Actors' Playhouse," Rothenberg remembers in his memoir. "Parole officers, elected officials, and judges revealed themselves in the audience and frequently joined us" in the post-performance discussions onstage."[39] Two formerly incarcerated men—Pat McGarry and Clarence Cooper—usually spoke on these Tuesday nights. Rothenberg himself acted as moderator, and by all accounts, they were productive, provocative, and exciting.[40] *The New York Times* covered these post-show talks and reported that "gradually, out of this experience, there grew the decision to 'do something' about prison reform. In November 1967, an organization took shape, its name derived from the play—the Fortune Society," a charity designed to help incarcerated men and women after they are released from prison, to speak to young people about the horrors of prison life, and to work for reform of the prison system itself.[41]

The establishment of this charitable and political organization designed to help improve the lives of prisoners came directly out of the publicity garnered by the first production of *Fortune and Men's Eyes* off-Broadway. Caoimhe McAvinchey credits Herbert's play for this effect, arguing that "*Fortune* dared to reflect a version of the world that was raw, brutalised and unjust and demanded that theatre audiences think about what happens in prison and *do* something about it."⁴² Theatre scholar Neil Carson calls *Fortune* a "hard-hitting drama about prison life" that "exhibits in a particularly emphatic way the violence and corruption of prison society." For Carson, the play is a meditation on dehumanization and the effects of incarceration; he asserts for example that "the significant human problems . . . are the problems which transcend sexual categories—the problems which arise in moments of crisis in war, in emergencies, in prison."⁴³ These discussions of the play frame *Fortune* as a very serious drama about conditions prisoners are made to suffer, and place the play in conversation with new debates in the late 1960s about prison reform and inhuman prison conditions.⁴⁴

Most New York theater critics, however, saw this first production differently. Dan Sullivan, in the *Times*, understood that Herbert intended the play as a critique of the prison system—"Obviously, he feels strongly about his subject; obviously, he wants us to feel as enraged, as disgusted at the system that breeds such corruption"—but he noted that, rather than accomplishing its critique, the play's "only live character . . . is an outrageously funny 'queen' played in the style of the immortal Mario Montez."⁴⁵ Edith Oliver of *The New Yorker* offered a similar critique, remarking that "the play appears to have been written in good faith; there was no evidence—to me, at any rate—of pornographic intent," but she added that "there is no overwhelming evidence of talent, either, in anyone concerned. *Fortune and Men's Eyes* is repulsive, but it is not disturbing, for beneath it beats a heart of corn."⁴⁶ Both Oliver and Sullivan see that the play aspires to seriousness but find those aspirations undermined by the attempted marriage of social critique and camp.

"The Boys in the Band Get Busted"

Whether viewed as serious, sensational, or sentimental, in this first production *Fortune and Men's Eyes* was a hit. But although advertisements for the play emphasized its profundity and gritty realism, comparing Herbert to playwrights Peter Weiss and Jean Genet (Figure 1.1), audiences for the play appear to have been overwhelmingly gay men.⁴⁷ Perhaps even more importantly, *Fortune* was unquestionably a play *about* gay men. In an opinion piece in *The New York Times* about gay characters in literature, a commentator who used a pseudonym complained that *Fortune* was yet another drama where gays are only shown in a negative light, and Margaret Harford, in her *précis* of the play for the *Los Angeles Times*, ignored entirely the

FIGURE 1.1: Ad for *Fortune and Men's Eyes* from page 28 of the *New York Times*, 3 March 1967

acts of rape in the play and stated that *Fortune* "deals with homosexuality and other indignities of prison life."[48] *Variety* even subtitled its review of *Fortune*'s film version "The Boys in the Band Get Busted."[49] If audiences understood that the 1967 production of *Fortune and Men's Eyes* was a piece about gay men—more interested in titillation than social justice—then the UK premiere in 1968 and Sal Mineo's productions (in Los Angeles and in New York City) in 1969 cemented this association.

In London, in a new production directed by Charles Marowitz, the director attempted an audience-immersion technique, fingerprinting audience members and posting ushers as prison guards. "The audience was assaulted by distant sirens, the sound of alarm bells and droning voices making prison announcements," but Marowitz also added an element of nudity never present off-Broadway.[50] *Variety* reported that "the play has been ballyhooed over a scene in which three men were said to emerge from a shower room and dry themselves." But although the *Variety* critic called the scene "over-publicized," his description is all the more aimed as a promise of titillation: "There are swift backviews of two of the men and only a theatergoer with swift, keen eyesight will catch a glimpse of the genitals of the other actor as he turns on stage." The critic all but invites those with exceptional abilities to test their skill! *Variety*'s review of the London production focused solely on sex and never on prison conditions, synopsizing that "the thin storyline concerns a young heterosexual serving his first reformatory term, sharing a dormitory with three convicted homos and swiftly becoming depraved."[51] Despite the director's stated intentions, in the popular press *Fortune* was not a play about social justice, it was a sexy play about gay life in prison.

Back in the US, Hollywood actor Sal Mineo—who rose to fame in Nicholas Ray's *Rebel without a Cause* (1955) but whose star had been on a slow fade since the early 1960s—directed *Fortune*'s West Coast premiere. Taking onstage male nudity several steps further than London for the Los Angeles production, Mineo, who played the rapist Rocky, "decided to strip at stage left and walk across the stage with just a towel tossed over his shoulder." Mineo biographer Michael Michaud describes the director's modified version of the rape sequence in the following way:

> [Rocky] then grabs Smitty, pushes him into the shower [onstage for this production], tears off his clothes, shoves him against the prison bars, and begins to sodomize him. A prison guard's whistle blows as the lights fade to black and Smitty painfully screams. Theater audiences had never seen anything like it before, and they had *never* seen a famous American actor (especially one twice nominated for an Academy Award) appear nude in a film or onstage.[52]

Mineo also changed the play's ending. In this production, after Mona was dragged offstage, Smitty masturbated as he listened to Mona being beaten by the guards, an "auto-erotic ending" that the *Los Angeles Times* clarified was "the director's idea, not the author's."[53]

Daily Variety was kind: "the controversial piece is handled with such good taste that it rises far above the somewhat objectionable subject and results in an entertainment that should assure tingling tills through a long run"; the trade paper also offered that the "simulated [rape] scene is candidly presented but so well blocked that it is in no way obscene."[54] Mineo, too, claimed to be more interested in the treatment of prisoners and prison conditions than in sexuality, visiting California's San Quentin prison in order to research the play and appearing extremely conscientious in all of the interviews he gave promoting it.[55] Mineo's changes to the show ostensibly involved an attempt at a greater degree of realism: he installed a working shower onstage and, as Marowitz had done in London, brought the prison setting out into the audience through the use of both scenic elements and ushers dressed as prison guards. Once again, however, the majority of critics focused on the play's eroticism. The *Los Angeles Times*, while mostly generous to Mineo, referred to "the cell's inmates" as "young perverts," and reported the staging as "graphic enough for reverse peristalsis."[56]

For his part, Mineo continued to emphasize the play's interest in prison reform, stating that "my intention was not: where can I put a nude scene. I didn't believe the kid's transition from a typical nice boy into a boy-slave—just like that—with no sign of it at all. I mean, they don't show anything in the original play—not one moment of physical violence."[57] As I noted earlier, Mineo's assessment of the offstage violence in Herbert's original text is accurate. The director's attempt to make the violence visible to *Fortune*'s audiences reflects, therefore, a particular ethical point of view related to representations of violence. For Mineo, the effects of the violence that Smitty experiences in *Fortune* ring false because the audience has not actually witnessed the violence to which Rocky subjects Smitty, and so the director aimed to place that violence where his audience could see it.

That these interviews about the ethics of onstage nudity and the importance of representing violence realistically were given to publications with a predominantly gay male readership such as *In*, *After Dark*, and *Avanti*, suggests, however, that Mineo was well aware of his play's intended audience. Michaud reports that "publicity targeted a predominantly homosexual demographic," also providing these magazines with titillating photographs of the cast taking showers and in various stages of undress, including nudes.[58] As with the first New York production, audiences were overwhelmingly male, and Dan Sullivan offers that "a tip-off to the essential thrust of this particular production . . . was the irreverent giggle heard from the audience recently during a tender scene between the boyish hero and [Mona]: 'Oh, give IN! I would!'"[59]

In Los Angeles, *Fortune and Men's Eyes* ran for seven months. The show did so well that Mineo found backing for a second production on the East Coast only two years after its first New York production. This time the show opened at Stage 73 on the Upper East Side, far away from the predominantly gay and trans neighborhood of Sheridan Square (which had been the site of the Stonewall Riots earlier in the year). Mineo kept all of the elements he had added in Los Angeles—the nudity, the onstage sexual violence, the autoeroticism—and also extended the rape scene from a brief one into a three-minute "gladiator battle in the shower."[60] This time, reviews were brutal. Clive Barnes in *The New York Times* said that "Mr. Mineo's version of this play is pure and tawdry sensationalism"; his bitter review included vilifications such as, "If this sounds like the kind of play you would like, it is to be found at Stage 73, . . . but Sir or Madam, I suggest that if this does sound like the kind of play you would like, you need a psychiatrist a lot more than you need a theater ticket."[61] A kinder but still dismissive *Village Voice* opined that "Mineo's lively presentation of prison life has all the authenticity, depth, and social consciousness of a gay-oriented 42nd Street novel on the subject."[62] In *Variety*, Richard Hummler described the revival as "crass sensationalism and a blatantly pandering production. It's poorly directed and even more poorly acted, but it has a lot of boxoffice impetus and should run indefinitely," he quipped acidly.[63] The *Los Angeles Times* referred to this revival of *Fortune* as "a play of singular sleaziness."[64] John Herbert himself even took the unusual course of writing an opinion piece in *Variety* criticizing Mineo's directorial choices and distancing himself from the production.[65]

Perhaps surprisingly, one of the chords consistently sounded in reviews of Mineo's 1969 production was its alleged departure from Herbert's original intentions. Barnes claimed that the play's "first production was fundamentally a serious indictment of the North American prison system," *Variety* seemed to remember the original *Fortune* as "a thought-provoking blast at the inhumanity engendered among inmates by prison life," and Sandra Schmidt claimed in the *Los Angeles Times* that even the fan dance that is such a centerpiece of act 2 "had nothing to do with the play," which she remembered as a drama about "the operation of power" and "the all-pervasive workings of love."[66] As we have seen, however, critics had been hostile to *Fortune* from the play's first production. *Fortune and Men's Eyes* had never been the ideal play about social justice in American prisons that scholars and critics wanted.

Despite the pans in the *Times* and *Variety*, the play ran at Stage 73 for nearly seven months. Mineo biographer Paul Jeffers attributes the show's longevity to gay male audiences, claiming that "gay men who hailed 'the Stonewall rebellion' considered it a duty and act of loyalty to flock to the box office of the small theater on 73rd Street."[67] Mineo's production may not have been to Clive Barnes's taste, but it had not offended New York's gay men; they plainly remained interested in what *The Village Voice*—despite its objections to the show—called "an honest, . . . accurate, portrayal of four homosexuals."[68] Audiences for productions of *Fortune and Men's Eyes*, at least in the United States, have *always* been overwhelmingly gay and male.[69] Herbert's play—with its campy humor, gay love story, and frank portrayal of sex exchanged for power—was, in fact, aimed at gay male audiences *as originally written*.

Perverting the Prison-Reform Play: Fortune's Legacy as Rape Drama

The remainder of this chapter will outline three important aspects that Herbert's play established for the prison dramas that would follow it and the widespread cultural implications of this dramaturgy for perceptions of prisons, the men they confine, and the sexual violence within their walls. The interpretive frame for male/male rape set up by these productions of *Fortune and Men's Eyes* between 1967 and 1970 ought not to be underestimated. *Fortune* is the first attempt by any dramatist at a portrayal of the damage caused by male/male rape, and its legacy was to have far-reaching effects. The play opened the door to prison drama about sexual violence, and it was released in a film version by MGM in 1971. *Fortune* was followed almost immediately by two other notable plays about prison life in the United States: Rick Cluchey's *The Cage* (1969) and Miguel Piñero's *Short Eyes* (1974), itself made into a film in 1977.[70] *Fortune*'s influence on both of these plays is undeniable, not because Cluchey or Piñero would necessarily have read Herbert's work—Cluchey had begun to sketch his play almost at the same time as Herbert finished his writing in Toronto—but because, as a public event, *Fortune* set up a series of expectations and paradigms for the new prison drama that deeply affected reception of *The Cage* and *Short Eyes*. Reviews of both plays frequently mention *Fortune* as an interpretive touchstone, often comparing the authenticity of the newer play with *Fortune*'s model. What I chart here is a shift in how prison dramas began to work in the years subsequent to Herbert's play.

Plays about prison in the US and UK have often included queer characters, but these dramas have, from the first, been documents interested in the brutality of prison life. *Fortune and Men's Eyes* marks a historical moment when dramatic representations of *the brutality of incarceration* transform into dramatic representations of *the brutality of prison sexual hierarchies*. Traditional realist prison dramas—beginning with John Galsworthy's *Justice* (1910) and including plays such as Martin Flavin's *The Criminal Code* (1929), Albert Bein's *Little Ol' Boy* (1933), Tennessee Williams's *Not about Nightingales*, and William Douglas Home's *"Now Barabbas . . ."*—all follow a similar pattern in which a young, innocent, or otherwise naive (white) protagonist is incarcerated and attempts to survive life behind bars.[71] Over this period that spans the first half of the twentieth century, these playwrights uniformly represent prison life as damaging. They document overcrowding, substandard living conditions, and mistreatment by guards and wardens. Although the protagonist in each play invariably tries to behave properly and stay out of trouble, he is uniformly crushed. This destruction is wrought by the prison system itself, which the playwrights indict as corrupt and damaging. Many of these protagonists have been killed by play's end; others have been transformed from good, honest people into hardened criminals.[72] In each case, the prison play engages in a call for social justice by using a kind of perverse bildungsroman in which the young prisoner is not allowed to come of age but instead either is killed or becomes an anti-social figure to be feared.

Fortune and Men's Eyes follows this traditional pattern of the prison-reform drama, and Herbert makes it quite clear in his play that what needs reform is the administration of the prison. The guards look the other way while Smitty is raped and possibly even rape Mona themselves; their actions condone all of the sexual violence that occurs in the prison. Mona, we find out by the play's end, has been incarcerated not for a criminal act but because of the failings of a justice system that sees an effeminate man as de facto deserving of incarceration. If, therefore, the play ends with Smitty vowing revenge against Rocky and Queenie, when he breaks the fourth wall he also looks out to the audience, promising to revenge himself on the entirety of the prison system and, by extension, society at large. As Herbert updated the social justice prison narratives of the 1930s and '40s, he naturally described the brutalities of carceral life that he experienced firsthand in Canada and that he saw as reflective of his contemporary moment in the 1960s. Understandably, then, the playwright's attempt at a realistic depiction of prison conditions necessitated a depiction of prison sexual hierarchies, the homophobia and transphobia of prison employees, and the ubiquity of sexual violence in prison systems. But critics' interest in the new politics of gay visibility outweighed any interest in prison rape prevention or the politics of prison reform. As Mariame Kaba and Kelly Hayes have argued, "Whether it's war, climate change, or the prison-industrial complex, Americans have been conditioned to simply look away from profound harms."[73] US American critics were interested in the sexual politics of the day, and in this way, the politics of prison reform were swallowed up by the more titillating and exciting new ideas about homosexuality then in circulation.

Rape Is a Homosexual Problem

I have already noted that the early critical reception of *Fortune* in the press focused on the play's attention to homosexuality, but the overwhelming majority of scholarly work on *Fortune* has also addressed the play from the point of view of the newly visible homosexual. Peter Dickinson notes that *Fortune and Men's Eyes* is often considered the beginning of "modern gay drama in Canada," and Alan Sinfield's catalog of gay and lesbian theater, *Out on Stage*, emphasizes sexuality as the play's most important subject.[74] Extraordinarily, in Sinfield's gloss of the play there is no reference to rape anywhere. Reading Sinfield, *Fortune* becomes a play about bullying: Rocky doesn't rape Smitty, he "exploits" him.[75] Sinfield's reading works rather to characterize the violence in *Fortune* as simply one more aspect of male homosexual relations.

I note Sinfield's conflation of male/male rape and homosexuality in *Fortune and Men's Eyes* because nearly every critic of the play's original production framed the play in exactly this way.[76] Martin Esslin, speaking about a growing trend of nudity in the theater, refers to the naked men "in John Herbert's play about homosexuality in a prison," and in *The New York Times*, Sylvan Fox referred to "the brutal, homosexualized world of a prison cell."[77] The *Los Angeles Times* claimed that the play examined the "dark side of gay life," and in her very perceptive piece for *The New York Times* titled "Up the Camp Staircase," Rosalyn Regelson offered that Herbert "equated the degradation of prison life with the homosexuality in the prison dorm."[78] These responses are typical of reviews for the productions of *Fortune* in London and Los Angeles, for both productions in New York, as well as for Harvey Hart's 1971 film version. For these critics, the prison is not a space that becomes a site for legally sanctioned sexual violence or racist discrimination. Instead, it is a breeding ground for "homosexuality." Put another way, male/male rape is here interpreted as a sexual act, and the rapist and his victim both as homosexuals. Such criticism makes no differentiation between the perpetrator of sexual violence and the man who is subjected to it.

It is fundamental to understand that in *Fortune and Men's Eyes* male/male rape and homosexuality were interpreted as though they were identical to one other. Because of this, reception of the play by both scholars and mainstream critics has focused not on the play's portrayal of male/male rape as one of the harrowing conditions obtaining in Canadian and US American prisons, but rather on the pernicious effects of homosexuality as such, as though what is wrong with American prison systems is homosexuality itself and not the conditions under which prisoners are forced to live. For the majority of critics, *Fortune* was a melodrama about homosexual sex much more than it was a play about the brutality of prison life, the flaws in American justice systems, or an inability to rehabilitate young criminal offenders. More pointedly, homosexual sex was interpreted *as equivalent to* the brutality of prison life, the flaws in American justice systems, and an inability to rehabilitate young criminal offenders. As the former warden at San Quentin prison put it in 1969, "There's plenty of sexual activity in our prisons, but it's the wrong kind. No inmate ... is entirely spared homosexual advances, and many succumb."[79] Rape, here, is not understood as rape but as homosexual sex, *and homosexual sex is what makes prison life brutal.*

If the play's reception deviated from Herbert's intentions, it is here, perhaps, where that discrepancy is most apparent. I have already claimed that *Fortune* attempted to follow a tradition of social-reform realism, but I want also to note briefly the way that Herbert's text attempts to portray rape and homosexuality as polar opposites. When Mona refuses to have sex with Smitty, he describes homosexual desire as something beautiful and precious, a kind of ideal love that he is unwilling to abandon. Mona says he loves Smitty, and when he characterizes himself as separating his real world from his dream-world, Mona places his love for Smitty in the dream-world and his experience of rape at the hands of other prisoners in the real world. "It's to the world I dream in you belong," Mona tells Smitty. "I won't let you move over, into the other, where I would become worthless to you—and myself. I have a right to save something."[80] In Mona's imagination, then, homosexuality is redemptive and beautiful, an ideal love set apart from the quotidian; male/male rape is this love's antithesis, a component of the violence and brutality of the world as it really is. In this way, Herbert places male/male sexual violence in stark contrast to gay desire. They are, in *Fortune*, each other's thematic opposites.

This aspect of Herbert's play appears to have made no significant impression on either reviewers or scholars. Many of the critics in the popular press saw homosexuality as a de facto component of the punishment of American prison systems, and this way of thinking was to become widespread across US American society; as noted earlier, accounts of prison sex in the 1960s and '70s were, according to Regina Kunzel, "newly ubiquitous, newly graphic and newly univocal in depicting sexual violence and brutality, so much so, in fact, that rape would come to be understood as the defining practice of sex in men's prisons."[81] Further, if to be raped was equivalent to a homosexual experience, then homosexuality was, again, reproducing itself, finding new recruits and converting them.

Homosexuality and male/male rape would remain equivalent to one another in the two prison dramas that immediately followed *Fortune*, Miguel Piñero's *Short Eyes* and John Cluchey's *The Cage*. In *Short Eyes*, for example, Paco attempts to seduce Julio (Cupcakes) in the shower by kissing his neck; Julio spurns his advances, but the two have a dangerous conversation where they frankly discuss male/male rape and link it explicitly to homosexuality.

> PACO: Man, cause I kiss you doesn't mean you're a faggot.
> CUPCAKES: It means you're a faggot... don't do it again... Leave me alone... déjame... You're sick.
> PACO: I'm what? Sick—don't you say that to me... Sick... Shit, I'm sick cause I'm in love with you... Push comes to shove, I'll take you. But I don't wanna do that cause I know I'm gonna have to hurt you in the doing. Look, man, I'll go both ways with you.[82]

Piñero describes rape here as an extension of homosexual desire: Paco offers Julio sex, then threatens to rape him, and then offers sex again, all while telling him that he loves him. Paco is willing to go both ways—he offers to allow Julio to penetrate him as well—but what Paco cannot earn through seduction he threatens to take through violence. In this shower sequence, Piñero figures rape as a clear result of Paco's frustrated homosexual desire for Julio, and Julio doesn't see his attempted rapist as a frustrated heterosexual; he explicitly identifies Paco as a "faggot."

Formally, *The Cage* is a more complex play than both *Fortune* and *Short Eyes*—it has a ritual, dreamlike quality to it that differentiates it from realism—but here too, sexual violence and homosexual sex are equivalent. Though Doc and Al are lovers at the beginning of Cluchey's play, Doc threatens Al with rape over the course of the narrative, and both of them threaten the new inmate, Jive. Their advances are seductive at first but grow violent when seduction doesn't work, using violence as a means to achieve sexual satisfaction.[83] In this way, the plays that immediately followed *Fortune* figured homosexuality and male/male rape as linked. So although *Fortune* attempted to articulate a clear distinction between homosexual desire and male/male rape, critics and later prison dramas emphasized them as identical.

Rape Is a Prison Problem

The second paradigm set up by *Fortune and Men's Eyes* was that it contained male/male rape within the walls of the prison. Herbert's placement of male/male rape inside a prison also worked to separate male/male sexual violence from an analysis of normative hydraulic sexual behavior. As critics discussed the brutal, "homosexualized" world of the carceral, they restricted male/male sexual violence to an activity created by the monosexual world of the prison, and they discursively cordoned male/male rape off from the world outside of this system. *Fortune*, *Short Eyes*, and *The Cage* all portray prison as a world entirely incommensurable with society at large. Each drama, in fact, is identical in its exposition, introducing a young, white, male prisoner who has never before been incarcerated. In all three plays this man is inexperienced and has no idea of the dangers, rules, or language of the prison. Another character in each play quickly explains carceral society to the new prisoner in the play's first scene. The audience, of course, needs these expository sequences in order for the plays themselves to work, but the very structure of these sequences requires an emphasis on the differences between society outside and society inside.

The effect here is to depict the world of the prison as a discrete, racially segregated system, populated by people very different from the audience, operating according to rules that differ widely from normative society and using a language only partially comprehensible to speakers of standard English. What is taken for granted in this prison world (dense argot, monosexuality, racial segregation, hierarchical structures of violence) is therefore represented as inherent to and the result of the processes of everyday life within prison society. As portrayed in *Fortune*, *Short Eyes*, and *The Cage*, male/male sexual violence is a product or consequence of the prison system, one, indeed, that appears to have been designed by the prisoners themselves. In this way, these theatrical representations give voice to male/male rape as a problematic and then locate that problematic within a community that needs reform but remains separate from normal society. As Kunzel argues, "Prisons were often represented as hermetic institutions in which residues of past and more primitive sexual cultures persisted and thrived."[84] In fact, prisons are designed to create a discrete field separate from that of the majority, and the dramaturgy of these three plays works to emphasize precisely such a difference. After the 1960s, populations of prisons in the United States grew increasingly Black, as media campaigns and daily police practices increasingly criminalized Black existence and incarcerated Black men and women.

This means, then, that even as productions of *Fortune* continued to be overwhelmingly populated by white actors, the *difference* of prison that the plays emphasized, was easy for audiences to imagine as a difference caused by the Blackness of prison. The plays characterize prison as a space for deviants and criminals, where activities take place that do not and never would take place among "normal" people. *Fortune* and its successors, then, ideologically place male/male rape *outside* the realm of possibility for normative white American society by placing it *inside* the four walls of the prison.

What *Fortune and Men's Eyes* and other early prison rape plays do not do—what, indeed, is entirely outside of their agenda—is question the binary structures of masculinity/femininity, of dominance/weakness, of penetration/impenetrability, of receptivity/aggressivity that adhere to representations of rape. Rather, because these dramas are focused on the damaging effects of incarceration and the failings of American justice systems, it is in the interest of these dramas to represent prison life as shockingly as possible. In this way, the plays portray prison rape as simply *the way things are in prison*, an attitude toward sexual violence that avoids interrogating rape as a problem inherent to societal structures formed and sustained *outside* of the carceral system. In 1968, therefore, when Rosalyn Regelson opined in *The New York Times* that "another interpretation of the action [of *Fortune*] might be that behind the brutal sexual assaults made on the weaker prisoners by the stronger was the need to assert our culture's sick idea of 'masculinity,'" she would be the lone voice in the medium of print to do so.[85] The overwhelming majority of critics saw the world of the prison in *Fortune* as unconnected to their own society, and neither *Fortune*, *Short Eyes*, nor *The Cage* discusses the hierarchical organization of prison sexuality as reflective of the masculinist hierarchies that structure the world outside of the carceral system. Instead, prison rape and the power that it produces appear to be sealed off from the very society that, in fact, creates and maintains the space that makes these power dynamics possible. In *Fortune and Men's Eyes*, prison sexual violence is not caused by gender dynamics that were invented outside of the prison but appears, rather, to have emerged, fully formed, from the discrete space of the prison itself.

Rape Authenticates Representations of Prison

The final aspect that I wish to emphasize about *Fortune* and the prison plays that immediately followed it is that in these plays rape is not a metaphor.

In this book's introduction I emphasized rape's consistent metaphorization and mobilization as a discursive device, so it is important that we note rape's dramaturgical function in these, the first dramas to treat the subject of male/male rape with any amount of frankness. As we shall see in the chapters that follow, later authors ask rape to stand in for numerous other concepts—genocide, barbarism, colonialism, depravity—but in these plays, the presence of sexual violation works, instead, to emphasize the *authenticity* of these dramas. Piñero, Cluchey, and Herbert do not present rape as though it signifies anything other than itself. Rather, in *Short Eyes*, *The Cage*, and *Fortune*, male/male rape is a fact of carceral existence, displayed mostly through realist social justice techniques and designed to demonstrate and expose the inhumane conditions of life behind bars.

The plays' frank portrayals of male/male rape as a normal and terrifying component of life in prison were so convincing that representation of rape would become a dramaturgical technique that worked to indicate a narrative's authenticity as a prison drama. The lasting effects of this authenticating gesture remain with us. After *Fortune*, mention of rape became a way for a representation of prison to demonstrate its authenticity, and references to prison rape would become commonplace in drama about prison. If *The Cage* and *Short Eyes* could not claim authenticity as prison drama without a portrayal of sexual violence among prisoners, virtually no play or film produced in the last fifty years with prison as its subject has been able to avoid some portrayal of rape or the threat of rape. Representations as different as Patricia Nell Warren's *The Front Runner* (1974), Ira Levin's *Deathtrap* (1978), David Mamet's *Edmond* (1982), William S. Yellow Robe's *The Independence of Eddie Rose* (1986), the 2004 science fiction movie *The Butterfly Effect*, the US television series *Oz* (1997–2003), and the 2008 stoner comedy *Harold and Kumar Escape from Guantanamo Bay* all explicitly include reference to rape as though it were a conventional even unremarkable aspect of prison life. In film and television, this list could go on almost indefinitely.

The link between rape and prison life has become so widespread that as long ago as 2001, Human Rights Watch confidently asserted that "judging by the popular media, rape is accepted as almost a commonplace of imprisonment, so much so that when the topic of prison arises, a joking reference to rape seems almost obligatory."[86] One recent example of this is a speech Donald Trump gave in 2022 in which he articulated his idea of the best way to get a journalist to reveal a confidential source: "And they say, 'We're not gonna tell you.' Then [you] say, 'That's OK. You're going to jail.' And when this person realizes that he is going to be the bride of another prisoner very shortly, he will say, 'I'd very much like to tell you exactly who that leaker [is].'"[87] Trump's audience laughed and applauded, easily interpreting "bride" to mean "rape victim," and understanding immediately that male/male rape is simply "what happens" in prison.

Fortune and Men's Eyes, though it has been all but forgotten by cultural theorists, has had a profound impact on the way that violent masculinity is figured in US American culture. The play's four important and very different productions in the late 1960s represented prison as a homosexual space where sexual violence was commonplace; by classifying male/male rape as simply one more aspect of the normal violence of life behind bars, these theatrical events crystallized popular discourses of the time, refashioning and sexualizing representations of prison life for years to come while simultaneously constructing these sexualized spaces as fundamentally different from the cultures that incarcerate young men and produce carceral spaces through legislative action. *Fortune and Men's Eyes* established a tradition of imagining sexual violence as something that burgeoned and developed within the walls of its prisons rather than locating the causes of sexual violence—male/male or otherwise—in a masculinity that structures and subtends our culture as a whole.

CHAPTER 2

How to Make a Man
Male/Male Rape in Mid-Century Fiction

> The moon runs down in a purple stream
> The sun refused to shine
> Every star did disappear
> Yes, freedom shall be mine!
>
> Didn't my Lord deliver Daniel
> Deliver Daniel, deliver Daniel?
> Didn't my Lord deliver Daniel
> And why not every man?
>
> —TRADITIONAL

This chapter turns to the fiction of the 1970s, primarily to James Dickey's *Deliverance* (1970) and James Baldwin's *If Beale Street Could Talk* (1974). I frame my analysis of these novels with two others written largely in the immediate post-war years of the late 1940s: Gore Vidal's shocking bestseller *The City and the Pillar* (1948) and the mostly ignored prison novel written by Chester Himes, *Yesterday Will Make You Cry*, which appeared posthumously in 1998 but was published in an abridged version in 1953 as *Cast the First Stone*. Central to all four novels—each of which includes male/male rape as subject matter—is the problem of US American masculinity, and this chapter explores the way each novelist uses rape as a limit case for what it means to be a man, testing his characters' masculinities by subjecting them to sexual violence or having them violate the bodies of others.

Vidal, Dickey, Baldwin, and Himes represent rape in strikingly different ways, and they ask male/male rape to mean very different things, depending on the use to which they put this fictional violence. I want to emphasize at the outset of this chapter, however, that although the discourse of *prison* rape crystallized over the course of the period from 1965 to 1971 in the wake of *Fortune and Men's Eyes*, the larger cultural poetics of male/male rape were not yet static. This same period in US American fiction saw images and sequences of male/male rape deployed to make meaning in a variety of ways, and the four novels examined in this chapter display a wide range of meanings, associations, and symbols rather than a consensus. Further, Vidal, Dickey, Baldwin, and Himes had radically different projects vis-à-vis US American understandings of masculinity, race relations, homosexuality, the criminal justice system, and the Vietnam War, and their novels—*The City and the Pillar Revised*, *Deliverance*, *If Beale Street Could Talk*, and *Yesterday Will Make You Cry*—ask us to look with new eyes at this nexus of issues and ideas.

For each novel I examine the body of critical analysis that has accumulated since its publication. The amount of scholarship written about these books varies from novelist to novelist: Dickey's and Baldwin's novels have been treated as literature—and therefore worthy of examination—in ways that Vidal's and Himes's novels largely have not. Himes, especially, has been ignored by scholars until only recently, and indeed *Yesterday Will Make You Cry* was only finally published in 1998. My goal here is to explore the meanings that scholars have found in the male/male rapes in these novels. I see the examination of scholarly interpretations as one way to take the temperature of changing ideas about male/male rape and its significatory power. But in nearly every case, scholars have studiously avoided examining the actual sequences of male/male rape in these novels, choosing instead to focus on rape as a meaning-bearing signifier for the larger, more important ideas to be taken from this literature. This means that the poetics of male/male rape have remained largely unexamined, even in books that have been key to the formation of US American ideas about—and cultural associations with—this violence. My analysis turns attention toward the sexual violence itself, toward the interpretive frames offered by these novelists, and toward their effects on the larger discourse of male/male rape in the United States.

Jim Willard and Mid-Century Masculinity

In 1965, after making a name for himself as a political commentator, television and film writer, playwright, and public intellectual, Gore Vidal returned to three of his earlier novels, revising and republishing them.[1]

Perhaps most notable among these was his *succès de scandale* from 1948, *The City and the Pillar*. A landmark in gay fiction, *City* was Vidal's third novel, but *The New York Times* had refused to run ads for the book because of its homosexual subject matter and—partially because of this—*The City and the Pillar* quickly became a bestseller.

Briefly, the book is about a young white man named Jim Willard who explores his burgeoning homosexuality over the course of six or seven years, coming to terms with his desires but pining, always, for his high school crush, Bob Ford, with whom he had a weekend of sex and play as a teenager. The city in Vidal's title refers to Sodom and Gomorrah, the fabled cities of the plain in the book of Genesis, but Vidal has always stated that the *pillar* in his title is more important to the novel's themes.[2] Jim Willard makes the mistake of continually looking back and, like Lot's wife in the story, he is paralyzed by this backward glance, unable to move forward with his life because he is fixated on the romantic ideas he has about Bob. At the end of *The City and the Pillar*, Jim finds his friend again and propositions him, wanting to renew their sexual relationship, but Bob rejects him: "'You're a queer,' he said, 'you're nothing but a damned queer! Go on and get your ass out of here!'"[3] Jim snaps and begins to fight Bob; he overpowers him and begins to choke him. Jim is stronger, and he kills his friend, all the while mourning the loss of his dream.

At least that's how *The City and the Pillar* ended in 1948. When Vidal revised the novel in 1965, he altered the ending so that instead of murdering his beloved, Jim overpowers Bob and then rapes him. As Vidal framed it rather acidly in his 1995 memoir *Palimpsest*, "To placate . . . those who felt that I was making a case that same-sexualists were homicidal psychopaths, I made it clear that Jim does not literally kill Bob, only the idea of him."[4] In the *Columbia Anthology of Gay Literature*, Byrne R. S. Fone claims that Vidal's novel *originally* ended with rape but that the publishers wanted a more violent ending.[5] Vidal has refuted this in his memoir and, as I argued in Chapter 1, male/male rape would have been understood by his readers in a very different way in 1948 than in 1965.[6] The discourse of male/male rape in the United States developed only in the mid-1960s, and prior to that time period, discussion of male/male rape was almost invariably framed as *homosexuality* rather than violence. Vidal reworked *The City and the Pillar* in 1965, altering the ending from murder and replacing it with male/male rape, but this literary maneuver did not return to some purer, more authentic version of the novel from the 1940s; rather, it was produced by and reflected new ideas about male/male rape that were emerging in the 1960s.

Critical consensus around the two different versions of *The City and the Pillar* is that the original ending is "melodramatic"—the word recurs with near-maddening regularity in literary analyses of the book—and that the revised ending is far superior from a literary standpoint.[7] Because of the coolly ironic tone of most of the novel, critics have found Vidal's newer version more detached, more plausible, and more in keeping with the novel as a whole. There are two other constants in critical analyses of *The City and the Pillar* in both its revised version and its original: scholars invariably discuss the novel's flat, unadorned prose; and they *always* focus on the masculinity of its protagonist, Jim Willard.[8]

It has seemed to most scholars that masculinity is the book's chief concern, and a majority of critics has remarked upon the fact that Jim Willard is a *normal* or *ordinary* young man who has homosexual desires. In one of the book's earliest reviews, critic Richard McLaughlin noted in the *Saturday Review* that "Unlike the usual characterization of the male homosexual in current novels, Jim Willard is drawn, with deliberate strokes, to appear the opposite of abnormal."[9] McLaughlin saw *The City and the Pillar* as a "problem novel" that was bound to shift attitudes about homosexual sex in the United States: "And with the help of the astounding revelations in the first report of the Kinsey group, a great many more people are soon going to be forcefully enlightened on the variety and changes in the American sex patterns and, furthermore, the necessity for greater public and private tolerance of the vast differences in the sex habits of Americans."[10]

Vidal takes pains to emphasize his protagonist's masculinity throughout *The City and the Pillar*, and Jim Willard regularly examines himself in order to reconcile his sexual desire for men with the societal assumptions about gender that are supposed to accompany those desires. Jim is clear about his homosexual desires, but he has trouble making sense of himself as a homosexual or as a member of the gay subculture with which he is familiar. Accordingly, Jim consistently refuses his own femininity. After spending time with the gay men he knows, "he would study himself in a mirror to see if there was any trace of the woman in his face or manner; and he was always pleased that there was not."[11] This passage has an ironic tone, and the narrator slightly mocks both Jim and his investment in his masculinity, but masculinity is nonetheless essential to Vidal's project in *The City and the Pillar*.

Critics have given a great deal of attention to Jim's masculinity. Citing earlier critics Susan Baker and Curtis Gibson, Claude Summers, Ray Lewis White, and Vidal himself, Angela Fratarrola points out just how frequently scholars have felt the need to refer to the *normality* and *ordinariness* of Vidal's protagonist.¹² Dennis Altman's analysis in *Gore Vidal's America* stands in for a large body of scholarship on *The City and the Pillar* and the masculine white man who has sex with other men. As he puts it:

> Jim Willard was a far greater threat to assumptions of sexual and gender normality than the fey creatures who waltzed through the pages of Truman Capote or Carson McCullers at the time. Within the confines of the period, [*The City and the Pillar*] rejected the stereotype of the homosexual as sissy, or the homosexual as victim, to foreshadow the sort of homosexual men whom the next generation of writers (Edmund White, Christopher Bram, etc.) would create.¹³

Vidal insists that there is no specific homosexual type, that simply because a man has sex with other men, that does not make him—to quote the famous passage in Foucault—now a species.¹⁴ Vidal articulates this using precise language in his 1965 afterword to *The City and the Pillar Revised*.

More recent critics have found this insistence on Jim's masculinity tiresome and its casual mockery of fey creatures (!) misogynist. Fratarrola's evidence in this area is overwhelming: critics have been intensely preoccupied with Jim Willard's distance from the effeminate gay men who defined homosexuality in popular media, and those same critics have often been outright dismissive of femininity.¹⁵ But feminine men populate *The City and the Pillar* as well, and Vidal's novel always treats them with derision. In a perceptive essay in *Twentieth-Century Literature* in 2013, Harry Thomas notes that:

> *The City and the Pillar* makes its case that Jim Willard can be both gay and masculine (and therefore normal) only by associating most other gay men with effeminacy (which is figured as abnormality). Rather than challenging mainstream culture's denigration of effeminacy, that is, *The City and the Pillar* seeks to normalize both Jim Willard's homosexuality and his masculinity by contrasting them to effeminate gay men who are themselves characterized as "strange womanish creatures."¹⁶

The City and the Pillar was a challenge to popular ideas about homosexuality, but it left unchallenged popular ideas about effeminacy or feminine men. And this is true of the novel in both its 1948 version and in *The City and the Pillar Revised*. Indeed, the revised version of the novel enlists male/male rape in its project.

Vidal's revisions lean further toward traditional white masculinity. He revised *The City and the Pillar* to tone down the "melodrama" of the original, to make his prose more flat and unadorned, and to transform "the murder of the beloved by the hysterical lover" into a violent purgation of nostalgic romantic fantasy.[17] Vidal is invested in conventional masculinity and in the (now more-or-less accepted) idea that a man can both practice homosexuality and be masculine according to mainstream criteria. But this position vis-à-vis masculinity and femininity is important because as Vidal added male/male rape to the plot of *The City and the Pillar Revised* in the mid-1960s, he did so according to the traditional associations that equate the violate man with femininity, powerlessness, shame, and humiliation. Vidal, in other words, uses male/male rape in conventional, easily decipherable ways, citing and contributing to a discourse that has been in place—as I noted in the introduction—since the ancient world.[18]

Like an ancient tragedy, *The City and the Pillar Revised* moves inexorably toward violent confrontation for the entirety of the novel, but once it arrives, the rape sequence takes up no more than a single page.[19] After Jim makes a pass at Bob, Bob hits Jim in the face and then tells him to leave his room. He then advances toward him, but Jim lunges at Bob and fights him, "overwhelmed equally by rage and desire." They grapple, in a sad echo of the novel's beginning, when the young men wrestled with sexual pleasure, and Jim overpowers Bob. The narrator reports the sequence with the same ironic detachment as the rest of the novel:

> Jim looked down at the helpless body, wanting to do murder. Deliberately he twisted the arm he held. Bob cried out. Jim was excited at the other's pain. What to do? Jim frowned. Drink made concentration difficult. He looked at the heaving body beneath him, the broad back, ripped shorts, long muscled legs. One final humiliation: with his free hand, Jim pulled down the shorts, revealing white, hard, hairless buttocks. "Jesus," Bob whispered. "Don't. Don't."
>
> Finished, Jim lay on the still body, breathing hard, drained of emotion, conscious that the thing was done, the circle completed, and finished.[20]

Within the novel as a whole, this is an emotionally difficult sequence because it is devastating for the protagonist. Jim is a wonderfully lovable and sensitive character. His dream of reconnecting with his beloved is shattered, and he responds in a surprising, violent way to this belated discovery.

But the details of the rape sequence in *The City and the Pillar Revised* reveal, further, a key for interpreting the protagonist's violence. Vidal's narrator not only describes Jim's rape of Bob, he also clearly offers a way for readers to make sense of it. The narrator links "rage and desire" here; Jim is "excited at the other's pain." And Jim desires Bob sexually: Bob's muscled legs, in particular, have been an object of Jim's fantasy for the entire length of the novel, and they appear again here for his—and our—visual pleasure. The narrator, even while speaking flatly, also takes care to describe Bob's buttocks using erotic language. Vidal emphasizes both sex and power in the passage; Bob is "helpless" and in pain, and Jim is stronger, "excited"—the word has an undeniable sexual valence—by his ability to hurt Bob.

In the context of this insistently masculine novel, Jim commits a performative act of gender as I've described it in the introduction. The narrator also understands Bob as *humiliated* by rape. Vidal's use of the word places Jim's rape of Bob within the long history of sexual violation as performatively shaming its victims. I discuss shame in more detail in Chapter 4, but it is worth noting here that the links between shame and rape are very old, described even in the fifth century, where Augustine's language in the *City of God* (413) characterizes rape as a performative that creates shame as an essential component of the violence it enacts.[21] Vidal's phrase "one final humiliation" makes this same move, explicitly attaching shame to victimization by rape.

The majority of this sequence is offered to us from Jim's perspective. The narrator tells us what's happening in Jim's mind, even when he is confused or when alcohol is making concentration difficult. Perhaps surprisingly, the narrator is not at all concerned with the *victim's* emotional experience of this sexual violence, but Vidal does offer more of Bob's responses as the sequence ends:

> Bob did not stir. He remained facedown clutching the pillow to his face while Jim dressed. Then Jim crossed to the bed and looked down at the body he had loved with such single-mindedness for so many years. Was this all? He put his hand on Bob's sweaty shoulder. Bob shied away from him: fear? disgust? It made no difference now. Jim touched the pillow. It was wet. Tears? Good. Without a word, Jim went to the door and opened it.[22]

Bob's disgust, shame, fear, and grief are reported to us but, significantly, we are given access to these emotions only from Jim's perspective, as he tries to recognize them through the filter of his own grief and frustration and anger. Identification with the rape victim, here, is made nearly impossible. The rape at the end of *The City and the Pillar Revised* is tragic, but it is important to understand it as a tragedy for Jim, whose story this is, and not for Bob, who is the object of desire not the subject of the narrative. My use of the word *tragedy* is purposeful here, as well. The narrator notes that Jim is "conscious that thing was done, the circle completed, and finished"; that is, both Jim and the reader achieve *narrative* closure through Jim's sexual violation of Bob.

The City and the Pillar, in both its original version and its revised version, is a novel about masculinity, specifically about a man coming to terms with his masculinity and his homosexual desire, neither of which he is willing to abandon. This is a novel that takes pains to shore up the boundaries of traditional US American masculinity through the disavowal of feminine men. Vidal is invested, here, in portraying a man who is decidedly *not* feminine, who refuses femininity, longing instead for something more like sexual brotherhood or the erotic life of the Sacred Band of Thebes. Within these terms, *The City and the Pillar Revised* must insist that Jim retain his masculinity. He must disavow femininity, and at the novel's conclusion he does so violently by sexually humiliating Bob.

What is extraordinary here is the way that *The City and the Pillar Revised* works to reconcile masculinity and homosexual desire in the person of the rapist. As Jim violates Bob, he is able to hold on to both masculinity and same-sex desire, though he is not able to satisfy his deeper longing for sexual brotherhood. It is easy to conceive of a version of this story, in which, perhaps, the gay protagonist finds himself overpowered and defeated in a violent confrontation with his beloved. This is precisely what happens to Mona in *Fortune and Men's Eyes*; he is beat up after being accused of making a pass at a group of straight guys. A version of this same story happens frequently in later cautionary tales about homosexual vulnerability with which we are all more familiar: when, for example, Adam/Felicia, Guy Pearce's character in *The Adventures of Priscilla, Queen of the Desert* (1994), is told to be more careful by his two friends but returns badly beat up after flirting with a group of straight men; or when Don Shirley, Mahershala Ali's character in *Green Book* (2018), is beat up by police after he is discovered having sex with another man; or when Nathan Stewart-Jarrett's character Jules is violently beaten by a man who checks him out in *Femme* (2023). In these more familiar stories, the feminine gay man is tempted by the eroticism of masculinity, he makes himself vulnerable to masculine violence, and he is physically injured by the forces of homophobia. Not so in *The City and the Pillar Revised*. Vidal's novel pries femininity and homosexuality apart, insisting instead on the violent, masculine domination of the straight man who calls Jim Willard a "queer."[23]

If Vidal separates homosexuality from femininity, however, he nevertheless attaches homosexuality to male/male rape. In *City Revised*, Jim is "excited" by the pain he causes Bob; he charges at him "with rage and desire" both. Jim dominates Bob using the sexualized terms of US American hydraulic masculinity, to be sure, but he also does this in a particularly *homosexual* way. Jim desires Bob sexually, and the rape he commits is not only an act of humiliation or anger; it is also sexually motivated. In fact, Vidal links homosexual desire and rape in another, earlier passage that he *also* added to the revised edition of the novel. Long before the final sequence of rape in *The City and the Pillar Revised*, Jim is in the Air Force and finds himself attracted to a young corporal named Ken: "Watching him through half-closed eyes, Jim felt desire. For the first time in months he wanted sex. He wanted the young corporal. Mentally, he raped him, made love to him, worshiped him; they would be brothers and never parted."[24] For Vidal's narrator, *worship*, *rape*, *lovemaking*, and *brotherhood* form a chain of terms that characterize Jim's sexual desire for Ken. This is only a fantasy of Jim's, of course, and it is articulated by the gently mocking narrator of *The City and the Pillar Revised*. Indeed, when he and Ken are drunk alone in a room together, Jim makes a pass at him, Ken rebuffs him, and Jim coldly takes the hint.

My point is not that Jim is essentially a rapist any more than he is essentially a homosexual; to the contrary, the author assiduously avoids the use of "homosexual" as a noun and was vehemently opposed to essentialism.[25] But Vidal, in this passage, places male/male rape in the same realm as sex, desire, worship, and brotherhood—as one more way that one man might connect with another on a masculine erotic plane. More simply put, Vidal describes rape as *one of the ways that men have homosexual sex*.

In this way, *The City and the Pillar Revised* aligns with the set of assumptions I discussed in Chapter 1 that followed in the wake of *Fortune and Men's Eyes*. In the popular imagination, rape becomes a homosexual problem, and Bob, the victim of rape in *The City and the Pillar Revised*, has been victimized by a violent homosexual with whom he got too close. Even more importantly, the rape in *City Revised* maintains the traditional assumptions and meanings attached to male/male rape: the novel asks us to see the man who has been raped as violently feminized, defeated, shamed, and humiliated, retreating into silence. Although *City Revised*, then, is unusually successful at decoupling femininity and homosexuality, it achieves this disaggregation by citing—and bolstering—the old cultural poetics of male/male rape, by violently feminizing the violate man.

Paddle Faster

I now turn to the novel that would come to serve as the urtext for the most spectacular male/male rape in all of cinema. The book was *Deliverance*, and its author was James Dickey, the well-known poet of the American South. It was made available to readers for the first time in the February 1970 issue of *The Atlantic Monthly*, and it would have a profound effect on cultural conceptions of male/male rape worldwide. Further, *Deliverance* would be adapted and referenced innumerable times and in various ways in the decades subsequent to its initial publication. *Deliverance* was published in its entirety in the summer of 1970. It received raves in the *Nation*, *The Washington Post*, *The New Republic*, and *The New Yorker*, and it quickly became a *New York Times* bestseller. Rights to a film version were secured nearly immediately, and the film of *Deliverance* was released in the summer of 1972.

The book had its detractors, of course, most notably Fredric Jameson, who called the novel "repellant" in the journal *College English*, and Anthony Thwaite, who scathingly remarked in *The New Statesman* that "though [the narrator] tells the story in a manner compounded of the rhetorical flatulence of Mr. Dickey's own poems, Hemingway and the King James Bible . . . his actual dialogue (and that of his companions) is banal, debased, the argot of . . . 'a high-school locker-room,' as is his philosophising."[26] Nearly everyone, however, agreed that the novel was enjoyable to read, and even its harshest critics acknowledged Dickey's abilities as a storyteller. The book, in fact, continues to delight readers. Forty years after the novel's first publication, *The New York Times* published a piece praising *Deliverance*: in 2010, Dwight Garner referred to it as "the kind of novel few serious writers attempt any longer, a book about wilderness and survival whose DNA contains shards of both *Heart of Darkness* and *Huckleberry Finn*. . . . It's lonely work looking for its serious successors."[27]

Although *Deliverance* is ostensibly a tale of physical and spiritual growth visualized through the feats of bravery and violence rendered as masculine, a considerable portion of the book's notoriety is due to its infamous sequence of male/male rape, a scene represented in detail in John Boorman's film of the novel. Boorman's movie, with its wide distribution and recognizable stars, has become a much more visible cultural product than Dickey's book, and the rape at the film's center has become the most famous of its scenes. For many, *Deliverance* is simply a film *about* male/male rape. Henry Hart reports that even while the movie was still in production, "[Dickey's son] Chris pointed out that audiences were going to come away from the film thinking of only one thing—the homosexual rape. His father disagreed."[28] History has proved Dickey incorrect. Pamela Barnett finds that "the rape scene in *Deliverance* has become a broadly shared cultural joke," and Jennie Lightweis-Goff notes that "at the mention of Dickey's *Deliverance*, there is often laughter. The film's rape, with its famous piglike squeals of pain and humiliation, has become a cultural point of reference."[29] J. W. Williamson states unequivocally that "the impact of *Deliverance* on popular culture cannot be exaggerated," and that "squeal like a pig," the phrase the rapist in the movie yells as he rapes his victim, "long ago entered the demotic vocabulary."[30] Even the "Dueling Banjos" theme music that recurs throughout the film has come to signify male/male rape: a connotation evidenced by the popularity of tee-shirts bearing the phrase "Paddle faster; I hear banjos!" (Figure 2.1). The link from banjo music to male/male sexual violation is hardly a natural one, but it has been cemented through popular repetition, and it indicates the discursive power of the male/male rape sequence in the film.

Underneath this considerable cultural baggage of mountain man references and jokes about banjos is Dickey's original novel, which I argue here takes a much different and more nuanced attitude toward male/male sexual violation than its popular use as a metonym for rape would indicate.[31] Critical analyses have often treated the novel and the film as though they are no different from one another, but the movie *Deliverance* and the book on which it is based diverge significantly in their depictions of sexual violation.[32] My discussion of *Deliverance* attempts to leave behind the cultural associations that have attached themselves to Dickey's story in the last fifty years, to examine the novel and the film separately, and to discuss the ways in which their treatments of male/male sexual violence are distinct. This chapter reads Dickey's original novel as an important event in the history of representations of male/male rape in its own right, and I postpone discussion of John Boorman's film version of *Deliverance* until Chapter 3.

I will be making what might at first seem an outrageous argument: that James Dickey's novel is interested in neither the misogyny nor the homophobia of which it has frequently been accused but argues instead for a revision of traditional white masculinity, spiritual growth, and a humble approach to the world in which we live. This chapter suggests that the

FIGURE 2.1: "Paddle Faster; I Hear Banjos" tee from supergraphictees.com

already existent trope of male/male rape into which *Deliverance* was introduced in 1970 constricted Dickey's actual project, one much more complex than years of scholarly exegesis on his novel have suggested. I do not make this argument in order to offer a "correct" reading of *Deliverance*; I wish, rather, to draw attention to the ways in which specific critical lenses intent on producing the novel's meanings have themselves emphasized the significatory power of male/male rape.

Essential to this argument is my resistance to reading male/male rape as a metaphor for something other than itself. An overwhelming amount of the scholarly analysis of *Deliverance* has made use of metaphors that feminize the violated body and insistently homosexualize the anus. But critics of *Deliverance* have been too quick to acquiesce to popular, masculinist interpretations of male/male rape, reading them into the book. I want to argue, instead, not only that Dickey's novel is not guilty of the misogyny and homophobia of which it has been accused, but also that it offers possibilities for a different kind of masculinity, a nontraditional version of adult maleness that understands the male body as capable of power while also remaining vulnerable, penetrable, even broken. In this way, *Deliverance* departs remarkably from the version of masculinity in *The City and the Pillar Revised* and offers us something else.

Deliverance follows Ed Gentry, an Atlanta businessman who seeks an escape from the middle-aged boredom of his office job and his no-longer-exciting marriage. The possibility of deliverance from this banality is provided by Ed's athletic friend Lewis, who proposes a canoe ride down the (fictional) Cahulawassee River before the river is destroyed by a government project that will dam it up to create a lake. Ed's friends Bobby and Drew go with them on their canoeing excursion. The novel is narrated in the first person and focuses on Ed's subjective experiences of the trip, particularly his attention to the natural world—the river, the wildlife, and the forest.

On their way down the Cahulawassee, the campers are accosted by a pair of mountain men. One of the men rapes Bobby, and Ed is forced to watch. While the other man prepares to rape Ed in turn, Lewis kills the first man, shooting him with an arrow; the second rapist escapes. The four suburbanites bury the man they've killed and continue down the Cahulawassee until they hit a bad patch of white water. The rapids pitch all four into the river, and when they find that Drew has been shot, the men realize that they are being hunted by the other mountain man. Lewis's leg is broken, Drew is dead, and Bobby is inept and terrified, so Ed embarks on a climb up a nearly vertical cliff face in order to find and kill the man who is hunting them. This climb forms an extensive portion of the book, and Ed reaches a new awareness of himself as a part of the natural world as he scales the cliff to hunt the rapist. He also experiences "a peculiar kind of intimacy" with the man he hunts, an understanding he describes as a kind of spiritual oneness.[33]

Ed kills the man; Bobby and Ed hide the corpse, canoe the rest of the way down the Cahulawassee, get Lewis to a hospital, concoct an explanation to appease local law enforcement, and head home to Atlanta. The entire experience changes Ed's life: he returns to his suburban existence with a new sense of himself and a renewed appreciation of his wife, son, and career. "The river," Ed says at the book's end, "became a possession to me, a personal, private possession, as nothing else in my life ever had.... The river underlies, in one way or another, everything I do."[34] Through his journey on the river, Ed has learned a new way to live, even in the boredom of his Atlanta suburb. Broadly speaking, the novel is, then, an exploration of manhood tested by intense physical and spiritual demands. *Deliverance*'s narrator is able to pass this series of tests, and he returns to his life better, wiser, and more aware of his own subjectivity.

Many critical analyses of *Deliverance* have interpreted the novel as a metaphor for the war in Vietnam and ethical exploration of the decision to commit violence.[35] Other critics have read *Deliverance* as a literalization of class conflicts in the United States.[36] Readings such as these—that concern themselves with war or class—are interested with the novel mainly as a large-scale metaphor for other conflicts. The critical tendency to understand *Deliverance* as an allegory has been used as a kind of hermeneutic method with which to address the novel's subject matter. This has been even more frequent in critical treatments of the novel as allegories for battles between masculinity and femininity or between "civilization" and "nature," and it is these treatments of *Deliverance* as allegory that have focused most on the meaning of the rape in the book.[37] The emblematic mountain man who rapes Bobby, shoots Drew, and who is eventually killed by Ed serves a *metaphorical* function in all of these readings, and critics designate rape as one single exchange of power in a whole series of skirmishes that constitute a larger conflict. Thus, in many analyses of the rape in *Deliverance*, the violence becomes less a physical event than a psychologically symbolic one, signifying the penetrability of civilization and its weakness in a confrontation with nature. It is the argument of this book, however, that discourses that address rape as a metaphor ignore the material and psychological effects of rape on violated bodies and psyches at the same time as they efface the ideologically charged sources of rape's power *as* a metaphor. Cultural taboos against male/male sexualities, anality, the penetrated body, and homosexual desire invest the rape metaphor with power, and these taboos are, in turn, reinforced and strengthened through the metaphor's use.

Readings that treat male/male rape as a metaphor use the standard interpretive frame for male/male rape that we find in *The City and the Pillar Revised* in order to make sense of *Deliverance*. Scholars describe Dickey as though he wrote a novel in which an act of penetration is able to establish permanent dominance and effect humiliation. Critics who read the novel in this way often attempt to criticize what they see as Dickey's misogyny, but the readings themselves uncritically re-inscribe the widespread understanding of hydraulic sexual hierarchies in which the partner who penetrates is powerful, whole, masculine, and the partner who is penetrated is weak, lacking, feminine.

Even the antagonism between nature and civilization, which has so often been excavated from *Deliverance* in analyses of the text, is one that has been produced more by critics than by Dickey himself. The novel, to the contrary, advocates a kind of merging, where Ed comes to understand himself as *a part* of the natural world and not in opposition to it.[38] In an extraordinary passage in the text, as the rapids dump Ed and his companions into the Cahulawassee, Ed struggles against the river but begins to realize that the only way to survive is to allow the river to command him. "I got on my back and poured with the river," Ed says, "sliding over the stones like a creature I had always contained but never released." And as Ed does this, he understands the river. The water is in complete control; Ed lets go of his need to dominate, and the river grants him knowledge: "Everything told me that the way I was doing it was the only way, and I was doing it. It was terrifyingly enjoyable."[39] This moment of communion with the river is echoed later in the novel as Ed prepares to climb the cliff face—"My heart expanded with joy at the thought of where I was and what I was doing . . . , not thinking of anything, with a deep feeling of nakedness and helplessness and intimacy"—and again as he nears the top of the cliff—"I lay there sweating, having no handhold or foothold. . . . Fear and a kind of enormous moon-blazing sexuality lifted me, millimeter by millimeter."[40] Finally, when Ed leaps from the cliff back into the river, he describes feeling "the current thread through me, first through my head from one ear and out the other and then complicatedly through my body, up my rectum and out my mouth and also in at the side where I was hurt." Ed feels the water going in "like an ice pick" but understands this pain as "almost luxurious."[41] Nature is not Ed's enemy in the novel. The river is Ed's teacher, a nonhuman force that helps him achieve his human potential.

In each of these passages, Ed submits to the world around him; he abdicates power, to use Leo Bersani's phrase from "Is the Rectum a Grave?" He sensitizes himself to his environment and chooses to follow rather than lead. Dickey describes each of these sequences using the terminology of pleasure (moon-blazing sexuality, enjoyment, intimacy, luxuriousness), and he also emphasizes Ed's vulnerability (helplessness, fear, nakedness) and penetrability (through his body, on his back, in at his side). Ed opens up to the power of his surroundings and divests himself of a need to control his environment. For Dickey, the men are at their best and human experience at its richest when they begin to understand themselves as in relationship with—and at the mercy of—the natural world.

Masculinity, Queerness, and the River

The reading of *Deliverance* as a metaphorical struggle is dependent upon a binary that sees Dickey's novel as symbolic for an ancient battle of the sexes. The terms for this reading are always the masculine and the feminine, where—as I noted in this book's introduction—the rapist is always asked to represent masculinity and the victim of rape made to represent femininity. The rape of Bobby by the mountain man, in these critical figurations, performs the work of gendering so that any metaphor the critic attempts to address is always already gendered by a focus on the rape as the novel's most significant sequence. Thus, Richard Calhoun and Robert Hill can say that Ed and Bobby "are confronted by two sardonically threatening backwoodsmen, who launch a kind of taunting homosexual attack on the effeminate Bobby," and Theda Wrede can argue that "the metaphor of the land as female lover . . . becomes one of the dominant images in the novel, fostering the hero's transition from figurative boyhood to manhood."[42] Pamela Barnett is perhaps the theorist who has most insistently described the rape in *Deliverance* as a creator or destroyer of masculinity. In her book *Dangerous Desire*, she argues that "the rape recognizes the city men as representatives of the powerful administrative class and then violates them as if to express that this social power, divorcing them from their brute bodies, is the root of their feminization and queering." Barnett is one of many critics who take this point of view toward the novel. *Deliverance*, these critics believe, "clearly portrays rape as an emasculating event" for the victim.[43] And as critics transform the rape into a metaphorical confrontation between Civilization and Nature—and therefore also the masculine and the feminine—they turn the novel toward meanings that are dependent on uncritical readings of male/male rape.

Rather than emphasize the gender binary, Dickey instead consistently avoids gendering the natural world in his text, associating the river, rather, with power and with beauty. As the campers first push out on the river, Ed says that "a slow force took hold of us; the bank began to go backward. I felt the complicated urgency of the current, like a thing made of many threads being pulled, and with this came the feeling I always had at the moment of losing consciousness at night, going toward something unknown that I could not avoid, but from which I would return."[44] A bit later he describes "the current enter[ing his] muscles and body as though [he] were carrying it; it came up through the paddle."[45] Dickey is clearly focused on his narrator's communion with the river, and the novelist decidedly eroticizes this communion, but neither the river nor the forest is gendered in these passages. Instead, Ed finds himself keenly aware of "the beautiful impersonality of the place."[46] Ed describes the river and its wild environs as fundamentally different from his experience of living in the city, and again Dickey figures this difference as neither masculine nor feminine.[47] The river and the forest exist simply as forces of otherness that remain mostly separate from Ed.

Deliverance, to be sure, is an exploration of masculinity; to suggest otherwise would be to misread the book completely. But unlike the more traditional, indeed, *classical* white masculinity we find in Vidal's *City*, Dickey never describes masculinity as a coherent concept in *Deliverance*. He allows none of his characters—neither camper nor mountain man—to achieve a concrete masculinity to which we might point as ideal. Joyce Pair has argued that when Bobby is raped and Ed is threatened with rape, Ed finds himself "robbed of his masculinity until he takes on Lewis's role and becomes the death-dealing commando," but Dickey never figures Ed as a commando, death-dealing or otherwise.[48] For all of the novel's possible links to the Vietnam War, Dickey describes both Ed and the man he kills as hunters; his interest in masculinity is linked to stalking, shooting, and killing animals not soldiers. Ed and his companions' weapon of choice is the bow, not the rifle. It is certainly possible to read the bow as signifying a particular image of white, colonial masculinity. We might, for example, see the bow and arrow as designed to link Ed with a "primitive" or "natural" masculinity, to read Ed's journey alongside, say, the hackneyed ideas of Jack London as some kind of "call of the wild" or a return to the "truer," native masculinity that we find in James Fenimore Cooper.[49] But, again: Dickey's protagonist is dominated by the river, the cliff face, and the forest; he does not dominate them. If Ed is able to become a man or find some version of masculinity, he does so by collaborating with the natural world and learning from it, not locating a "true" essence of manhood inside of himself.

Neither should we interpret the threat of rape as able to rob Ed of his masculinity. Rape cannot take Ed's masculinity from him because Dickey never describes him as having it in the first place. Long before the mountain men appear in the novel, Ed, enjoying his own presence in the forest, tells us that, "I touched the knife hilt at my side, and remembered that all men were once boys, and that boys are always looking for ways to become men."[50] Dickey makes clear not only that Ed has not quite achieved masculinity but that Ed *understands himself* as not having achieved it, that this is one of the continual projects of his own life. This jells perfectly with Dickey's first epigraph for the novel, a passage from Georges Bataille that he renders in French and that translates to "There exists a principle of insufficiency at the base of human life." In the original, Bataille continues: "In isolation, each man imagines the others incapable or unworthy of 'being.' ... A burst of laughter, an expression of repugnance greets gestures, sentences, failings in which my deep insufficiency is betrayed."[51] Dickey draws readers' attention to a lack—*insuffisance*—at the center of "each man" even before the novel begins.

I have argued that a persistent critical focus on the image of rape in the first half of the novel has led, because of the gendering power of an act of rape, to the frequent assertion that gender is the lens through which the novel ought to be read. Dickey's novel, however, works to resist an easy translation into metaphor, insisting instead on experience rather than a coherent set of symbols from which meaning can be excavated. Dickey himself always argued that *Deliverance* was about a ritual transformation. In a letter to John Boorman, for example, Dickey writes, "What I really have in mind for the whole story, both in the novel and the film, is an updated version of Van Gennep's *Rites de Passage*: 'a separation from the world, a penetration to some source of power, and life-enhancing return.'"[52] I propose to accept Dickey's own frame for the novel, and to turn, now, to the rite of passage, shifting our attention toward the phenomenal experience of male/male rape in the narrator's "life-enhancing return." This shift will allow us to move away from readings of this infamous rape sequence as a signifier for something other than itself and in the direction of something much more complex.

It is essential to understand that Dickey's characters treat the act of rape as a fundamentally serious one. There are no jokes about banjos here. Drew refers to the rape as "sexually assaulting," and after it is over, Ed is concerned about Bobby's physical health.[53] The men consistently describe the rape as a physical act and not a metaphorical one, and not one of the men understands the rape as a sex act; Ed's descriptions are completely devoid of any eroticism whatsoever and focus rather on the possibility of damage done to Bobby's body. In *Deliverance*, rape is unquestionably an act of violence.

Additionally, Dickey's focus is on the narrator's experience of rape, the perspective, that is, of a witness. Before the rape, as Ed becomes aware of the danger he and Bobby share, he tells us that "I shrank to my own true size, a physical movement known only to me."[54] And when the mountain man draws a knife-blade across Ed's chest, he reports that he "had never felt such brutality and carelessness of touch, or such disregard for another person's body," a description commensurate with what Jean Améry has called "the first blow," an act of violence that "brings home to the prisoner that he is *helpless*. . . . They are permitted to punch me in the face, the victim feels in numb surprise and concludes in just as numb certainty: they will do with me what they want."[55] As the two mountain men move toward Bobby, Dickey focuses on the moment when it becomes clear what it is that the men want:

> The white-bearded one took [Bobby] by the shoulders and turned him around toward downstream.
> "Now let's you just drop them pants," he said.
> Bobby lowered his hands hesitantly. "Drop . . . ?" he began.
> My rectum and intestines contracted. Lord God.
> The toothless man put the barrels of the shotgun under Bobby's right ear and shoved a little. "Just take 'em right on off," he said.[56]

Dickey attends to Ed's physical responses here, registering, through a description of his bowel contracting, Ed's understanding that Bobby, and probably he, too, will be raped.

When the mountain man violates Bobby, Dickey avoids a description of the violence itself. Instead, the narrator tells us, "A scream hit me, and I would have thought it was mine except for the lack of breath. It was a sound of pain and outrage, and was followed by one of simple and wordless pain. Again it came out of him, higher and more carrying. I let all the breath out of myself and brought my head down to look at the river."[57] Ed literally looks away from the act of violence, and Dickey asks his readers to look away from it, as well. Instead of describing a visual representation of the rape, he reports Ed's identification with Bobby, *a shared experience of pain* that is both Bobby and Ed's.

After he is raped, Bobby is confused and ashamed. Ed describes him as "furiously closed off from all of us," noting that "he stood up and backed away still naked from the middle down, his sexual organs wasted with pain."[58] The description echoes Ed's own earlier experience of shrinking to his "own true size," as well as the contracting he felt in his own anus and intestine during the violence. Ed and Bobby both become literally smaller. Their experiences, here, are not identical, however; as the campers bury the body, Ed actively "move[s] away from Bobby's red face. None of this was his fault, but he felt tainted to me. I remembered how he had looked over the log, how willing to let anything be done to him, and how high his voice was when he screamed."[59] Ed begins to distance himself physically and psychically from Bobby through the logics of traditional masculinity.

For Pamela Barnett, "*Deliverance* has had amazingly persistent cultural resonance, perhaps because it responds to a prevailing set of concerns about white men as victims in the postsixties era. True to his cultural moment, Ed perceives himself as feminized[,] and feminization is insistently figured here as queer. Homosexual rape is the ultimate threat to his masculinity."[60] Barnett's diagnosis of white male victimhood is borne out in my analysis, but queerness and feminization, here, are the critic's fantasy and not Dickey's own. Queerness simply does not appear in the novel, although the figuring of men as homosexual was, at the time, a quick rhetorical way to emasculate them. "Fag" and "faggot" were common terms in US American popular parlance even in the 1960s (as, indeed, they are in the twenty-first century), and though it would have been quite easy for Dickey to figure Bobby as queer, he never chooses to do so.[61] The difference between the men is not a metaphorical one but one related to their different experiences of the rite of passage. If Bobby is closed off from his companions, it is not because the men suddenly understand him as queer but rather because he is in pain and they are not. *Deliverance*, again, avoids metaphorization, turning its attention, rather, to the anguish experienced by the victim and the difference and distance experienced by the witnesses.

Against claims, such as Barnett's, that "misogyny and homophobia . . . drive the plot" of *Deliverance*, I want further to argue that Ed and *Deliverance* are in no way opposed to homosexual sex or even queerness.[62] Quite to the contrary, Ed Madden has argued that Dickey, even in the book's first chapter, "renders sexual arousal as anal not phallic, not through the erect penis and the desire to penetrate but through a 'deep and more complex' thrill of an organ more frequently tied to being penetrated."[63] Madden refers specifically to Ed's sexual attraction to a female print-model in the novel's first chapter; the narrator describes this feeling "as if something had touched me in the prostate," and Ed's attention to anality returns time and again throughout *Deliverance*.[64]

Critics have consistently pointed toward Ed's awareness of his own anality as though these moments rupture the homophobic metaphors of *Deliverance* as a whole.[65] Such readings, however, assume that Dickey intended something different from what his novel contains, as if the critic has seen through the author's masculinist posturing to the true homoeroticism beneath. But Dickey was, without question, aware of his novel's insistence on anality. Hart reports that:

> Throughout his career Dickey wondered and worried about his love of the male body.... Because Dickey cultivated the mystique of an avid womanizer, gay literary friends like Richard Howard found Dickey's interest in homosexuality and his friendliness toward gay men surprising and charming. Other friends found Dickey's attitude toward homosexuality divided and disturbing. He propositioned men (sometimes crudely and in jest), he claimed to have had sex with men (partly to shock), and he discussed homosexuality as if it might deliver him into a new region of risk and inspiration (he romanticized the breaking of all taboos in such a way).[66]

Dickey later told John Boorman, "I have never made love to a man, but if it gave me the slightest pleasure I would do so immediately."[67] Perhaps most strangely, after the release of *Deliverance*'s film version, Dickey even "told several people that he had had a homosexual affair with Burt [Reynolds] in order to 'save the movie.'"[68]

The author of *Deliverance* was prone to wild claims, and he was an extraordinarily complex and contradictory individual. I report these elements of biography not in order to make an argument for James Dickey's homosexuality—on the contrary, he actively cultivated a flamboyantly heterosexual image—rather, I wish to argue that Dickey's version of masculinity was itself deeply inflected with anality. Barnett finds it "shocking" that Ed should describe his penetration by the river as pleasurable, "since Ed has spent the novel trying to distance himself from his raped, feminized friend," but Ed's pleasure at being penetrated is only surprising if the critic interprets, as Barnett and Pair do, "the mountain man's anal rape of Bobby [as] situating him forever outside the phallocentric group."[69] If, instead, we avoid translating the rape in *Deliverance* into a signifier for something other than itself, it becomes possible to read the figuration of desire in Dickey's novel as both phallic *and* anal, and to read the rape committed on Bobby as productive of neither femininity nor queerness. Neither Dickey nor his protagonist appears disgusted by the idea of being anally penetrated. On the contrary, anal penetration as a rite of passage *is incorporated into* Dickey's concept of masculinity.

What Ed says terrifies him is not a fear of penetration *per se* but the rapists' violence, their brutality and disregard for the bodies of others. Further, Dickey's sequence of male/male rape focuses consistently on the victims' perspective of pain and terror, refusing to sexualize the event. And if the men in the novel are, finally, silent about what they experienced while canoeing down the Cahulawassee, this silence is caused by a need to cover up the violence they have committed in order to save their own lives, not by a fear of femininity or queerness. When Ed describes Bobby's reasons for silence at the end of *Deliverance*, Dickey provides us the image of rape for a final time in the novel. Ed tells us that he knows that "what would keep [Bobby's] mouth shut about the truth was himself kneeling over the log with a shotgun at his head, howling and bawling and kicking his feet like a little boy. He wouldn't want anybody to know that, no matter what; no matter how drunk he was. No."[70] This final rendering of the rape in the novel is a complex one, certainly, and one that reflects Ed's feelings of derision toward Bobby at the end of the novel, but neither femininity nor queerness appear in this last image, and Dickey again avoids conflating rape and homosexuality. Instead, he draws our attention, not to Bobby's penetration, but to the violent potentiality of the shotgun at his head and a figuration of Bobby as a child. If Bobby ultimately does not achieve masculinity, it is not because he is a woman or a homosexual or even because of weakness or powerlessness—indeed, weakness and powerlessness are neither queered nor feminized in the novel—but because Bobby is still the petulant "little boy" he was when he left Atlanta in the first place.[71] Unlike Ed, Bobby has not learned from the ritual process to which *Deliverance* subjects him, and it is this refusal to change that Dickey's novel criticizes.

Critics who have insisted on translating the rape in *Deliverance* into a metaphor have missed the novel's much more phenomenological approach to the violence of rape, its attention to bodies in space, and its focus on the emotional experience of rape's victims. I make this claim only about the novel and not the film, but male/male rape in *Deliverance* is not about sexuality or femininity; it is not about nature and civilization, and it is not about homophobia. Rape in *Deliverance* is about suffering pain and bearing it bravely. It is about becoming a man *through* suffering and learning to abandon the male fantasy of inviolate wholeness in order to transform into something more fluid. Ed finds power through the dissolution of the self, what Darieck Scott calls "extravagant abjection." He gives up but finds power "at the point of the apparent erasure of ego-protections, at the point at which the constellation of tropes that we call *identity, body, race, nation* seem to reveal themselves as utterly penetrated and compromised, without defensible boundary."[72]

We are discussing white masculinity here, of course, but *Deliverance*'s version of white masculinity is invested in coming to terms with the vulnerability of men to violence, exploring penetrability, and abandoning the masculine fantasy of wholeness. This is not to say that I do not share José Muñoz's anxiety about "recuperating the term *masculinity* because, as a category, masculinity has normalized heterosexual and masculinist privilege." Muñoz has argued that "masculinity is, among other things, a cultural imperative to enact a mode of 'manliness' that is calibrated to shut down queer possibilities and energies. The social construct of masculinity is experienced by far too many men as a regime of power that labors to invalidate, exclude, and extinguish faggotry, effeminacy, and queerly coated butchness."[73] *Deliverance* is certainly no celebration of faggotry, but rather than shoring up traditional masculinity, the novel consistently describes masculinity as incoherent and inchoate.

I thus take issue with Barnett's contention that "the novel is, of course, resistant to the idea that masculinity needs to be shattered and thus remade."[74] To the contrary, the novel insists upon the shattering and restructuring of masculinity. Far from having an interest in bolstering the social construct of "manliness" criticized by Muñoz, *Deliverance* repeatedly figures the masculinity it describes as helpless, naked, relaxed, vulnerable, and, indeed, even penetrable. The novel's critics have seen the rape as a metaphor, reading the violate man as a signifier for powerlessness. These readings re-articulate precisely the assumptions that they accuse Dickey of exploiting, and in this way critical interpretations of the novel have still further cemented our association of the violate man with weakness, femininity, deviance, brokenness, and shame. Dickey, on the other hand, imagines the violate man not as permanently excluded from the category of maleness but rather as capable of rebirth and reconfiguration.

The People vs. Alonzo Hunt

In December 1969, between the publication of his fourth and fifth novels, *Tell Me How Long the Train's Been Gone* (1968) and *If Beale Street Could Talk* (1974), the cultural critic, playwright, novelist, and public intellectual James Baldwin directed his first play. Baldwin was persuaded by his friend Engin Cezzar, one of the dedicatees of *Train*, to direct *Düşenin Dostu*, or "Friend of the Fallen," during his time in Istanbul. The play was in Turkish, and Baldwin worked with a translator throughout rehearsals. *Düşenin Dostu*, however, was not a translation of one of Baldwin's own plays; Baldwin's directorial debut was a Turkish translation of *Fortune and Men's Eyes*.[75]

Melinda Plastas and Eve Allegra Raimon have argued that Baldwin's writing about prison in the 1970s and his direction of the play "served as vehicles for contemplating sexual alterity and for imagining a morally and politically renovated social order."[76] Their article on the subject, "Brutality and Brotherhood," argues that Baldwin uses "prisons and the specter of incarceration as a vehicle for commenting on love, desire, sexuality, and their relationship to power more broadly."[77] In Chapter 1 I described how John Herbert's play thematically opposes an ideal and redemptive homosexual desire to the brutality of sexual violence—an opposition clearly in alignment with Baldwin's own thinking on the subject, and one that is evident, for example, in *Tell Me How Long the Train's Been Gone*.[78] Plastas and Raimon's discussion focuses on the first of these opposed terms, on Baldwin's attempts to rethink male intimacy and the erotics of homosociality. Their focus accords with what Baldwin himself emphasized in his direction of *Düşenin Dostu*. As Magdalena Zaborowska reports it in *James Baldwin's Turkish Decade*, Baldwin attended most carefully to the casting and performance of Mona, the figure in the play who best articulates the redemptive and beautiful qualities of gay desire and male femininity.[79] Although critics and directors often overlooked Herbert's opposition between homosexual desire and sexual violence, as I note in Chapter 1, these ideas appear to have been central to Baldwin's own interpretation of the text.

Düşenin Dostu was a hit in Turkey, running for 103 performances, but Baldwin's direction of Herbert's play was barely remarked upon in the United States.[80] I am less interested, then, in the impact Baldwin's production of *Fortune* had on male/male rape discourse in the US than I am in its influence on Baldwin's own thinking about sexual violence in prison.[81] This is especially intriguing because Baldwin's fifth novel, *If Beale Street Could Talk*, explicitly discusses male/male rape in the New York prison system. Baldwin's descriptions of prison sexual violence in *Beale Street* also differ significantly from the interpretive frames set up by *Fortune and Men's Eyes* that I described in Chapter 1, and in their focus on the violence of police forces and prisons, they are more in line with *Fortune*'s own critiques of the criminal justice system. In this way, Baldwin's novel is a unique contribution to US American discourse about male/male rape, and it functions as a rebuttal to the way the discourse around prison sexual violence crystallized in the years following *Fortune*.

As Patrick Elliot Alexander has argued, "Prison preoccupied the literary imagination of James Baldwin."[82] Alexander's book *From Slave Ship to Supermax* is particularly concerned with what he calls "survivor testimony," and he asks us to examine how *If Beale Street Could Talk* speaks against the carceral state and white-supremacist police brutality. Baldwin's writings frequently and damningly describe racism and racist violence, of course, but critics have also demonstrated that his work is frequently preoccupied with sexual violence and, in particular, the sexualization of anti-Black violence. Ernest L. Gibson, for example, discusses Rufus's sexually violent treatment of Leona in *Another Country* (1962) with sensitivity and nuance, arguing that Baldwin is using descriptions of sexual violence in order to explore some of the tragic aspects of interracial desire and Black manhood that are so central to that novel.[83] David Marriott's masterful reading of *Going to Meet the Man* (1965) also demonstrates Baldwin's perceptive understanding of how racist violence is sexualized, as Jesse attempts to deal with his oedipal fantasies through the persistent sexualization of—and white-supremacist violence against—Black men.[84] And Marlon Ross notes that in "texts of the mid to late twentieth century by James Baldwin, Chester Himes, Eldridge Cleaver, and many others, race rape and male same-sexuality constitute a theme deeply embedded, though rarely commented on, in the black male protest tradition."[85]

Baldwin describes his own experiences and fears of sexual violence in several of his essays; he also discusses the rape sequence in David Lean's *Lawrence of Arabia* (1962) and argues that it "cannot be used to justify the bloody course of Empire."[86] *If Beale Street Could Talk*, however, is Baldwin's most pronounced discussion of male/male rape in print; the topic of rape appears sporadically throughout this short novel, a story about the destruction wreaked by the US criminal justice system on Black manhood, Black love, and the Black family.[87] *Beale Street* is divided into two sections: "Troubled about My Soul," the first portion, comprises nearly 90 percent of the novel, with the final section, "Zion," taking up the short remainder. The book is narrated by Tish Rivers, who describes growing up and falling in love with Fonny Hunt, the beauty of their relationship, their troubles with their families, and their attempts to begin a life together. When the novel begins, Fonny has already been unjustly imprisoned—accused of raping a woman he does not know at all—and *Beale Street* moves back and forth in time as Tish remembers her childhood with Fonny, their first home, and beginning their life together. Meanwhile she visits him in prison and works to secure his release, marking the time until the baby she's carrying will be born.

Prison and policing in the United States are the central subject matter of *Beale Street*, and in early drafts Fonny was imprisoned in Attica before Baldwin moved the site of his incarceration to The Tombs, a prison officially named the Manhattan Detention Complex.[88] Rape is not the subject matter of this novel *per se*, but in many ways rape functions as its central theme. Fonny is in jail on a trumped-up rape charge, and much of the action of the novel involves attempting to find the woman who has accused Fonny in order to convince her to recant. Phony rape charges, of course, have a particular history in the United States, as Black men have been accused of raping white women in order to justify both their legal and extralegal killing. Baldwin's choice of a rape charge, here, places Fonny within a history of state violence committed against Black men; Baldwin explicitly draws a parallel between men lynched in the southern United States for rape and men whose lives and families are destroyed by the New York City criminal justice system.[89] "*You won't hang me*," thinks Fonny near the end of the novel.[90]

Baldwin also places the false charge of rape used to threaten Fonny next to the actual violence of rape with which Fonny contends while in The Tombs. Through this juxtaposition, Baldwin describes Fonny and other Black men as forced to defend themselves from being *victimized* by sexual violence in prison because they have been falsely *accused* of committing sexual violence outside. *Beale Street*, then, articulates precisely Tommy Curry's description of Black male precarity, in which "the convict-criminal is a category endemic to Black maleness that makes Black males vulnerable to repetitive sexual repression, violence, and rape."[91] As Curry says in *The Man-Not*:

> The Black male is therefore vulnerable to racism and the rationalizations of a white-supremacist society that make him into a lustful raping beast because he has sexual desires. . . . Under the guise of repressing his savage nature, white men and women are able to "fuck" the Black male into submission. He is now able to be raped, used for the sexual pleasure of the order, because his nature demands punishment for its sexual inclinations.[92]

This is not symbolic language, despite Curry's ironic quotation marks. Rape is a metaphor neither in the philosopher's analysis nor in Baldwin's novel. Black men's incarceration and societal position make them vulnerable to actual sexual violence.

Fonny is not raped in prison, or, if he is, Tish doesn't know about it and cannot tell us. But incarceration traumatizes Fonny; the experience alters him fundamentally, and this, too, is related to sexual violence. Tish tells us at the end of *Beale Street* that "He is placed in solitary for refusing to be raped. He loses a tooth, again, and almost loses an eye. Something hardens in him, something changes forever, the tears freeze in his belly. . . . He is fighting for his life."[93] The threat of rape hovers over Fonny while he is incarcerated, and Tish and the reader understand that victimization by sexual violence is an ever-present possibility for Fonny. We know this explicitly because Fonny's friend Daniel has been raped in prison, and Daniel's experiences with violence at the hands of the police recur repeatedly throughout *Beale Street*. The "hardening" that Fonny experiences as he fights for his life is prefigured for the reader by Daniel's experience of state-sanctioned violence, and I want to turn now to Daniel, a character in the novel who has largely escaped critical examination.

When we first meet Daniel he has recently gotten out of prison, and Tish says she "can see to what extent he has been beaten." She recognizes this, notably, by looking in Fonny's eyes. "I could not be indifferent to Daniel," she tells us, "because I realized, from Fonny's face, how marvelous it was for him to have scooped up, miraculously, from the swamp waters of his past, a friend."[94] Daniel is deeply troubled, and he struggles throughout the sections of *Beale Street* in which he appears, to speak to Fonny about what he has experienced. Tish puts it this way:

> Daniel tried to tell Fonny something about what had happened to him, in prison. Sometimes he was at the house, and so I heard it, too; sometimes, he and Fonny were alone. Sometimes, when Daniel spoke, he cried—sometimes, Fonny held him. Sometimes, I did. Daniel brought it out, or forced it out, or tore it out of himself as though it were torn, twisted chilling metal, bringing with it his flesh and his blood—he tore it out of himself like a man trying to be cured[95]

At this early point in Daniel's story, Baldwin postpones literal description of the violence that has affected his life, but *Beale Street* describes that violence precisely as penetrative, as something needing to be forced out of Daniel's body. The image is one of violent stabbing, and Tish describes Daniel's body as wounded and penetrable.

Tish tells us, and Daniel tells us himself, just how frightened he has become because of his experiences. In this section of the novel, before we know what has happened to him, he tells Fonny, with tears streaming down his face, "Man, I know what you're saying. And I appreciate it. But you don't know—the worst thing man, the *worst* thing—is that they can make you so fucking *scared*. Scared, man. *Scared.*"[96] Daniel has become so frightened that Fonny accompanies him to the subway so that he doesn't have to walk the streets alone.

Daniel struggles to put his experience into words. What is significant about this is that Baldwin consistently frames Daniel's attempt to deal with the history of violence committed on his body as a physical effort. It is a struggle he experiences repeatedly, and it is one with which Fonny and Tish assist: "Daniel was trying very hard to get past something, something unnamable: he was trying as hard as a man can try. And sometimes I held him, sometimes Fonny: we were all he had."[97] The final time Tish describes Daniel's struggle is positioned at the end of *Beale Street*'s first section. Baldwin places it, in other words, right before the police come to arrest Fonny. The passage where Daniel tells Tish and Fonny about one of the worst things that happened in prison forms the final passage in part one:

> He was a little drunk. He was crying. He was talking, again, about his time in prison. He had seen nine men rape one boy: and *he* had been raped. He would never, never, never again be the Daniel he had been. Fonny held him, held him up just before he fell. I went to make the coffee.
> And then they came knocking at the door.[98]

It would be difficult to overstate the structural importance of this passage to *Beale Street*. Because of where this sequence is situated, "Zion," the very short second part of the novel, is framed by this description of gang rape. The novel, quite literally, takes a pause here—to give us time to think about the violence Daniel experienced. This is one way that Baldwin articulates the stakes of incarceration—not just for Tish and for their new family, as well as for their parents and extended family—but also for Fonny's own body and subjectivity. In addition, the narrative emphasizes Fonny's care for Daniel. As Ernest Gibson points out in his analysis of the novel, this passage emphasizes what he calls "Fonny's salvific role. Through Tish's perception, which we might read as a kind of deified narrative voice through its discerning capacity, we learn how Daniel's deliverance ought to come through Fonny."[99]

It is fundamental to note that Baldwin does not use male/male rape in *Beale Street* as a mere plot point; neither does he describe male/male rape in order to authenticate his prison setting, a narrative technique that I argued became common in post-*Fortune* representations of incarceration.

Beale Street's focus, rather, is on the effect of sexual violence on the male body and psyche, on Black men's vulnerability to police violence, and on the extraordinary violence of prison itself. Fonny is fighting for his life, and his vulnerability to rape in prison is part of this fight.

The violence of the prison system rests in a white supremacy that simultaneously sexualizes and brutalizes the Black male body. Although this particular antiracist frame was uncommon in the contemporary literature on prison rape, as I noted in Chapter 1, in *Beale Street* Baldwin always frames the violence of the prison as white violence exercised on Black bodies, and he is careful always to mark the sexual aspects of that violence. Trudier Harris, for example, has pointed out that Bell, the white policeman who organizes Fonny's arrest, uses his eyes to "convey the possibility of symbolic rape."[100] In fact, Bell's sexualization of Fonny and his threat of rape are explicit in Baldwin's text. "Bell's eyes swept over Fonny's black body with the unanswerable cruelty of lust," Tish tells us. "*I'm going to fuck you, boy*, Bell's eyes said. *No you won't*, said Fonny's eyes."[101] Again, this is not a metaphor; the rape is not symbolic. Fonny is fighting here quite literally against a sexual violence threatened by this white policeman.

In *James Baldwin, Toni Morrison, and the Rhetorics of Black Male Subjectivity*, Aaron Ngozi Oforlea has written specifically about the prison sexual violence in *Beale Street*, and he suggests that perhaps:

> the men [in prison] who attempt to rape Fonny think of themselves as straight and him as weak or feminine, which reveals the confusing pliability of constructions of masculinity and sexuality in the service of hegemony. Fonny fights them—defends himself and maybe even his sexuality—but he doesn't judge them because he sees himself in them and his plight in their condition.[102]

Oforlea's approach to the novel attempts to make sense of male/male rape in *Beale Street* but, in order to do so, Oforlea accepts the meanings attached to it by mainstream culture—the ideological connections between masculinity, heterosexuality, and wholeness that I described in the introduction. Careful attention to Baldwin's descriptions of male/male rape, however, reveals that *Beale Street* makes use of male/male rape to prompt us to think about it in ways that differ from these traditional connections between victimization and whiteness or masculinity and aggression. Baldwin's novel asks us to refuse some of the assumptions that were already ingrained in the US American imagination by 1974.

In Oforlea's reading, those who attempt to rape Fonny are other incarcerated men, and Fonny finds identity with these men even while defending himself. But Baldwin is, in fact, careful not to say who attempts to rape Fonny or who rapes Daniel. Even the nine men whom Daniel describes as raping a boy are not identified in the text. Rather than blame other incarcerated men for the rapes in the novel, Baldwin consistently racializes violence in *Beale Street* as white, and Fonny does not identify with those committing rape. Further, the anti-Black violence in the book is also consistently sexualized. In addition to the "cruel lust" that drives Bell to want to fuck Fonny in the passage cited earlier, Daniel says that when he is arrested, the cops find marijuana in his back pocket: "man, do they *love* to pat your ass," he says.[103] Later he describes sitting in a police van with a young Black man who is sick and in pain, and Daniel insistently characterizes the officers as sexually aroused by the violence they commit on the Black men they've imprisoned: "the mothers who put him in this wagon, man, they was coming in their pants while they did it. I don't believe there's a white man in this country, baby, who can even *get* his dick hard, without he hear some n[—] moan."[104] *Beale Street* repeatedly emphasizes that the male/male rapes it describes are the responsibility of white officers erotically invested in violating the Black male body. Rape is always committed in *Beale Street* by white officers and the violence of the white-supremacist prison system itself; those vulnerable to rape are Black men.

More pointedly, Baldwin consistently links this sexual violence to the hegemonic masculinity that dominates society *outside* of the prison. All of Bell's interactions with Fonny and Tish occur prior to his arrest in the streets of New York, a city Tish describes as "the ugliest and dirtiest city in the world."[105] Rape in *Beale Street* is neither a "homosexual problem" nor a "prison problem": it is a problem of white supremacy that simultaneously sexualizes and attempts to violate Black men. Baldwin uses male/male rape in *Beale Street* to illustrate the vulnerability of Black men to the violence of white supremacy, but I want to stress that male/male rape in Baldwin's novel is not a *metaphor* for white-supremacist violence or carceral power. To the contrary, male/male rape in *Beale Street* is one of white supremacy's numerous literal *manifestations*, along with daily harassment, medical neglect, racial profiling, and carceral violence.[106]

At the end of *Beale Street*, Tish gives birth, and so the novel directs our attention toward the future. As I noted earlier, the short final section of the novel is titled "Zion," and thus the novel's conclusion also points toward the city on the hill, the possibilities of new life and new social arrangements.[107]

Beale Street's closing image is beautiful and complex: "Fonny is working on the wood, on the stone, whistling, smiling. And, from far away, but coming nearer, the baby cries and cries and cries and cries and cries and cries and cries and cries, cries like it means to wake the dead."[108] *Beale Street* ends with an image of Fonny free and happy, but this is coupled with an image of the baby's anguish or grief—or perhaps protest.

And although Fonny is *Beale Street*'s central character, for my own analysis, I want briefly to return to Daniel, the violate man who serves such a key role for understanding the dangers of the prison system into which Fonny has been remanded. The novel includes a similar image of anguish-grief-protest for Daniel earlier in *Beale Street* and, in it, Baldwin cleverly twists "deliverance," James Dickey's title, toward the music of Black protest. Tish tells us that Fonny walks with Daniel to his subway stop after their first evening back together again:

> And Fonny, who is younger, struggles now to be older, in order to help his friend toward his deliverance. *Didn't my Lord deliver Daniel? And why not every man?*
>
> The song is old, the question unanswered.[109]

This section of *Beale Street*, especially, is filled with music, most of which is contemporary—"Compared to What," "What's Going On," and, hilariously, "Funny Girl"—but here Tish's own narration *moves into song* and moves, more specifically, into the language of Black protest music. As with the conclusion of the novel as a whole, Daniel's future is ambiguous. The Lord has delivered Daniel; he is free from prison. But he is also not yet free. True deliverance is still afar off. Daniel has been deeply wounded, and how he will deal with that in the future Tish does not know; Baldwin leaves the question unanswered because it's a question only we can answer as we work toward building Zion.

Beale Street treats male/male rape in a fundamentally different way than the other rape discourse in this book. Baldwin uses representations of male/male rape to analyze Black male vulnerability and state violence. Baldwin's treatment of Black male vulnerability to sexual violence was extremely rare for the 1970s, and it remains so now. His analysis of the United States in this novel has not been taken up by mainstream "wisdom" about prison life and police violence. To the contrary, Baldwin's understanding of the problem of prison rape in the United States remains as a direct rebuttal to the received and persistent mainstream point of view about prison sexual violence.

A further lesson we can take from both *Beale Street* and *Deliverance* is that these novels ask us to let go of the assumptions we bring to an author's treatment of male/male rape. There is an overwhelming ideology attached to male/male rape that accepts the fantasy of masculine wholeness, that asks us to see rape as feminizing and that racializes sexual violence so that Black men are its perpetrators and white men are its victims. We bring this ideology with us to the novels we read and the movies we watch—even critics do this, as I've been demonstrating. But both *Beale Street* and *Deliverance* attempt to describe male/male rape in ways that depart from the traditional associations we have with rape and rape narratives; they ask us to move past male/male rape as either a metaphor or a mere plot point and turn our attention to those characters who narrate their experience of sexual violence; both novels, in other words, teach us that male/male rape can and should be discussed otherwise.

What Can and Cannot Be Said

This chapter concludes with Chester Himes, a novelist who was mostly done publishing fiction in the 1970s but who was widely known as the author of a series of hardboiled pulp novels following the Harlem detectives Grave Digger Jones and Coffin Ed Johnson. Two film adaptations from the series appeared during this period—*Cotton Comes to Harlem* (1970) and *Come Back Charleston Blue* (1972)—and Himes's reputation as a novelist is largely dependent on these novels. Like James Baldwin, Chester Himes was a Black American ex-pat living abroad, and I want to turn now from Baldwin's novel about The Tombs to Himes's novel about the Ohio State Penitentiary. Himes was imprisoned there in 1928, was transferred to the London Prison Farm in 1934, and was finally released in April of 1936.[110] He began writing while incarcerated, and he may have completed the first version of his novel about his prison experiences as early as 1936.[111] This novel had a great deal of trouble finding a publisher, and Himes had already published *If He Hollers Let Him Go* (1945) and *The Lonely Crusade* (1947) by the time his prison novel finally saw the light of day as *Cast the First Stone* in early 1953. The novel had been significantly altered from its original version—publishers had objected to its dark treatment of prison life, its emphasis on homosexual romance, and its intriguing portrait of masculinity.

In 1998, however, editors Marc Gerald and Samuel Blumenfeld published Himes's original manuscript under his title *Yesterday Will Make You*

Cry, and we are now able to compare what Himes wished to say in the 1940s with what publishers would allow to be said in the 1950s. In this way, although neither his portrait of life in prison nor his treatment of homosexuality is strictly contemporary with those of James Baldwin or John Herbert, Himes's perspective fascinates because his ideas about these topics were there all along, silenced by cultural forces that shaped US American attitudes toward prison, masculinity, homosexuality, and male/male rape. Himes's novel waited to be read for half a century, and although it was unable to influence the other fiction in this chapter, and although it, indeed, made no impact on US American discourse, *Yesterday Will Make You Cry* provides an intriguing picture of how our ideas and attitudes might have turned out differently.

Yesterday begins with its protagonist Jimmy Monroe's first night in prison, and the book ends with Jimmy's transfer to the Prison Farm.[112] The novel is narrated in the third person, and this voice reports Jimmy's experiences carefully, attempting to get at something very close to the emotional life of a prisoner of the state. As Clare Rolens notes in a wonderfully insightful essay in *Callaloo*, "Like many prison novels, [*Yesterday*] is not tightly structured around a linear plotline, but rather seeks to capture time as it passes for prisoners behind bars—perceived not as an unbroken chain of events but rather as loosely linked brutal episodes.[113] Still, the novel has a clear structure. It is divided into four parts, three of which are of relatively equal length and one that is slightly shorter and takes place outside of the prison. This shorter section, "A Flood of Tears," describes Jimmy's childhood and the life he had before he got to prison. "Flood of Tears" appears as the novel's second part; it works to link prison life to life outside, and these chapters are filled with Himes's insights about the state, criminality, and masculinity. It was entirely cut from *Cast the First Stone* when it was published in 1953.[114]

The other three sections of *Yesterday* follow Jimmy's day-to-day experiences of life inside, his friendships with various other men, his gambling, his regrets, the brutality he witnesses on the part of the guards, a description of the famous Easter Monday Fire of 1930, the softball team, and his romances with two or three other men.[115] The final section of the novel comprises Jimmy's romantic and sexual relationship with Prince Rico, the last of these, and with Rico Jimmy focuses his energy, takes up writing, and finds hope before he is released. *Yesterday*, the novel's original version, is an extraordinary text. It's an autobiographical novel narrated in the third person about the brutalities of prison and the criminal justice system. It also narrates a man's gradual acceptance and embrace of love and sex between men because of the limits placed on incarcerated men. Jimmy finds his relationship with Rico frustrating and maddening; he has a tendency toward bitter jealousy, as indeed Himes did with his female partners outside, but this pettiness and jealousy is reported unsparingly by the narrator, who always tries to understand Jimmy's behavior, even at its most juvenile. In this way, the novel, as Rolens puts it, "centers on the contradictions and myriad ideals that make up masculinity in crisis both inside and outside the prison."[116] The homosexual relationship that makes up so much of the fourth section of the novel was also largely altered for the original 1953 publication.

Male/male rape does not take up a large amount of the emotional space in *Yesterday*, and there is no stark scene of sexual violence in *Yesterday* comparable to those in *Deliverance* or *The City and the Pillar*, but rape is an ever-present possibility in the book, and the idea of it looms over Jimmy's time in the Ohio State Penitentiary. In his analysis of *Yesterday* in *Slaves of the State*, Dennis Childs argues that "while prison rape moves at the margins of a story based on the redressive capacities of his love affair with Rico, the unspeakably banal practice of sexualized and gendered carceral terror completely encircles the romance plot in *Yesterday*."[117] Both Childs and Rolens have carefully and thoroughly analyzed the novel's treatment of Black masculinity and the stark difference between salvific homosexuality in Jimmy's relationship with Rico and the "institutionally sanctioned rape and domination" endemic to the prison.[118] I want to examine the way that Himes thinks through the topics of masculinity, homosexuality, prison, and rape, and how *Yesterday* places Himes's ideas about these topics in a different relationship than any author we have seen thus far. In this way, Himes's novel offers a unique perspective on mid-century masculinity, one that was carefully kept from the eyes of the public by the novel's mid-century publisher.

In contrast to the common wisdom of prison wardens and other commentators about prison sexuality in the 1940s and '50s, when Jimmy Monroe and Prince Rico talk about rape, they understand the difference between rape and homosexual sex. On nearly every occasion that the topic arises in *Yesterday*, Himes places them next to one another, contrasting the two rather than conflating them. This is clear, for example, in a sequence when Rico tells Jimmy about his past and describes getting both of his legs broken. "I was riding a freight coming out of Pittsburgh and got to fighting with a guy," Rico says. "We were in a box car and he wanted to make me, so we got to fighting and he knocked me off the train." Rico's description of refusing a violent sexual encounter causes Jimmy to react jealously: "The picture came unbidden; against his will it came. He could see Rico riding freights with different fellows, some of whom he must have liked, some of whom he must have kissed, or had allowed to fondle him in the corner of some damp, chilly box car, on some sacks or straw, perhaps. He cursed himself and cursed his thoughts."[119]

Himes here contrasts an image of rape with images of Rico as a desirable sexual object and a desiring sexual subject. The stark difference between sex and rape comes up again later in the same conversation, as Jimmy acknowledges the sexual violence ubiquitous in the prison and Rico describes sexual pleasure in contrast:

> "You must have had it tough in all those joints," Jimmy observed. He did not want to say it, but he could not help himself. "With your sensitive mouth and the way your eyes get sometimes."
>
> "The year in Florida was the toughest," Rico confessed. "Those wolves down there will try to rape you and the guards don't give you much protection if you're from the North. I carried a big shiv with me and they knew I would use it. But in the reformatory it was different. I wanted sex there, but I wanted to be the man. They were all trying to make me, so I just played the field and took everything and never gave anything."[120]

This long conversation reflects Jimmy's growing understanding about Rico and homosexual desire, and all of these discussions of violence in *Yesterday* are in the context of Jimmy and Rico's own love affair, the romantic language of which has been difficult for some critics to reconcile with the violence of the prison. Jimmy is falling in love, and the narrator tells us that "Everything touched Jimmy that spring. He was too emotional; he had never been so emotional. Everything was soft inside of him and at the slightest touch he'd bubble over, like foam."[121] The contrast here with the insistent hardness of the prison is remarkable.

Rico's phrase *I wanted to be the man* in this passage cites the conventional associations of masculinity with activity in sexual relationships and femininity with passivity. These associations arise repeatedly in *Yesterday*, and they are shorthand ways of describing positions in anal intercourse.[122] But masculinity itself is not so easily achieved in *Yesterday*, and—as with *The City and the Pillar*, *Deliverance*, and *If Beale Street Could Talk*—Himes's novel is fundamentally an exploration of his protagonist's relationship to manhood. *Yesterday* constantly puts masculinity under a microscope, and Jimmy struggles with it from a very young age. Always more interested in books than his classmates, Jimmy is mocked by his peers, who call him "Sir Galahad." As a boy he begins to fight anyone who makes fun of him: "He didn't want to fight. No one ever really knew how much he hated fighting, and how sickeningly afraid he was to fight. But when some one hurt you, you fought them. That was what all the heroes and knights did. And if you won they stopped."[123] Jimmy models his masculinity on Achilles, the hero of the *Iliad*, but he finds himself punished for behaving and punished for misbehaving both: "Be good, they said. But what was that? Something that when you were, people thought you queer. And when you weren't, they merely thought you bad. And if you had a choice to make, you'd always rather be bad."[124] Jimmy is forced as a boy to prove that he isn't a sissy, but he has no idea how to do that.[125] What Himes does in these passages is demonstrate that the world of the prison is not topsy-turvy or an inverted version of US American culture. These passages, which were excised from the 1953 version of the novel, explicitly link traditional US masculinity with the sexual hierarchies of the prison. In fact, in his memoir *The Quality of Hurt*, Himes says quite bluntly, "Nothing happened in prison that I had not already encountered in outside life."[126] Rather than portraying "the upside-down world of prison life," *Yesterday* sees the values of mainstream society as extending *into* the prison and influencing it.[127]

Jimmy's path toward the theft that has landed him behind bars is due largely to his struggles with how to get by in a society that demands that he be a man according to its terms. That same society then turns around and incarcerates him for it. As Jimmy thinks about it in a profound passage much later in the novel, "It seemed so illogical to punish some poor criminal for doing something that civilization taught him how to do so he could have something that civilization taught him how to want. It seemed to him as wrong as if they had hung the gun that shot the man."[128] Clare Rolens has argued that an even more important passage in *Yesterday* occurs after Jimmy and Rico's fellow prisoners get angry at them and the captain tells Jimmy he's going to report Rico on a sex perversion charge.[129] Jimmy, in an act of defiance and protection of Rico, tells the captain, "if you write him up, write me up; he couldn't do it by himself."[130] Jimmy, in other words, claims identity with Rico as a "sex pervert," altering his own status in the prison. This act of solidarity, which on the surface appears very small, changes both men and becomes a turning point in the novel. Jimmy and Rico are sent to the hole, and they get time added to their sentences. Rico understands this as something Jimmy has done for him, for their love, but as Jimmy thinks about it, he decides that "the thing he had done, he had done it for himself. He had done it because in his warped and unmoral way it made him something; it made him a man. . . . He had served plenty of time and he could serve plenty more. But the way he thought of it, he could not have waited until later to have been a man."[131] Jimmy finds that he must reject traditional masculine values in order to become a man. He knows that this is "warped and unmoral" according to the ideals he has been taught—both in prison and outside of it—but he departs from his society's values and comes, instead, to his own version of what it means to be a man.

As it articulates its own deeply moral version of maleness, *Yesterday Will Make You Cry* rescripts the value systems of mid-century masculinity. Himes's protagonist is a primarily heterosexual man who is in love with—and in a sexual relationship with—another man; he has been imprisoned by the state for attempting to live according to society's masculine ideals, but he eventually rejects those values, finding in that rejection a different, alternate version of what it means to be a man. Jimmy Monroe does not execute a tragic reconciliation of homosexuality and masculinity like the rape Jim Willard commits in *The City and the Pillar*. And his masculinity rejects the white-supremacist fantasy of the sexually violent police officers in *If Beale Street Could Talk*. *Yesterday Will Make You Cry* proposes, instead, an abandonment of those terms from the perspective of an incarcerated man in the 1940s.

US American publishers were not interested. As I've argued in this chapter, even when a novelist like James Dickey tried to think about male/male sexual violence as a rite of passage or a submission to the natural world in order to emerge different on the other side, critics insisted on interpreting the violence in *Deliverance* according to the masculinist terms with which they were already familiar. Even when critics read an antiracist novel like Baldwin's *If Beale Street Could Talk*, they can't help but imagine the rapists in his novel as Black men. It is interpretations such as these that would most impact US American discourse about male/male rape. Although novelists throughout the 1960s and '70s, then, were experimenting with different ways of thinking about masculinity, homosexuality, sexual violence, and the criminal justice system, the US American discourse about the violate man became further restricted, established along strict lines of weakness, whiteness, femininity, homosexuality, and brokenness.

CHAPTER 3

After the Production Code
Male/Male Rape in 1970s Cinema

> It is an ancient litigation,
> this turning of horror into stories,
> and it is a lonely piece of work,
> trying to turn the stories back into horror
>
> —TONY HOAGLAND, "Fire"

R. Barton Palmer has referred to the rape sequence in John Boorman's *Deliverance* (1972) as "a scene with no antecedents in the American cinema," but this was not the first male/male rape sequence put on celluloid.[1] In Chapter 1, I noted that Harvey Hart's film version of *Fortune and Men's Eyes* was released in the summer of 1971, a year before *Deliverance* appeared in theaters. But it would have been fairly easy for most moviegoers to miss *Fortune*: Addison Verrill's review in *Variety* expected the film to do well only in urban gay markets.[2] In addition, the only onscreen rape in *Fortune* is very brief and significantly obscured; it makes sense that the rape in this Canadian film has been considerably less widely remembered than the one in *Deliverance*.

There is, however, another male/male rape sequence that predates *Deliverance* in the history of US American cinema, one that is also consistently forgotten in discussions of on-screen sexual violation. That no one seems to remember this is especially fascinating since the audience for this particular film was much, much wider than *Fortune*'s. In fact, although it was released with the prohibitive X rating in 1969, this film made nearly as much at the box office as *Deliverance* would three years later with its rating of R. The film to which I refer is John Schlesinger's *Midnight Cowboy*, whose protagonist, played by Jon Voight, is raped in a nightmare sequence in the middle of the film. *Cowboy* was released in the summer of 1969, did extremely well at the box office, and won three Academy Awards, including the Oscar for Best Picture.

The year after *Deliverance* was released, 1973, saw yet another depiction of male/male rape at the movies: this time in a frightening scene in Jerry Schatzberg's unjustly forgotten *Scarecrow*, a picaresque story of two drifters, played by Gene Hackman and Al Pacino, who become friends and hitchhike their way across the country. These three cinematic representations of male/male sexual violence differ significantly but examining them together will illuminate a great deal about the discourse of male/male rape in what would quickly come to be called the New Hollywood or the Hollywood Renaissance.

Midnight Cowboy, *Deliverance*, and *Scarecrow* were all made as part of what the film industry—even at the time—understood as the New Hollywood. All three are mentioned in the first few pages of Peter Biskind's bestselling history of this period, *Easy Riders, Raging Bulls*, and the three films star some of the key New Hollywood actors: Gene Hackman, Jon Voight, Dustin Hoffman, and Al Pacino.[3] The hallmarks of the New Hollywood were, most importantly, the collapse of the Motion Picture Production Code and a new belief in the director as auteur. The films that mark the beginning of this period—*Bonnie and Clyde* (1967), *The Graduate* (1967), *The Wild Bunch* (1969), and *Easy Rider* (1969)—are instantly recognizable as departures from the types of films Hollywood had made before, and they are notable, especially for their new approaches to sex and violence on-screen. The new Motion Picture Association of America (MPAA) rating system and the overthrow of the Production Code (PCA) had shifted what audiences were permitted to watch and, therefore, what filmmakers were able to do. This period in Hollywood has, by now, been well documented, and it has come to represent a kind of legendary golden age of US American moviemaking.[4] Indeed, the influence of the New Hollywood on later filmmakers would be hard to overstate, as Quentin Tarantino has documented in *Cinema Speculation*, his own book on the period.[5]

This chapter focuses on the effect of the New Hollywood on the discourse of male/male rape in the US. We have seen how theater and fiction have affected this discourse in the years 1965–1974. This same period coincides with the rise of the New Hollywood and with new cinematic possibilities for the representation of violence. Although the three films differ significantly, *Midnight Cowboy*, *Deliverance*, and *Scarecrow* each contribute to this discourse. The differences between the ways the films present male/male rape are most significant at the level of the formal techniques their filmmakers employed. Each film figures male/male rape using distinct styles and conventions that considerably impact the ways in which audiences are asked to understand this sexual violence. Importantly, these techniques have had an enormous effect on how this violence has been remembered by audiences. The visual rhetoric employed by Schlesinger for the rape in *Midnight Cowboy* has allowed it to be all but forgotten by cinematic history, and the rape in *Scarecrow* went unremarked even at the time of its release, while the stylistic amplitude of *Deliverance* has elevated it to what many still reference as the most spectacular male/male rape in cinematic history.

Following Stephen Prince's pathbreaking scholarship on film violence, this chapter examines, especially, the stylistic shift that the *Deliverance* sequence marks. The important question here is *how* male/male rape is represented in *Midnight Cowboy*, *Deliverance*, and *Scarecrow*, how the filmmakers communicate the violence to us, and what that violence is asked to mean for the narrative. Because of the enormity of its impact, *Deliverance* is my natural point of departure here, but this chapter plays close attention to these other two early representations of male/male rape in film. This chapter develops a language for the way post-PCA, New Hollywood cinema mediates male/male rape narratives, as well as how audiences and critics put these narratives to their own use. Part of my argument here will be that because metaphors are everywhere in movies, and because filmmakers represent rape *through* metaphor as often as they ask rape to work *as* a metaphor for something other than itself, the *meaning* of male/male rape on screen will often work to distance us as viewers from rape as an act of violence in the real world.

Joe Buck's Nightmare

In *Midnight Cowboy* the main character, a neglected young man named Joe Buck (Voight), is gang-raped by a group of men who discover Joe and a young woman (Jennifer Salt) kissing in a truck at night. The men, attired in cowboy hats, denim, and boots, separate the two lovers, drag Joe from behind the wheel, rip off his jeans, bend him over the hood of his vehicle, and rape him. This plot sequence, in many ways, is quite straightforward. The sequence in *Midnight Cowboy* is also surprisingly graphic, and there can be no doubt for members of the audience that what we are watching is a rape. Furthermore, the scene contains no hint of eroticism: the male/male rape in *Midnight Cowboy* is contained within a violent sequence that depicts no more or less than sheer terror for its victim.

But if the narrative details of the rape in *Midnight Cowboy* are simple, the way Schlesinger relates the violent attack on Joe is anything but straightforward. The cinematic techniques the director employs to tell the story of Joe Buck's rape allow viewers a certain distance between ourselves and the attack on Joe. In the timeline of the film's events, Joe's experience of rape occurs before *Midnight Cowboy* begins. The audience, however, doesn't find out about the rape until halfway through the movie, long after Joe has left the desert to move to the bustling streets of New York. Schlesinger presents the rape in a nightmarish flashback sequence intercut with other childhood memories and confused dream imagery. This flashback is narratively framed with images of Joe falling asleep and beginning to dream and an image of him abruptly waking up. The nightmare, further, is filmed in black-and-white, and it is the only sequence in *Midnight Cowboy* not in color. Occasionally in color films, black-and-white photography can work as a filmic indication that what the audience sees happened in the past—as with *American History X* (1998) or *Memento* (2000)—but unlike these films, *Midnight Cowboy* contains numerous flashback sequences, and all of them are in color; the rape sequence is the only one Schlesinger presents in monochrome.

While telling the story of Joe Buck's rape, Schlesinger also makes use of a cinematic technique that Stephen Prince calls *metonymic displacement*, "a form of spatial displacement in which the occlusive or evasive composition contains some object or action that stands in for the violence that is occurring out of view."[6] In order to keep a violent image off-screen, metonymic displacement substitutes the violence with a coded image that an audience can easily read as though it were physical violence. (One example of this might be, say, a shot of a man about to fall from a tall building that cuts to a shot of an ice cream cone hitting the pavement and splattering.) Prince argues that "these metonymic elements are typically quite explicit and denotative.... Too much subtlety in their design, in fact, will tend to nullify the purpose and utility of this code." *Midnight Cowboy*'s metonymic displacement of male/male rape is fascinating and extremely complex.

The sequence moves very, very quickly, and the rapid editing has a disorienting effect.[7] As Joe and his girlfriend kiss in their vehicle, they are discovered by the gang of men; in the dream-logic of the flashback, however, Joe is surprised, not by his rapists, but by his grandmother Sally (Ruth White). The image appears to be a memory, perhaps one of Sally

FIGURE 3.1-7: *Midnight Cowboy* (1969), Joe Buck's Nightmare

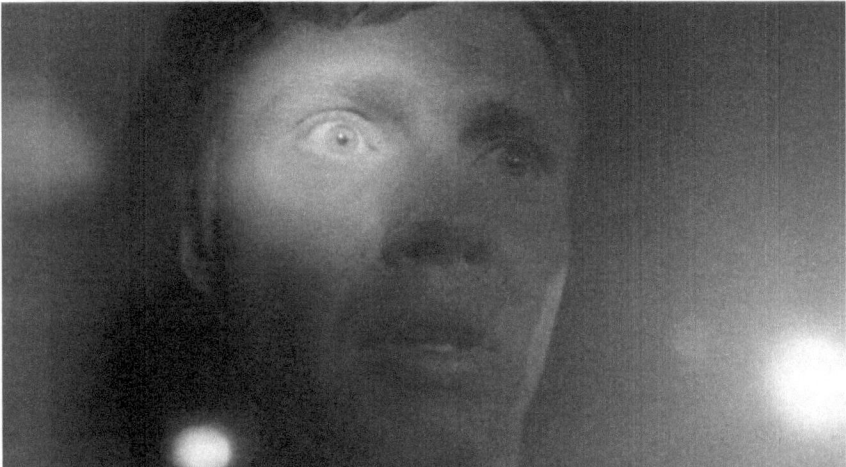

FIGURE 3.2

discovering Joe masturbating in his bedroom or happening upon him while he is in bed with a different lover. Joe's grandmother turns on the light in the bedroom (Figure 3.1); the light becomes the rapists' flashlights as they shine them in the young couple's faces (Figure 3.2). As the men drag Joe and his girlfriend from the car, they pull down Joe's pants, exposing his underwear (Figure 3.3); the film cuts immediately to an ostensible memory of Sally spanking a very young Joe on his bare buttocks (Figure 3.4). Throughout this rape sequence, Schlesinger intently studies the rape victim's emotional

After the Production Code 101

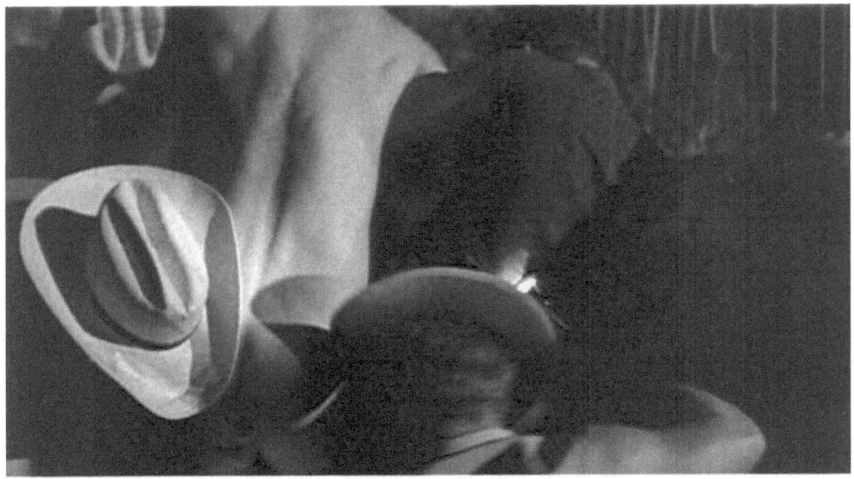

FIGURE 3.3

FIGURE 3.4

and physical anguish by focusing the camera on Joe's face as he struggles to break free of the men (Figure 3.5). Next, the camera displays Joe's bare legs as the men wrench them apart. The moment of Joe's penetration is again metonymically displaced with a memory of Joe's grandmother as she prepares to give the young Joe an enema (Figure 3.6); the film then cuts quickly back to Joe's face as he is raped by the first of his assailants (Figure 3.7).

From this point in the flashback, what has so far appeared to be a memory becomes increasingly confused and bizarre as a group of policemen enters

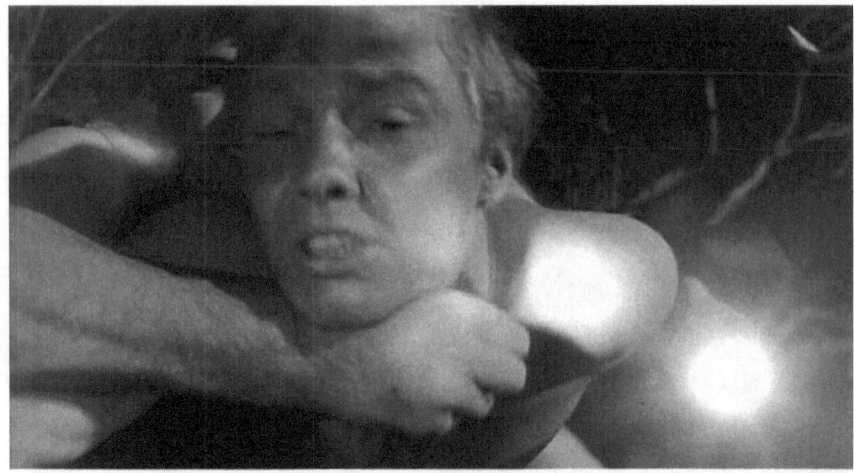

FIGURE 3.5

FIGURE 3.6

the scene. Included in this group of policemen is Joe's companion Ratso (Dustin Hoffman), whom he has only just met in New York and who could not possibly have witnessed the rape. The dream switches to other possible memories or fantasies here, as well: Joe appears to go to jail, his girlfriend is taken away in a car, his grandmother chews sadistically on a piece of candy, and (still in black-and-white) a building is demolished by a wrecking ball. The entirety of the dream sequence lasts ninety seconds, with the rape consisting of a maximum of one minute. It is also important to note

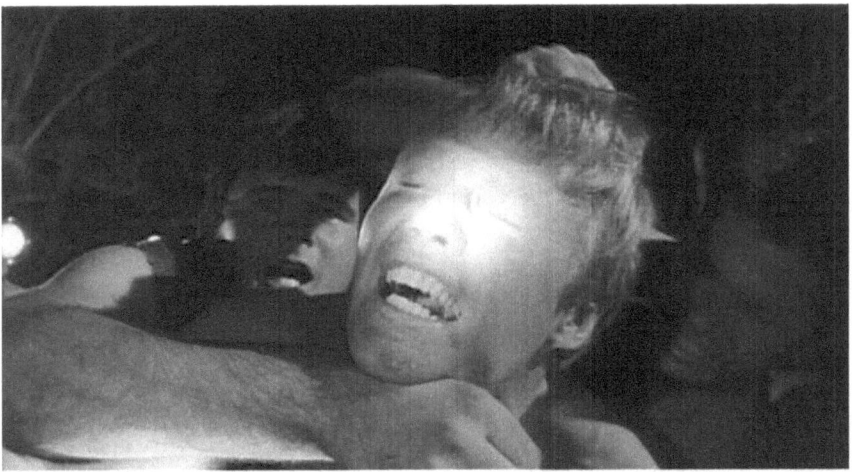

FIGURE 3.7

that although this nightmare sequence includes images of both Joe and his girlfriend screaming, in what would certainly have been a loud struggle, we cannot hear their anguish; the soundscape of the nightmare consists primarily of electronic effects, plucked wires, and a single moment of breaking glass. There are no cries for help, and we do not hear the voices of Joe, his girlfriend, or their assailants. Schlesinger portrays few things distinctly in this sequence, and the film neither names nor characterizes the men who commit this sexual violence, but the suffering of the rape victim is quite clear in *Midnight Cowboy*. The director's focus is on Joe's experience of the violence of the event and the physical pain the rape causes; the camera maintains an intent gaze directed at Joe's anguished, terrified face.

I am highlighting Schlesinger's complex and dizzying filmic technique in order to demonstrate how stylistically distinct this sequence is, not only from other films at the time but also from other sequences in *Midnight Cowboy*. Schlesinger distinguishes the flashback of the rape from Joe's other memories by switching from color to black-and-white film, and he displaces the violence metonymically by intercutting disturbing childhood memories of Joe and his grandmother with Joe's memory of the rape. Schlesinger, importantly, undermines our ability to trust the entire sequence's authenticity by introducing the anachronistic presence of Ratso into the memory. Each of these techniques works to confound the audience's comprehension of—and emotional responses to—the male/male rape on-screen. The *Los Angeles Times*'s Charles Champlin, for example, found the flashbacks "fragmentary, almost inchoate," adding that they are "frequently difficult for the watcher to decipher until he can at last assemble the whole mosaic in his own mind."[8] Champlin's response describes the confusing effect of the entire nightmare sequence, which leaves the viewer with an idea of what has happened—or what might have happened—only after the sequence has ended and its mnemonic pieces can be puzzled out through the viewer's memory. *The New York Times*'s Vincent Canby does not mention the rape sequence at all, but he refers to the film's narrative digressions as "abbreviated, almost subliminal fantasies and flashbacks."[9] For Canby, then, the difference between memory and fantasy in *Midnight Cowboy* is unclear. In fact, because this technique was quite new in 1969, every review of the film in the major papers noted this effect. Louise Sweeney in *The Christian Science Monitor* found the film "chaotic and confusing as it substitutes abrupt flashbacks and intercuts for the linear effect of [James Leo Herlihy's] novel," and *The Washington Post* objected to the flashbacks, calling them repetitive and digressive.[10] In his history of the shooting of *Midnight Cowboy*, Glenn Frankel reports that the entire idea of these flashbacks was that "they were processed directly through Joe's psyche, not as traditional flashbacks but as memories and experiences that Joe was thinking about as we watch them happen."[11]

It is worth noting that although Louise Sweeney is certainly correct when she refers to the novel's linearity, the rape sequence in Herlihy's book is just as unclear as it is in Schlesinger's film. In the novel, the story is told from a third-person perspective very close to Joe Buck and, because Joe himself doesn't understand exactly what is happening when he is raped, Herlihy's prose is as confused as Joe's experience. The narrator refers, for example to "soft damp hands . . . all over his back and along his thighs," but before the reader can decipher what is happening, Herlihy describes "a crash in which everything was at once obliterated, and instantly re-created, but in a totally different perspective."[12] The narrator's description stays firmly in the realm of nightmare, and Joe's relationships to space and to what is happening to him are ambiguous. For Joe, "the room had become a hole, shaped something like a well, and Joe was lying in the bottom of it, looking up. . . . And then the opening at the top of the hole was completely covered over by this fat form darkening everything so that it was no longer possible to see." Joe becomes "aware that some effort was being made up above, someone was trying to release him from the anguish and the darkness. . . . He fought hard to cooperate with the force that was drawing him upward, straining every muscle in order to help. And then, just as it became clear what exactly was being enacted upon him, something broke deep inside of him." Although the rape sequence in the film, then, left critics confused as to whether they were watching a memory or a fantasy, Schlesinger and screenwriter Waldo Salt's choice to use short flashbacks and complex imagery cleverly attempts to match the effect of the film's source material.

Variety, the only periodical other than the *Los Angeles Times* even to mention the movie's gang-rape sequence, uses language that directs the reader away from the gender of the rape victim, referring with intentional euphemism to "cruel group ravishments and forced colonic irrigation."[13] These flashback sequences, though they may have annoyed critics, irrupt constantly during the film's narrative, and they provide *Midnight Cowboy* with a protagonist who seems constantly lost, who cannot get a purchase on his present because of the repetitive insistence and lingering importance of his past. As Frankel puts it, "they are meant to be as puzzling and disturbing to us as they are to Joe when he experiences them. And they are faithful to the novel because they keep us inside Joe's head, . . . explaining Joe's mood of loneliness and despair."[14] What remains fundamentally unclear throughout *Midnight Cowboy*, however, is whether or not these sequences that Joe Buck appears to remember ever actually happened.

Midnight Cowboy, in other words, certainly represents a male/male rape, but although Schlesinger focuses his camera on Joe Buck's face, emphasizing the painful and haunted experience of the violate man, the final effect of *Midnight Cowboy*'s rape sequence is to leave viewers confused, never quite sure whether the gang rape actually occurred or whether Joe's fears of being violated have simply come to life in a nightmare. Bracketed by images of Joe falling asleep and waking up and intercut with so many other strange and confusing images, the rape sequence in *Midnight Cowboy* is easy to construe as a nightmare rather than a memory. Joe literally wakes up from these terrifying images of sexual violation, he removes himself from them, away from any immediate danger, and finds himself back in the relative safety of Ratso's squat in Manhattan. Further, the rape sequence is tiny in proportion to the rest of the movie, and because the rapists are nameless and nearly faceless, the film allows them to remain relegated to the unreal world of the dream. As oneiric manifestations, they are free to function as figures of terror, embodiments of immaterial drives or inchoate forces. The male/male rape in *Midnight Cowboy* is significantly *less* real than the real world of the film itself, and it remains a part of the realm of fantasy, psychically and symbolically but not physically threatening.

Rape as Metaphor in Deliverance

In Chapter 2 I argued that, on the page, *Deliverance* treats male/male rape as a rite of passage or test, but British filmmaker John Boorman, who directed the Warner Bros. film version of the novel, saw the sexual violence in Dickey's tale as a metaphor, a symbolic attack committed by the natural world upon men from civilization who were bent upon the destruction of nature. In his autobiography he explains his interest in *Deliverance* by saying, "its themes coincided with my own: man's relationship to nature, the attempt to recover lost harmony, the Earth's anger at the despoiling human race. At its centre was the rape of the city men by the mountain men. It was a metaphor for the rape of America."[15] Boorman was critical of what he saw as the desecration of the North American continent by its "civilized" inhabitants, and his movie explores this destruction in explicit terms.

The film *Deliverance* begins with shots of a man-made lake: bulldozers and trucks move dirt as they transform the land. Over this, we hear three men talking. Lewis (Burt Reynolds) describes the Cahulawassee River as "just about the last wild, untamed, unpolluted, un-fucked-up river in the South," telling us that "they're gon' stop the river up. They ain't gon' be no more river. There's just gon' be a big, dead lake." As the men argue, Lewis's voice again dominates, and we hear him say, "You just push a little more power—you push a little more power into Atlanta, little more air-conditionin's for your smug little suburb, and you know what's gon' happen? We're gon' rape this whole *goddamn* landscape. We're gon' *rape* it." The other men protest this as an "extreme" point of view, but as the argument ends, Boorman punctuates what we're hearing with a bang. We watch as explosives detonate, destroying a portion of the land about which Lewis is speaking.

Lewis's reference to the river as *un-fucked-up* and his repetition of the word *rape* in the film's opening sequence set the terms for the movie; they frame the film with rape as a metaphor. As Boorman speaks of the *despoiling* of the continent, and as he has Lewis speak about *raping* the land, Boorman metaphorizes rape. As I argued in the introduction, the use of the word *rape* does the ideological work of asking us to respond to something that is not a sexual violation as though it were violently sexual. Boorman introduces rape as a metaphor in *Deliverance* long before he presents his viewers with the images of rape at the film's center. The director's treatment of rape, then, is fundamentally different from the way Dickey approaches it in his novel, and it is difficult to argue with critics of the film who saw the mountain men/rapists as "symbols for the evil in 'nature,'" or those who understood that "what happens to the Ned Beatty character, Bobby, in the rhododendron hell on the banks of the river . . . is not the only rape. There is a larger one that in Boorman's eyes ought to make us just as queasy."[16] Critics interpreted the rape of Bobby in the film as the landscape's metaphoric revenge for the suburbanites' "rape" of the river because that is precisely what Boorman intended his audience to understand.

If critics, however, found themselves reading the rape at the center of *Deliverance* as a metaphor for something else, audience members have had more visceral reactions to the violence in the film. Carol Clover notes that the film has often been experienced by audiences as a horror film, arguing that "although *Deliverance* is commonly taken less as horror than as a 'literary' rumination on urban masculinity, its particular rendition of the city–country encounter has been obviously and enormously influential in horror—so much so that it is regularly included in cult/horror lists."[17] Clover's book *Men, Women, and Chain Saws* is the foundational text for discussions of gender as it is mobilized in the horror genre, and the amount of space her book devotes to reading *Deliverance* (much of its long third chapter) is indicative of the film's powerful effect *qua* horror film on audiences and later filmmakers in the genre.

For the essayist David Griffith, *Deliverance* "remains unmatched in American film for its ability to make men groan and turn away from the screen," and he is not alone.[18] Director Stanley Kubrick, who staged the unforgettably disturbing rape scene in *A Clockwork Orange* (1971), has described *Deliverance*'s rape sequence as "the most terrifying scene ever filmed," and in 2005 the men's magazine *Maxim* unironically named Bobby's rapists as the number one film villains of all time, referring to the phrase "Now let's you just drop them pants" as "undeniably the most terrifying words ever spoken on celluloid."[19] I don't wish to create an opposition between audience responses to metaphor and audience responses to realistic depictions, but it is fundamental to remember that although critics interpreted *Deliverance*'s rape sequence, as Brownmiller acerbically puts it, "as some sort of metaphor for the rape of the environment," audiences have tended to respond viscerally and emotionally to the film rather than to consider its symbolic meanings.[20]

I will return to rape's symbolic meanings at the end of this chapter, but I want at this point to examine *how* the film approaches its subject matter. Clover's focus on the influence that the film has had on the horror genre draws attention to the way the scene in *Deliverance* is shot and edited—how the film styles its violence for viewers. Film scholar Stephen Prince refers to these techniques of representation as *stylistic amplitude*. He argues that "once filmmakers learn compelling ways of styling violence, the methods can't be unlearned. They go into the storehouse of cinema syntax and stay there, available to subsequent filmmakers whose interests incline them in this direction."[21] For Prince, images that indicate violent action, even those that represent violence using the language of metaphor, such as a round of machine-gun fire ripping into a plaster wall or a man banging away furiously on a drum set, can be enormously effective at communicating the experience of violation to an audience. The visual rhetoric of filmic violence is, for Prince, more important to a film's reception than whether or not a film is violent *per se*.[22] By exploring *Deliverance*'s stylistic amplitude and describing Boorman's approach to the rape at the film's center, this chapter also attempts to articulate the terms used in the representation of male/male rape for the movies that will follow *Deliverance*. The importance of this film to the history of violence in cinema cannot be overstated; the visual rhetoric for male/male rape in *Deliverance* will be used again and again by filmmakers after Boorman—from artists as diverse as Barbra Streisand and Edward James Olmos to Quentin Tarantino and the creators of *South Park*.

In contrast to *Midnight Cowboy*'s ninety-second nightmare/flashback (less than 1 percent of the film's length), the rape of Bobby in *Deliverance* lasts over four minutes. After the attack, it takes Bobby an additional five minutes before he is completely dressed, and the full sequence concerning the rape and its immediate effects lasts a punishing thirteen minutes. This is followed with an additional nine-minute sequence during which the four suburbanites argue about how to dispose of the rapist's body before they bury it. In total, the encounter between the film's four suburbanites and the rapists takes up more than twenty minutes of *Deliverance*. If critics and audiences have remembered the male/male rape sequence in *Deliverance* much more vividly than they have remembered the rape in the film adaptation of *Midnight Cowboy*, one reason for this is that *Deliverance* simply devotes much more time to the subject than its predecessor. As I noted earlier, for Boorman rape is the central image and overriding metaphor of *Deliverance*, and the sequence in his movie is not only longer than other male/male rape sequences from the time period, it also takes up more space, proportionally, than does this same series of events in Dickey's novel: a sequence that composed less than one-eighth of the book's length takes up more than one-sixth of the film.

Obviously, the medium of film has the capacity to literalize acts of violence in visual ways that differ drastically from the capabilities of a novel, and this was especially true three years after the fall of the PCA, but Boorman's visual approach to the rape in *Deliverance* also differs from the novel's portrayal of sexual violation. In the previous chapter, as I described the rape in Dickey's novel, I pointed out that the protagonist looks away from Bobby as he is being violated and turns his gaze, instead, toward the river, toward the possibility of being rescued. Rather than a description of Bobby as the man rapes him, Dickey relates an experience or sensation of anguish that both Ed and Bobby *share*: "a sound of pain and outrage, . . . followed by one of simple and wordless pain."[23] Boorman's film, by contrast, visualizes the act of rape in detail. Indeed, *Deliverance* is fundamentally invested in this visualization of male/male sexual violence. For although the rape scene has no overt erotic charge (Brownmiller calls it "one of the ugliest rapes committed by some of the ugliest rapists in cinematic history. . . . In no way can it be construed as a sexual turn-on."), Boorman asks his viewers to look at Bobby frequently, both before and during his violation, and the director does not avert his camera or metonymically displace the act of violence as Schlesinger does in *Cowboy*.[24]

The rape of Bobby as adapted for film is very similar to its source material in respect to the actual violence that occurs. The additions Boorman makes to his film version, however, are what give the movie its terrifying quality and make the sequence harrowing enough to be so frequently classed as a horror film. As in the novel, Ed (Jon Voight) is tied to a tree while Bobby (Ned Beatty) remains untied. "Now let's you just drop them pants," the first rapist (Bill McKinney) says to Bobby. The second man (Cowboy Coward) adds that he should take off his shirt, and finally the first rapist growls, "them panties: take 'em off." The film keeps Bobby in a medium shot while he undresses, and the audience, the rapists, and Ed all watch him as he disrobes (Figure 3.8). Bobby also prays while he removes his clothing, and his prayer can be heard distinctly on the film's soundtrack, even when the camera focuses on the rapists and Ed as they watch Bobby undress.

Immediately after the rapist tells him to remove his underwear, Bobby turns and begins running away. The chase sequence that follows is a departure from Dickey's novel, and Boorman uses both medium-shots and close-ups for this sequence. The rapist follows Bobby up a hill, smacking his buttocks and tugging him back down the slope again. He grips Bobby's chest and belly (Figure 3.9), and then, in the film's most memorable departure from the novel, the rapist begins to refer to Bobby using pig imagery.

FIGURE 3.8: *Deliverance* (1972), Bobby disrobes

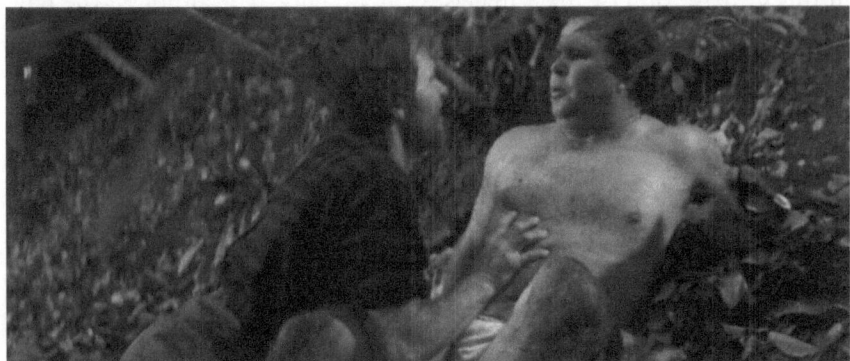

FIGURE 3.9: *Deliverance* (1972), the attack on Bobby

FIGURE 3.10: *Deliverance* (1972), porcine imagery

FIGURE 3.11: *Deliverance* (1972), the other man laughs

"You look just like a hog," he tells him, and then he calls Bobby "piggy, piggy," pulling on his nose to make a snout and forcing him to give him a ride as though he were a pack animal (Figure 3.10). Next, in a longer shot, we watch as Bobby struggles and even escapes momentarily before he is caught again. At this point, the rapist says to his companion, "looks like we got a sow here instead of a boar." He grabs Bobby's ear, saying "I bet you can squeal like a pig. Squeal, now. Squeal." Bobby squeals desperately as the rapist begins to remove his own overalls, and the film looks away from Bobby for a moment, finding the man with the gun laughing heartily—at his friend's pleasure or Bobby's agony or both (Figure 3.11). As the man brings Bobby down to his knees and places himself behind his victim, he and Bobby both continue to squeal; Bobby's squeals are consistently high-pitched and desperate.

Boorman gives his audience one last instruction as to how we should watch the next few shots by cutting to an image of Ed as he stares helplessly at this scene. Ed clutches the tether at his neck and attempts to escape: he would help his friend if he could, but he cannot. He must simply watch (Figure 3.12). The rape itself is shot using four single shots—a separate close-up or medium close-up for each of the actors—and Boorman cuts back and forth between these shots (Figures 3.13–3.15). The rapist, sweaty and terrifying, squeals throughout, as his companion with the gun laughs. In the film version of *Midnight Cowboy*, Schlesinger metonymically displaces the moment of penetration by presenting the audience with an image of Sally giving young Joe an enema instead of an image of rape. In *Deliverance*, Boorman effects no such displacement. The scene unfolds in real time, and the camera does not cut away.

112   THE VIOLATE MAN

FIGURE 3.12–15: *Deliverance* (1972), reaction shots

FIGURE 3.13

FIGURE 3.14

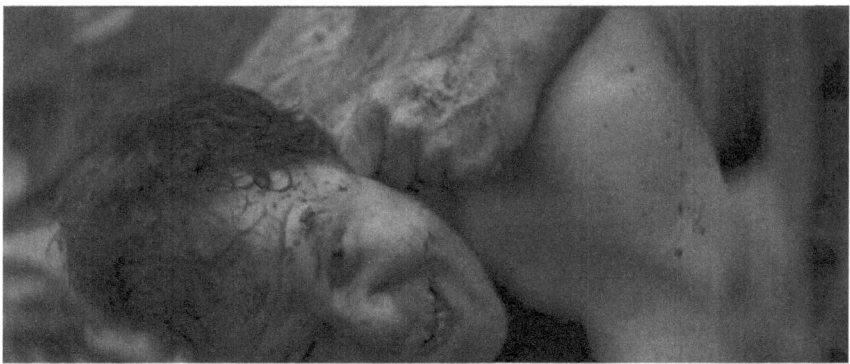

FIGURE 3.15

The rapist continues to squeal almost rhythmically, with Bobby steadily repeating him. A viewer might even become slightly accustomed to the shrill sound that the man makes, as it is followed, at regular intervals, by Bobby's own squealing. As the rapist squeals a final time, however, Bobby lets out a different sound altogether, a low, dissonant, irregular cry of pain that lasts much longer than his squeals did. In the next shot we see the man with the gun look lecherously at Ed (Figure 3.16). Because this close-up is shot from Ed's perspective, the man with the gun looks directly into the camera and at the audience, toothlessly grinning with pleasure at the rape we have all just watched and also, presumably, at the violation he imagines he will commit on Ed. Finally, Ed looks away from his friend and toward the river, and the film resumes the novel's approach to the event, asking the viewers, too, to turn our gazes away from the violate man (Figure 3.17).

After the toothless man threatens to rape Ed orally, uttering the now-infamous line "He got a real pretty mouth ain't he?" Boorman returns to the plot points of the novel. Lewis shoots the rapist with an arrow, the other man flees, and the suburbanites argue about whether or not to bury the body or alert the authorities. In a fascinating bit of staging, Boorman focuses for an extended period of time on the rapist as he dies from his wound, and the director keeps the man's dead body in nearly all the shots of the men as they discuss what to do with the corpse (Figure 3.18). The effect here is to emphasize the gravity of the situation, the violence that has been done to the dead man, and the moral conundrum the men face.

The film approaches the attack on Bobby as an event to be *endured* by the audience. More than one reviewer remarked on the discomfort that *Deliverance* appears to want to engender in its audience, and the film is able

FIGURE 3.16: *Deliverance* (1972), the other man looks at the camera

FIGURE 3.17: *Deliverance* (1972), Ed looks away

FIGURE 3.18: *Deliverance* (1972), the corpse stays in the picture

to create this feeling by insistently turning its gaze toward the act of rape. When Boorman aims the camera away from the attack itself, he directs it either at Ed or at the man with the gun, both of whom stare intently at Bobby and his rapist. In this way, even when the film appears to avert its gaze from the rape, it does not completely look away, registering instead either Ed's horror or the toothless man's pleasure. And, as I noted earlier, the film sustains its visualization of the rape for over four full minutes.

Deliverance sets itself apart both from its contemporaries in the cinema and its source material through the use of yet another formal device. I remarked that we can plainly hear Bobby praying as he is forced to remove his clothing, and in fact, the entire time that the rapist chases Bobby up the hill, Bobby is muttering the words "no" and "don't." These words are constantly repeated, mantra-like, in a manner evocative of and continuing the prayer he uttered as he undressed. In this way the film underlines the terror of the situation, as Bobby unsuccessfully pleads with the rapist. It is extremely significant that we hear Bobby's anguish in this sequence. According to Stephen Prince, "empirical studies of viewer reactions to screen violence have shown that when expressions of pain and suffering are present in a scene, viewers tend to attribute a greater level of violence to the depicted action."[25] Prince also reports that by the mid-1930s, "the evolving politics of screen violence" had resulted in a widespread "suppress[ion of] the use of sound to delineate physical suffering. This suppression would," Prince says, "have lasting consequences for American film, helping to make screen violence into the largely pain-free phenomenon that it remains even today."[26]

Prince's argument in regard to the auditory information of violent action on the screen draws attention to just how unaccustomed movie audiences are to the sound of a victim's pain. This tradition of occluding the auditory information related to pain and anguish can be traced back to the first years of the Production Code in the 1930s. In 1972, the PCA had only recently been dismantled, and *Deliverance*'s sound information broke startlingly with filmic convention; as I have noted, even *Midnight Cowboy*, only three years earlier, did not include the sound of pain in its staging of sexual violence. Boorman's cinematic choices, then—his sustained and insistent attention to the act of violation, his staging of the terrified victim as he attempts to escape the rape, his inclusion of the sounds both of Bobby's resistance and his anguish, his decision to shoot the sequence in real time without a blackout, and the bizarre quality of the pig imagery and the squealing—explain both the scene's formal influence on the horror genre and the lasting impression it has had on audiences in general.

The total unexpectedness and dehumanization of the rapist's use of porcine imagery and his command that Bobby squeal like a pig also work both to racialize *Deliverance*'s male/male rape and to place it into the realm of the fantastic.[27] The rapists—with their odd language, inscrutable motivations (the attack does not appear to be spurred by homosexual desire), unknown origins, and scant attention to hygiene—might be better described as wood-demons or creatures than men. Rodger Cunningham argues that Boorman's film explicitly links the rapists with the forest, remarking that "the campers, and Lewis in particular, are generally shot in front of the green of the forest, standing out against it. In contrast, the first rapist is initially seen moving *within* a wall of green, as if belonging to it, a 'living extension' of its threat."[28] More importantly, as Carol Mason notes, "Appalachia is one of the 'backward' places to invoke if [a writer] want[s] to depict sadism and coerced sex as inevitable and inherent. Sexual deviance is portrayed as endemic to the region and its people."[29] The rapists, in other words, *are not the same kind of people* as the campers. Queer theorist Mel Chen's analysis in *Animacies* helps us to see, further, that the porcine imagery and the insistent racialization of the rapists as not-quite-white in *Deliverance* work to place them lower on a hierarchy of animacy than the white men at the film's center.[30] Queerness, racialization, and animality work together in *Deliverance* not only to present male/male rape as an attack against the civilized whiteness of the campers but also to shore up whiteness as such and to present rape, the threat of rape, and its causes as something apart from "normal" hydraulic sexual activity. It is especially important to notice the racialization and animacy hierarchies present in *Deliverance* because the rapists in both *Midnight Cowboy* and *Deliverance* are nameless, apparently impoverished, uneducated white men, and their appearance in these two movies will begin a long tradition of racialization of the rapist in film, one we will see repeatedly in the films of the 1990s.

For all the immediacy and terror of the act of rape in *Deliverance*, the film's unmistakable treatment of the rapists as subhuman works to distance the act of male/male rape from the realm of the possible, framing it as something that happens in the forest or in nature, far away from civilization. *Deliverance* locates male/male rape in the realm of the fantastic, firmly outside of the realistic world inhabited by the film's intended urban and suburban audiences. As Allison Graham argues conclusively in *Framing the South*, "the cretinous redneck would become an increasingly popular film villain" in the late 1960s and early 1970s.[31] In Clover's influential study, horror films with hillbilly villains invest the city/country axis with violence (sexual and otherwise) as a way of exploring "the confrontation, cast in almost Darwinian terms, of the civilized with the primitive. The scenario to which city/country horror obsessively returns is one in which the haves, the civilized urbanites, are separated from the system of supports that silently keep their privilege intact."[32] This racialized confrontation between the civilized and the barbarous is plainly evident in horror films such as *The Texas Chain Saw Massacre* (1974) and *The Hills Have Eyes* (1977), but it is also recognizable in films from the period classified under more respectable movie genres such as *In the Heat of the Night* (1967) and *Easy Rider* (1969).[33] Each of these narratives involves an urban protagonist who travels to the South and must confront, in a situation always fraught with metaphorical signifiers, the "uncivilized" or "backward" residents of the "country" and learn what he or she can. In *Deliverance*, male/male rape becomes one more indicator of this city/country divide.

Already a Cliché

Jerry Schatzberg's *Scarecrow* begins with two men, Max (Gene Hackman) and Francis, nicknamed Lion (Al Pacino), hitchhiking somewhere in California. They are not friends, but they become friends in the first few minutes of the movie because, although Max is loud, talkative, and will pick a fight with anyone who looks at him sideways, Francis makes him laugh and gives Max his last match when he doesn't have a light. *Scarecrow* is a more-or-less aimless modern odyssey following the two men as they hitchhike and freight-hop their way through Denver, St. Louis, and Detroit. Max's plan is to open a car wash in Pittsburgh. They take odd jobs as they travel the country, picking peaches and washing dishes, but there is not really a plot to the film, as such. The story is essentially about the two very different men—one angry and determined and one a sensitive comedian—learning to trust and care for one another despite their dissimilarities. *Scarecrow* ends in a downbeat mood typical of the New Hollywood style, as Francis, the younger and more sensitive of the two, becomes catatonic after a mental breakdown, and Max vows to stay with him and take care of him.

Early in the film we learn that Max has recently gotten out of prison, and, setting up *Scarecrow*'s later violence, the two men have the following exchange while walking along some railroad tracks:

> FRANCIS: Hey Max, I been meaning to ask you.
> MAX: Yeah.
> FRANCIS: In the joint . . .
> MAX: Yeah.
> FRANCIS: No women, right?
> MAX: No.
> FRANCIS: So how'd you get laid?

Max stops walking and just stares at Francis. It's a moment filled with meaning, although Max does not answer Francis's question. Indeed, it is unclear why Francis has asked the question, except perhaps because he's a joker and he wants to tease his friend. After a pause, Max smiles, and the two keep walking:

> MAX: Hey, I'm gonna have that car wash. Yeah. And a deep freezer full of steaks. And *ass*, buddy! I mean *ass*!
> FRANCIS: You should be more careful where you drop your drawers. Some scorpion'll put a lip-lock on your big ass.
> MAX: Uh-huh. Well, it'll be his funeral.

This kind of exchange is typical of the conversations in *Scarecrow*. The two men talk about all sorts of things and get to know each other while they travel.

The exchange about prison sex takes on a different valence, however, as Max and Francis find themselves incarcerated for a month in a Denver prison farm because Max has started a fight outside of a restaurant. To make matters worse, Max unaccountably blames Francis for their incarceration and stops speaking to him. Francis, friendly throughout, and constantly attempting to convince Max to stop being angry at him, is befriended by Riley (Richard Lynch), another man at the prison farm. In a shocking episode in this episodic film, Riley brutally beats Francis and rapes him. *Scarecrow*'s treatment of this violence is quite different from that of *Midnight Cowboy* and *Deliverance*, although it should come as no surprise that Riley is coded, like the rapists in the other two films, as a hillbilly (see Figure 3.19).

In *Scarecrow*, the male/male rape occurs while the characters are incarcerated and, accordingly, Schatzberg and screenwriter Gary Michael White represent prison rape using the tropes established by *Fortune and Men's Eyes* that I described in Chapter 1. The rapist in *Scarecrow* is coded as a homosexual, rape is a fact of prison life, and rape functions to authenticate the

FIGURE 3.19: *Scarecrow* (1973), Riley

film's prison narrative. The way the filmmakers represent Riley's rape of Francis to us, however, makes use of *classic* film violence techniques much more than it does the styles of New Hollywood that we see in the rapid editing of *Midnight Cowboy* or the multiple perspectives and long duration of *Deliverance*. These techniques work to lessen the emotional effect of the sexual violence in *Scarecrow*, even if the narrative itself is no less shocking.

In the scene, Riley has gotten Francis drunk, and the two men are laughing very hard in a kind of workshop in the prison farm, with Francis, as usual, clowning around. Riley propositions Francis casually—"Hey, how about it, huh?"—but Francis doesn't seem to understand what Riley is asking, even though the audience, because of the familiar narrative conventions I've described, can be reasonably expected to know what Riley means. Riley touches Francis's face, but he shrugs him off. Then Riley attempts to kiss Francis on the mouth. Francis again moves away, but he doesn't treat the situation as if he is in danger; instead, he attempts to deflect Riley's seduction with humor. Riley persists, saying, "Don't make fun of me. I mean, don't make fun of me, you know, it's . . . ." and then the scene becomes scarier. Riley backs Francis into a corner and stands up on a bench with his clothed crotch in Francis's face. Francis is afraid now, and he says, "I'll bite it off, you fuck!" (Figure 3.20). He gets Riley off him but accidentally hurts him in the process. Francis, always kind and generous, goes to Riley with concern: "Riley, I didn't mean to hurt you. What's the matter with you?"

But Riley has become terrifyingly violent, and Francis's care for his companion has been gravely misplaced. Riley beats Francis's head onto a worktable filled with wrenches and other equipment. He has him bent over the worktable, and he then turns Francis around and begins hitting him

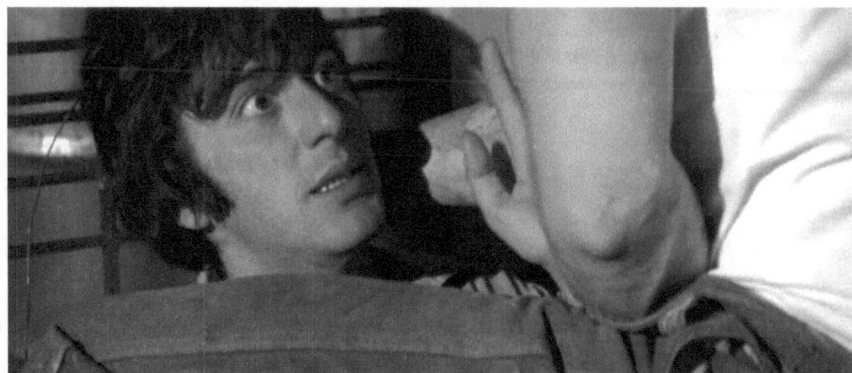

FIGURE 3.20: *Scarecrow* (1973)

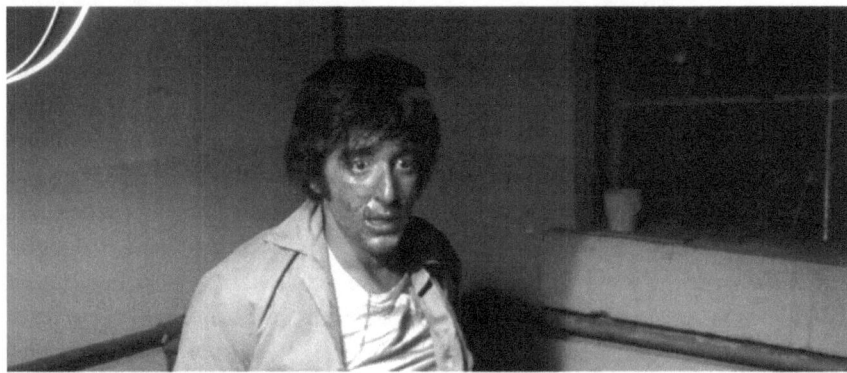

FIGURE 3.21: *Scarecrow* (1973)

in the face, saying, "Mama's boy likes to play, but doesn't pay—." Francis pushes Riley off him, and the camera shows Francis's face, covered in his own bright red blood (Figure 3.21). It's a brief moment before Riley again grabs Francis around the neck and begins to hit him. It's a brutal and terrifying scene, but it ends there, abruptly, as Riley hits Francis in the stomach repeatedly.

The next scene moves much more slowly, giving us time to make sense of what has happened. Francis walks gingerly into the dormitory where Max is asleep. He can barely stand up, and he holds onto the wall for support (Figure 3.22). He has been beaten very, very badly. He crashes to the floor and calls out to Max for help, slurring his words. Max slowly goes over to him, but when he realizes what has happened, he holds Francis's face in his hands. "Jesus Christ," he says. Francis's eyes are purple, and his

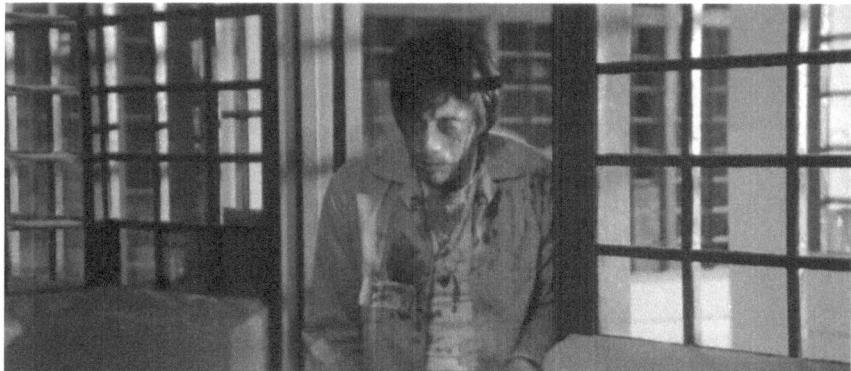

FIGURE 3.22-23: *Scarecrow* (1973), immediate aftermath

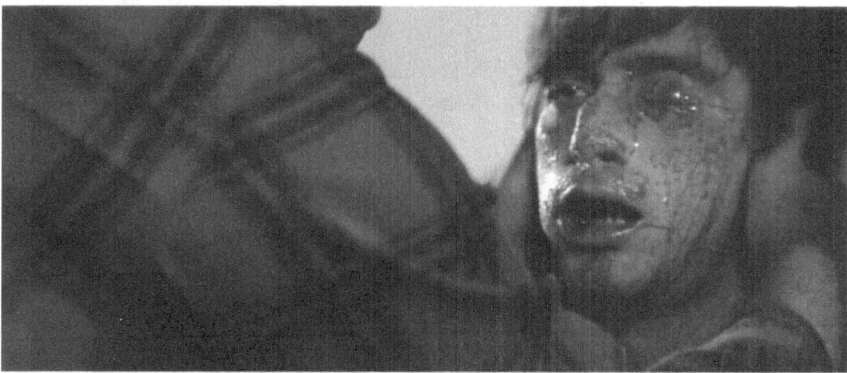

FIGURE 3.23

mouth and eyes have cuts around them (Figure 3.23). His jaw is swollen, and he is covered in blood. Ever the clown, Francis makes a heartbreaking riff on the old "you should see the other guy" joke:

MAX: Who did . . . ?
FRANCIS: Riley tried to fuck me, so I had to kick the shit out of him, you know?

Francis is weeping, and Max hugs his friend's bloody face to his chest.

In the next scene, Max finds Riley outside and asks him, "You gave it to my partner, Lion, didn't ya? Didn't you, Riley, didn't you give it to him?" Riley tells Max to "fuck off," but Max grabs Riley, and we watch him pummel Francis's rapist in a longshot. The two men leave the prison farm in the next scene, and the friends seem to return to their usual antics, with Max brawling and Francis making jokes, but Francis has been deeply altered by the event. His face is still badly bruised and cut, and he has become quieter. A few scenes later, in a bar in St. Louis, Max, in order to stop a fight, teasingly takes off his clothes while "The Stripper" plays on the jukebox: it's a delightfully funny sequence, and the entire restaurant is laughing at Max's antics, but Francis stands by the door thinking and troubled. After this, Francis seems to weaken and lose his nerve. He goes to pray in a cathedral, and then, after having traveled across the country to Detroit for the sole purpose of visiting his child and ex-girlfriend, he changes his mind and decides to call instead, even though he's just across the street. After this, he has a real breakdown: scaring some children and parents at the James Scott Memorial Fountain and then holding onto a stone lion for dear life, he becomes catatonic.

Critical responses to *Scarecrow* avoided the rape and its effect on Francis; they also described the prison sexual violence in the movie as if it were a boring commonplace—even as early as 1973. In *The Boston Globe*, Kevin Kelly's frustrated review complains that *Scarecrow* "draws on cliches. At the Honor Farm, for example, Pacino is badly beaten by an inmate whose sexual advances he resists. The experience draws him to the paternal warmth of Hackman, but it still seems like a copped inclusion for the usual sensationalism."[34] Rex Reed's hostile review in the *New York Daily News* phrases it this way: "They end up in a model prison near Denver, Lion gets his face beat in for resisting a sexual assault, his wife has re-married and although we see his infant son on the floor near the phone, she tells him his child is dead. It's *Midnight Cowboy* with varicose veins."[35] In other words, not only are these critics impatient with the male/male rape scene in *Scarecrow*, they report it as if Pacino's character is not a victim of a rape. They see the rape as an attempted seduction, one successfully resisted by the character. This seemingly willful avoidance of *Scarecrow*'s male/male rape, in turn, makes the film much more difficult for the critics to understand. Kelly, for example, finds that: "Two scenes later, at *Scarecrow*'s end, Pacino is locked in catatonia, the implication that he's paralyzed in guilt, and it just doesn't ring true."[36] Because the critic has not understood the sexual violence experienced by Francis, he can't acknowledge its possible effect on the character, and the entire film loses its credibility for the critic.

The critical blindness here is partly due to the filmmaking techniques used in *Scarecrow*. The film does not actually show Riley rape Francis, and unlike *Cowboy* and *Deliverance*—with their intense studies of the victims' faces during the assaults in those films—*Scarecrow* avoids showing this violence outright. Instead, it moves quickly past what might have been a much more harrowing sequence to the *effect* of the rape on the violate man. The scene remains unsettling and sad because of how keenly Schatzberg focuses on the character's brutalized face, but *Scarecrow* is more interested in Francis's fear of Riley before the sexual violence and his ongoing pain after the violence. The rape itself is kept off-screen. This is a narrative technique perfected during the classic Hollywood era. Representations of sexual violence (always against women) were expressly forbidden and always happened off-screen under the PCA; audiences were simply expected to understand— this is what happens, for example, in the rape sequences in Ida Lupino's *Outrage* (1950) and Elia Kazan's *A Streetcar Named Desire* (1951). So, unlike the New Hollywood representations of male/male rape in *Cowboy* and *Deliverance*, *Scarecrow*'s filmmakers opted for aesthetic techniques from the previous era, offering critics the ability to ignore what *Deliverance* wouldn't let any of its viewers avoid. In Kelly's review, and in most contemporary US American reviews of *Scarecrow*, one finds a refusal to see the violate man at all. For so many critics in 1973, prison rape is just a boring cliché. Worse yet, the rape victim becomes instead someone who "gets his face beat in for resisting a sexual assault" or a "naive" character who is forced to deal with "a prison farm trusty who fancies" him—anyone other than a violate man.[37]

Male/Male Rape and the Buddy Film

Although it shared the top prize at the 1973 Cannes Film Festival and was well appreciated in Europe, critics in the United States didn't care for *Scarecrow*.[38] In 2013, in a rave that coincided with a re-release and restoration of the film, the British critic Peter Bradshaw calls Schatzberg's film "a jewel of American cinema" but he notes that the country's critics have largely ignored it, remarking that "in his *Easy Riders, Raging Bulls*, Peter Biskind said *Scarecrow* was part of a body of 1970s work which was of 'secondary' significance. That judgment looks way off. *Scarecrow* is simply a masterpiece of the American new wave, a rangy, freewheeling tragicomedy in which Hackman and Pacino give effortlessly charismatic performances."[39] Critics in the US seemed frustrated by *Scarecrow*'s superficial similarities to *Midnight Cowboy*. Nearly every review of *Scarecrow* compares the two films— and always unfavorably—as in Rex Reed's labeling of *Scarecrow* as *Midnight Cowboy* with varicose veins cited earlier. In the *Los Angeles Times* review of

Scarecrow, Charles Champlin mentioned *Cowboy* three times.[40] Reviews by Gene Siskel in the *Chicago Tribune*, John Huddy in the *Miami Herald* (a rare rave), and Roger Ebert all refer to Schlesinger's film by name.[41]

Comparisons of *Scarecrow* to *Midnight Cowboy* also generated extended and surprising discussions of the "buddy film" in this period. In a *New York Times* opinion piece titled "Boy Meets Boy—Where the Girls Aren't" in January of 1974, Aljean Harmetz noted the trend: "Elliot Gould and Donald Sutherland. Robert Redford and Paul Newman. Gene Hackman and Al Pacino. Dustin Hoffman and Steve McQueen. These are the new romantic teams of the 1970s—the replacements in our fantasies for Katharine Hepburn and Spencer Tracy, Mickey Rooney and Judy Garland, Ginger Rogers and Fred Astaire."[42] Harmetz singles out *Scarecrow* for discussion, and she is intrigued by the possibility of platonic love between men. As she puts it:

> Our culture regards deep male friendships after adolescence with uneasiness. In my circle of acquaintances, it is the women who have emotionally penetrating relationships, while the men stay relentlessly on the surface with each other.
>
> In that sense, the often adolescent and sometimes silly relationships between the protagonists of these films may be a psychological step up.[43]

But Stephen Farber, in a May 1973 article about the buddy movie in *The New York Times* that also re-reviews *Scarecrow* (Vincent Canby had already reviewed it for the *Times* in April), calls Schatzberg's film "a tedious, pretentious, ultimately dishonest saga of two down-and-out rovers adrift in Middle America."[44] I want to spend a little time with Farber's review because it is specifically about male relationships and because his article discusses *Midnight Cowboy*, *Deliverance*, and *Scarecrow*; few critics connected these three films in 1973, and few have done so since.

Farber's frustration with *Scarecrow* is both entertaining and insightful—even if I do not share his overall assessment of the film:

> Beyond the failures in acting and direction, what makes the film insufferable is its dumb, dreamy celebration of male camaraderie. *Scarecrow* is in a long tradition of popular movies about male partners—from *Boom Town* and *Of Mice and Men* through *The Professionals*, *Butch Cassidy and the Sundance Kid* and *Husbands*. These gruffly tender male love stories delight audiences who want to retreat into reveries of summer camp, locker room and Army barracks, the rugged world of adventure on the open road or the high seas.[45]

FIGURE 3.24: *Scarecrow* (1973), best friends

The buddy film is, in Farber's view, a misogynist fantasy, one that avoids adult responsibilities, opting instead for permanent boyhood. As he caustically puts it, "American men yearn for the breezy, undemanding liaisons of a 12-year-old's life; they want to flee the threat of deeper involvement." In the buddy film, the bonds between the men are threatened chiefly by women, who always make too many demands on the movie's men. The male bonding in these movies is also always threatened by the specter—even the mere possibility—of homosexuality. Indeed, it is one of the central arguments of Eve Sedgwick's *Between Men* that: "'obligatory heterosexuality' is built into male-dominated kinship systems, [and] that homophobia is a *necessary* consequence of such patriarchal institutions as heterosexual marriage."[46] There is no continuum that links loving, sexual relationships between men on the one end and men supporting men's interests on the other. Homophobia, Sedgwick argues in that foundational book, is necessary in order to disrupt the continuum that would see homosexual sex as a logical extension of male team sports, business partnerships, or all-male seminaries. The possibility of gay sex must be disavowed—as we saw in the Idaho locker room in this book's introduction—if the buddy film is to work.[47]

As Farber points out, the possibility of *homosexual* affection between Max and Francis, is everywhere in *Scarecrow* (see Figure 3.24), and this is, of course, also true of *Midnight Cowboy*, whose characters so insistently try to avoid being seen as "fags." In order to disavow the possibility of homosexual desire, then, the films introduce an image of homosexuality that the characters reject. In Farber's severe judgment of *Scarecrow*, "The only purpose of a ridiculous, protracted, sensational, prison episode—in which a sadistic homosexual attacks an astonished Lion—is to underscore the boyish innocence of Max and Lion's relationship. The filmmakers want to make absolutely certain that no one in the audience mistakes Max or Lion for a homosexual." Farber is, in many ways, correct about this. Disavowed images of homosexuality *do* work to straighten up buddy films.

It is incorrect, however, to say that the only purpose of the male/male rape sequences in *Midnight Cowboy*, *Deliverance*, and *Scarecrow* is to heterosexualize the relationships at the center of these movies. Indeed, since these three films appeared, critics—Farber included—have read homosexuality *into* them, often believing themselves to have discovered something about which the filmmakers were unaware. The difference here is that what these films represent is male/male rape rather than homosexuality per se, and representations of male/male rape do not make meaning in the same way that representations of homosexuality do. Representations of male/male rape, to the contrary, work to undermine fantasies of masculine wholeness and solidity, they function instead, more like Kaja Silverman's description of historical trauma in that they "bring a large group of male subjects into such an intimate relation with lack that they are at least for a moment unable to sustain an imaginary relation with the phallus and so withdraw their belief from the dominant fiction."[48] In this way, the male/male rapes in *Cowboy*, *Deliverance*, and *Scarecrow* function perfectly for the cinema of male loneliness and lack that characterized the New Hollywood.

Fundamental to the films of this period and their use of male/male rape is that critics have all understood that rape *means* something. That is, rape, in these critics' evaluations—and sometimes also in the filmmakers' stated intentions—becomes important as a symbol. This is especially true in critical readings of *Cowboy* and *Deliverance*, where rape has often been read as a figure for repressed sexuality, but we can also see it in the idea that rape is a symbol for the dangers of homosexuality threatening the male camaraderie of *Scarecrow*. Rape does not mean rape in these films, or rather, we are invited to see it as something other than what it is and, in this way, we are permitted to avoid taking it seriously as an image of male vulnerability. As I have argued, the intellectual rush to read metaphor into *Deliverance* is the quickest way to deal with the emotional disruption of on-screen sexual violence. More important than the idea that the male/male rapes in these films represent a threat of homosexuality, then, I'm arguing that reading rape as a symbol or metaphor has had an effect on rape's unreality. We take rape *less* seriously when we make it into a metaphor. As we transform rape into a symbol, we look away from the pain on the faces of the men in *Cowboy*, *Deliverance*, and *Scarecrow*. But in New Hollywood's portraits of lonely and disaffected men, it is with their pain, to the contrary, that these filmmakers have asked us to identify.

Laughing at Pigs

Another way to cope with the images of male vulnerability offered us by *Midnight Cowboy*, *Scarecrow*, and the much more memorable rape sequence in *Deliverance* has been laughter. By the mid-1990s, there were countless references to *Deliverance* in US American popular culture, and most had rape as their punchlines. Richard Linklater's now-classic high school comedy *Dazed and Confused* (1994) includes a sequence in which an older bully played by Ben Affleck spanks new freshman Jeremy Fox and tells him to squeal like a pig, saying "Squee! Squee!" The camera pans away, and we watch from the perspective of the young man's two companions, who watch him get beaten. This works to great comic effect. In a 1995 episode of the sitcom *Married with Children*, Al and Bud, the show's main character and his son, are camping alone in an ostensibly scary forest. They are not frightened by the hoot of an owl or the sound of crickets, but when banjo music strikes up, both men jump out of their sleeping bags and Bud covers his (clothed) rear end with his hand.[49] A year later on *Married with Children*, when the family goes on vacation to Branson, Missouri, they stay at a place called the Deliverance Inn. The man at the front desk predictably promises Al that "you'll squeal like a pig at our hospitality."[50]

Perhaps the most iconic *Deliverance* citation is Damon Wayans and David Alan Grier's exchange from a 1992 "Men on Film" segment of *In Living Color* in which the delightfully flamboyant Blaine Edwards and Antoine Merriweather review films on videocassette "from a male point of view":

> BLAINE: My favorite love story video is *Deliverance*. Now this—this is a film about love and camping, but the movie really doesn't start off until they meet up with them little dirty hillbillies, who teach these mens about how to rough it in the great outdoors.
> ANTOINE: Mmph. Just make me wanna squeal like a pig. Soooieeeee![51]

I could probably go on indefinitely citing humorous references to *Deliverance* in popular culture. The film has remained a source of anxiety for decades. Even the animated movie *Shrek Forever After* (2010), a film presented in 3D and marketed primarily to families with young children, contains a sequence where the King and Queen walk into a scary forest while "Dueling Banjos" can be heard in the background. The filmmakers of *Shrek Forever After*, in other words, amuse the audience with the possibility of their characters becoming victims of rape.

Popular culture has a fascinated and ambivalent relationship with *Deliverance*, and the film's most memorable components—"squeal like a pig," "purty mouth," and "Dueling Banjos"—have become punchlines on television, but the causes of this laughter are very complicated, and they differ according to the subject doing the laughing. Where, after all, does the laughter that is apparently aimed at *Deliverance*'s rape victim originate? Freud suggests that the production of the comic is deeply linked to the unconscious. If the vulnerability of the violate man is what produces this laughter, Freud suggests that we laugh "even if we have to confess that *we* should have had to do the same in that situation." But Freud offers that:

> We only find someone's being put in a position of inferiority comic where there is *empathy*—that is, where someone else is concerned: if we ourselves were in similar straits we should be conscious only of distressing feelings. It is probably only by keeping such feelings away from ourselves that we are able to enjoy pleasure from the difference arising out of a comparison between these changing cathexes.[52]

Here Freud notes that as we laugh, we feel profoundly our own vulnerability ("inferiority") first and then laugh because we are not obligated to feel the distress that should accompany those feelings. Put another way, when I laugh, *I experience myself as though I am the person at whom I laugh*, but I am able to laugh because I have not materially experienced the distress suffered by the object of my laughter.

Alternatively, however, we might see laughter directed at Bobby's squeals in *Deliverance* as simply about mocking Bobby for his own weaknesses (which are, we should remember, purely fictional). Freud understands this as "comic unmasking," which he argues is "the method of degrading the dignity of individuals by directing attention to the frailties that they share with all humanity, but in particular the dependence of their mental functions on bodily needs."[53] In other words—and here Freud again focuses on the identification of the person laughing with the object of his laughter—we are permitted to laugh at Bobby *because he is like us*, because he has been proven to possess frailties that we, too, possess.

I have suggested, following Kaja Silverman, that the rape sequences in these films—and especially the one in *Deliverance*—disrupt "the dominant fiction" of masculine wholeness, impenetrability, and able-bodiedness. Laughter is a technique for what Freud would call *binding* that event, of bringing a series of unwieldy or intense feelings under control. This involves not only a transformation of something over which the man feels he has no control into something over which the man has power, "but also the gradual reaffirmation and reconstitution of the dominant fiction": in other words, the widespread fantasy that men actually *do* possess the phallus, that they *are* inviolable, inviolate, able-bodied, whole, and can rightfully, therefore, claim to be powerful.[54]

The quantity of laughter at the events in *Deliverance* directs our attention toward an enormous cultural concern that persists in relation to this film and, indeed, toward the fragility of traditional masculinity, despite its apparent hegemonic power. Both disavowed and claimed, metaphorized and literalized, the rape of Bobby is something from which US American masculinity has been unable to look away and with which it has been forced to cope. The constant reiteration of the "joke" of *Deliverance* in popular culture—whether in the form of "squeal like a pig," "you've got a purty mouth," or "Dueling Banjos"—betrays a persistent masculinist need to deal with what none of us can forget happened to Bobby on the banks of the Cahulawassee River, to contain this spectacularization of male vulnerability and integrate it back into a fantasy of able-bodied masculine identity, to bind it through laughter. That this single cinematic representation of an act of male/male rape has maintained its power to threaten hegemonic masculinity by exposing it as a fiction for fifty years attests not only to the filmmakers' abilities to visualize this violence on-screen but also to the vulnerability of dominant masculinity as such.

CHAPTER 4

Revenge Tarantino-Style

Male/Male Rape in 1990s Cinema

> It is precisely *because* rape is the most quintessentially feminine of experiences—the limit case of powerlessness and degradation—that it is such a powerful motivation, such a clean ticket, for revenge.
>
> —CAROL J. CLOVER, *Men, Women, and Chain Saws*

The most significant and impactful male/male rape sequence on film in the 1990s was the violation of the gangster Marsellus Wallace by the security guard Zed in the basement of the Mason-Dixon Pawn Shop in Quentin Tarantino's *Pulp Fiction*. This sequence, which is a small segment of *Pulp Fiction*'s interconnected but temporally disjointed narrative, has also been the most influential male/male rape sequence to be seen on a screen in the last thirty years. Two decades after the debates about movie violence in the New Hollywood period—when critics and audiences discussed the work of Arthur Penn and Sam Peckinpah—Tarantino's *Reservoir Dogs* (1992) heralded another extraordinary shift in the history of screen violence. Discussions of what has been called a new brutality or hyperrealism in movie violence proliferated during the 1990s, and many of these debates centered on the early films written or directed by Quentin Tarantino: *Reservoir Dogs*, *True Romance* (1993), *Natural Born Killers* (1994), and *Pulp Fiction*. At the same time as the arrival of this new approach to film violence, the 1990s also saw a proliferation of male/male rapes at the movies. The rise in "ultraviolent" cinema and an increase in on-screen representations of male/male rape were, in other words, simultaneous. I will make some arguments about the connections between the two later in this chapter, but for now I will simply say that male/male rape in popular US American cinema in the 1990s constituted one part of a larger trend whereby, as Manohla Dargis puts it, "the Reagan hardbody once idealised by Schwarzenegger and Stallone is transformed into something vulnerable, soft, as if masculinity itself were being battered into new shapes."[1] A new masculinity was on the rise in the 1990s, a maleness represented as vulnerable to sexual violation.

The films in the 1990s that feature male/male rape differ widely by genre: *Pulp Fiction* is a darkly comic gangster flick, *The Shawshank Redemption* (1994) is a Capra-esque morality tale, *American Me* (1992) is a biographical Chicano crime film, *The Prince of Tides* (1991) is a romantic drama, *Sleepers* (1996) is a rape-revenge film that doubles as a courtroom drama, and *American History X* (1999) is an uneven amalgam of public service announcement and racist tirade. But their approaches to their rape narratives also have much in common, and together these six films—the "children of *Deliverance*," as Joe Wlodarz has called them—form a discourse that shaped a late twentieth-century way of thinking about male/male rape, who commits it, where it happens, whom it victimizes, what its long-term effects are, and how best a man ought to respond to rape or the threat of rape.[2] As in the films of the 1970s I discussed in Chapter 3, in each of these films from the 1990s, the rapist is a white, frequently Southern, man; just as frequently the rapist is characterized as a homosexual figure, motivated by (perverse) gay desire. Most importantly, though, this chapter argues that the male/male rape films from the 1990s—unlike those of the 1970s—are revenge films, anxiously focusing on retribution for the violence committed and asking the audience to take pleasure in the destruction of the rapist. Some are, of course, more complex than others, but these US American films from the 1990s establish a pattern in which violent revenge is articulated as the only viable response to rape.

This chapter devotes a specific section to each of these six films but pays especial attention to *Fiction* and *Shawshank*. It is clear, more than twenty years later, that Tarantino's work has been much more influential among filmmakers and much more popular among audiences than films like *Sleepers* or *American History X*, and although Frank Darabont's style has acquired fewer devotees among filmmakers, his film *The Shawshank Redemption* has become an enormous audience favorite. Both were released in 1994, and both were nominated for Best Picture at the 1995 Academy Awards (they lost to Robert Zemeckis's *Forrest Gump*).[3] Both *Fiction* and *Shawshank* also gained their enormous popularity on home video over a long period of time. *Shawshank*, in particular, had trouble connecting with audiences in theaters, but "since then year-by-year, the critical stock of the film has steadily risen to current top ten status in public polls of all-time favourites."[4] This fact is, perhaps, less surprising when one considers that neither of these films relates in any specific way to its own time period or even location. In both *Fiction* and *Shawshank*, as in the postmodern films Fredric Jameson describes in his critique of the cultural logic of late capitalism,

> the setting has been strategically framed, with great ingenuity, to eschew most of the signals that normally convey the contemporaneity of the United States in its multinational era: the small-town setting allows the camera to elude the high-rise landscape of the 1970s and 1980s . . . , while the object world of the present day—artifacts and appliances, whose styling would at once serve to date the image—is elaborately edited out. Everything in the film, therefore, conspires to blur its official contemporaneity and make it possible for the viewer to receive the narrative as though it were set in some eternal thirties, beyond real historical time.[5]

Consider briefly the vintage toaster in Butch's apartment, Jules's Jheri curl, the cartoons on the television, or the entire setting of Jackrabbit Slim's in *Pulp Fiction*. The film might take place in the past just as much as the present. *Shawshank*, even more urgently, asks to be evaluated apart from the society into which it was released. Operating in the improbable space of a post-race American prison in the 1940s, '50s, and '60s, it relates to the society of the 1990s in almost no way at all. I will discuss this in more depth with each film, but both *Pulp Fiction* and *Shawshank*, in fact, succeed through the use of an intertextuality that refers not to the societies in which their audiences watch them, but to images and ideas from other movies.

This chapter is intended as a supplement to the important readings of these films we already have. In his excellent essay on *Sleepers*, for example, Joe Wlodarz has described the way Barry Levinson's film carefully distances itself from homoeroticism by locating its violence in the homosexual male body, and in *The Bronze Screen* Rosa-Linda Fregoso rightly critiques the way *American Me* places blame on the Chicano family unit rather than on institutional structures that cause gang violence. Because my focus, however, will be on the rape sequences in these films and the ways that each film describes the consequences of these rapes, my analysis will differ considerably. This is a move away from the meaning of these movies, toward the various ways they ask us to encounter *affectively* the specific scenes of sexual violence they portray.

In the previous chapter, I noted that although *Deliverance* aimed for deeper meanings about "man" and "nature," audience reactions were primarily visceral: they responded to *Deliverance* as though it were a horror film, one of the "body genres," like pornography, that Carol Clover, and Linda Williams after her, have argued aim to have a direct, physical effect on the bodies of viewers.[6] The fact that we respond affectively to what we watch does not mean, of course, that films aren't understood intellectually as well as emotionally, but here I am interested in thinking through the emotions that the male/male rapes in 1990s cinema attempt to elicit from their audiences.[7] Throughout this chapter, I focus on the way filmmakers capture the face of the violate man. I noted this tendency in the 1970s films in Chapter 3, as well, but we will see the New Hollywood focus on faces filled with terror and anguish replaced, in the 1990s, with the faces of violate men experiencing shame.

My arguments in this chapter concern the way that the pleasure of violent revenge is designed to organize and cope with the shame that accompanies the experience of watching a male/male rape on screen. In other words, if viewers have had trouble coping with *Deliverance*'s threat to masculinity, filmmakers in the 1990s actively attempt to deal with that threat—and they do so in surprisingly similar ways. These films do not shy away from the victim's experience of shame; they rather ask us to *share* in the victim's experience of shame, and then they propose violent solutions for dealing with that shame. Before we move to the films this chapter describes, then, I want to offer some theoretical tools for understanding how shame works, and how audiences are asked to share in the shame experienced by the characters on the screen.

Shame and Silence

"Few words," Sedgwick argues in *Touching Feeling*, "could be more performative in the Austinian sense than 'shame': 'Shame on you,' 'For shame,' or just 'Shame!', the locutions that give sense to the word, do not describe or refer to shame but themselves confer it."[8] To refer to something as shameful or to say that someone ought to be ashamed, does not, in other words, simply designate an object or person as shameful, it also makes that shame appear. The phrase "shame on you" actually possesses the power to attach shame to the object or person. Sedgwick, additionally, articulates not only the simple power of this word but also the infectious quality of shame itself. As an emotional response to actions or performatives, shame lingers. It is as easily conferred as language, "flood[ing] into being as a moment, a disruptive moment, in a circuit of identity-constituting identificatory communication."[9] Shame for Sedgwick "is the place where the *question* of identity arises most originarily and most relationally."[10] This feeling is related fundamentally to how we understand our very selves.

Sedgwick's work on shame is indebted chiefly to the mid-twentieth-century psychologist Silvan Tomkins, whose theories about the affects—there are nine in Tomkins' work—describe them in great detail and include the physical movements and facial expressions that attend each.[11] *Affect* in Tomkins's work refers to a physical response in the body that actually constitutes the feeling (a word that describes a corporeal sensation as well as an emotional one). As Tomkins describes it, "the shame response is an act which reduces facial communication. . . . By dropping his eyes, his eyelids, his head, and sometimes the whole upper part of his body, the individual calls a halt to looking at the other person, particularly the other person's face, and to the other person's looking at him, particularly his face."[12] Shame is a hiding of the self—a reduction but not a complete refusal of communication—and this reduction is accomplished by covering the face, covering the genitals, hiding the eyes. For Tomkins, "In contrast to all other affects, shame is an experience of the self by the self. At that moment when the self feels ashamed, it is felt as a sickness within the self. Shame is the most reflexive of affects in that the phenomenological distinction between the subject and object of shame is lost."[13] It is, in other words, a profoundly individualizing gesture in which one feels one's self intensely while simultaneously feeling disgust toward oneself.

Sedgwick, however, proposes that at the same time shame interrupts identification, it also "makes identity. In fact, shame and identity remain in very dynamic relation to one another, at once deconstituting and foundational, because shame is both peculiarly contagious and peculiarly individuating."[14] In other words, because shame is contagious, we connect with shame in other people—we form identity with them—but when we feel shame, we experience ourselves as alone. As Douglas Crimp puts it, "in the act of taking on the shame that is properly someone else's, I simultaneously feel my utter separateness from even that person whose shame it initially was. I feel alone with my shame, singular in my susceptibility to being shamed for this stigma that has now become mine and mine alone."[15] This contagious but simultaneously individualizing quality of shame is particularly relevant for thinking about how film audiences respond affectively to representations of violation such as rape. In these accounts of how shame works, because shame is bound up fundamentally with *who one is*, shame works always to refer back to a kind of originary moment when shame flooded the body. The experience of shame, as Sedgwick describes it, is a kind of revisiting of a consciously forgotten but unconsciously remembered scene of ur-shame.

In a discussion of James Weldon Johnson's *Autobiography of an Ex-Colored Man* (1912), for example, Darieck Scott describes a moment when the narrator witnesses a lynching for the first time and is flooded with the experience of himself as a Black man, violable and fragile. Scott describes this as simultaneously an affective experience of identity and an understanding of vulnerability; in Scott's reading, the narrator experiences this recognition affectively as shame: "the shame of this intimate, bodily knowledge of suffering, the shame of not being able effectively to separate this suffering from himself, not being able to project it out onto something that is the not-self: the shame of having to harbor in his body the abject, the unassimilable." Although the white witnesses of the lynching are able to perceive themselves as different from the murdered man, the narrator "does not have available to him the psychic mechanisms of the white spectators" and identifies with the violate man and his violability.[16]

The *Encyclopedia of Rape* notes that the stigma surrounding rape remains "a pervasive and persistent phenomenon whose peculiarity becomes evident when one realizes the difference between the attitude toward rape survivors and that reserved for victims of nonsexual assaults."[17] As I argued in the introduction, the anus often functions, for both men and women, as a physical symbol of bodily integrity, as a "guarantor of privacy," and as a site of shame.[18] An act of violence committed on this area of the body, considered private in the extreme, cannot help but induce a shame–humiliation response in a victim. Shame, therefore, is nearly impossible to separate from any incidence of male/male rape, including images of its representation. The ability to produce a shame–humiliation response in a victim through an act of rape makes that act of violence akin to the locutionary performatives Sedgwick describes in *Touching Feeling*. Put another way, an act of rape confers and is intended to confer shame on the body of another through a method uncannily similar to the linguistic performative "shame on you."

Shaming the body of the victim—as the white witness-participants of the lynching do in Johnson's novel—is one of the intended effects of an act of rape (whether or not the victim themself feels ashamed).[19]

Despite increased media attention directed toward acts of rape and the presence of rape in US American society, anti-rape activist Michael Scarce reports that for many male victims of rape "the involvement of body parts that our culture deems to be 'sexual' or 'private' . . . hamper[s] survivors' ability to speak openly about their experience."[20] The *Encyclopedia* notes that "due to the stigma attached to being a male rape victim . . . , many men do not report rape or tell anyone about their experience. . . . Lack of reporting and community awareness creates a lack of visibility of male rape and reinforces the isolation and silence of all victims."[21] Silence, as has been argued by Elaine Scarry, is essential to pain itself; the destruction of language and the enforcement of silence are an integral part of what the creation of pain works to do. For Scarry, silence is the direct result of power that creates pain, and "the difficulty of articulating physical pain permits political and perceptual complications of the most serious kind. The failure to express pain . . . will always work to allow its appropriation and conflation with debased forms of power."[22] If pain works actively to destroy language, the silences surrounding rape are often also the direct result of the shame intended by the act of sexual violence: head down, eyes averted.

It is the project of this book to think ethically about male/male rape discourse, and part of that project is to document the ability that representations of male/male rape have to confer shame onto bodies. As we continue, it is important for us to consider images of shame *as both constative and performative*: these images not only represent shame, they also assign it. It is essential that we question portrayals of rape, interrogating their ability to encourage and enforce the very silences they appear to break. It is crucial, too, that we articulate the ways in which our culture encourages and enforces silences related to the violated body and the body in pain. With relative frequency, cultural productions that represent male/male rape ostensibly give voice to the experiences associated with rape, while at the same time they articulate violence, silence, and disavowal as the appropriate responses to those experiences. In each of these representations, shame and silence are the natural responses to having been violated. Because of the contagious nature of shame, these 1990s films have the ability to *produce* shame in their audiences by encouraging and enforcing silence about rape.

Marsellus Wallace

It would be difficult to over-emphasize the importance of *Pulp Fiction* to the new wave of violent cinema in the 1990s. In addition to the film's numerous nominations at the 1995 Academy Awards, the film was awarded the Palme d'Or at the 1994 Cannes Film Festival, and it was also named Best Picture by the National Society of Film Critics, the National Board of Review (tying with *Forrest Gump*), and the Los Angeles Film Critics Association. The film was both a critical and popular success. *Fiction*'s rape sequence occurs near the end of the film's second act, and it is memorable not only for its surprising brutality but also because the sequence begins with a stunning peripety.[23] In rapid sequence, Butch (Bruce Willis), one of the film's protagonists, kills Vincent (John Travolta), the film's other protagonist, and then is suddenly confronted by Marsellus Wallace (Ving Rhames), the powerful mobster whom he has double-crossed. Everyone in the film describes Marsellus as both volatile and dangerous—he has had a character thrown from a building for allegedly giving his wife a foot massage, and we know that he has ordered numerous hits, including one on Butch.[24] Although everyone in the film thus far has been associated with Marsellus, Tarantino's camera hasn't allowed a clear view of him up until this point two-thirds of the way through the film, and so Butch's confrontation with the "big man" as the script calls him, is also the audience's first real introduction to him.[25] The rape sequence in *Pulp Fiction*, then, is set off by narrative devices that lend gravity toward what follows: we have been waiting to meet Marsellus for the entire film, and now when we meet him he is sexually violated in the back room of a North Hollywood pawn shop.

The first notable thing about this rape-revenge sequence is that it is interracial; further, not only does Tarantino script a scenario in which two white men rape a Black man, he also explicitly racializes Marsellus's rapists (their names are Zed and Maynard) as "hillbillies." He marks them as Southern and racist through the image of the Confederate flag—a large one hangs behind the counter in the Mason-Dixon Pawn Shop—and by having Marsellus refer to Zed specifically as "hillbilly boy."[26] Indeed, the rape sequence is staged with overt nods to Boorman's *Deliverance*, a reference that no one at all seems to have missed.[27] The shot of Maynard (Duane Whitaker) watching Zed (Peter Greene) commit the rape, in particular, recalls *Deliverance*'s shot of the Toothless Man watching his companion (Figure 4.1). For most critics, the citation of *Deliverance* reminds audience members that what they're watching is not real. It's just movie

FIGURE 4.1: *Pulp Fiction* (1994), Maynard recalls *Deliverance*

violence.[28] But audience members did not respond in the same way as critics who decoded the reference; Joseph Natoli describes Zed and Maynard as "our worst nightmares. In point of fact, they are our cultural nightmares, whether they are stalking you in real life or on the net, their sexuality is wrapped in incomprehensible, alien, distorted desires."[29] For Jim Smith, the sequence "twists into a kind of Tobe Hooper pastiche exploitation horror with hillbilly rapist murderers, and abasement in dungeon basements."[30] This is intended, then, not only as a citation of Boorman's film but also as a way of achieving visceral sensations similar to those an audience might experience while watching *Deliverance*—a film Tarantino apparently saw when he was only nine years old.[31]

Unlike *Deliverance*, however, *Pulp Fiction* explicitly homosexualizes its rapists by framing their violence as motivated by sexual desire for their victims *as well* as sadism. Zed and Maynard gag Marsellus and Butch using bright red ball gags associated with BDSM practices, and the two apparently keep as a pet a grown man on a leash whom they call The Gimp (Stephen Hibbert). The script explicitly describes The Gimp as "dressed from head to toe in black leather bondage gear"; he speaks no lines, and his only real function in the film is to help us better understand the rapists.[32] I do not wish to make an argument that Zed and Maynard are either secretly or "really" gay men, but visually the ball gags and the leather gear link the two with gay male sex practices, and this homosexualization of the rapists seems to have connected with most viewers of the film. Both Allan Campbell and Marsha Kinder refer to the scene's homoerotic aspects, and bell hooks calls the scene "overtly gay-bashing."[33] *Pulp Fiction*, then, manages to describe the violence of rape as both a kind of deviant sexual practice preferred by

Southern hillbillies *and* linked in spirit to kink and fetish communities that practice consensual sado-masochistic sex.

In Devon Jackson's reading of the racial dynamics of this sequence in *The Village Voice*, "Willis going back in to save Rhames has nothing to do with loyalty and everything to do with the bond among heterosexual men that says: male viewers, fret not, for I shall send Butch back into the bowels of that faggot hellhole for a most necessary, most logical *Death Wish/ Deliverance*-style retribution."[34] For Jackson, this sequence is about Tarantino linking white masculinity with Black masculinity and asking a kind of inherent Black coolness to rub off on those white men who can "speak the lingo"—like Butch and Vincent and Tarantino himself. Jackson sees *Pulp Fiction*'s constant deployment of the N-word as indicative of the film's surface-level engagement with issues of race in the US during the 1990s. As I noted earlier, both *Pulp Fiction* and *Shawshank* actively avoid reference to the world outside of their films, confining their references to popular culture and film history.

As a Black, male victim of rape, Marsellus is a first in 1990s cinema, where male/male rape victims are almost exclusively young and white. And since the rapists' motivation is apparently homosexual desire, Marsellus is eroticized as well. Zed, as he chooses which of the men to rape, counts off "eenie, meany, miney, moe," substituting for the more traditional word *tiger* the racist slur so common in Tarantino's films. Zed is clear, in other words, about which of the two men has piqued his interest, and the rape is overtly both sexualized and racialized.[35] Zed and Maynard's violation of Marsellus reproduces precisely the situation of Black men murdered and sexually violated by white men under Jim Crow. This racist violence is also a sexualized violence that Tommy Curry, using a Fanonian analysis, has referred to as "the lust—the libidinal desire—for the Black man's body that serves as the motivation behind his condemnation and death."[36] Curry argues that one of the central components of US American racist ideology "erases the sexual vulnerability that Black males historically have endured at the hands of white men and women" and that our culture refuses to see Black men as possible victims of sexual violence.[37] But although *Pulp Fiction* might seem to articulate Black vulnerability to white violence, the film instead portrays the Black man's sexual violation only to refuse again his vulnerability.

Curry's work—and the work of Carlyle Van Thompson, Vincent Woodard, and Sharon Holland—help us to see that "the killing of Black males has always involved an erotic obsession with their Black flesh."[38]

Indeed, I argued in Chapter 2 that this is precisely how James Baldwin frames anti-Black violence in *If Beale Street Could Talk*. But rather than describing white libidinal investments in Black death and dismemberment, representing this violence as motivated both by white-supremacist and homoerotic fantasies, *Pulp Fiction*'s portrayal of male/male rape *enacts* those fantasies for its audience, while simultaneously blaming them on *other* racialized, homosexualized subjects. *Pulp Fiction* does nothing to draw attention to the way racism eroticizes Black men's bodies and then uses those erotics to justify their murder. To the contrary, the film actively isolates the racist erotics that animate everyday white-supremacist violence in the United States, such as police brutality and mass incarceration, by ascribing those drives to the two homosexualized hillbillies whom Butch and Marsellus kill. If we consider the film's own libidinal investments, we find that *Pulp Fiction* views Marsellus as a kind of apex of masculinity; he's the "big man" in Tarantino's script. Other characters repeatedly describe him as unreasonably violent, and a terror of Marsellus motivates many of the characters' actions. The scene in the pawn shop basement unreflexively uses the traditional ideological links between feminization and rape, disability and rape, and deviance and rape precisely to attack Marsellus's reputation as a man. *Pulp Fiction*, in this way, fulfills a fantasy of taking the big man's masculinity down a peg and doing so in a way that disavows the racist and erotic pleasure in watching the Black man's violation that it provides. This fantasy is further fulfilled when the "butch" white man returns to kill the rapists and save the Black man's life.

Instead of escaping from the shop, Butch interrupts Zed in the act of sexually violating Marsellus by killing Maynard with a katana. As Butch enters the scene, the camera looks into Marsellus's face. He is wincing in pain and there are tears in his eyes (Figure 4.2); the film's sound information also emphasizes Marsellus's anguish. After Butch kills Maynard, he holds Zed at sword-point, threatening him. Behind Butch, Marsellus picks himself up, grabs an enormous pump-action shotgun, and orders Butch to "step aside," at which point he shoots his rapist in the genitals.[39] Zed goes down screaming, but he is still alive. "You okay?" Butch asks Marsellus. "Naw man. I'm pretty fuckin' far from okay," comes the reply. The remainder of the scene is shot with Marsellus in the foreground.[40] He looks slightly down and to the left of the camera, never taking his eye off his rapist, who is out of the frame (Figure 4.3). Butch is in the background of the shot behind Marsellus's right shoulder. Both men's chests are turned toward the camera, but although Butch looks at Marsellus throughout this

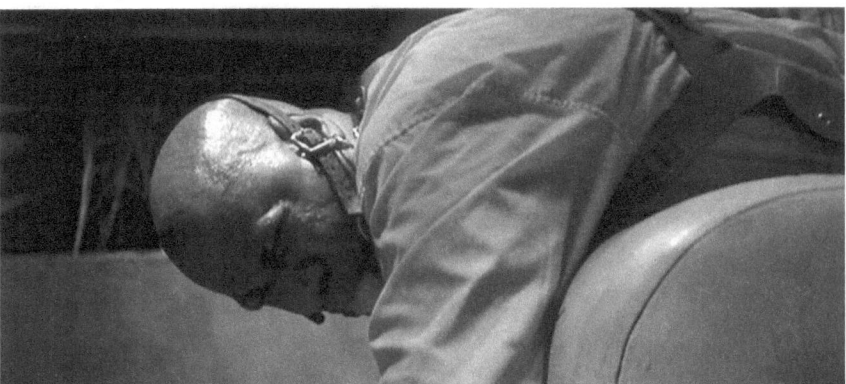

FIGURE 4.2: *Pulp Fiction* (1994), Marsellus Wallace

conversation, Marsellus never looks at Butch. He speaks to Butch without even once allowing him to see his face or eyes. This turning away, which gives *Pulp Fiction*'s audience access to Marsellus's face while preventing Butch from having the same contact, is a complex staging of the physical shame–humiliation response described by Silvan Tomkins: eyes down, head down. In this iteration of the response, the character conceals his face from the other character in the movie, but the filmmaker does not hide that same face from the audience.

In answer to the question "What now?" Marsellus describes what he's going to do to revenge himself on his rapist—it involves a blowtorch and a pair of pliers—but that isn't what Butch is asking; he wants to know if rescuing Marsellus has squared things between them. Marsellus agrees, but he has a condition: "Don't tell nobody about this," he orders Butch. "This shit is between me, you, and Mister soon-to-be-livin'-the-rest-of-his-short-ass-life-in-agonizing-pain Rapist here. It ain't nobody else's business."[41] Marsellus also tells Butch that he is to leave town immediately. Butch agrees and goes; Marsellus raises his hand as a goodbye but never turns to look at him (Figure 4.4).

Marsellus and Butch's lack of facial communication might seem like a logical way to end the scene, but notably this is not how the scene ends in the shooting script. On paper, after the two men make their final agreement, Tarantino writes that "The two men shake hands, then hug one another," then Marsellus says "Go on now, get your ass outta here."[42] In a film in which traditional masculinity is so important, it is fairly easy to see why the handshake and hug were eventually jettisoned, but I describe their absence from the finished film in order to note that Marsellus's refusal to

FIGURE 4.3-4: *Pulp Fiction* (1994), Marsellus avoids Butch's face

FIGURE 4.4

show his face to Butch is a conscious choice made by the filmmakers; it was certainly not the only possible way to end such a sequence.

As it stands, the scene's ending works on an emotionally vulnerable register while also reinvesting Marsellus with the power his unseen image wielded for the first two-thirds of the picture. Marsellus's shame at having been raped is evident both to Butch and to the audience watching the movie, but Marsellus channels this feeling into action: "I'm gonna git medieval on your ass," he tells his rapist, and "the big man" becomes terrifying once again. This mobster's power, however, is also now dependent, at least partially, on Butch's silence about what Zed and Maynard did. Marsellus hides his shame by hiding his face, and he also hides his shame by keeping silent—and insisting on Butch's silence—about the violence that has occurred in the pawn shop.

In many ways, *Pulp Fiction* is a film about violence and the material vulnerability of human bodies to drugs and weapons, especially firearms. Immediately prior to the scene in the Mason-Dixon, for example, Marsellus shoots a bystander in the hip. And in the sequence preceding that one, Butch shoots and kills Vincent using a machine gun. *Pulp Fiction* articulates violent revenge as the appropriate response to *every* slight, real or imagined, that a person might suffer, but the male/male rape sequence is given a place of special gravity in the narrative, and Marsellus's response to being violated is one of the film's definitive moments.[43] In effect, *Pulp Fiction* momentarily represents the Black male body as vulnerable to sexual violence only to reassert the ideological necessity of maintaining its imagined invulnerability. Marsellus is "pretty fucking far from okay," but he picks himself up off the ground immediately and moves into action, castrating Zed with the shotgun and instantly beginning to plan tortures for his rapist. *Pulp Fiction* puts Marsellus's shame on display, but the film also articulates this affective response as something that can and should be overcome through violent masculinity. Marsellus overmasters his feelings, and he mobilizes his shame into both an injunction of silence and an act of revenge.

Andy Dufresne

In *The Shawshank Redemption*, Frank Darabont's adaptation of a Stephen King novella, the main character Andy Dufresne (Tim Robbins) is raped repeatedly by a group of men known as the Sisters. We are told in voice-over that these assaults happened for the first two years of Andy's incarceration, but the rape storyline in *Shawshank* occurs so early in the movie that the entirety of the film's short plot about rape is over before the film's second act. Unlike *Pulp Fiction*, in which the male/male rape is a shocking twist and a kind of interruption of the slickness of the movie, *Shawshank* is a prison film, and it deals with the issue of male/male rape almost at once. In Darabont's film rape is no surprise or shock; it is a fact of prison life.

In his book on *Shawshank*, Mark Kermode offers that "The rapidity and forthrightness with which the theme of sexual abuse is established and explored is particularly unusual for a film which has developed such a reputation for mainstream palatability."[44] He finds it "remarkable ... that *The Shawshank Redemption*, which is not widely remembered for its frank sexual forthrightness, should handle such potentially controversial material in such a remarkably matter-of-fact manner."[45] As I argued in Chapter 1, however, after the 1960s, portrayals of male/male rape worked to authenticate prison narratives. By the time *Shawshank* was released in theaters in 1994, film references to prison as a location rife with male/male sexual violence had become common. In movies including *Murphy's Law* (1986), *The Principal* (1987), *Kinjite: Forbidden Subjects* (1989), *Hard to Kill* (1990), *King of New York* (1990), *Reservoir Dogs* (1992), and *True Romance* (1993), all of which predate *Shawshank*, prison is figured as a place where men get raped. Many of these films from the late '80s and early '90s are crime capers, with action stars such as Charles Bronson or Steven Seagal, but even romantic comedies like *Death Becomes Her* (1992) contain references—often jokes—to prison as a place where men get raped.[46] By 1994 any filmmaker would have found it difficult *not* to refer to male/male rape as a standard component of carceral life. It is neither extraordinary nor even unusual that *Shawshank* should represent sexual violence. The matter-of-factness that Kermode sees in the film is, in fact, a cliché—Kevin Kelly said as much about *Scarecrow* in 1973. We know, from years of big-budget Hollywood movies telling us so, that what happens to clean-shaven white men in prison is that they are subjected to sexual violation. Rather than challenging audience expectations of prison or the prison film, the rape sequences in *Shawshank*, which all take place off-screen, confirm for us what we already think we know.

The rape plot in *Shawshank* comprises approximately six or seven very short scenes. On Andy's first night in Shawshank Penitentiary, he and the other new prisoners are tormented by some of the older prisoners with threats of rape. In particular, Heywood (William Sadler), a character we will come to love, taunts a new prisoner nicknamed Fat Ass (Frank Medrano) by saying "I know some big ol' bull queers who'd *love* to make your acquaintance . . . especially that big white mushy butt of yours."[47] Fat Ass responds to this by breaking down; he is so distraught that he cannot seem to respond to the demands made by Captain Hadley (Clancy Brown), the most violent of Shawshank's prison guards. Hadley beats Fat Ass to death in this early scene.

On what appears to be the next day, a man named Bogs (Mark Ralston) addresses Andy in the shower: "Anybody come at you yet? Anybody get to you yet? Hey, we all need friends in here . . . I could be a friend to you." Andy walks away without saying anything, and the camera illogically remains with Bogs in the shower as he says to himself, "Hard to get. I like that" (Figure 4.5).[48] In the next daytime scene, Red (Morgan Freeman) refers to Bogs and his gang as "The Sisters," explaining to Andy that they've "taken quite a liking to you. Especially Bogs."[49] Later, three men trap Andy

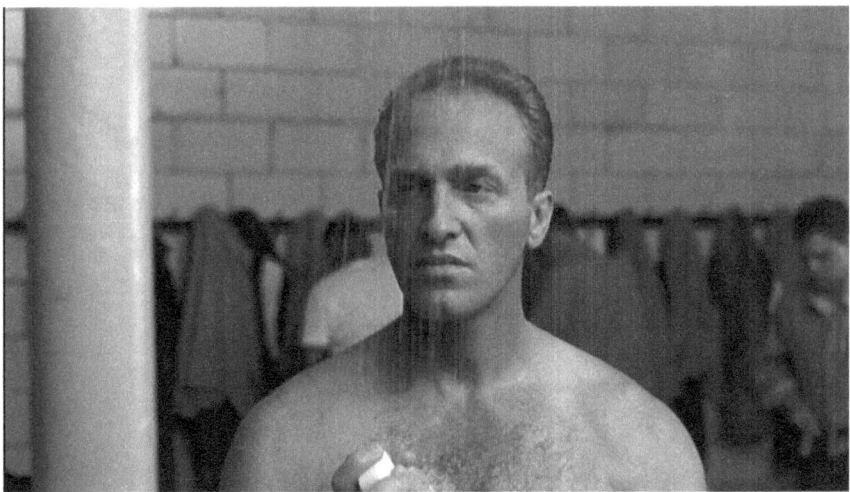

FIGURE 4.5: *The Shawshank Redemption* (1994), "Hard to get. I like that."

alone in a storage room; they rape him while Andy struggles, punching and kicking the men until they restrain him. As Mark Browning remarks, these acts of violence "mostly occur off-camera and are suggested by sound effects rather than direct visuals."[50] Using techniques from classic Hollywood, *Shawshank* never shows any of the sexual violence it describes. The sequences, however, are, as Kermode says, "explicit enough to leave the viewer in little doubt as to the nature of the attack, a brutal truth driven home by Freeman's voice-over, which intones, 'I wish I could tell you that Andy fought the good fight, and The Sisters let him be, but prison is no fairy-tale world.'"[51] We know that Andy is being assaulted repeatedly over a period of two years, and we see him physically defend himself against the Sisters in three different and very brief scenes but, unlike *Pulp Fiction* or the three films in Chapter 3, Darabont's film focuses neither on the act of rape nor the victim's emotional responses. In many ways, although the rape plot of this film takes up a significant amount of time, *Shawshank* consistently apostrophizes rape by moving it always outside of the camera's gaze. As in *Midnight Cowboy*, rape in *Shawshank* is metonymically displaced, and the audience is not confronted with any images of sexual violence. Darabont substitutes rape with standard images of violence conventionally seen in any movie—punching and kicking (Figure 4.6).

Prison, indeed, is not a fairy-tale world, but *The Shawshank Redemption* certainly is. This is a movie in which hundreds of prisoners stop everything

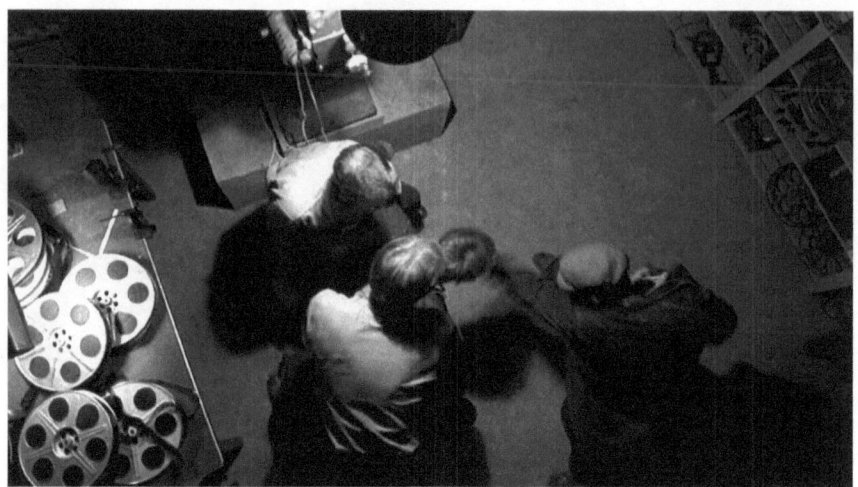

FIGURE 4.6: *The Shawshank Redemption* (1994), punching and kicking

and turn their eyes to the sky in rapt, united attention while they listen to a duet from *The Marriage of Figaro* in a language they don't understand. *Shawshank* even adds a pat Hollywood ending to King's novella. In Kermode's sardonic description of this sequence, "a beaming, shoeless Red strolls toward the white-clad form of Andy, earnestly sanding a boat. As the men's eyes meet their faces break into radiant smiles; and as they walk toward each other, the camera flies exultantly heavenward, all ambiguities resolved."[52] But it isn't simply the sentencious, Capra-esque treatment of its narrative that places this movie in the realm of the fairy tale; *Shawshank* doesn't so much as tell the story of a prison as it tells the story of a *movie* prison. Like *Pulp Fiction*, Darabont's film is filled with movie references. The posters on Andy's wall of Rita Hayworth, Marilyn Monroe, and Raquel Welch are obvious references to famous films, but Browning reminds us that the baby crow Brooks (James Whitmore) adopts is a citation of John Frankenheimer's *Birdman of Alcatraz* (1962), and Andy dumps plaster into the yard through his trouser legs exactly like the ingenious prisoners do in John Sturges's classic prison film *The Great Escape* (1963).[53] For Michelle Brown, "The truly amazing thing about such a production is not simply *Shawshank*'s intense level of self-reflexivity in its invocation of classical prison cinema, but the absence of any irony or commentary in such a reproduction. In this way, the 'real' that *Shawshank* imitates is not real at all but a celluloid fantasy—built upon the memories and conventions of past prison films."[54] The rape sequences in *Shawshank* work in a similar way.

Shawshank's rapist is, in fact, a very familiar figure. Darabont says that he cut a scene from his screenplay in which Bogs blows Andy a kiss because "it made Bogs out to be some sort of demented gay," and he further protests that "the film takes pains to draw a distinction between a homosexual and a prison rapist." In 1996, with apparent exasperation he said, "let me state it one last time for the record: Bogs as a character does not represent homosexuality; he represents the predatory sexual violence of rape."⁵⁵ To be sure, when Andy finds out about the Sisters, Darabont has Red tell us that these men are not homosexuals: "You have to be human first," he quips. "They don't qualify."⁵⁶ Darabont claims to understand these men as sadists, who only enjoy rape *as* rape and wouldn't enjoy a willing partner. According to Red, "Bull queers take by force, that's all they want or understand."⁵⁷ Perhaps this is true in King's novella, but in the film, Bogs is not so inscrutable. In his first scene he quite plainly attempts to seduce Andy ("I could be a friend to you") in a nonviolent way, and the camera stays with him after Andy leaves so that we can see his disappointment. If the film reminds us that Bogs is dangerous and violent, it also plainly feminizes him: "Honey, hush," he calmly tells Andy when he attacks, and his gang is pointedly gendered as "sisters." *Shawshank* presents Bogs as a discouraged homosexual seducer who becomes a rapist because of his frustration, not because he gets pleasure only from force.

In an even more familiar gesture, the film also associates Bogs with the "hillbilly" rapists of *Deliverance, Midnight Cowboy, Scarecrow,* and *Pulp Fiction*. Faced with being forced to fellate Bogs, Andy convinces his assailant, in their final scene together, that "serious brain injury causes the victim to bite down," and that sexually assaulting him might be very dangerous. "Where do you get this shit?" Bogs asks him. Andy replies, "I *read* it. Know how to *read* you ignorant fuck?" Bogs looks confused. "Honey," he says again, "you shouldn't," before he and the other Sisters start beating Andy.⁵⁸ Bogs is not overtly coded as Southern or Appalachian, but with this simple exchange, *Shawshank* taps into the now typical image of the male/male rapist as an ignorant hillbilly. The film's racialization of Bogs here is especially interesting because *Shawshank* is, for the most part, silent on the topic of race, and the prison is not racially segregated. Further, Darabont's film switches the racial identity of Red, the narrator of King's novella, and along with that switch comes another alteration. In the novella, the Irish Red tells us that he has also been raped by the Sisters, but in the film Red gives us no hint that he has been victimized by sexual violence.⁵⁹ There is only one rape victim in *The Shawshank Redemption*, and he is the typical victim of prison

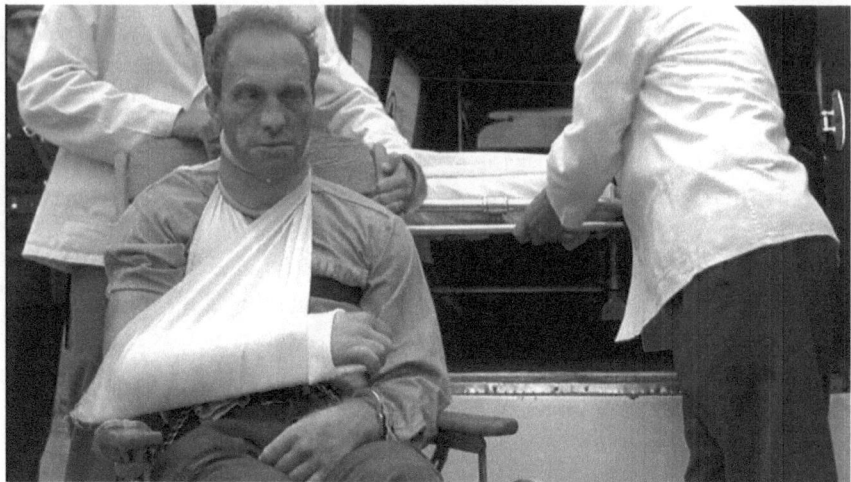

FIGURE 4.7: *The Shawshank Redemption* (1994), Bogs is disabled by violence

rape in film: a young, handsome, middle-class white man. Black men in *Shawshank*, as in the US American imaginary writ large, are unimaginable as the victims of prison sexual violence.

Revenge is meted out in a way that will become traditional, as well. Bogs is brutally beaten by the violent Captain Hadley, whom Andy has helped become $35,000 richer in a scene on Shawshank's rooftop.[60] Andy comes under the protection of the prison guards by providing financial services for them, and in this way the film settles its score with Bogs. Andy isn't present to take part in the pleasure of enacting this violent revenge, but the film presents it for the audience's enjoyment nonetheless. The camera lingers on Bogs getting beaten, and we watch him reach out of his cell for help before, as Darabont puts it, his body "vanishes abruptly from view like some hapless swimmer in *Jaws*."[61] The revenge is sweet, and in voice-over, as we watch a begauzed, immobilized Bogs get packed into an ambulance, Red tells us that the Sisters never touched Andy again and Bogs never walked again (Figure 4.7). With the breaking of Bogs's body, *Shawshank* dispenses with its rape plot.

For Tony Magistrale, *Shawshank*'s rapists "represent the masculine and patriarchal at its worst," but the film doesn't associate Bogs or the other Sisters at all with the patriarchy.[62] The Sisters' desires are deviant, and they possess a vicious homosexuality that the film links explicitly with a lack of education. When Bogs is beaten so that he will never walk again, he is not beaten by a group of prisoners rebelling against violent masculinity. On the contrary, he is beaten by those same representatives of the patriarchy who killed Fatso in the film's first few minutes. Further, Andy is protected by the prison guards precisely because he hails them across a class divide with the promise of making them richer. Andy Dufresne, a wealthy banker who from the start knows more about the workings of power in the outside world than the guards or his fellow prisoners do, garners the protection of the institution by offering the guards access to knowledge he possesses because of his position within the patriarchy.[63] In other words, *Shawshank* does not somehow take pleasure in the defeat of patriarchy and masculinity when Captain Hadley beats Bogs within an inch of his life. To the contrary, it is patriarchy and masculinity that do the beating, and *Shawshank* asks its audience to take pleasure in this violent revenge, to believe again in the compulsory heterosexuality and able-bodiedness that comprise a traditional fantasy of masculine wholeness.

I am emphasizing the *disabling* power of masculine revenge in *Shawshank* and *Pulp Fiction* because both films so clearly focus on the broken bodies of their white, homosexual rapists after their victims get revenge. If we look with particular care at the image of Bogs as the men in white coats wheel him into Shawshank's ambulance, we might also consider the way the image of the hospitalized white gay male body was more commonly circulating in US American culture in 1994. In newsmedia images, like Theresa Frare's famous photograph of David Kirby and his family in *Life* and in films such as *Longtime Companion* (1989) and *Philadelphia* (1993), the image of the disabled, hospitalized young man was, in the 1990s, more frequently asked to stand in for the contemporary HIV/AIDS crisis.[64] This is not to say that *The Shawshank Redemption* attempts to say something about HIV/AIDS; indeed, as I have already noted, the film takes place neither in the 1990s nor in the real world, and it seems actively to avoid comment on the society in which its audience lives. However, as disability theorists teach us to consider the way injury, illness, and debility are frequently used by cinema to represent contagion or threat, we can begin to see this final image of Bogs as an image that calls to mind not only the many people living with and dying from HIV/AIDS in the United States in the 1990s but also the other prisoners that *Shawshank*—and US American society as a whole—would prefer to forget.[65]

Consider, for example, Victoria Arellano, a twenty-three-year-old undocumented transgender woman, who died in an ICE-run detention facility in California in 2007 because she was refused the life-saving medication that was helping her stave off HIV-related infections. If Bogs is not an undocumented trans woman of color living with HIV whose medical care was fatally neglected by the state, in *Shawshank* he functions nevertheless as a trans figure, a Sister with homosexual desires, whose expulsion from the film's narrative is accomplished by agents of the state and works as a containment of the threat to the prison system and to the film's white, middle-class protagonist. As Michelle Velasquez-Potts argues in her essay about Victoria Arellano, "HIV/AIDS continues to be attached to trans/queer bodies and imagined as a threat to Western society. The trans/queer body with HIV/AIDS is used as a site of regulation and management, imbricating sexuality, gender, and race in ways that make legible who, as well as which acts, falls outside the lines of normative citizenry."[66] Bogs is *The Shawshank Redemption*'s serial rapist and major villain, but the threat he represents is not that of masculinity or patriarchy, it is one of perversion and contagion. He turns out to be the queer/trans body that threatens all of society with violence and infection, and his destruction in the film's first act banishes our fears of that perversion and contagion beyond the prison walls along with the forgotten lives of trans prisoners of color whose stories the film seems—only on the surface—to ignore.

Tom Wingo, Lorenzo Carcaterra, Montoya Santana

Shawshank and *Pulp Fiction* cemented a tradition in US American movies in which violent, murderous revenge becomes the customary way to deal with a (usually Southern, usually homosexual) man who rapes another man. In *The Prince of Tides*, *American Me*, and *Sleepers*, however, the victims of rape are almost all young boys, and so these films study their victims very differently than *Fiction* and *Shawshank*. Each of these movies represents the pain of victimization by rape as residing in the body and psyche of the adult. These three films focus intently on the way the violation he has suffered haunts the protagonist, and through the use of flashbacks, each film continually reminds us of the child that that man once was. I want to describe a pattern here, and so I will describe each of these films only briefly, but it is worth saying at the outset that because of their investments in the experience of the victims, *The Prince of Tides*, *American Me*, and *Sleepers* all deal with sexual violation in much more nuanced and interesting ways than do *Fiction* and *Shawshank*. These three movies are fundamentally invested in the toll that sexual violation takes on its victim, and each uses the techniques of film in order to convey those psychic and physical difficulties to the audience. Still, all three films are careful to destroy the rapists quickly and definitively in what I am arguing is an attempt to restore (masculine) bodily integrity to the protagonist–victim by breaking the body of the rapist.

The plot of Barbra Streisand's *The Prince of Tides* is fairly simple. Tom Wingo's marriage is in trouble, and his twin sister has attempted suicide and is in a coma in New York City. Tom (Nick Nolte) goes North at the request of his sister's psychiatrist, who asks him to be his sister's memory. He stays in the city to tell her what he can, he and Dr. Lowenstein (Streisand) fall in love, and Tom has many realizations about his own life before his sister gets better and he can return again to the South and to his family. Central to the film is a secret that Tom and his sister have been keeping since adolescence. After many weeks of seeing the therapist, Tom finally breaks his silence about this experience. He tells Lowenstein that when he and his sister were thirteen, she and their mother were raped by three men who had escaped from the nearby Callanwolde prison.[67] Tom, however, keeps silent about his own violation when he describes the event.

Flashbacks are used repeatedly throughout *Prince of Tides* as Tom remembers events from their childhood. So, as he begins to narrate the attack, Streisand's film tells the story both in the present and the past by using this (color) flashback technique. In this crucial sequence, the camera in Lowenstein's office sits in midshot, with Tom's chest and most of his body visible. With the camera on her, Lowenstein asks, "You said before that *three* men came in. What happened to the third man?" and the film cuts back to Tom in close-up. His eyes move rapidly but nothing else moves in his face (Figure 4.8). "Tom?" she says. "Where was *he*?" Then we cut to the past.

In the flashback, the third man shoves thirteen-year-old Tom (Trey Yearwood) up against a table, breaking several glasses. The camera movement in the flashback is very shaky, and the editing is rapid. Tom speaks in voice-over: "He said 'You move I'll slit your throat.' Raw meat. Called me raw meat. 'There's nothing I like better than fresh, raw meat.'" In the present the camera stays in a tight close-up on Tom as he says, "What was happening to me . . . was *unimaginable*, literally. I didn't know it could happen to a boy" (Figure 4.9). The film immediately cuts back to thirteen-year-old Tom, with the rapist behind him, screaming in pain with tears in his eyes. "All I wanted to do was die," Tom says in the present. Next, Tom's older brother (Chris Stacy) enters the house with a shotgun, shoots Tom's rapist in the genitals, and then another one in the head (Figure 4.10). Tom's mother stabs her rapist in the back.

FIGURE 4.8-9: *The Prince of Tides* (1991), studying Tom's face

FIGURE 4.9

The plot of *Prince of Tides* is rooted in Tom's *mother's* shame-inducing response to this violation. She demands that the children tell no one, even though both Tom and his sister are seriously injured by the violation both physically and emotionally. No one calls the police, and they clean up the carnage and bury the bodies before Tom's father gets home. "I think the silence was worse than the rapes," Tom tells Lowenstein, and *Prince of Tides* understands the powerful effect that the shame of having been

FIGURE 4.10: *The Prince of Tides* (1991), Tom's brother shoots the rapists

raped has had on Tom. The filmic images from the past intrude onto the present, like difficult memories, shaky and hazy; their style is designed to induce a panic and confusion in the audience that parallel Tom's own. But once Tom breaks his silence about this violation, he seems to have freed himself of the power these memories had over him. The film does not return to the subject matter of the rape, and Tom's sister immediately begins to recover. What is fascinating about this portrayal is its focus on and interest in the effect of rape on the violated *man*. *Tides* is interested in the violated *boy* only insofar as that boy has become the man at the center of the film, and the movie asks its audience to study Tom's adult face intently (in tight close-up) in order to see what remains of this violence in his body.

Barry Levinson's *Sleepers* is completely structured around sexual violence; the plot of this movie is the systematic and repeated rape of four boys at a juvenile detention center followed by their revenge against their rapists a decade and a half later. *Sleepers* is divided into three clear acts: one in Hell's Kitchen, in which the four friends enjoy their childhood and accidentally kill a man; a second at the Wilkinson Home for Boys, where they are subject to numerous beatings, rapes, and other humiliations by four male guards; and a third courtroom/cloak-and-dagger section, in which the now-grown boys get revenge on the guards and cope with the violations they have suffered. Each act has a distinct style.

FIGURE 4.11: *Sleepers* (1996), Shakes looks away from Father Bobby

The film's first act opens with Frankie Valli singing "Walk like a Man," and we see the four boys sunning shirtless on a rooftop. The boys are photographed lovingly by the camera, and this is meant to evoke a desire for life lived idyllically—Levinson made his name directing nostalgia pictures such as *Diner* (1982), *The Natural* (1984), and *Avalon* (1990)—and so the effect is nearly erotic. Indeed, one of the boys in *Sleepers* is played by Brad Renfro, who had become a star as a teen heartthrob in the previous year's *The Client*. Levinson also shows the teenagers diving into the East River in their underwear, and the sunning-on-a-rooftop image is repeated near the end of this first act. This section of the film describes the boys and the world they live in as pure and innocent, and even though the film's visual content gives the lie to this—a man is shot four times, another is lynched for dealing drugs on a street-corner, and the boys deliver money to crooked cops for the local mafia—both the voiceovers and the film's music (the Beach Boys' "Good Vibrations" also makes an appearance) incongruously insist upon the benignity of all of this.[68]

The second act is much darker. On their first night at the Wilkinson Home for Boys, Shakes (Joe Perrino), the film's protagonist and narrator, is made to undress completely while the guard Nokes (Kevin Bacon) watches him. Soon after, the boys are taken into a storage room and forced to fellate the guards. The film is explicit about this, and the sequence is quite scary. The camera tracks through the basement tunnels of the school so that the audience loses a sense of time and location but also understands what is happening as a terrifying shift in the lives of the boys. The boys are raped and beaten repeatedly at Wilkinson. Although the voice-over in these reformatory scenes is vague and sententious, with lines such as "It was my

FIGURE 4.12-15: *Sleepers* (1996), the boys are haunted

FIGURE 4.13

fourteenth birthday. And the end of my childhood," the film's dark visuals leave no doubt as to the violations that are occurring and the effects they are having on the four boys.[69] These effects are both physical and emotional, and *Sleepers* pulls no punches here. When their Hell's Kitchen priest, Father Bobby (Robert De Niro), comes to visit, Shakes hides his face (Figure 4.11). He tells us that he can't look at the priest, afraid that he will "see right through [him]." Later the boys decide as a group that they want no one to know what has happened to them at Wilkinson. "We've got no choice but to live with it," they agree. Already they appear haunted by the violations they have endured, with sunken, terrorized eyes (Figures 4.12–4.15). They all agree to keep silent.

The film's third act begins when two of the boys (Billy Crudup and Ron Eldard), now adults, run into Nokes in a restaurant and shoot him in the

FIGURE 4.14

FIGURE 4.15

genitals at point blank range before killing him. The men are put on trial for the murder, but their friends Shakes (Jason Patric) and Michael (Brad Pitt) concoct a plan to acquit them and also get revenge on the other rapists. It works. They arrange for one of the assailants (Jeffrey Donovan) to be murdered by gangsters; another (Lennie Loftin) is arrested for crimes unrelated to the rapes, and the third (Terry Kinney) testifies in court about the sexual violence at Wilkinson, making both his guilt and Nokes's a matter of public record.

Although the film's action is driven by the desire for revenge, what is intriguing here is the way Levinson presents these violated men. *Sleepers* sees all four as damaged, haunted by what has been done to them. The camera studies the men intently, searching their faces for information, but none

Revenge Tarantino-Style   157

FIGURE 4.16-19: *Sleepers* (1996), the men are haunted

FIGURE 4.17

of their faces gives anything away (Figures 4.16–4.19). Each seems, on the very surface of his face, still to be trying to figure out what happened. And lest the audience think Shakes, apparently the most resilient of the boys, is less haunted than the others, Levinson intercuts a scene of Shakes praying in the present with a flashback in which Nokes and the other three guards rape him with a truncheon. This and other flashback sequences make clear that the rapes are not over, that their effects have been lasting, powerful, and deeply wounding. Like *The Prince of Tides*, *Sleepers* also presents silence about the rapes as part of the damage they caused. Late in the film, Michael's former love interest tells him "If only you told me, I think things could've been different." She says this to Michael, but Michael keeps his face averted and does not look at her.

FIGURE 4.18

FIGURE 4.19

Sleepers, then, presents speaking about sexual violence as one possible antidote to shame, but the men, in fact, stay silent. What happens instead is that Shakes only tells other characters about the rapes in order to facilitate his revenge, which the film articulates as a necessary feat that the men must achieve. *Sleepers* transforms into a revenge film by its third act, and although the characters themselves appear not to benefit from this vengeance—we learn at the end that two of the men die before turning thirty—for the film's audience, the revenge is quite satisfying: watching a rapist turn into a puddle in court or get riddled with bullets certainly *feels* like justice.

It is this feeling on which I want to focus, because if *Sleepers* is invested in representing the effects of rape as damaging, the film also makes an attempt to assure its audience that the offenders are destroyed and that the future is safe. Further, as Joe Wlodarz argues in his brilliant essay on *Sleepers*, the film attempts a "massive recuperation of Catholicism," performing an "erasure of pedophilia from its most likely candidate" by turning the focus away from both the home and the American Catholic Church.[70] Even more damningly, James Kincaid notes that, in the ideological project of the film, nothing "is as important as child abuse—not drug dealing, not organized crime, not murder," and when a voice-over tells us that all of the *other* boys at Wilkinson were violent offenders and belonged there, the film is saying "we needn't concern ourselves with any thing outside the immediate psychodrama: the institution is just fine, the system is fine, and so are we."[71] To put it another way, although the film's characters are, in fact, men broken by the institutional violence of the criminal justice system, *Sleepers* uses the generic logic of the thriller to recuperate Catholicism, to reassure us that the criminal justice system works, and to valorize the usual suspects of violent masculinity in the 1990s: organized crime and vigilante justice.

Edward James Olmos's *American Me* deals in even more complex ways with sexual violence as a fundamental element in the lives of its characters. Olmos's film is structured around four separate acts of rape, two of which are rapes by males of males. In fact, each of the movie's three acts begins with a rape. At the start of the film we are shown that the protagonist, Montoya Santana (Olmos) is the child of rape. Santana's mother is assaulted by white sailors during the so-called Zoot Suit Riots, while his father is being beaten.[72] This causes a rift from the first with his father, who doubts the boy's paternity. Santana is himself raped on his very first night in a juvenile detention center—by a young white man (Eric Close). Immediately after being raped at knifepoint, young Santana (Panchito Gómez) stands up, wrestles the young man to the bed and then stabs him in the neck, killing him. This begins his prison career.[73]

Finally, in the most memorable sequence in *American Me*, Santana is out on a date with his (female) love interest after his release from prison, and the two have sex for the first time. The sequence of their first sexual encounter is crosscut with the rape and murder of an Italian prisoner named Tony (Michael Shaner) by Santana's gang, La eMe, at Folsom Penitentiary. This sequence is incredibly complex, and I will describe it in detail.

As Santana and Julie (Evelina Fernández) spend the evening together, the film cuts back to the prison several times, setting up the parallels between the two events over the progress of the evening. The men in the prison drink together at the same time as Santana and Julie drink together. As

Santana and Julie begin to have sex, she asks him if he's ever had sex with a woman before; he does not answer. Meanwhile, the gang pulls off Tony's pants and stuffs a handkerchief in his mouth. The scene cuts back and forth regularly. They tie his arms with rope so that he is bent over several burlap sacks of rice, while Santana and Julie clasp hands during their lovemaking. One of Tony's assailants sticks a knife into the bag of rice directly under his face, slitting it open, simultaneously signifying and preparing us for the violent penetration the film will shortly represent. In a striking close-up, Tony screams in agony while his mouth and face are covered in dry, white rice. As with other close-ups of this type from the period, the camera is focused primarily on Tony's anguish (Figure 4.20). The scene cuts back to Santana, who flips his girlfriend over, clearly indicating that if he hasn't had sex with a woman he is not without sexual experience. Julie cries for him to stop, but he anally rapes her. Back at Folsom, one of the men gets out a massive knife shaped like a Christmas tree and holds it directly below Tony's anus (Figure 4.21). The film cuts away at the moment of the knife's penetration.

Within the plot of *American Me*, this rape sequence is the beginning of a change for Santana. He has ordered the rape and murder of Tony because he wishes to take over drug trafficking in East Los Angeles, and he decides to teach Tony's father, an Italian mafia boss, a lesson. Instead, he causes a war: the mafia boss starts selling extremely pure heroin, killing many of the Chicanos on the East side, including Julie's brother.

For Frederick Luis Aldama, *American Me*'s rape sequences "reproduce the anal encounter as abnormal and perverse—as an act of physical violence that leads to the mass destruction of the heterosexual matrix."[74] In Aldama's reading, "when the double-anal-rape scene leads to an apocalypse in the barrio, one can't help but read this against our AIDS-panicked mass culture that associates anal intercourse . . . with suicide and disease, especially in poor ethnic enclaves."[75] I am in complete agreement with Aldama here and, as I argued in my analysis of *Shawshank*, fear of male/male rape in both films displaces and figures a cultural fear of HIV/AIDS. Aldama's analysis next moves toward understanding *American Me* as the story of Santana's transformation into a queer mestizo figure. For Aldama, Santana "comes to inhabit a transecting sexual and gender (even a trans-Chicano/Latino/Carib) identity that . . . exists as an alternative 'originating force' to the traditional vagina/penis binary system."[76] Aldama's understandable focus on the queer desire in *American Me*, however, occludes the film's own fundamental interest in rape as violence, as well as the horrifying way that Olmos stages each of the film's rapes. Indeed, because Olmos's

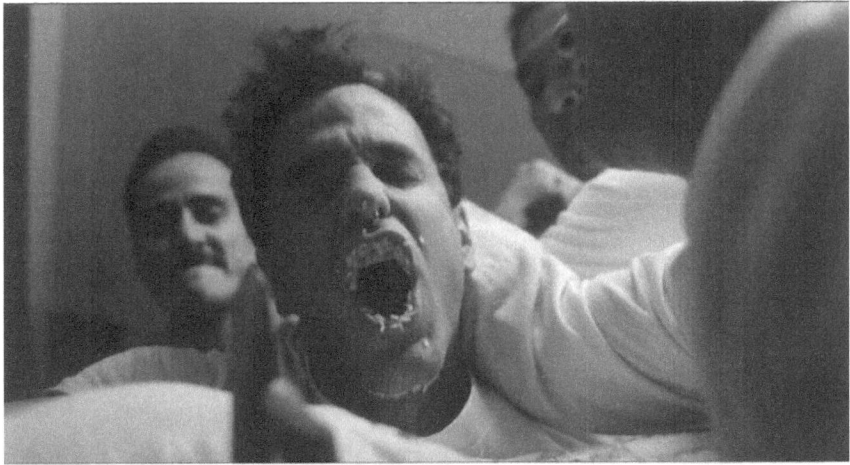

FIGURE 4.20: *American Me* (1992), close-up on Tony's anguish

FIGURE 4.21: *American Me* (1992), the knife emphasizes the violence

film, unlike all of the other films in this chapter, makes explicit equations between female rape victims and male rape victims, *American Me* consciously treats rape primarily as an act of violence and not as a sex act. If, in other words, the film eroticizes the homosocial relationships between Santana and the members of La eMe with the "little pecks on the cheek" and "longing glances" that Aldama describes, *American Me* is also careful to make a stark distinction between pleasurable sex and rape. *American Me* understands rape as brutally violent in each of the violations it stages: both of the male/male rapes in the film end with the death of either the victim or the rapist, and both scenes use knives to underline the deadly force of these encounters.

Olmos's film is, as Rosa-Linda Fregoso says, an "unflinching treatment of Chicano masculinities," with a "shrewdly oblique refusal to romanticize the defiance of the masculine heroic figure."[77] The film clearly understands Santana as a wounded boy—like the characters in *Prince of Tides* and *Sleepers*—still dealing with having been raped as a child. Pace Aldama, the subjectivity Santana has created isn't queer or trans so much as it has been forged by the violence to which he has been subjected, violation that the film stages unsentimentally. As Julie says in an early voice-over, Santana is "two people. One is like a kid—doesn't know how to dance, doesn't know how to make love. That's the one I cared about." And by the end of *American Me*, Santana desires to break the structures of domination, penetration, and violence that are cited and perpetuated both by the rape to which he has been subjected and the acts of rape he has committed.

These three films—*The Prince of Tides*, *American Me*, and *Sleepers*—establish a discourse in the 1990s for the way that rape affects the bodies and psyches of male victims. In each film, the rapes that the boys are made to suffer have long-lasting effects, and each film makes clear that silence about sexual violence is an important component of this damage. All three make the argument that silence, and the shame that silence maintains, increases the harm caused by rape. The movies, in this respect, are fascinated by the damaged body, but they also work very hard to contain, cinematically, the threat of sexual violence that they portray. Although we are asked to feel vulnerable as we identify with a raped protagonist, as soon as the rape is over, these films offer again the spectacle of male wholeness, as we watch the rapist's genitals get blown off (*Tides* and *Sleepers*) or get stabbed in the neck (*American Me*).

American Me's portrayal of rape is the most sustained and haunting of the three. If the movie is without hope, as Fregoso and others such as Luis Valdez have complained, this is because Olmos also takes us past the standard rape-revenge plot.[78] Olmos's film is not content with an ideological fiction that, in fact, substitutes one type of violence as the solution to another. *American Me* remains with its character long enough for Santana to understand his own violent contributions to US American masculinity. Early in the film, Santana gets revenge for the rape he suffers, and he is convinced by the law this violation articulates, perpetuating it and evaluating others based upon a masculine fantasy of wholeness, hardness, and impenetrability. What Santana decides at the end of *American Me* is to step away from this fantasy, and this is why he must be murdered, finally, by his own gang. If the film is bleak, and if some have found it difficult, this is because Olmos does not allow his audience the closure offered by the rape-revenge narratives of *Sleepers*, *Pulp Fiction*, and *Shawshank*; *American Me* refuses to offer audiences the fantasy of a masculine wholeness that can be contrasted with the broken body of the rapist after he has been castrated, riddled with bullets, or otherwise vanquished. Olmos's film fundamentally resists the idea that an act of violence can make a person whole again.

Derek Vinyard and Rape Without Revenge

This chapter concludes with *American History X*, the final 1990s film with an important male/male rape sequence. In Tony Kaye's extremely violent movie, we follow a white supremacist named Derek Vinyard (Edward Norton) who bullies his family, hurls racist insults at everyone he meets, vandalizes grocery stores, and finally—in a sequence almost too unbearable to watch—commits a horrific murder motivated by hate and anti-Black racism. Once in prison, however, Derek is raped by his own gang of Aryans. They violate him in order to teach him a lesson, an attempt to shame him and reassert their own authority over him. The rape causes Derek to turn his life around. He decides to leave behind his racism, and he tries to extricate his younger brother (Edward Furlong) from his neo-Nazi associations. Structurally, the rape in *History* functions to indicate a turning point in Derek's faith in white supremacy. He is thoroughly, brutally betrayed by the men he thought had the most principles and the people with whom he identified most completely. As a plot point, then, *History*'s male/male rape sequence stands in for the corruption and perversion of racist beliefs, rooted, not in respectable values, but simply in violence and hatred.

If this sounds, as it did to Manhola Dargis, "like one of those j.d. movies from the '50s," that is because this is how *American History X* wants to work.[79] The critical consensus around the film is that its public-service-announcement style failed, and this failure was primarily due to the dynamism with which Kaye directed the film. *History*, as it turns out, makes Derek's tirades against people of color much more convincing than his conversion to nonviolence and harmony. The film positively luxuriates in the pleasure of the violence and racism that make up more than half of *History*'s length (Kaye, for example, chooses to underscore a neo-Nazi victory in a racist basketball game with triumphal orchestral music), and Dargis rightly argues that "Derek is peddling malevolence, and Kaye can't see that he's helping to nail the sale."

Unlike the other violence in *History*, however, its male/male rape sequence is filmed with sensitivity and care. For Janet Maslin, this sequence "has been so strikingly photographed by Mr. Kaye himself that it makes up for the facile nature of the film's prison interlude."[80] The rape takes both the audience and Derek by surprise; no threats of rape precede it, and the sequence is over very quickly. Derek is showering after a basketball game, all of the other men leave silently, and then five white men enter without saying a word while the guard quietly exits. Derek is raped brutally by one man, while the others pin him to the shower wall. After he is raped, Derek's assailant (Nicholas R. Oleson) slams Derek's head into the tiled shower wall. He hits the ground unconscious, and the room fills with the steam of the showers, framing Derek's injured form in mist. The camera lingers on tight close-ups of his bleeding face, his naked buttocks, blood streaming onto the floor from under his genitals, and the "white power" tattoo on his right bicep.

In the next scene, Derek's high school English teacher, Sweeney, played by Black actor Avery Brooks, enters the prison. "How is he?" he asks the doctor. "He took six stitches," we are told. Derek lies face down on a hospital bed. He looks at Sweeney and the camera and then looks away. Sweeney puts his hand on the man's back. Derek begins to cry, hiding his face. It is a very powerful scene, and because of the rapidity of the scene previous, Derek's sobbing functions as an emotional release from the tension built up during the rape sequence.

Most intriguingly—and this is perhaps one reason why the film seems unconvincing to many viewers—Derek does not seek revenge for the violation he suffers. After he is raped, he cuts off contact with the Aryans altogether, turns his life around, and by the end of the film's third act, he has convinced his brother to eschew racism, as well. *History*, unlike the other male/male rape films in this chapter, does not attempt to make the body whole again through an act of revenge, and this is fundamentally different from how cinema in the 1990s trained audiences to watch male rape victims respond to violation. Kaye's choice to avoid the typical revenge plot here is not only rare, it also points us toward our own feelings about male victims who *don't* fight back, who don't attempt to refashion their own bodies as whole through violence.

As Dargis describes this transformation between "Derek the Hater" and this new, reformed version, she says that "Norton seems to shrivel back to character-actor size. He doesn't just look smaller, less brutal, built and sexy, he actually starts to look like an extra: He shrinks to fit the movie."[81] Perhaps so. It is certainly one of the film's failings that the film sees Derek the antiracist as a much less dynamic figure than Derek the neo-Nazi, but we are also speaking about a man whom we have seen raped. Whether or not the film does this well, *American History X* portrays rape as something that fundamentally changes Derek, injuring him and transforming him into a different person. If Derek seems smaller after he has been raped, this is because the movie of which he is the star has not attempted to reassert his inviolability. He seems "less brutal, built and sexy" because *History*'s project strives to avoid reclaiming the fantasy of white-supremacist masculinity that saturates the film's first half.

Even more importantly, the shame that the film indicates as Derek turns his face away and hides his head in his hands is a shame with which *American History X* asks its audience to identify without disavowing it. In Douglas Crimp's important essay "Mario Montez, For Shame," he describes his experience watching Montez's humiliation in Andy Warhol's film *Screen Test #2* (1965). Warhol, for his movies, discusses looking for a kind of shock or embarrassment that surprises with its "realness." For Crimp, however, *Screen Test #2* produces a disquiet that lingers in the body of the viewer. This, he says, is:

> our encounter, on the one hand, with the absolute difference of the other, his or her "so-for-realness," and, on the other hand, with the other's shame, both the shame that extracts his or her "so-for-realness" from . . . Warhol's performers, and the shame that we accept as also ours, but curiously also ours alone. I am thus not "like" Mario, but the distinctiveness that is revealed in Mario invades me—"floods me," to use Sedgwick's word—and my own distinctiveness is revealed simultaneously.[82]

Crimp's is a description of a shame that is extraordinarily productive. The viewer is simultaneously ashamed and proud, connected to Mario in *his* shame and alone with his own shame but reveling in the experience of both. Crimp experiences shame as something that both makes him himself and has the ability to alter the way he thinks of himself. Shame, here, is something that affects Crimp as he watches—lingering and unsettling but working to shift his subjectivity in ways he cannot predict or control. In their various ways, *American History X*, *American Me*, and *The Prince of Tides* invite just such complex identifications with the violate man. These three films to varying degrees also allow for their protagonists to remain broken, to refuse the fantasy of closure that destructive revenge seems to offer. The films perhaps even invite their audiences to remain open to the unsettled, lingering shifts in subjectivity that Crimp describes in his essay.

This is not true of *Pulp Fiction*. To the contrary, Tarantino forecloses a similarly complex response for the viewers who watch Marsellus as he is raped by Zed. Marsellus hides his face from Butch and immediately transforms himself through an act of violence (shooting his rapist in the genitals) from the broken, allegedly passive victim of rape into a subject whose body is inviolate, whole, impenetrable. *Pulp Fiction* represents shame as unproductive and toxic, needing to be excised from who one is, distanced from the self as quickly as possible, so that a fantasy of masculine subjectivity can be reasserted. If watching Marsellus's shame floods its audience with the same affect, Tarantino's film asks us immediately to disregard that shame, to put it aside, and to take pleasure in watching Marsellus (with Butch's help) reassert himself as inviolate.

In this way *Pulp Fiction* re-legitimates the men's response in Boorman's *Deliverance* by, twenty-two years later, articulating that same response to sexual violation as necessary and appropriate: Utterly destroy the men at whose hands you suffered and then tell nobody. As for the audience, shame's quality of contagiousness means that *Pulp Fiction* works hard to invite its audience to share in the feeling of shame that we see on the face of Marsellus Wallace. And once we are flooded with shame, a shame that becomes both Marsellus's and our very own, Marsellus shows us, immediately, how we ought best to cope with that feeling—with a pair of pliers and a blowtorch.[83]

These films, narratives in which responses of silence and violence are proposed as logical, natural, and even poetically just, further work to teach audience members how to approach shame in our own lives. As Sedgwick warns us, however:

> the forms taken by shame are not distinct "toxic" parts of a group or individual identity that can be excised; they are instead integral to and residual in the processes by which identity itself is formed. They are available for the work of metamorphosis, reforming, refiguration, *trans*figuration, affective and symbolic loading and deformation, but perhaps all too potent for the work of purgation and deontological closure.[84]

The possibilities for being flooded with shame that Sedgwick imagines are extraordinary and productive, describing transformative versions of working through or therapeutic binding. *History*'s Derek Vinyard and *American Me*'s Montoya Santana attempt versions of this, incorporating their shame into new, less masculine subjectivities that they craft for themselves. *Fiction*, *Shawshank*, and *Sleepers* offer instead a kind of false deontological closure, imagining that shame can be separated from the subject through an act of violence, as though when Marsellus shoots Zed in the groin—or John and Tommy shoot Nokes in the genitals or Andy has Bogs beaten by the guards—he could destroy his own shame along with the body of his assailant.[85] *Fiction*, *Shawshank*, and *Sleepers* attempt to sell us the masculinist fantasy that we can somehow rid ourselves of shame, that silence and violence are the correct responses to the emotions that flood the body during and after an experience of violation.[86] But silence and violence, far from achieving closure, compound the experience of shame by denying its existence and projecting it outward onto the broken body of another. The responses to violence in which these films are invested can only ever be a failed attempt—as an act of rape is—to shore up the boundaries of the masculine subject by shaming someone else through yet another violation.

CHAPTER 5

Testimony and Television
Male/Male Rape on Cable and Network TV

> HOWARD BEALE: The only truth you know is what you get over this tube. Right now there is a whole, an entire, generation that never knew anything that didn't come out of this tube! This tube is the Gospel, the ultimate revelation. This tube can make or break presidents, popes, prime ministers. This tube is the most awesome god-damn force in the whole godless world.
>
> —PADDY CHAYEFSKY, *Network*

With the turn of the new century, representations of male/male rape proliferated at the movies. There are male/male rape sequences in *In Too Deep* (1999), *Animal Factory* (2000), *Lockdown* (2000), *I'll Sleep When I'm Dead* (2003), *The Mudge Boy* (2003), *The Butterfly Effect* (2004), and a threatened rape in *Felon* (2008). Most of these follow the typical patterns for rapists, victims, and narrative tropes for containing and disavowing shame enumerated in Chapter 4. In a prison sequence in *The Butterfly Effect*, for example, Evan (Ashton Kutcher) is raped by two members of an Aryan gang, whom he then stabs with a shiv, and in *Lockdown*, an Aryan named Graffiti (David Shark Fralick) repeatedly rapes the new prisoner Dre (De'Aundre Bonds) before he is finally killed. In these stories the threat of male/male rape is contained—and the masculinity of the rape victim restored—by the rapist's eventual murder.[1]

Perhaps the most surprising development of this history of male/male rape discourse was the rise of the prison rape *comedy* as a kind of subgenre appearing annually—including *Let's Go to Prison* (2006), *The Ten* (2007), *Harold and Kumar Escape from Guantanamo Bay* (2008), *Big Stan* (straight to

DVD in 2009), and *I Love You Phillip Morris* (2009)—in which lengthy plots or subplots limn male/male rape for its comedic potential. Male/male rape jokes were, of course, hardly a novelty in the 2000s, as I noted in both Chapter 3 and in the discussion of *Hit & Run* in the introduction, but comic subplots entirely about prison rape and explicit, comedic references to prison rape, some of which are even visualized in these films, were certainly a new phenomenon for the new millennium. This comedic discourse worked in the 2000s, as it did with the jokes about *Deliverance*, to contain a collective anxiety in the United States, especially around prison sexual violence, related to the astounding increase in prison populations in the US.

In addition to these comedies, at the turn of the century male/male rape would also find sustained representation on television with the debut of Tom Fontana's prison program *Oz* on the cable network HBO. *Oz*, which aired from 1997 to 2003, was the first hour-long drama series produced by Home Box Office, and it would soon be followed by the hit shows *The Sopranos* (1999–2007), *Sex and the City* (1998–2004), *Six Feet Under* (2001–2005), and *The Wire* (2002–2008), heralding a takeover of "quality" television by non-broadcast networks not subject to Federal Communications Commission (FCC) regulations that has continued into the present. As Mark Simpson reported in the *Guardian* at the time of *Oz*'s debut in Great Britain:

> *Oz* can afford to be much more explicit, much more macho than American broadcast TV (which has to think of women, children and advertisers). The language is foul, the sex [sic] is graphic, the violence is extreme—one man is torched to death with lighter fluid; another has his penis cut off and stuffed in his mouth—and, most offensive of all for American TV, there is no happy ending.[2]

Oz was the first in a trend of no-holds-barred television series that were to become the stock-in-trade of the cable networks and that would soon be representing all manner of sexual activity, nudity (full-frontal male nudity included), graphic violence, drug use, and explicit language. Even in Simpson's very brief description here, it is evident that *Oz* already set the bar for shocking content quite high when it debuted in 1997. Over the period of seven years that *Oz* was on the air, images and explicit discussions of male/male rape were common, even *de rigueur* on the show. The sexual violation of one male by another, such a taboo topic in the mid-1960s, had become, by the summer of 1997, an almost weekly subject of discourse on cable television.

After *Oz* ended in 2003, male/male rape plots continued to appear sporadically on cable TV shows. In season three of the award-winning FX series *The Shield* (2004), one of its main characters was raped at gunpoint by a gang member, and things took a shocking turn on *Six Feet Under* when a character was raped and terrorized in the show's fourth season (also 2004).[3] Perhaps most surprisingly, in May 2010, ABC's daytime soap opera *General Hospital* began a storyline in which one of the show's beloved teenagers, Michael Corinthos Quartermaine (Chad Duell), was badly beaten by his protector Carter (Josh Wingate) during a brief stint in prison.[4] Because of the generic conventions of the daily afternoon serial, the story developed over an extended period of time, with Michael keeping silent about what actually happened. The episodes in which the violence occurs were not explicit, and so audiences in 2010 were left to their assumptions—assumptions I have described in detail in Chapter 1. Months later, in 2011, *General Hospital*'s writers brought the story back: after witnessing the attempted rape of the woman he was seeing, Michael revealed that what happened in prison was that he was raped.[5]

More recently on network TV, ABC's Emmy-nominated second season of *American Crime* revolved around the rape of a young man at a wealthy Indiana high school and the cover-up perpetrated by the school. The show's ripped-from-the-headlines timeliness seemed to reference rape/sex scandals at St. Paul's, an elite boarding school in New Hampshire, and St. George's, a private boarding school in Rhode Island, while simultaneously addressing issues of bullying and homophobia.[6] The *Guardian* called this season of *American Crime* "the first must-watch TV show of 2016," and in *USA Today* Robert Bianco referred to it as "one of the most astonishing, moving and timely dramas on TV, one that can match any for stylistic flair and tops most for substance."[7] Season two of *American Crime* aired on broadcast TV in a 10:00 P.M. prime-time slot on Wednesday nights, and male/male rape as an extended topic of discussion had arrived on network television.

This chapter begins, however, with a brief description of three television events in the mid-1980s, the first narrative treatments of male/male rape on broadcast television. Each of these stories of sexual violence is discrete, relegated to a single evening of television, but these brief storylines on network TV set up a pattern for what audiences could be led to expect from representations of male/male rape. Next, I describe and analyze storylines of male/male sexual violence in both *Oz* and *American Crime*. By carefully following these two series, we will chart a history of television discourse around male/male rape developing from 1997 to 2016 as the topic moved from cable to network television and from stories set in the relatively discrete space of a New York prison to a story taking place in the homes of middle- and working-class families in Indiana. Because of the medium of the television series, sustained portrayals of characters over long periods of time allow for—even if they do not always achieve—a much more thorough and complex portrayal of the physical and psychological effects of rape on male victims. This chapter, accordingly, turns its attention to the televisual representation of therapy and the discourse of truth in regard to male/male rape. I argue that the very form of the dramatic television series is predisposed to treating rape using the psychoanalytic language of trauma and the narrative form of the confession. My analysis of *Oz* and *American Crime* charts the rise of this demand for confession in male/male rape narratives in the first decade of the twenty-first century.

I close this chapter with four short case studies, all of which are recent examples of confessional narratives. These are Garrard Conley's gay conversion-therapy memoir *Boy Erased* (2016), Jonathan Parks-Ramage's neo-gothic novel *Yes, Daddy* (2021), Michaela Coel's confessional series *I May Destroy You* (2020), and Richard Gadd's Netflix series *Baby Reindeer* (2024). The male/male rape narratives in these books and television series evince the continuing influence of the confessional mode on these narratives and the extraordinary impact of television on male/male rape discourse.

Television Patterns and the Basic Plot

Lisa Cuklanz's 2000 study *Rape on Prime Time* argues convincingly that rape plots on television—from 1976 to 1990, the years of her study—"use the subject matter of rape in order to spotlight the performance of hegemonic masculinity. As models of this ideal, detectives and male police officers serve as clear moral contrasts to rapists."[8] Cuklanz's study surveys hundreds of episodes of network television, including police procedurals, legal dramas, situation comedies, medical series, and detective shows. She finds that when rape is a topic on these shows, the sexual violence against the female victim is almost always present in order to demonstrate the successful masculinity of the protagonist male characters in the show; these honorable men are clearly contrasted with the violent evil of the rapists. The actual victim of sexual violation in these episodes, however, is often merely a catalyst for the episode's plot, and she frequently appears only at the beginning of the hour to put the plot in motion. Cuklanz's study describes a basic pattern: the typical episode with rape as its subject matter demonstrates a "lack of focus on the victim"; it will almost always portray "rape as a violent stranger attack"; and it will invariably portray "the show's protagonist as the enlightened protector of the victim."⁹ The centrality of questions of masculinity to each of these narratives cannot be overstated, and this same pattern holds for narratives about male/male rape, as well. The very purpose of the episodes Cuklanz studies is to contrast different men with one another as popular ideas about masculinity fluctuated.

Underlining the importance of female rape storylines to *male* protagonist detectives, the earliest representation of male/male rape on TV appeared in a police series with two female protagonists, *Cagney & Lacey*.¹⁰ This single-episode storyline in 1985 follows exactly the basic plot Cuklanz describes in *Rape on Prime Time*: the deeply traumatized victim appears in a single scene early in the episode but then disappears; the rapist is unremittingly malevolent; and the causes of rape are demonstrated to be evil men (described as "animals" in this episode). Since this rape storyline has a male victim, however, there are some key differences from the usual pattern found in Cuklanz's study. Indeed, this *Cagney & Lacey* episode falls into the patterns I've articulated for male rape victims, especially in Chapter 1. The victim in this episode is an inexperienced young white man. Sixteen-year-old highschooler Dwayne Patterson (Doug Savant) is booked as an adult and accidentally spends the night in Rikers Island prison where he is violently raped over a four-hour period. This is network television, so only the aftermath of the rape appears on screen, evident in the young man's traumatic response to the violence he has endured.

As always with male/male rape storylines, race is central to the episode's plot, even though both the rapist and his victim are white men. During Cagney and Lacey's investigation, Dwayne's white cellmate Eddie Stutz (Gregory Sierra) accuses "three soul brothers" of having committed the rape, and he offers to testify against them; that is, he raises the specter of the Black male rapist with the idea of getting his own conviction overturned. But Cagney and Lacey discover that it was Eddie himself who "instigated the rape." Stutz is unapologetic, even arrogant. He claims he'll have a nice time in Attica, "as long as you keep sending me those nice, young boys." He notes, as well, that boys aren't his preference, and he slides his hand up Cagney's arm to make a pass at her. Cagney, in turn, threatens Stutz with rape in a well-established pattern linking Black men, prison, and sexual violence: "We're gonna put the word out about how you tried to set up the blacks, Eddie," Cagney tells Stutz. "You're gonna be a big hit in Attica. They're gonna be calling you the Queen of Soul." In other words, despite the vivid presence of an unrepentant white rapist in the scene, Cagney's threat raises the specter of the apparently even more dangerous Black prisoners in Attica, effectively confirming, again, what we all know about who commits rape in prison and who is victimized by it.

With her phrase "Queen of Soul," Cagney also casually links male rape victims and homosexuals. It's a common association, of course, and it is used here as a threat against a violent, malevolent villain. But the link to homosexuality is not isolated; the episode includes another character making an explicit link between homosexuality and victimization by rape. Dwayne's father—angry at the police for taking his son to Rikers in the first place—yells at the detectives: "You turned my son into a faggot!" It's an extraordinarily unsympathetic and homophobic response to a rape victim by a man who disavows his son's experience. Indeed, Dwayne's father gets this last word about his son; no one disputes his judgment of the situation; and by this point in the episode Dwayne himself has disappeared.

There were two other male/male rape plots on television within one year of this *Cagney & Lacey* episode. In an episode of the prime-time show *St. Elsewhere* that was written by *Oz* creator Tom Fontana, one of *St. Elsewhere*'s main characters, Jack Morrison, is raped and very badly beaten when he does a stint volunteering at a prison.[11] The rapist in the episode is a white, incarcerated, apparently homosexual career criminal who articulates his sexual attraction to his victim as well as his desire to humiliate him; he matches, in other words, the characteristics of the rapist on *Cagney & Lacey* and, indeed, all the rapists I describe in Chapter 4. The character who is sexually violated—played by series regular David Morse—is raped at the end of the episode and then does not appear in the final three episodes of the season, returning only in the following season in 1986. Again, as with the pattern Cuklanz describes in *Rape on Prime Time*, rape works as a discrete event, and these television series do not spend time with the victims, their feelings, or their recovery.

Finally, there is the made-for-television film *The Rape of Richard Beck*, directed by frequent *Cagney & Lacey* director Karen Arthur, which aired on ABC in May of 1985. This film won Richard Crenna an Emmy Award; it was generally dismissed by critics as preachy, but *The Rape of Richard Beck* also successfully critiques the misogynist and careless treatment of (female) rape victims by police.[12] The film, in fact, reflects a growing sensitivity to feminist activism around rape that Cuklanz finds more broadly in television of the late 1980s.[13] Unlike the episodes of *Cagney & Lacey* and *St. Elsewhere*, *The Rape of Richard Beck* is not set in prison. Still, the rapists who violate

Richard accord perfectly with the patterns set up for television sexual violence; they are represented as white career criminals very similar to the male/male rapists in the films I analyze in Chapter 4. Indeed, the men who rape Richard repeatedly call him a "pig," say that he will "squeal," and repeat the knife gesture (this time with a gun) from 1972's *Deliverance*.

There is one other key element that I'd like to highlight in *Richard Beck*. In this TV movie, when Richard's father (Pat Hingle) finds out that he's been raped, the two men have the following heated exchange:

> FATHER: You let 'em take your gun. Let 'em . . . do things to you.
> RICHARD: I didn't *let* 'em do anything! They did it! Them! Not me. They beat the hell out of me. They were gonna kill me. I didn't wanna die—can't you understand that?
> FATHER: No . . . I can't understand that.
> RICHARD: Dad! I—Dad?

Richard's father doesn't reply, walking away from him instead. In his severe judgment, the male rape victim is worthy of death. With its new feminist ideas about sexual violence, *The Rape of Richard Beck* portrays Richard's father's view as extreme, a relic of outdated ideas of masculinity, but it also treats this point of view as one that is common and in need of reform.

These three early representations of male/male rape appeared on network TV between March 1985 and March 1986.[14] This is a key period in Cuklanz's history of rape on television—when feminist activism around date rape, marital rape, and male rape victims had begun to have an effect on television's representational practices. In these episodes, however, male/male rape conforms to the set of established patterns for what we think we know about male/male rape. The episodes of *St. Elsewhere* and *Cagney & Lacey*, especially, use typical *narrative* structures that align with representations of rape with female victims, and at the same time they also import the traditional set of *thematic* associations that link male victims to whiteness, prisoners to Blackness, and victims and perpetrators both to homosexuality. These links would persist.

Emerald City and Carceral Economies

When *Oz* premiered at the late hour of 11:30 P.M. on July 12, 1997, before settling into its first-season 11:00 P.M. time slot, it was advertised as a gritty, no-frills examination of day-to-day life in the (fictional) Oswald maximum-security penitentiary. The language used by the characters and the descriptions of the occurrences in *Oz* are much more graphic than those explored so far in *The Violate Man*. Every episode of the series involves numerous, sensational acts of violence; murders are frequent in Oswald, and mutilations and severe bodily injuries are equally commonplace. As early as episode 1, for example, one man is burned alive and another suffocated. In what would become a dramaturgical staple of the more recent HBO drama *Game of Thrones*, *Oz* also kills off its characters mercilessly. The protagonist driving the narrative for much of the first episode is dispatched by its end, and as *Oz* continued, even the show's lead characters weren't safe from being killed.[15] But the "realism" of *Oz*, though it was much touted in its promotional material and even by several television critics, was never credible.[16] Bill Yousman runs the numbers in his book *Prime Time Prisons on U.S. TV*. Counting violent incidents on *Oz*, he finds that their frequency is not only "almost three times greater" than most prime-time programming but that "'reality' is amplified to the extent that severe distortions result."[17] He notes, for example, that "Murder accounts for three out of every four deaths in *Oz*, while the most likely cause of prisoner deaths in the real world—suicide, disease, and old age—*combined* account for only 8% of the deaths on *Oz*."[18] In another piece on *Oz*'s unrealistic portrayal of prison life, Lara Stemple offers a list of the items to which prisoners appear to have access in Oswald. Her hilarious compilation includes "ten-inch kitchen knives, ballgowns, rat poison, a hospital medicine cabinet evidently run on the honor system, a video camera, straight razors, a gun, fishnet stockings, bomb-making supplies, and a personal cappuccino machine," to which later episodes would add psychedelic pot brownies, a pool table, including standard cues and balls, and more heroin than most people have ever seen.[19] Later episodes in the series involve medical trials of a drug that prematurely ages prisoners, a holy man who literally vanishes into thin air, a production of *Macbeth* with a real knife, and a photo shoot for a magazine using death-row prisoners as fashion models. Hard-bitten realism is less of a priority here than sensationalized, unusual images of violence and shocking storytelling.

Rape is a constant occurrence at Oswald. In the first two seasons of the show, there is a reference to sexual violation in every episode but one, and over the course of the program's six seasons (fifty-six episodes) *Oz* features at least a dozen distinct storylines involving rape, each of which spans multiple episodes. As I argued in Chapter 1, rape plots since the late 1960s work to lend credibility to prison narratives, but *Oz*'s depictions of sexual violation differ markedly from those we have examined thus far. From the first episode, *Oz* treats rape as a component of prison life and, more importantly, as an event that affects and changes the prisoners in Oswald rather than, as with the films of the 1990s I described in Chapter 4, something that can be surmounted or otherwise disavowed. Unique among film and television representations of prison rape, *Oz* also demonstrates a real interest in the traumatic effects of sexual violence on its victims, paying close attention to the men as they deal with and respond to the violence that they have experienced.

The main rape narrative on *Oz*—a plot that begins in *Oz*'s first episode and is sustained for the entire series—follows a white, middle-class lawyer named Tobias Beecher (Lee Tergesen) and his relationship with the white-supremacist Vern Schillinger (J. K. Simmons). Upon arrival, Beecher is immediately threatened by a Black inmate who gets into his cell. The terrified Beecher is promptly offered protection by Schillinger and immediately accepts that protection. Once transferred into the neo-Nazi's cell, however, Schillinger rapes Beecher. The violation is not shown on-screen, but in a brief sequence, the camera shows Beecher's bare buttocks as Schillinger tattoos a swastika onto his right cheek.[20] Later in the episode, Beecher appears miserable, alone in his cell, lying in bed during his free time. In this way, *Oz* takes care to indicate that depression and shame have resulted from Beecher's experience. In a number of subsequent episodes, Schillinger humiliates Beecher, requiring him to clean his boots with his tongue in public, forcing him to dress in drag, and making him sing in front of the entire prison.[21] Schillinger also uses rape as a tool to blackmail Beecher, threatening to have his sons, who are on the outside, rape Beecher's wife and daughter.[22]

In this narrative arc, Schillinger repeatedly rapes Beecher, although the show makes this explicit only one other time in *Oz*'s first season. The episodes do not focus on Beecher's violation by Schillinger but instead represent other ways that Beecher suffers humiliation. And rather than spectacularizing Beecher's experience of physical pain, *Oz* turns its attention to the traumatic effects of these sexualized humiliations. The narratives that involve Beecher for the remainder of the first season detail his process of coping with rape-trauma and his forced transformation into a "prag," a term introduced by *Oz*'s narrator Augustus Hill (Harold Perrineau) and probably invented for the show.[23] Beecher begins using heroin in the show's third episode, and when confronted about this drug use by the prison counselor, Sister Pete (Rita Moreno), he tells her, "You don't know what it's like here"; the episode clearly describes drug use as a component of the rape-trauma Beecher is experiencing.[24] As the season concludes, Beecher becomes mentally unhinged. In a bizarre sequence from which the camera does not shy away, Beecher assaults Schillinger, kicking him, placing a weight on his chest, and then defecating in his mouth.[25] For the remainder of seasons 1 and 2, Beecher also cannot bear to be touched, even by his friends. He responds to touch by instantly recoiling and occasionally becoming violent. *Oz* demonstrates that all of these new aspects of the character are the direct result of the trauma he is experiencing. This is an important shift for representations of rape in the US. *Pulp Fiction* and *The Shawshank Redemption* focused on rape as a violent assault that could be overcome by its masculine victims through violent revenge. These narratives were uninterested in trauma. Other films from the 1990s occasionally describe the anguish of rape victims, but as I argue in Chapter 4, these films avoid exploring the experience of that trauma by violently destroying the perpetrators of rape.

Although *Oz* treats Schillinger's rape of Beecher as traumatic, and though it finds the traumatic effects of this particular rape storyline worthy of dramatic attention, the show approaches the other rapes in seasons 1 and 2 from an entirely different point of view. In season 2, Schillinger rapes intellectually disabled Cyril O'Reily (Scott William Winters) and, as with Schillinger's assaults on Beecher, this rape happens off-screen. *Oz* substitutes language for violence: "I gave him the royal welcome," he boasts to the Aryans in the mess hall.[26] Cyril is terrified and visibly traumatized by the rape, even though he does not seem fully to understand what has happened. But when his brother Ryan (Dean Winters) asks unit manager McManus (Terry Kinney) to move Cyril to a safer area of the prison so that he can protect his brother, McManus bargains with him. He offers to transfer Cyril if Ryan confesses to a murder that he committed. When Ryan refuses to confess, McManus uses rape as a bargaining chip in the exchange, saying, "Well, then, your brother stays in Vern Schillinger's ever-loving arms." In this story arc, Schillinger rapes Cyril as a way of attaining power over Ryan; he plans to use sexual assault to bargain with Ryan for drugs or to blackmail him into committing acts of violence. But if Schillinger mobilizes rape as a kind of currency, so does the unit manager. Though he is not himself raping Cyril, McManus has the power to stop the rapes and knows he has this power; instead of doing so, he uses the threat of rape to purchase something that he wants. Even in the contrived world of *Oz*, prison rape is only possible when those in charge of the prison turn a blind eye toward the violence inside its walls. Although *Oz* usually avoids placing direct blame on the corrections officers or the unit managers of Oswald for the rapes that occur inside the prison, time and again those in charge of the prison are manipulated or compensated so that they tacitly allow or even openly condone the rape of one prisoner by another.

Both of the rape storylines I've described thus far from seasons 1 and 2 are perpetrated by the prison's Aryan gang, run by the vicious Vern Schillinger. *Oz* purports to be a realistic prison series, and so Oswald is presented to its audience as divided along strict racialized lines. The Italian American prisoners don't usually spend time with the religious Nation of Islam group, who do not usually associate with the other Black prisoners or the Latino prisoners. *Oz* presents the Aryan gang as a slightly special case. Nearly all of these groups commit violent crimes, but the Aryans are especially sadistic, and this sadism is frequently sexualized. Following the racialized pattern of *Midnight Cowboy*, *Deliverance*, and *Scarecrow* from the 1970s, *Cagney & Lacey* and *St. Elsewhere* in the 1980s, *Pulp Fiction*, *American History X*, and other films of the 1990s, as well as every single prison film from the 2000s that I described at the beginning of this chapter, nearly all of the rapes in *Oz*'s six seasons are perpetrated by members of the Aryan Brotherhood. There are only a few exceptions to this rule (one of which I discuss later in this chapter), and on the rare occasion when a rape on *Oz* is committed by a Black man, his victim is nearly always a white man.[27] As with the scenario between Schillinger and Beecher in *Oz*'s first episode, these white rapists follow a typical pattern: they stoke their white victim's fear of Black male sexuality, and then, in exchange for protection from "Black rapists," they coerce their victims into sex, violate them, and publicly humiliate them. In the racially segregated space of the prison on *Oz*, rape is almost exclusively portrayed as something that happens to helpless young white men.

In many ways this is a citation of the discourse (discussed in Chapter 1) that permeates prison narratives beginning in the late 1960s. *Oz* apparently wants to avoid the overt racism of a piece like Alan Davis's 1968 *Trans-Action* article, but the show's portrayal of rape remains highly racialized. Young white characters on *Oz* seem to enter the prison already accepting Davis's contentions about the racial dynamics of rape behind bars. These white characters assume that the threat of sexual violence will come from the prison's Black residents. Almost all of Oswald's sexual violence, however, is committed by white men, and this is a kind of dramaturgical sleight of hand: Fontana assumes his audience's racist assumptions and then undermines those assumptions by showing us that the "real" threat is from the Aryan Brotherhood. *Oz*, branding itself as an unvarnished depiction of carceral realities, rearticulates much of what we all already think we know about the threats to young white men that exist behind bars, but it pointedly attempts to alter the source of that threat. It does so by giving us precisely the rapist with which we are most familiar, the homosexualized uneducated white man we know from *Deliverance*, *Pulp Fiction*, and *The Shawshank Redemption*. The violate man on *Oz* is as old as the 1960s, as well. He's the vulnerable naïf I described in Chapter 1, a white man who has accidentally found himself in the dangerous space of the prison—a place where nice, middle-class white men don't truly belong and a place that will destroy him. Accordingly, Black men remain as specters of the threat of sexual violence on *Oz*, and men of color are nearly invisible as possible victims of sexual violence. As *Oz* represents the "realities" of carceral life, it portrays prison as a dangerous, segregated space in which most men of color and some (racist, Southern, uneducated) white men know how to survive, but where no judge should ever send a nice, middle-class white boy.

Oz and Traumatized Subjects

In the only rape that is actually shown on-screen in the first two seasons, Yoruba prisoner Simon Adebisi (Adewale Akinnuoye-Agbaje) rapes his rival drug dealer, Italian American Peter Schibetta (Eddie Malavarca). Unlike the sympathetic point of view that *Oz* takes toward Tobias Beecher and Cyril O'Reily, however, the show treats the rape of Schibetta as though it is primarily his own fault. After the rape, Warden Leo Glynn (Ernie Hudson) and Officer Burrano (Skipp Sudduth) speak in an extraordinarily detached manner about Schibetta as he lies in a hospital bed:

> BURRANO: Pancamo and Schibetta were found unconscious, Schibetta's rectum bleeding; he could've been raped.
> GLYNN: What do you mean could've?
> BURRANO: Well, he says he doesn't know what happened. He won't talk about it.
> GLYNN: Ah, he knows. He's too ashamed to admit he took one up the ass. He won't talk; he'll just get even.[28]

The men do not describe rape as an act of violence done to the victim but rather as something that Schibetta *allowed* to happen to him ("he took one").

The warden shows no sympathy for the victim, and the show does not mitigate this opinion by introducing any of *Oz*'s other voices.

Later in the episode, it becomes clear that Schibetta has been severely traumatized by the rape. He repeatedly begs Burrano not to tell his (deceased) father about the rape, demonstrating both his mental instability and the shame he feels about having been sexually violated. The rapist Adebisi, on the other hand, struts arrogantly around the prison and is in no way punished for the rape. In fact, the episode reflects without criticism the entire structural economy by which rape attains its power in the prison. In this way, *Oz* actually reinforces the traditional associations of rape and power, masculinity and femininity. Adebisi gains power by committing rape, Schibetta loses power through having been sexually violated, and neither the show itself nor any character on the show demonstrates any sympathy toward the victim. Schibetta is sent to the psychiatric ward and doesn't speak another word for the remainder of the second season. In season 3, the Italians, who had been led by Schibetta, partner with Adebisi in order to sell drugs. Their humiliated former leader is forgotten in the psychiatric ward, and he does not appear for the remainder of season 3 or for any of season 4.

Surprisingly, however, Schibetta returns in season 5. Unit manager McManus introduces this plot development to the Italians, Chucky Pancamo (Chuck Zito) and Don Zanghi (John Palumbo), in his office:

PANCAMO: Schibetta? I thought he was in the loony bin.
MCMANUS: Well, not anymore. He's undergone long-term therapy, and I'm happy to say he's recovered.
ZANGHI: You mean, he got over being raped by Adebisi?
MCMANUS: I don't wanna minimize his trauma or pretend that he's exactly the way he was before, but he's learned to accept and deal with the situation. . . . It's gonna be rough on him for a few days, so all I ask is that you tread lightly.[29]

Schibetta is immediately reintroduced into the ward, but he remains the silent, stunned-looking character from season 2 for the remainder of the episode.

This changes when we next see him, as Schibetta makes a move to take over the gang of Italians again. Zanghi advises against it: "Adebisi took you down, man," he says, but Schibetta plans to change his status by parlaying with the head of the Muslim faction in the prison, Kareem Saïd (Eamonn Walker).[30] Again, however, *Oz* reminds us that in the hierarchies of the prison, a victim of rape ought not to get any respect. Saïd refuses to help, emphasizing not the act of violence itself but Schibetta's transformation into something other than he was before the rape.

SAÏD: You were raped by Adebisi.
SCHIBETTA: Yeah . . . well . . . I'm asking, uh . . .
SAÏD: I'm answering. You look like you may have resolved the rape in your own head. It doesn't change the facts. Here in Oz, you will always be known as one of Adebisi's bitches. No matter what you do, you cannot change that.
SCHIBETTA: No. I can.
SAÏD: Good luck.

Frustrated, Schibetta attempts to prove his mettle by means of a violent attack on the Aryans, but this does not work either. Schibetta is overpowered by three Aryans and is raped again—three and a half years after his first rape—this time by Schillinger.

The show's response to the violence done to Schibetta differs slightly in season 5 from the response in season 2. This time, the two people discussing the violence are the prison's doctor and its counselor—both women—and this time they care for Schibetta, stop the bleeding, and send him to the psychiatric ward. But if the characters care more about Schibetta in season 5, the storyline ends with an image that reinforces the same morality as that from season 2. The new chief of the Italians, Chucky Pancamo, looks at Schibetta through a window into the hospital unit and shakes his head. Just as it had in season 2, the show treats Schibetta as a case study for sexualized hierarchies, demonstrating how the violence of rape works to structure relations between prisoners. This season 5 episode underlines that Schibetta should have learned his lesson the first time and understood his place in the prison hierarchy. In this way *Oz* uncritically demonstrates that this violent sexual hierarchy, indeed the very system of sexual abjection that attaches power to violent acts of rape, is logical, even natural, and cannot be challenged successfully.

This point of view, however, shifted over time. In *Oz*'s early seasons, rape serves a strictly narrative function, giving various characters motivations for the acts of violence or other machinations they effect; in the show's final two seasons, however, *Oz* begins telling rape narratives about healing. The dramaturgical trajectory of rape in Oswald becomes one focused on processing and psychological binding rather than revenge or rage.

One can see a hint of this already in the episode in season 5 in which McManus reintroduces Schibetta into the prison: he refers to "trauma," and he says Schibetta has "learned to accept and deal with the situation." After he is violated in season 2, Schibetta is whisked off-screen and ignored, made superfluous to the show's storylines by the fact that he is no longer a player in the characters' power struggles. In season 5, by contrast, after Schibetta is raped he remains on the show, and *Oz* begins to focus on the process of his healing. Indeed, the question of how to recover, how to work through this traumatic experience, becomes Schibetta's weekly narrative arc.

The discourse also shifts in discussions among Oswald's staff members. When Sister Pete asks Warden Glynn to investigate the violation committed on Schibetta, his response is that the crime is beneath investigation, even after she reminds him that his own daughter has been victimized by rape:

GLYNN: This is different: this is Oz.
SISTER PETE: Rape is rape, Leo.
GLYNN: I don't agree. Here rape has a *leveling* effect. Peter Schibetta, from the day he arrived, wanted to be a tough guy, wanted to follow in his father's footsteps: running things, hurting people. Well, he got stopped by Adebisi. Now he got stopped again.[31]

This logic might explain Glynn's behavior, but *Oz* presents the warden as more and more out of touch with cultural mores as seasons 5 and 6 progress. "A leveling effect?!" Sister Pete rages at him, "You want rape to do your job?" And at the end of this episode in which Glynn has glibly described rape as just one more aspect of "survival of the fittest," the camera focuses on the bloody face of yet another weeping young white man who has been stripped, raped, and severely beaten by the Aryans.

Sister Pete's opinion is the point of view the show comes to endorse. If rape is a reality at Oswald, by the show's final season *Oz* has dispensed with '90s revenge plots and their "leveling effects." Now when we see Schibetta we see him dealing with having been raped: working through his feelings about having been violated, dealing with taunts from his rapist, in therapy with Sister Pete, deciding when to see his wife, but never plotting retaliation for the rape. *Oz* asks us to invest in the work of recovery. Indeed, in season 5, even Beecher and Schillinger begin meeting regularly with Sister Pete to discuss psychic healing from season 1's sexual violence. And in its final season—after Schibetta is killed unceremoniously by the other Italians—*Oz* introduces yet another rape–healing narrative as former rapist

James Robson (R. E. Rodgers) begins to talk about the violence he endured in a coercive sex relationship with another Aryan.

The Robson plot takes place over the final seven episodes of the series. It is the best example of *Oz*'s late-season conscientiousness toward male/male rape and the shift in focus toward psychology and testimony, and so it merits special attention, particularly because Lara Stemple, formerly of the advocacy group Stop Prisoner Rape (now Just Detention International), has called the main episode in this storyline "the most accurate and riveting fictional treatment of prisoner rape I've seen, read or heard."[32] Before I address the scene that Stemple cites—a sequence of group therapy led by Sister Pete and attended by Robson—I'll briefly explain the series-long narrative concerning this character.

We first meet Robson as an Aryan rapist who orally violates Beecher in the first episode of season 2. Beecher retaliates by (improbably) biting off the tip of Robson's penis.[33] Robson, however, heals from this wound, and in season 3 we find him socializing with the Aryans and taunting Cyril O'Reily with rape.[34] Throughout seasons 3, 4, and 5, Robson is a minor character seen almost exclusively with Schillinger. Threatening younger white prisoners with rape is part of his character's *modus operandi*. This happens explicitly in season 5, for example, when he says "I love a man who sweats," to a new prisoner and threatens, "There's two ways this can go, precious; and they both end up with my dick in your ass."[35] For most of seasons 2 through 5, in other words, *Oz* presents Robson as a two-dimensional image of homosexual predation analogous to Bogs in *Shawshank*.

This changes when Fontana gives Robson his own storyline in season 5. In a truly ludicrous plot twist, Schillinger and the other Aryans abandon Robson after he undergoes oral surgery for a gum transplant but is unable to verify that his new gums came from a white person. Desperate, Robson hacks at his gums with a razorblade, and after returning from the medical unit, he asks another white prisoner, Cutler (Brendan Kelly), for protection.[36] Cutler demands sex as well as humiliation. In a grotesque scene that emphasizes Cutler's unpredictability and sadism, Robson submits to being sodomized with a spoon, and we watch him scream in agony as he is penetrated.[37] Over the subsequent two episodes, Robson consents to various sexual acts with Cutler in order to gain protection. He also switches to wearing lipstick and earrings, as Beecher did in season 1. Finally, Robson murders Cutler, making it look like a suicide, and the Aryans inexplicably welcome him back, apparently forgetting why they abandoned him in the first place.

Robson begins seeing Sister Pete regularly, and he confesses to her that he was sexually molested as a small child. During a visit with his wife some time after Cutler's death, Robson becomes violent and his wife gets angry; she calls him a "cocksucker."[38] Robson is furious, but because he has begun visiting with Sister Pete, they discuss his anger together. Through tears he tells Sister Pete that Cutler raped him. This isn't precisely accurate according to the government's definition of rape, but *Oz* presents Robson's confession as the accurate reading of what the audience saw in previous episodes.

Next, Robson begins attending a therapy group led by Sister Pete, in which five men who are not regular characters on *Oz* speak candidly about having been raped.[39] An older Black prisoner, for example, tells the group that his rapist: "bought me for two cartons of Kools. . . . I was rented out. . . . Three dollars for a blow job, five for anal sex." A young white man says:

> I came to Oz nine months ago. I—I was a virgin, so right away I was targeted. So, I kept breaking the rules, refusing to go to work or take a shower, shit like that. They put me on Special Restrictions. I figured I'd be safe locked in my cell all day. But then . . . they put this lowlife in my cell, and he . . . he beat me till I said yes. As he was doing it, I could hear the TV in the C.O.s' office. They were watching *I Love Lucy*.

The other three men tell their stories, as well, and the sequence ends as each prisoner says the phrase "I had no choice." Robson joins in: "I had no choice."

The sustained focus on rape in this episode is unique for *Oz*. Although rape had been a large component of the show's subject matter since its first episode, no episode with Schibetta or Beecher ever spent this amount of airtime on the emotional difficulties of having been sexually violated. For Stemple of Stop Prisoner Rape, the stories told in this group therapy session truthfully depict rape survivor testimony: "SPR couldn't have done it any better," Stemple says, "and I wouldn't be surprised if the research for this scene included the letters from survivors that SPR posts on its website."[40] This therapy sequence occurred midway through one of *Oz*'s three final episodes, and its treatment of male/male rape was an important contribution to the discourse of male/male rape in the United States, airing over a year prior to the rape plots on both *The Shield* and *Six Feet Under*.

The group therapy sequence on *Oz* charts four very important developments in US American discourse about male/male rape in the early 2000s.

First, *Oz* turns away from the attitude that rape might have the "leveling effect" proposed by the warden. The young white man who is targeted because he is young and inexperienced certainly doesn't need to be stopped from trying to consolidate power in the prison; the older Black man who is purchased and then rented out is not trying to be "a tough guy." *Oz* is clear that rape cannot be mistaken as somehow "good" for prisoners or in any way a valid part of their punishment. Second, by placing these rape stories in a group, by dealing with them as similar to one another, the episode rejects the idea that rape is something that happens to one man because he is weaker or whiter or more "feminine" than other prisoners. (Incidentally, the warden's flawed argument is precisely the opposite—that a man is raped because he is too strong, not because he is too weak.) By placing these very different narratives of rape next to one another, *Oz* makes an argument that *rape* is the problem rather than any particular characteristic possessed by or any particular action made by the violate man. The common denominator in the stories is how violent they are.

The episode makes a third point by underlining repeatedly that rape in prison is condoned and facilitated by the very guards who are supposed to be preventing violence among these prisoners, as well as the men and women responsible for the administration of the prison. I quoted the narrative in the group therapy sequence in which the guards blithely watch *I Love Lucy* while a man is raped; in another of these narratives, a prisoner says, "I asked for a kit to collect evidence to prove what happened. The C.O. waited two days to take me to the infirmary. . . . By the time the nurse examined me, there was nothing left to find"; in yet another story in the sequence, a prisoner reports that "The hack told me 'Quit whining,' to stand up and fight." This episode of *Oz* makes the argument that rape is preventable and that accusations of rape are verifiable—if only the men and women running the prison were interested in rape prevention.

As a part of this argument for similarities among rape victims, Robson's inclusion in the group therapy session makes a fourth and final important point: *Oz* understands Robson's coercive sex relationship with Cutler—in which he *technically* consented to sex with the other man—as rape. Robson says, "I had no choice," and the show's writers treat this without irony or skepticism. I noted in this book's introduction that discussions of consent appear almost nowhere in male/male rape discourse, and this scene in *Oz* is one of the first to treat the topic. Importantly, the sequence is *critical* of consent as a rubric for evaluating harm. Robson and the other men's repetition of "I had no choice" takes a point of view of prison sexual activity that is in disagreement both with the US government's definition of rape, which hinges on consent, and with theories of prison sexual activity such as Mark Fleisher and Jessie Krienert's—theories that argue that most sexual contact in prison is either consensual or coercive and that the word *violent* is an inaccurate descriptor for most sex in prisons.[41] In *The Myth of Prison Rape*, Fleisher and Krienert argue that coercive sex is nonviolent: it is sex initially performed or submitted to against the will of the victim, but this sex is agreed to as a part of prison culture and prison economy, and violence is not necessarily a component of such activity. For Robson on *Oz*, such a description makes no sense. He may officially consent to being sodomized with a spoon, but the event is certainly not pleasurable for Robson, and he would never have consented to it under circumstances other than those created by his incarceration. In other words, Robson may appear to have had the illusion of consent, but he does not exaggerate when he says he didn't have a choice. To modify slightly an argument from rape scholar Ellen Rooney, a "subject who can act only to consent or refuse to consent is in fact denied subjectivity."[42] Robson consents *against his will* to a relationship with Cutler, and this episode contends that coerced sex is rape.

More important to the history of male/male rape discourse than the claims and arguments this episode makes, however, are the narrative techniques *Oz* uses to make those claims. Over time *Oz*'s treatment of rape shifted from representations designed to entertain through terror or titillation to those designed to entertain through emotional identification and the pleasures of the confession. This move began as early as season 5, in which Schibetta and Beecher both discussed the experience of having been violated with Sister Pete but, in season 6, confession and testimony are the chief elements of the Robson storyline. This was a component, documented by Joe Wlodarz, of a larger generic shift for *Oz* as Fontana transformed the show into more and more of a soap opera, but it also coincided with a change in the larger culture of the United States, in which men were becoming legible as potential victims of rape and male/male rape was emerging as a criminal, psychiatric, and sociological issue.[43]

I argued in Chapter 4 that an injunction to silence is already embedded in the act of rape, and I noted as well the *Encyclopedia of Rape*'s statement that "Lack of reporting and community awareness creates a lack of visibility of male rape and reinforces the isolation and silence of all victims."[44] Indeed, one finds in almost all of the sociological and criminological literature on male/male rape what appears to be an exasperated frustration with victims' desire not to report the violence they have experienced to the "proper authorities."⁴⁵ I want to avoid, however, the implied judgment made by the *Encyclopedia* and other resources that silence about rape is incorrect or "closeted" behavior and that speaking out about rape is always "the right thing to do." We would certainly all understand the phenomenon of male/male rape better if we had more data and information on its incidence, its circumstances, its perpetrators, and the experiences of its victims. But this desire for more information is a testament to our own wish to understand male/male rape, to make it speak and testify to its own meaning; it is not necessarily linked with rape victims' own desires.

Indeed, it is worth asking how this injunction to speak, to heal oneself through testifying to the injury one has suffered, is linked to the power-knowledge Foucault says is embedded in the apparatus of the confessional. Foucault describes the requirement for confession in the first volume of his *History of Sexuality*, where he finds that:

> The obligation to confess is now relayed through so many different points, is so deeply ingrained in us, that we no longer perceive it as the effect of a power that constrains us; on the contrary, it seems to us that truth, lodged in our most secret nature, "demands" only to surface; that if it fails to do so, this is because a constraint holds it in place, the violence of a power weighs it down, and it can finally be articulated only at the price of a kind of liberation.⁴⁶

The idea that "confession frees, but power reduces one to silence" is repeated frequently in rape-survivor literature, but as Foucault charts the history of Catholic penance in *Abnormal*, his 1974–1975 lectures, he finds that the topic of the confessional has, for centuries, been specifically a confession of *sexual activity*, a series of "offenses against a number of sexual rules."⁴⁷ The injunction to confess, to testify to the details of rape or to speak of oneself as a rape victim or rape survivor, then, is fundamentally related to our curiosity about and interest in the supposed inscrutability of male/male rape and, concomitantly, to our society's concepts of "truth" and the normal. Male rape victims, in the name of healing themselves, are asked to speak their truth, to explain, to make sense *for us* of what has happened to them.

Foucault locates in this an "examination [that] is a meticulous passage through the body, a sort of anatomy of the pleasures of the flesh."⁴⁸ The confessant is asked to describe the experience of his body through anatomization and articulation. This injunction, which demands that the victim speak, makes perfect sense as an antidote to the confusion many express about how to handle male rape victims and the desire for silence that many rape victims describe (given the cultural taboos that place responsibility for having been raped with the victim and also relentlessly feminize those victims). While rape itself, then, works to confer silence and shame onto the violated body, apparatuses associated with psychiatry, the law, and news-media attempt to capture, transform into meaning, and otherwise exert power over those same violated bodies through the demand to confess.

The representation of this injunction to confess sexual violation, however, arrives contemporaneously with the move of male/male rape to television. It appears nowhere in the films of the 1970s we examined in Chapter 3 or those of the 1990s in Chapter 4. As discourse about male/male rape adapted to the new medium, confession would become the obvious paradigm for how to speak about violation. Television, as the performance theorist Christopher Grobe argues, has been teaching us "to look at life as though it were a confession" at least since the mid-1970s.[49] In 1990s cinema and in early episodes of *Oz*, men get revenge on their rapists. On television in the twenty-first century, by contrast, men *confess* to having been raped. This new method for the discursive examination of male/male rape, so clear in the final two seasons of *Oz* in 2002 and 2003, would become typical of television's later treatment of the subject.

The Basketball Team Testifies

On season 2 of John Ridley's *American Crime*, the injunction to confess takes center stage. The ten-episode season describes the reverberations and effects of a late-night sexual assault on a fifteen-year-old male by a seventeen-year-old male. *American Crime* is an anthology series, where each season tells a different story; season two's plot takes place at a wealthy private high school in Indiana called Leyland and concerns, more than anything else, the members of the school's basketball team and their parents. The rape itself happens at an annual event called the Captain's Party where, it is revealed later, male members of the team typically coerce younger high school girls into sex as a Leyland school tradition. The Captain's Party never appears on-screen in *American Crime*, even in flashback. Instead, Ridley treats the party as a crime scene, so that "the truth" of what happened on the night in question seems permanently irrecoverable; the show's narrative instead consists of characters attempting to describe the events of the party in different ways and from different perspectives—with the goal of changing the story, shifting focus, or affixing blame for what happened onto characters other than themselves. To Ridley's credit, however, even as *American Crime* gets more and more complex, the young victim and his assailant stay central to the story, and there is no episode without reference to the violence committed on the boy's body.

As a substitute for showing its audience what happened at the Captain's Party, *American Crime* instead reveals—over the course of its ten episodes—what different people *say* happened, making confession rather than action the focus of the drama. Television is, of course, a medium that frequently has been concerned with disciplinary apparatuses—police stations, hospital wards, emergency rooms, legal offices, courtrooms, high schools—with the plot of the procedural so often consisting of the diagnosis and description of outliers from an imagined populace of viewers, the abnormal, the undisciplined, the criminal. In *American Crime*, all of these apparatuses are on display, but because the teenagers at the center of the drama are rarely interested in communicating with their parents or other disciplinary authorities, the show stages the increasing hysteria of its adult characters as they attempt to capture, understand, and manage their children, with—most important for the dramaturgy of *American Crime*—the demand that these young people speak.

American Crime's second season begins in darkness. Title cards flash the text of a 9-1-1 call on the screen. The operator asks the nature of the emergency, and we hear the voice of a woman say, while we simultaneously read on the screen: "I want to report a rape." The quotation marks around the phrase are included on the title card, and this punctuation seems to work from the very beginning to frame this phrase *as something said by someone else*. The audience cannot see the speaker and does not yet know who will say these words. "I want to report a rape" is a disembodied phrase, here, marked from the first as a citation. This moment sets up the content of the episode very clearly: We know that a rape has occurred or that accusations about a rape will be made, but we do not know what has happened.

The episode moves in a linear fashion beginning some days after the incident. We see blurry pictures shared on cellular devices, and the camera focuses on white teenager Taylor Blaine (Connor Jessup) looking troubled and terrified. Early in the episode he tells his mother (Lili Taylor), "I never should have gone to that school . . . I don't want to go back to that place. I don't."[50] Taylor is plainly distraught, and we hear his voice break and witness his inability to speak. The audience, of course, can already surmise what has happened—Taylor has been raped. The suspense and pleasure of the first episode, in other words, are built around the audience waiting for the boy to tell someone else a secret that the audience itself already knows. Structurally, the episode does not ask us to witness a rape, nor does it attempt to surprise us with the rape as a plot twist. Instead, the audience is asked to anticipate the confession: *I was raped*.

This confession happens no fewer than five times in episode 1. In the first of these, Taylor's girlfriend confesses to Mrs. Blaine that they went to the Captain's Party. She shares photos with Mrs. Blaine, which the camera shows us. The second confession is at home with Taylor himself, who tells his mother quite plainly that he doesn't know what happened, saying instead that "Everything got messed up. . . . I don't know. I don't remember." Finally he says, "I wasn't lying. I just—I didn't tell you because I was . . . I was ashamed, I was . . . Mom, I . . . I think they did something to me . . . I think someone did something . . . to me."

The episode's third confession occurs when Mrs. Blaine comes to see Leyland's headmaster, Dr. Graham (Felicity Huffman). This is the confession most important to the show's plot and the one to which the episode devotes the most time. Mrs. Blaine confesses what has happened to her son, and *American Crime* displaces the experience from Taylor onto Mrs. Blaine. She confesses her son's rape as though it were her own. "My son was assaulted," Mrs. Blaine says definitively. Again, the episode focuses on confession itself, the slow unfurling of the "truth" of what happened:

MRS. BLAINE: And then they assaulted him.
DR. GRAHAM: Physically assaulted. [*Pause.*] Sexually assaulted?
MRS. BLAINE: Sexual.

It is plainly difficult for Mrs. Blaine to say this, but then Dr. Graham asks about Taylor's own confession:

DR. GRAHAM: What did he say that makes you believe that?
MRS. BLAINE: It's what he didn't say. It's things he couldn't talk about.

Taylor isn't talking; Taylor doesn't want to speak: "I don't want to deal with the police," he will tell his mother in episode 3, "I just want it to be over."[51] But later episodes make it even clearer that instead of waiting for her son to speak, Mrs. Blaine chooses to speak for him, deciding what he would say if he were to speak.

Taylor and his body are asked to speak again and again as the show continues. In episode 2, the police say they can do nothing unless Taylor himself talks to them about what has happened. An examining nurse explains that "we're going to take a look at your anal area," a phrase pronounced very clearly on the soundtrack as the camera watches Taylor's face and a tear hangs in his eye.[52] Taylor's girlfriend, too, asks him how he is. Then there are Taylor's therapist and a counselor at Taylor's new school, as well as the detectives who begin to work on the case. For her part, Mrs. Blaine constantly asks Taylor to explain himself. Even when Taylor confesses to her, in episode 4, that he has been experimenting with homosexual sex, she responds only with the demand that he speak more: "Why didn't you tell me the truth?" she asks her son. "Did you think that I wouldn't—did you think that I would feel different? Did you think that I wouldn't love you because of the way you felt? Do you think that—do you really think that I can't love you?"[53] Four questions in rapid succession—she doesn't tell him that she loves him or assure him that things will be fine; she asks for more information. Taylor doesn't respond.

Taylor's rapist is revealed to be an angry young man named Eric (Joey Pollari) whom we have met in the show's first episode and who comes out as gay in episode 4. The sequences surrounding Eric, like those related to Taylor, are focused on the scene of confession and not on the plot twist. In fact, the audience has already been told—as early as episode 2—that Eric is meeting men for anonymous hookups via Grindr. The audience, again, is not asked to wait to know if Eric is gay but rather to wait for Eric to *confess* that he is gay. The audience can easily deduce that Eric is Taylor's rapist; we look not for the truth but for the confession. In episode 4 Eric confesses to one of these but not the other.

The disciplinary apparatus, perhaps not surprisingly, finds a much more willing confessant in the rapist than in the boy who was raped, and Eric is quick to justify his conduct to Leyland's basketball coach (Timothy Hutton):

COACH: Did you assault that boy?
ERIC: He wanted it.
COACH: Aw, jeez. You sound like a rapist.
ERIC: I didn't rape him. He wanted it. He wanted to hook up. Me and Taylor . . . he planned it. He—we were supposed to meet up that night. He was texting me, emailing.

The reason Eric says that he did not say anything sooner is because "Then everyone would know I'm gay." Circumstances have forced Eric to confess not that he is a rapist but that he is gay. Or, to put it another way, Eric is forced to confess not that he *did* something but that he *is* something.

When I cited *The History of Sexuality* in Chapter 2, I noted Foucault's famous description of the epistemological mutation of the sodomite (who has committed a crime) into the homosexual (who is a species): "the practice of sodomy" ceases to exist and becomes instead "homosexuality," a description of an interior compulsion.[54] I wish here to connect Foucault's description of the creation of the homosexual with a similar proposal he made the year prior to *The History of Sexuality*. In the latter half of *Discipline and Punish*, Foucault argues that "the penitentiary apparatus" and "the whole technological programme that accompanies it" do not apply themselves to a "convict" and certainly not to an "offence." The penitentiary applies itself to, and thus is productive of, "a rather different object, one defined by variables which at the outset at least were not taken into account in the sentence, for they were relevant only for a corrective technology. This other character, whom the penitentiary apparatus substitutes for the convicted offender, is the *delinquent*."[55] As Foucault describes him, the delinquent becomes indistinguishable from his crime so that (like the homosexual) his crime describes not an activity but an essential component of his subjecthood: "The introduction of the 'biographical' is important in the history of penality. Because it establishes the 'criminal' as existing before the crime and even outside it. And, for this reason, a psychological causality, duplicating the juridical attribution of responsibility, confuses its effects."[56] For Foucault, the "biological"—under which might fall case studies, family histories, attributions of the term "at risk," as well as diagnoses by psychiatrists and behavioral therapists—opposes itself directly to a notion of responsibility: no longer is the criminal responsible for the punctual act of his crime; instead the delinquent is identified with that which makes him delinquent. The delinquent *is* his crime, and those who commit crimes are delinquents—criminals in their essence, prior to the crime itself.

Accordingly, the question of whether or not Eric raped Taylor begins to recede in importance for *American Crime* as each of the boys becomes a kind of person, identified with a sexuality defined by people other than themselves. Taylor, for his part, consistently denies that he is gay, and although Eric frequently claims that identity, he tells the men he meets on Grindr that he just likes to kiss. Both of these young white men, however, become "gay" in the eyes of the disciplinary apparatuses working to capture them.[57] Perhaps even more troubling for the question of violation, as the young men begin to share the identity "gay," the possibility that one of them has committed violence and that the other has been the victim of that violence begins to seem less and less plausible. As Lynn Higgins has noted in an excellent essay on rape in film, "rape is a special kind of crime in relation to narrative" because "a rape defense can rest on the claim that what occurred was not a rape and so the question is not *who committed* the crime, but *whether a crime occurred at all.*"[58] By mid-season, most of the characters on *American Crime* have given up finding the truth of what happened at the Captain's Party. Whether or not Eric raped Taylor becomes merely a question of perspective. While everyone—including the medium of television itself—demands that both boys testify to their "truth," the rape is "discursively transformed into another kind of story."[59]

Disciplinary Structures

Although *American Crime* uses the injunction to confess in order to tell its story of male/male rape, it uses more traditional narrative techniques to analyze what it sees as the causes of the rape: the homophobia already at work at Leyland, the misogynist and violent sentiments held by the basketball team as a collective, and the almost total denial of affection on the part of the boys' families. It is these that finally become the subject of *American Crime*. If Eric is afraid that he will be ostracized by his team for being gay, his fears are immediately confirmed by the coach when he abandons the young man and leaves the room after Eric tells him he's gay. Indeed, both Eric's and Taylor's families respond with homophobia. The school administrators, the police department—all of them treat both Eric and Taylor in ways that seem designed to make the boys feel as though they've been keeping a guilty and dirty secret. Eric's family is particularly virulent, with his brother tagging "GOD HATES FAGS," a phrase popularized by the Westboro Baptist Church in 2001, on a wall at his school.[60]

That one of the young men sexually violated the other becomes less important to everyone than the idea that two young men might want to have sex with one another. But this slight shift in *American Crime*'s perspective illuminates male/male rape as an extension of structural elements already component to the way young men are frequently socialized in groups. One of the reasons *American Crime* struck some critics as timely or "ripped from the headlines," was that in January 2016, the month *American Crime* first aired, newsmedia reported the rape of a young man of fifteen with a pool cue at a Tennessee high school. The boy, a freshman on the basketball team, had been attacked just before the Christmas holidays by three older male athletes. The story, in fact, uncovered "an ongoing pattern of assaults allegedly committed under the guise of hazing, in which younger basketballers were regularly raped by varsity players."[61] In April 2015 the *Dallas Observer* much more pruriently reported a separate case in which five male volunteer firefighters were arrested for the rape of a male trainee. The girlfriend of one of the rapists, who filmed the assault, was also arrested. The Texas news outlet described the rape in graphic detail, reporting that "the men committing the assault initially planned on using a broomstick before deciding a link of chorizo in the fridge was a better choice."[62] Eight people were eventually indicted in the case, after the chief and assistant chief of the Ellis County Emergency Service District 6 Volunteer Fire Department met with the assailants in an effort to cover up the rape, referring to it as "funny shit."[63] These two news stories contemporary with *American Crime* describe lower-level authority figures who bullied others while higher-level authority figures condoned their activities or feigned ignorance. Rape, in both of these of these cases, is not aberrant; neither does it appear to be understood as homosexual sex. To the contrary, rape, in each of these incidents, is an appalling but logical extension of a regime or structure of sexualized bullying already at work in the humiliation and discipline of teammates or recruits.

What is notable about these stories of violation from 2015 is the simultaneous ubiquity and disavowal of sexuality embedded in the very structures of these organizations. The newsmedia recounting these incidents generally take a shocked tone, and most report the rapes with care and delicacy, but the astonishment expressed at each of these incidents betrays a willful ignorance of the ways that masculinist organizations such as volunteer fire brigades and high school sports teams are structured by the men who run them. Even in relationships in which penetration does not figure explicitly, in which *the loser* is not explicitly equated with *the screwed*, or in which masculinist bullying has not "gone this far," power relationships are frequently figured using sexualized (and often gendered) binaries. The queer theorist Michael Moon describes these relations as something we might best call sadomasochism, noting the very real presence of sadistic and masochistic pleasures in ostensibly nonsexual power relations:

> [Sadomasochistic] object-choices flourish in many institutional settings; relations of inflicting and receiving psychological and physical pain, with the sexual element of this interchange suppressed or not, are considered

not shocking aberrations but ordinary and even necessary practice in the military, in prisons, in many corporate organizations, athletic teams, and schools of all levels. It is the domestication of many of these procedures into "discipline," the daily practice of institutional "law and order," with only those interchanges that are most flagrantly sexually enacted isolated and stigmatized as "sexual perversion," that conduces most of us to disavow our insiders' knowledge of sadomasochistic pleasures most of the time.[64]

Moon's argument here ought to suggest to us that male/male rape exists on a continuum of "ordinary and even necessary practice[s]" in many homosocial settings, and that rape does not necessarily occupy a position apart from this continuum.

Moon offers a way for us to consider sexual violation as an extension of the everyday—indeed almost banal—practices of sadistic and masochistic pleasure that undergird male homosocial relations in the most quotidian of situations: the football field, the boardroom, a game of pool in a local bar, the floor of the New York Stock Exchange. Moon's analysis asks us to *re*-sexualize these situations, to begin to note the erotic dimensions of, say, a hostile takeover, a basketball victory, or a cornhole match. We might, in other words, begin to think of an act of rape committed by a man against another man as one more way of *screwing* an opponent, a complex but concrete extension of the erotics already embedded in structures of male power.

American Crime exposes these structures in many intriguing ways throughout the season, but they become central to episode 6 when, after Eric returns to Leyland and the basketball team, his teammates decline to speak to him and refuse to pass him the ball during a game. As they lose the game, Eric hears an attendee yell the epithet *fag* at him. The crowd's hostility, however, is not aimed at Eric alone: someone else yells (as an insult), "Way to go, ladies."[65] This same episode finds Taylor visiting an older man who helped raise him and with whom he used to attend Indianapolis Colts games as a younger boy; Taylor tells him that the reason he stopped wanting to go see the Colts play was that on one occasion this adopted father figure, upset with the team, began to yell, repeatedly, "You guys are playing like a bunch of queers." These insults that refer to sportsmen as "ladies" or "queers" are homophobic, certainly, but they are also almost unremarkable as that simple, standard misogyny that equates losing players to women, an invective tradition often directed at sports teams who aren't playing as well as their fans would like them to play. A gendered and sexualized hierarchy related to winning and losing is not only, then, a structural component of the team's own dynamics but also part of the larger culture of masculinity for whom the game is designed as entertainment.

The boy who is the primary target of this abuse on *American Crime* himself underlines this masculinist structure. As Eric returns to the basketball team, Leyland's headmaster asks him to do an interview with a gay journalist and, in a fury, Eric tells the reporter: "I'm gay, but I'm not a faggot!" *American Crime* aired on network television, and the show bleeped out the expletives *asshole* and *shit*, but the explicitly misogynist terms *fag*, *faggot*, and *bitch* crossed the FCC-regulated airwaves as clearly in 2016 as on *Cagney & Lacey* in 1985. Later in the episode, as the basketballers (sans Eric) commiserate over the lost game at a pizza parlor, the team captain delivers an extended tirade about Taylor and "bitches," complaining, "You know what the messed up part is? It doesn't matter how crazy they are, you gotta treat 'em like they're real people. You have to. Back in the day be like— [*here he gestures three slaps*]—handle your business; it's done. But now man, it's just—bitches just get to act how they act." The episode ends with four members of the team finding Taylor and beating him severely. Eric himself facilitates this violence by phoning Taylor and asking him to meet. "They were looking to mess somebody up," Eric tells the police in a later episode. "It was Taylor, or it was me. Far as they cared, any fag'll do."[66] The team, in other words, *produces* the "fag" through an act of violence. This time the violence results in a bruised face and a bloody lip rather than torn anal tissue, but what occurs in the episode is that Eric attempts to rejoin his team by helping four of them break the body of another. Eric grabs at the possibility of becoming something other than a "faggot"; he can see himself as a man again by helping the others hurt Taylor (again). If *American Crime*, in its later episodes, begins to see both boys as possessing an identical sexuality, the show is also clear that this identity with one another does not protect them. Instead, the masculine structures already embedded in the basketball team's values work to differentiate between bodies, including some and excluding others.

Discourse about male/male rape has markedly shifted from 1990s revenge stories that focus on the suffering male body into a new 2000s trend toward confession and a search for the "truth" of rape, but all of these narratives continue to describe the breaking of one body in order to restore the wholeness of another as central to the fantasy of masculinity. The violate man is produced so that another might momentarily convince himself of an inviolability he can never truly possess. Although the final episodes of *American Crime* move ever further away from the act of male/male rape with which the season began, the show's focus on the team as a whole continually highlights the structures, values, and practices that created that act of sexual violence in the first place. When Eric says "I'm gay, but I'm not a faggot" he articulates a logic that on the surface could seem nonsensical. To the disciplinary apparatuses attempting to capture Taylor and Eric, after all, men who have sex with men all seem to be identical to one another. But this isn't quite true in US American culture, and *American Crime* parses the distinction carefully. In the violent, masculinist logic that the show describes, some men are actually "bitches," and one way a man can prove that he isn't one is to demonstrate—through rape, through winning at a sport, through beating up a rival—that someone else is.

Performing Confession

To illustrate the continuing power of confession as central to the way we consume male/male rape in the period following the early 2000s, I close this chapter by discussing two recent books—with two very different aims—and two extraordinary British television series. This is properly a chapter about US American TV, so none of these four narratives truly belongs, but together, these four texts—*Boy Erased* (2016), *Yes, Daddy* (2021), *I May Destroy You* (2020), and *Baby Reindeer* (2024)—map the influence of early 2000s televisual treatments of male/male rape. These four texts illustrate our current discourse around male/male rape in the twenty-first century, our fascination with confession, our insistence on truth and testimony, and the different possible futures we imagine for the violate man.[67]

Boy Erased, Garrard Conley's memoir about undergoing gay conversion therapy at an organization called Love in Action, coming out as gay to his Baptist family, and growing into his twenties, had a powerful impact on the conversation in popular media about ex-gay movements, and especially on laws banning "therapeutic" treatment of LGBT youth in the mid-2010s.[68] Conley's memoir was understood, in large part, to be "testimony," designed to communicate the truth of these religious organizations. Reviewing the book for the LGBTQ website Edge Media Network, Noe Kamelamela writes, for example, that "Testimonies like *Boy Erased* are a necessary part of getting rid of ex-gay ministries or, really, any kind of program in which the explicit aim is to change the identity (in this case, the sexuality) of the subjects." Kamelamela sees *Boy Erased* as coming "from Conley's need to purge himself and raise public awareness of the harm he suffered in a Love in Action program."[69] The book is, indeed, a testimonial narrative, in which Conley recounts his experiences with his religious family, his struggles with his parents, his doubts and self-hate, as well as his experience of being raped by a friend at a Presbyterian college.

Of course, the entirety of *Boy Erased* is a confession; this is basic to the form of the memoir. Conley tells his story in the first person, and it is the truth of his story that is so emotionally powerful and has connected so well with readers. Importantly, however, Conley also recounts his experience of rape using many of the confessional storytelling techniques that we can see at work in *American Crime*. Like the events at the Captain's Party, we learn that Conley has been raped by his friend David *before* he tells us how it happened. This means, as I noted earlier, that sexual violence does not function as a plot twist, nor do we anticipate the event of the rape as a kind of ancient tragic reversal like we do in a novel like *The City and the Pillar Revised*. Instead, we wait for the violate man to confess his violation. Conley tells us the end before he tells us the story itself by setting us up for what will happen: "I sometimes believed he might not have raped me just a few months later . . . if I'd only chosen to carry my own boxes into the dorm."[70] At this point—in the space of the ellipsis in the quotation—Conley tells us in vivid detail what physically happened and the violence David committed. Conley's memoir then narrates his relationship with David, their church attendance, their burgeoning friendship, and David's strident religious convictions; the rape that we know will happen hangs over these interactions as he tells them, before Conley again describes his experience of the rape for his readers some twenty pages later. It is also important to note that in the text of the memoir we're reading Conley confesses, but within the story he is telling us he doesn't confess to having been raped; instead—and here too you should see echoes of *American Crime*—he confesses to being gay.[71] He wonders if the rape has made him permanently gay, if he is somehow at fault for the violence enacted upon him.[72]

Boy Erased explores in rich detail what it means to be a survivor of rape, how a person might build a life as a survivor. Rape is, in no way, the end of Conley's world in *Boy Erased*. By placing Conley's memoir within the context of the new confessional mode for male/male rape narratives, it is not my aim to critique the narrative choices made by Conley in his memoir—it's a moving story to which I relate very strongly, and it's well told. I want, rather, to be clear about the storytelling modes in operation in the second decade of the twenty-first century. *Boy Erased* mobilizes a recent popular interest in consuming the confessions of male/male rape victims. It responds to a demand that the violate man tell the truth about rape, that he confess not only his sexuality but also his experience of violation.

Male/male rape confessions are multiplied exponentially in Jonathan Parks-Ramage's critically acclaimed but extraordinarily shallow 2021 novel *Yes, Daddy*. The book's protagonist, Jonah, is drugged and raped repeatedly by a gang of wealthy, older men, who imprison him in the Hamptons. The novel in its entirety is told as a confessional—in the second person—as a letter to Mace, a fellow rape victim, and we learn of the rapes on the first page of the book's prologue as Jonah describes going to a rape trial where he's a witness. He is to testify to the rapes he and Mace experienced in this first trial, but he lies on the stand, claims that Mace is lying—this is a man who saved his life and was a survivor of systematic rape and imprisonment—and says that nothing happened. As in *American Crime* and *Boy Erased*, early confession of the rape in *Yes, Daddy* necessitates its *retelling*, and much of the remainder of the novel directs its attention toward anticipating the rapes, when they will happen and how they will happen, toward, in other words, Jonah's next confession.

After escaping the rapists but lying about them on the witness stand, Jonah begins writing exposés of sexual abuse for an online news agency—coercing others to confess to having been violated—then he gets canceled by folks on Twitter who find out about his lies, becomes an alcoholic, and joins a Christian megachurch in which he makes a vow of celibacy. At his new church, Jonah testifies even more. He tells his Christian support group about having been raped, but in this confession, rape becomes one part in a longer story of a "sinful" life prior to his life in the church: "I told them my entire story, the plot to my private horror film that started with my childhood, climaxed with Richard [one of his rapists], and ended with the miracle where I was saved by Christ, saved by the people with kind faces who sat across from me week after week."[73] The pastor then convinces Jonah to share his "testimony" with the church as a whole. He does this partly because he's in love with Matt, another ex-gay parishioner who has taken a vow of celibacy: "I told my story again and again onstage at the Hammerstein Ballroom—at the ten A.M. service, the noon service, the two P.M. service, and the five P.M. service. . . . I delivered my testimony four times in one day as Matt led the rock band behind me."[74] Jonah tells his story to the megachurch as a kind of penance for having lied about his fellow victim, Mace, on the witness stand, but the confessions in these latter chapters of *Yes, Daddy* are confessions of guilt about homosexuality to a homophobic church. The sexual violence he suffered becomes part of a litany of his own sexual "sins," rooted in Jonah's homosexual desires. Near the end of the novel—in one of the many echoes of *Boy Erased* in *Yes, Daddy*—Matt, the celibate ex-gay Christian whom Jonah loves, rapes him the evening after his long day of church testimony.[75] This sexually violent betrayal prompts Jonah, finally, to come clean about having lied on the stand. He issues a public statement confessing to having been raped, naming one of his rapists (but not the others), and telling the truth about his own lies in the earlier rape trial.

Yes, Daddy exploits almost every male/male trope I've described throughout this book. Rape stands in for homosexual sex in Parks-Ramage's novel; the two are conflated not only by the homophobic churchgoers but also by the homophobic protagonist.[76] The (several) rape victims in this novel are all young, white, and good-looking. At the novel's end, Jonah even gets revenge on one of his rapists by burning down his house in the Hamptons and nearly killing him. But the most pernicious and troubling of the male/male rape tropes exploited by *Yes, Daddy* is the novel's refusal to imagine a future for the violate man. Jonah, Parks-Ramage's reprehensible protagonist, returns to his family at the end of *Yes, Daddy*, and his belief in Christianity seems strengthened, but Mace, the young man he accused of lying about his victimization, commits suicide after Jonah's final confession. Confession doesn't save Mace, and he gets no revenge. He writes to Jonah and forgives him for everything but, in a devastating twist, he gets addicted to methamphetamines and slits his wrists in a condominium in Albuquerque. In many ways *Yes, Daddy* understands victimization by rape as the end of the world, and although the novel can imagine one very strange religious and celibate future for its protagonist, it relegates Mace to a bloody, hopeless death. In *Yes, Daddy*, the violate man is a man without a future.

In a very different mode and medium, Michaela Coel's series *I May Destroy You*, which aired on BBC One in the UK and HBO in the US beginning in June 2020, is a show that centers on various incidents of sex, consent, sexual assault, and rape. *I May Destroy You* is fundamentally confessional: Coel began writing the series after she was drugged and raped while working on her earlier series *Chewing Gum*, and Coel plays a version of herself in the show. She has been open about her experience as a rape survivor, and part of the publicity surrounding *I May Destroy You* involved Coel discussing her experiences. As she told Anne McElvoy in an interview in the *Guardian*, "If you are alive to reflect on a dark time, and keep returning there, it means you've survived it and you can keep going there until you've got what you need from returning."[77] What's extraordinary about *I May Destroy You* is that, although its focus is on Coel's character Arabella, her discovery of having been drugged and raped, her experience with the police, and her attempts to move forward with her life, nearly each episode includes a new and different twist or event, in which questions of sexual assault, consent, and rape become more complex. Arabella's experience of having been drugged and raped fundamentally transforms her world into an unsafe space, one in which she finds herself and her friends confronting and transgressing boundaries she had never before even considered. *I May Destroy You* is fascinating, frank, and smart, and it is also unsparing in its examination of its protagonist and her own failings.[78]

In the fourth episode of the series, Arabella's friend Kwame (Paapa Essiedu) is sexually violated by a hookup following a consensual sexual encounter. We see the violence on-screen, and it happens in real time without cuts. Kwame says, quite plainly, "We are not having sex again," but Malik (Samson Ajewole) says, "This isn't sex." Malik pins him down with his entire body and humps him. Kwame is plainly in distress, and he escapes from the apartment as soon as he can.[79] In the following episode, Kwame goes with Arabella and their friend Terry (Weruche Opia) to see the police about her case. The officers talk about different acts that qualify as rape, including nonconsensual condom removal. Kwame's eyes are very large during the entirety of this discussion. He's clearly thinking about something, wondering if what happened to him could be considered rape by the police. Kwame goes back to the police at the end of the episode to report a crime, but the policeman who takes his information is callous and homophobic. He wants to know specifically whether or not Malik penetrated him, and when Kwame isn't quite sure, the policeman becomes apathetic to the young man's distress, making the situation impossible for Kwame.[80] This is an *interrupted*, unsuccessful confession, for both the audience and for the character.

Although confession and truth are central issues for *I May Destroy You* as a whole, Kwame's storyline is fundamentally about neither, and it refuses confession as a narrative mode. Instead, the series focuses on the different ways Kwame is silenced, by both the police and his friends; in episode 6, Terry tries to describe to Kwame what is happening to Arabella. She lectures him:

> I'm saying our nervous systems also shut down to safety mode when it's overloaded with too much stimulation, too much, too much danger. Hashtag trauma, hashtag double click for double rapey shit that she's been

through. So, no, she's not fine. She's vacant, she's empty, she's a shell of herself, she's dying inside, but if you aren't looking for it, you ain't gonna see it.[81]

Kwame stares at her, looking vacant, empty, a shell of himself. He is not doing well, but his friends do not seem to notice. In other words, rather than framing Kwame as needing to confess in order to help himself move on, *I May Destroy You* shows the specific ways Kwame is enjoined *not* to speak.[82]

Talking about what happened to him helps Kwame deal with the assault, but the series doesn't ask the audience to anticipate his confession, and, in fact, it doesn't present his confession to us at all. In episode 7, when Kwame tells Terry what happened, the show skips past the confession altogether, and we instead move forward to a scene in which Terry helps her friend process the assault.[83] *I May Destroy You* is already unique for its descriptions of Black male vulnerability to sexual violence, but its refusal of the confessional mode is an extraordinarily rare and refreshing choice for male/male rape discourse in 2020. Rather than dwell on what Kwame must confess to us, *I May Destroy You* instead places different sexual assaults beside one another, asking us to think about how the police's responses (and our own) differ depending on the gender of the victim, the type of sexual harm, and whether or not the victim has previously had consensual sex with the assailant.

Although *Yes, Daddy* cannot imagine a future for its violate man, *I May Destroy You* is quite sincerely about how we live with having experienced rape and other sexual violations. Coel's series is fundamentally about the future, about processing and moving forward from the experience of sexual harm. The final episode of the series involves a range of possible outcomes for Arabella and her rapist. *I May Destroy You* shows us four different possibilities, each one more radical than the next. The first is a typical rape-revenge drama, in which she and her friends drug and murder the man. In the second, much more challenging scenario, she starts to empathize with her rapist, to begin to see that he, too, has experienced harm in various ways. In the third, she meets him at the bar and seduces him, and then they make love in her bedroom. In the fourth and final scenario, she decides not to go back to the bar at all; she stays home and plays video games with her flatmate instead.[84]

In an absolutely extraordinary interview with E. Alex Jung in *Vulture*, Coel describes what she was trying to do in the finale as "radical empathy":

It's really hard. This area feels very delicate. For me, this is the thing that needs a trigger warning, empathy, because . . . it's a really uncomfortable arena. I spent a lot of my life asking, pleading, hoping for empathy. I am aware of this phrase "Do unto others as you would have done unto yourself," and yet these two things don't always connect. I'm saying "Empathize with me." I'm saying "How would you like it if you felt like this and put your feet in my shoes?" If I am pleading for people to do this for me, then it only feels fitting for me to try to do the same thing, to know what that might be like, the act of putting your feet in somebody else's shoes. I think this is radical empathy, isn't it?[85]

Coel's questions resonate deeply with the abolition work of activists like Mariame Kaba and Andrea J. Ritchie.[86] These ideas are, perhaps, difficult to hear, and she acknowledges that with her invocation of the trigger warning, but Coel's proposal is about how we move forward from having experienced harm. Her protagonist decides to try to let things go. Coel admits "that there is a way of viewing that which is deeply offensive," but she offers this possibility as one way to keep going, one that she says is working for her.

Finally, and most recently, Richard Gadd's seven-episode series *Baby Reindeer* appeared on Netflix in April 2024 and quickly became a surprise hit. Like *I May Destroy You*, *Baby Reindeer* is a British series, beginning its life in theater and fringe theater spaces. The series is based on Gadd's performance pieces *Monkey See Monkey Do* and *Baby Reindeer*.[87] As with *I May Destroy You*, Gadd's series is fundamentally confessional. Gadd plays Donny Dunn, a version of himself, and the poster for *Baby Reindeer* prominently bills the series as "a captivating true story." (Indeed, the "truth" of *Baby Reindeer* has caused Gadd and Netflix a great deal of trouble, as some particularly captivated viewers have attempted to track down the real people behind *Baby Reindeer*'s thinly veiled fictions.[88]) Confessions abound in the series, and the entirety of *Baby Reindeer* is told through voice-over, as Donny relates the story of being stalked by a woman and their interactions become more and more complex. The series also begins with a scene of confession, as Donny visits the police to report that he's being stalked. The policeman's first response is *Why'd it take you so long to report it?* and this question hangs over the first three episodes.[89] At the end of episode 2, however, Martha sexually assaults Donny by grabbing his clothed genitals in an alleyway, and he immediately freezes up in response.[90] As always—this is a constant in *Baby Reindeer*—the camera focuses intently on Donny's face. He looks terrified. This is a person who has been assaulted before.

Episode 4 begins with a title card—"The following contains depictions of sexual violence which some viewers may find troubling"—and in this episode, Donny tells us about his relationship with Darrien (Tom Goodman-Hill), a fifty-five-year-old writer, who gives Donny drugs over a period of several months and begins sexually violating him while he is passed out.[91] In one sequence, Darrien gives Donny acid and a shot of Gamma-hydroxybutyrate and then Donny passes out while Darrien caresses him and pulls off his pants. Donny wakes up coughing and wheezing, and the camera shows Darrien raping Donny. The next morning, Donny takes a shower, but when the hot water touches his back, he screams in pain. Covering his mouth and crying, Donny covers his anus and sits on the edge of the bath. But he doesn't leave Darrien's apartment. "I would love to say I left," he tells us, "that I stormed out and never went back. But I stayed for days afterwards." Donny confesses all of this to the TV audience at home, but he doesn't tell anyone inside the narrative. In this way *Baby Reindeer*, as with many of the television narratives we've examined thus far, anticipates the confession. Donny confesses to us, and then we wait for Donny to confess to the other people in his life what we already know.

Donny confesses in episode 6; in fact, he performs his confession publicly after freezing up during a comedy routine he's supposed to be doing at a very big competition.[92] This is a powerful sequence, and Donny tells the audience about being raped and how it happened. He blames himself, and he explores the ways that his own desire for fame made him vulnerable to violence. The audience sits and listens to Donny's confession. It's almost kind the way they let him continue; only a few people get up and leave. Everyone else sits, in what seems to be something akin to generous patience. What's happening, however, is testimony as *entertainment*. In episode 7 we learn that a random audience member has recorded him on the sly and uploaded the video to YouTube, where his confession goes viral. Donny tells us, "I couldn't keep up with it all, everything that was happening. It was like my life began three decades in, and all I needed to do to achieve it was to be honest with myself."[93] But this isn't an accurate assessment. Donny has confessed not to himself but more or less to the entire internet. The confession onstage in Gadd's performance piece *Monkey See Monkey Do* has been transmuted into Donny's theatrical performance for the unsuspecting audience at this comedy show and, of course, Netflix viewers watching at home. We've been asked to anticipate this confession, and it arrives with healing power for Donny and narrative satisfaction for *Baby Reindeer*'s audience.

There are further confessions in episode 7, as Donny must also confess to his parents before they see it on YouTube. This is one of the most moving episodes in the series, and it's worth focusing on a bit more carefully. Like the boys in *American Crime* and like the violate men in *Boy Erased* and *I May Destroy You*, Donny confesses his queer *sexuality* to his parents before he can tell them about the violence he experienced. When he tells them about being sexually violated, he is most concerned about their perception of his masculinity, but their responses are surprising:

> DONNY: I just feel so fucking embarrassed, and I guess I never wanted you to know because I didn't want you to think less of me, you know . . . as a man.
> MOTHER: Oh, darling, of course we don't! You're our son, whatever happens.
> DONNY: I just feel less of one, having let something like that happen to me.
> MOTHER: But you didn't let it happen. You weren't to blame.
> FATHER: Would you see *me* as less of one?
> DONNY: What?
> FATHER: Would you see me as less of a man?

Donny's father tells him that he grew up in the Catholic church, and though he doesn't say more than this, he lets us understand that he has been working to incorporate his vulnerability to violation into his sense of manhood. Unlike the boys on *American Crime*'s basketball team, he doesn't look for someone else to be less of a man in order to understand himself as one.[94] This scene breaks with decades of tradition in the discourse of male/male rape, most notably the 1980s television representations I describe at the beginning of this chapter. In *Baby Reindeer*, Donny's father doesn't simply pity his son or accept his son, *he identifies*. It's an extraordinary moment in the history I've been charting throughout this book. Our media have, since the 1960s, actively worked to disavow the violate man, to foreclose the possibility of identifying with him. *Baby Reindeer* has another man—the violate man's own father, no less—say *me too*.

In 2024, *Baby Reindeer* follows the confessional narrative mode to which we have become well accustomed in male/male rape discourse, and the series mostly leaves behind older representational strategies for male/male rape. Donny, for example, considers getting revenge on his rapist, and in a troubling scene, he goes to confront his rapist but leaves shaken and in a panic. The show also avoids insisting on heterosexuality, and Donny emerges at the end of the series claiming his bisexuality and his deep love for his transgender ex-girlfriend. Perhaps most importantly, following the lead of *I May Destroy You*, *Baby Reindeer* tells the story of someone for whom rape is not the end of the world. Both Gadd's and Coel's series are focused on how to move forward in society as a survivor of sexual violence. The questions remaining at the end of *Baby Reindeer* are about how Donny will craft a new life, what choices he will make in the future, and how he will learn to live without a concept of himself as autonomous and inviolable but instead with a new understanding of his vulnerability.

CHAPTER 6

On Closure and Openness

> You tell me it gets better, it gets better in time
> You say to pull myself together, "Pull it together; you'll be fine"
> —LADY GAGA, "Til It Happens to You"

I end *The Violate Man* with a meditation on closure and openness—on the possibilities of power through dis-closure and the open-endedness of survivorship. Since I began doing research into the discourse of male/male rape roughly fifteen years ago, I have been consistently startled when a colleague has delicately or not so delicately asked me some version of the following question: "So . . . I study Caribbean literature because I'm from the Caribbean, and I have to ask: How did you get started researching *your* topic?" The questions should not have surprised me; in 1975 Brownmiller opened *Against Our Will* by telling us that "Have you ever been raped?" was "the question most often asked of me while I was writing this book."[1] I have fielded similar requests for me to describe my own relationship to sexual violation in one form or another at least a dozen times, and it is a question that asks me to play my part in the drama of confession that I described in Chapter 5 and that we now treat as essential to rape survivorship. I assume that my interlocutor expects to hear that my relationship to this subject matter is deeply personal—that I have experienced sexual violence or that I have friends or lovers who have experienced sexual violence. I also hear in this question a desire for me to reassure the person asking the question, to articulate a narrative of personal triumph in which the violate man transforms his private anguish into academic, artistic, or political work that has value to the public, in which good defeats evil through the power of the human will. This version of the story would, in many ways, be a nonviolent variation on the rape-revenge narratives I described in Chapter 4, a version in which everything happens for a reason, and I put myself back together by transmuting pain into purpose—or one in which a performed confession, like perhaps the one in *Baby Reindeer*, becomes art.

It is possible, however, that I misinterpret the reasons behind my interlocutors' questions. By introducing the topic of male/male rape into conversation, it is really I, of course, who have raised the specter of the violate man. They have perhaps already begun to hear a confession even as I broach the topic—simply by virtue of me describing my research. Imagining that I am someone who has experienced rape might reasonably cause my interlocutors to react with compassion and empathy; reassuring them that I have never been the victim of an act of sexual violation and that they needn't worry about me and my anguish might conceivably relieve a lot of anxiety. Brownmiller does precisely this for her readers at the beginning of *Against Our Will*—even before she begins the book's introduction—by saying directly and clearly that she has never been raped. Other scholars writing about rape often state whether or not they have experienced rape just as directly as Brownmiller.[2]

Whenever I am asked this question, I opt, as politely as I can, to avoid the role of confessant. It is not the duty of a survivor of sexual violence to reassure his society that "it gets better" or that she'll "be fine." Further, even if I could convincingly say, with Brownmiller, that I have not been raped, any such reassurance ought necessarily to ring hollow. In the first place, as we move through the world, the potential that violence might be done against us always exists. I might say today that I have not been raped, but this might not be true in a year or six months.

More importantly, however, my preference not to answer this question takes a cue from Robert McRuer, who, in a section in *Crip Theory* titled "Coming Out Crip," argues that the oppositions we create between queer, disabled, noncitizen bodies and "the rest of us" are no longer sustainable and—more to the point—that "if it's not even *conceivable* for you to identify as or with [for example] Brazilian, gay, immigrant workers with multiple sclerosis, then you're not yet attending to how bodies and spaces are being materialized in the cultures of upward redistribution we currently inhabit."[3] Although this book has focused on the discourse of male/male rape, it has also described numerous real incidents of violence, and if many of *The Violate Man*'s readers have only encountered sexual violence at the level of discourse, the experience of such violence is a material reality for many of us, no matter our genders. An enormous component of the cultural power of male/male rape is related to the ways that we, as an entire society, refuse to identify with the violate man. It was clear to Brownmiller that identifying as a survivor of violation was not a prerequisite for writing about rape, but, adapting McRuer, I want also to argue that if we cannot yet identify with—or as—the man who has been violated, we still have a good deal of work to do as we reimagine the gendered bodies that inhabit our societies. In a twenty-first century wracked by military hostilities and mass incarceration, in which bodies are being broken through everyday police violence, torture, bombing, ICE raids, and sexual violence, this work of identification is all the more necessary.

This question—"Have you ever been raped?"—makes evident that the specter of the violate man continues to retain a great deal of power in US American culture. In our discourse, the violate man—broken, ashamed, and irredeemably queer—haunts and undergirds US American masculinity. It is imperative that we find ways to talk about the violate man without hiding him, shaming him, or attempting the false deontological closure promised by acts of violent revenge. Even more, it is important that we begin to find ways to identify with him. Almost all of the narratives in this book involve the explicit *disavowal* of the violate man. He is pitiable, perhaps, but he cannot be understood and cannot be reincorporated into society. He has been transformed into something other than he was, changed forever by the violence he has experienced. Frequently, he is himself accused of having somehow caused the violence that was committed against him. Incarcerated men, especially, are treated as though rape is one of the things they ought to have considered before they committed their crimes; rape is understood as a just and reasonable component of their punishment.[4] If they suffer rape, it is their fault. This is true not only in rape narratives on television or in fiction; even occasionally in scholarly explanations for the causes of male/male rape we can find the responsibility for the violence placed with the victim.[5]

Identifying with the violate man might, in fact, mean identifying with brokenness.[6] It is true that much of the stigma surrounding male victims of sexual violence in the United States and elsewhere is related to societal perceptions of them as no longer men or "downgrading [them] to a lower (subordinate) masculine status."[7] Our associations with the violate man exclude him from dominant masculinity because of the ableism, homophobia, shame, and misogyny that are component to our ideas about male/male rape. But this doesn't mean that figuring out how to return the violate man to masculine status would be some type of solution to this problem. The strategy outlined by the films of the 1990s I described in Chapter 4 explicitly avoids opening up to the transformative possibilities that shame and the disruption of traditional masculinity offer us. The characters in these films, and the viewers they hail, are asked, once again, to disavow the violate man and the brokenness he experiences. Identifying with the violate man, on the other hand, could mean refusing this attempt to rebuild maleness as wholeness. Identifying with the violate man might mean learning to abandon the fantasy of wholeness as a pretense. It could mean reimagining maleness as a subjectivity that incorporates brokenness. It might even mean seeing brokenness itself as power, as beauty, as desirable.

I have often been frustrated, while reading scholarly descriptions of male/male rape, to find sentences such as: "Obviously, in America's patriarchal society, violently sodomizing a man with a foreign object is perhaps one of the most humiliating, physical, and psychologically harmful acts for a married heterosexual man with children to endure," or "As a heterosexual male victim his physiognomy as well his psychology conspire against coming to terms [with] this oddity."[8] Why privilege "heterosexual" victims or those who are married with children? Why ought we to imagine that victimization by rape is somehow more difficult for "heterosexual" men than it is for others? My resentment of these statements' erasure of non-heterosexual rape survivors, though, perhaps obscures something these theorists are stating obliquely, namely that this *might* be more difficult for those men particularly attached to heterosexual ideology. It is also true, in other words, that some queer and non-heterosexual men have already begun to incorporate openness, penetrability, perhaps even brokenness, into their subjectivities.

Obviously, queerness *per se* is no panacea. Queer communities are frequently virulently racist, and they're quite adept at reinforcing masculine codes and other sexual hierarchies, including those dependent on ableism, wholeness, and impenetrability. But queer communities need not be the only groups that construct and develop alternative masculinities. Indeed, much of this work is being done in communities of color where alternative masculinities have already been theorized. Much of this work begins from a place that recognizes the specific *vulnerability* that Black men, Indigenous men, and other men of color experience in US American society.[9] A true identification with the violate man would mean an active identification with brokenness and vulnerability—beginning to see oneself as penetrable and refusing to attempt to resolve that brokenness through the breaking of others. An active identification with brokenness would also be a fundamental refusal of the cultural value we place on wholeness, purity, able-bodiedness, aggression, and impenetrability, the discursive value system, in short, that lends rape the power it claims to possess in the world, the discursive value system that rapists cite when they commit violations.

As I conclude this book, I want to turn to two artists who use images of the violate man but who attempt to avoid many of the traditional discursive tropes described in this book's chapters. I wish to make no arguments for the "right" way to represent the violated male body, but what I appreciate in the works of both Kevin Kantor and Benjamin Peterson is that they ask us to think differently about the violate man, to discard what we think we already know about the broken male body and to see it in new ways.

Vasses

In 2016 the ceramic, video, and performance artist Benjamin Peterson began exhibiting a series of earthenware figures he campily calls *Vasses* (Figure 6.1). Peterson's *Vasses* are a perverse, even shocking, transformation of the ceramic vase, a practical decorative object traditionally employed by the US American housewife in a bourgeois domestic space. The *Vasses* introduce into that domestic environment the figure of the violate man, and because Peterson's *Vasses* are practical objects, they invite performance or interaction from the viewer. A vase exists in dynamic relation with the objects it contains: its very purpose is to hold and display other decorative objects, complementing the beauty of those objects with its own beauty.

Peterson's *Vasses* were first exhibited in January 2016 at the LeRoy Neiman Gallery in a show titled *LOVE 2016* curated by Rachel Stern, and they appeared one month later in Berlin at ROCKELMANN & PARTNER for the *Unearthed* exhibition curated by Geo Gonzalez and Dan Halm. The *Vasses* were also included in an "adult-themed" ceramics show juried by Laura Henkle called *Sweet and Slippery Slope* at Clay Arts Vegas's Victor F. Keen Gallery.[10] The ceramic *Vasses* are naked, life-like male figures with unexaggerated anatomies and undistinguishable facial features. Each man turns his anus upward; he supports his back with his hands, shoulders, and elbows, and he splays his legs in the air. The pose appears voluntary, or rather, because each man supports his own body, he seems actively to be attempting to hold the precarious position in which he has found himself. The clay men are unglazed and white, but Peterson has drawn attention to their anuses

FIGURE 6.1.: Benjamin Peterson, *Vasses with Roses*, 2016. Porcelain, glaze, gold luster, 9 × 5 × 5 inches each. Image courtesy of the artist

by glazing each figure's interior with a bright color and allowing this glaze to drip out of the anal cavity onto the exterior of the body.

The different *Vasses* are decorated in various colors including gold, green, white, pink, and bright red. Each color, of course, is evocative in its own way—Peterson says that variations in color mean that the pieces have the ability to "slide between being a violent or a pleasurable content"—but the dripping glaze implies a lack of care, a disregard for the man who has been penetrated, a possibly pleasurable or possibly violent sexual humiliation.[11] A *Vass* with a red glaze, however, is nearly impossible to read as anything other than an image of violation, one, indeed, that draws attention to the violable potential of all male bodies.

We might also see Peterson's *Vasses* as actively inviting the viewer to come into relationship with the violate man. These are practical objects designed to contain and display other objects. For the artist, the open anus that serves as the vase's mouth "creates an invitation for the user to participate in the transgression. Either by filling it with flowers, decorating the anus, or by pouring fluid into or out of the anus. In either case the viewer/user is required to participate or reject this visual statement."[12] In this way, each *Vass* functions as what the performance theorist and historian Robin Bernstein has called a "scriptive thing," things that "invite—indeed, create occasions for—repetitions of acts, distinctive and meaningful motions of eyes, hands, shoulder, hips, feet."[13] Each *Vass* is a piece that already possesses its own culturally defined script, requesting particular behaviors from those who come into contact with it. We know how we are supposed to interact with a vase: the object offers itself as a thing to be filled and then displayed. Each *Vass* requests not only that we look at it but that we interact with it. Whether we choose to sodomize the *Vass* by filling the cavity offered to us or refuse to follow this script, the *Vass* itself nudges its users toward troublingly violent participation.

Although Peterson's ceramic figures appear designed to agitate or confuse, they are also arrestingly beautiful, and they invite a different way of looking at the violated male body. These violate men—none of whom, I should note, is explicitly decorated in violet—support themselves.[14] They invite interaction, not scorn, and they make a spectacle of themselves, displaying the violated male body without shame as aesthetically arresting and, even more, as a receptacle for another decorative object. They turn the anus, that "essentially private" part of the body frequently understood as shameful, toward the viewer. Each *Vass* is a *beautiful violated male body* designed to exist in dynamic relation with other objects of beauty.

For exhibition at *LOVE 2016* and *Sweet and Slippery Slope*, Peterson filled the *Vasses* each with a single rose, but these flowers do not cover over the violated male body, they do not transform violence into beauty or pain into pleasure. Indeed, as displayed, the *Vasses* avoid narrativization, seeming frozen in contorted poses of display. What these pieces imagine, instead, is the violate man as a body that has not attempted to remake itself *as* a man, through violence, closure, or isolation. These male bodies remain violated and violable, penetrated and penetrable, supporting themselves and displaying themselves precisely as broken bodies, open and vulnerable. Peterson's work is a challenge for us to love these broken bodies, to place the violated body in relationship with other beautiful objects, to find a place for these bodies in our very homes, and, ultimately, to expand our definition of beauty to include the violate man.

"People You May Know"

In the early months of 2015, Kevin Kantor, who winkingly identifies as a poet, actor, and trans nonbinary phenom, became something of an internet sensation when a performance of their piece "People You May Know" at the College Unions Poetry Slam Invitational was circulated on BuzzFeed via Facebook and other social media.[15] In the poem, Kantor speaks about being raped by an acquaintance, and they describe the skepticism they faced from both law enforcement and acquaintances. Kantor tells us, too, that even their brother wondered why they hadn't put up more resistance against their rapist, and the poem ends as Kantor tells their brother that performance is itself a method of fighting back:

> Right now
> I promise
> Every day I write a poem titled
> *Tomorrow*
> It is a handwritten list of
> The people I know
> Who love me and
> I
> Make sure to put my own name at the top[16]

Performance is, for Kantor, one way of responding to and refusing victimization by sexual violence. Kantor has described poetry as a way to "work through" and "unpack" experiences.[17] But "People You May Know" is, notably, not simply words on a page. The poet has chosen, specifically, to attach their own face to their writing, speaking their experience aloud to groups of people as testimony. Indeed, Kantor also performs a poem at the beginning of "Season Two: Episode Four" of *American Crime*.

Kantor performs as a person who has been violated, and they respond to the people who want them to be silent, to their brother, to the police, not only by testifying to the violence they experienced but by performing this testimony, by asking audiences to see them as violate. Further, coming out as a survivor of sexual violence is linked in many ways, for Kantor, to coming out as trans nonbinary at age twenty-two. In an interview with Kerry Lengel in the *Arizona Republic*, Kantor says that as "People You May Know" went viral, it was "being held up as a piece on male survivorship in particular, and I found myself having to be in conversation a lot more with my gender identity as someone who was being perceived as—labeled as—a cis man, particularly in regards to my experience with rape culture."[18] Coming out as a survivor, already an act of gender nonconformity, became for Kantor a prompt for something else: "I really began to recognize this dissonance and felt the need to address it, and I came out as trans nonbinary that year." Coming out both as a survivor and as nonbinary is,

Kantor says, an attempt to be visible in society as well as to advocate for victims within US American society writ large, especially those who are trans and gender-nonconforming. If rape, as I have argued, is an attempted act of violent gender *performativity*, Kantor's work demonstrates the world-making possibilities of gender *performance*.

Rather than emphasizing a masculinity regained, as so many of the narratives we've examined in this book have done, Kantor emphasizes a trans femininity that is strong in and of itself, and Kantor speaks about being a survivor publicly and often. Visibility has become a priority for many victim advocates, and male, nonbinary, and trans victims of rape are becoming increasingly visible via national media, In a powerful contribution to the discourse of male/male rape, Kantor appeared with forty-nine other survivors onstage alongside Lady Gaga as she sang the song "Til It Happens to You" at the 2016 Academy Awards ceremony. Gaga's song was written (with Diane Warren) for the documentary *The Hunting Ground*, a film that reports on some of the methods that universities across the nation have used to cover up accusations of rape, including male/male rape, at their institutions. The film also documents the fights that a group of courageous young women waged against these universities using Title IX of the Education Amendments of 1972.[19] Lady Gaga has herself discussed surviving sexual violence, and "Til It Happens to You" is intended as both testimony and artistic expression. The song was nominated for an Oscar, and Gaga used this widely televised moment to stand united with rape survivors and bring visibility to a national problem, one particularly affecting young women on college and university campuses. In a 2016 interview with Bill Leff and Wendy Snyder of WGN in Chicago, Kantor described standing onstage with Gaga and fellow survivors as "empowering" and "validating," but as Leff and Snyder end their WGN interview they ask Kantor about their rapist. They ask if Kantor thought about their attacker while they were onstage at the Oscars. Snyder's question attempts to frame Kantor's experience using the terms of revenge and retribution established by cinema of the 1990s when she poses the question: "Did it give you some validation to show, 'Hey, I'm standing up to this; I'm on stage with Gaga, what are *you* doin'?'" Kantor's response is generous. They say simply: "I don't reframe any of my experiences through the lens of my attacker." Snyder's question asks Kantor to place the experience of violation within the usual narratives we have become accustomed to consuming because of the male/male rape discourse this book has described. Kantor carefully avoids this.

The poet also shies away from encouraging rape victims to report their experiences to law enforcement or to choose visibility over silence. Kantor offers that there is no "correct" way to respond to sexual violence; they clarify that their "goal is . . . that all survivors know that their only responsibility they have is to themselves to do what they think is best for them, and if that means reporting or not reporting or sharing or not sharing or going through the legal system or finding counseling . . .—that is what they should be doing." In other words, in addition to avoiding the masculinist demand for a kind of violent closure that we see in revenge films of the 1990s, Kantor also sidesteps the twenty-first-century demand for the survivor to confess that we've seen in *Oz*, *American Crime*, and *Baby Reindeer*. Kantor asks us to treat survivors as complex beings who ought to have the ability to process their experiences in their own time and in their own ways. Kantor's attitude follows activist and advocate Rousse Arielle when she says, "The image of the Survivor as ever strong and confident is a mistakenly idealized identity that cannot encompass the diverse narratives of those who have experienced sexual violence. . . . The Survivor should not be a victory to be achieved—survivors, in all their complexity, are entitled to an identity of survival simply because of their experiences."[20] Kantor and Rousse ask us to avoid thinking about survival through the terms of restored wholeness, masculinity, or strength.

But in the interview on WGN, Leff and Snyder continue to insist on the language of victory and triumph as they assure their audibly uncomfortable guest: "You *won*, Kevin," they say more than once. One suspects that Leff and Snyder would be hard pressed to say just what Kantor had won by appearing onstage at the Academy Awards or, indeed, how winning or losing relate to Kantor's experience of surviving rape. As I note in this book's introduction, however, winning and losing are embedded in the *poetics* of rape, even if they may have nothing to do with how survivors of rape have experienced it.

If we return to Kantor's poem, we find that "People You May Know" is less a poem about Kantor's connection to an attacker than it is about their own subjectivity and the skepticism they faced from the people whom they tried to tell—police officers, their brother, and four people who said they should have kept silent. Similarly, the lyrics of Gaga's song ("You tell me hold your head up, hold your head up and be strong, / 'Cause when you fall you gotta get up, you gotta get up and move on") are *not* an attempted victory over perpetrators of sexual assault; they are rather an indictment of a misunderstanding and ineffectual society. Leff and Snyder use the language of struggle, the common discourse of winning and losing that I have described throughout this book, but both Kantor and Gaga describe the real fight as one taking place at the level of the culture at large, a struggle between those who have experienced the violence of rape and a society that tells victims to deal with that violence quietly, all the while blaming victims themselves for the violation. The battle, for Kantor and Gaga, is one fought at the level of discourse.

The activism and performance poetry of Kevin Kantor and the scriptive beauty of Benjamin Peterson's *Vasses* break with the standard discourse for the violate man that this book describes. These pieces offer us, instead, a set of different possibilities for thinking about the violate man's place in US American culture. Certainly, these art works remind us that all men and boys are vulnerable to violation—as we have seen from the previous chapters, all representations of male/male rape have the ability to do this. Both artists' works, however, avoid the standard insistence on masculine wholeness and able-bodiedness that commonly accompanies male/male rape discourse in the United States. These pieces abandon the masculinist fantasy that a man can or should be without shame, that we can separate ourselves from femininity, queerness, or abjection. They remind us all of our violability, but they do not ask us to distance ourselves from that vulnerability. Theirs are not violate bodies that have been made "whole" again through revenge or disavowal; wholeness is only a fantasy of able-bodied masculinity. Both artists instead allow us to imagine the violate man as strong on his own terms, as making space for himself, insisting on his beauty and value.

Notes

INTRODUCTION

Epigraph. Toby Keith, "Courtesy of the Red, White, & Blue (The Angry American)," *Unleashed* (Nashville, TN: DreamWorks Records, 2002).
1. Michael Scarce, *Male on Male Rape: The Hidden Toll of Stigma and Shame* (New York: Insight Books, 1997).
2. Matthew Hay Brown, "Baltimore Sailor Says He Was Told Not to Report Rape," *Baltimore Sun*, March 13, 2013, https://www.baltimoresun.com/2013/03/13/baltimore-sailor-says-he-was-told-not-to-report-rape-3.
3. Nathaniel Penn, "Son, Men Don't Get Raped," *GQ* 84, no. 9 (2014): 244.
4. Deborah Sontag, "Push to End Prison Rapes Loses Momentum," *New York Times*, May 13, 2015, A1.
5. The Taguba Report contains a litany of such abuses. The testimony of Kasim Mehaddi Hilas is particularly damning. See Antonio M. Taguba, "Executive Summary of Article 15-6 Investigation of the 800th Military Police Brigade," International Committee of the Red Cross, accessed June 21, 2025, https://casebook.icrc.org/case-study/united-states-taguba-report.
6. Chris Fry, "Fire Department Accused of Forcible Sodomy," Courthouse News Service, June 9, 2011, https://www.courthousenews.com/fire-department-accused-of-forcible-sodomy. The use of the word *sodomy* makes the details of the case vague, but that a young man was forced to do things he did not wish to do is quite clear.
7. Allie Grasgreen, "Victims Too," *Inside Higher Ed*, December 3, 2012, https://www.insidehighered.com/news/2012/12/03/college-cases-highlight-complexity-same-sex-male-victim-sexual-assaults.
8. Noreen Abdullah-Khan, *Male Rape: The Emergence of a Social and Legal Issue* (London: Palgrave Macmillan, 2008).
9. Edward Said, *Orientalism* (New York: Vintage Books, 1979), 21.
10. Yet another phrase lurks beneath *The Violate Man*. As I've worked on this book for the last decade, I've had an alert set to receive notifications whenever the phrase *violate man* appears in a news article. Because of the way the words are set beside one another in my title, the articles sent to me invariably describe the same legal finding: "Judge Rules Officers Didn't Violate Man's Rights"; "Jury Finds Lafayette Police Officer Didn't Violate Man's Rights in Federal Excessive Force Case"; "Warrantless Vehicle Search That Produced Loaded Firearm Did Not Violate Man's Constitutional Rights, COA Affirms."

Because of the phrasing of the alert I set, I never received notifications for news articles in which judges or juries found that "officers *violated* man's rights"; the phrase itself selected articles with this particular judicial finding. But this is a book about the ways we talk about violated men, and it has been a bitter irony for me to work with this title that only ever calls up news reports where the finding is that the man's rights weren't actually violated despite his arguments to the contrary. See Sean Batura, "Judge Rules Officers Didn't Violate Man's Rights," *Livingston [MT] Enterprise*, June 7, 2024, https://www.livingstonenterprise.com/news/judge-rules-officers-didn-t-violate-man-s-rights/article_dab4c840-24d9-11ef-8942-b34b09604f31.html; Kate Gagliano, "Jury Finds Lafayette Police Officer Didn't Violate Man's Rights in Federal Excessive Force Case," *Acadiana [LA] Advocate*, December 22, 2023, https://www.theadvocate.com/acadiana/news/courts/jury-in-lafayette-federal-lawsuit-finds-no-excessive-force/article_b230668e-a056-11ee-a68c-ef02f26cb44e.html; Alexa Shrake, "Warrantless Vehicle Search That Produced Loaded Firearm Did Not Violate Man's Constitutional Rights, COA Affirms," *Indiana Lawyer*, October 26, 2023, https://www.theindianalawyer.com/articles/warrantless-vehicle-search-that-produced-loaded-firearm-did-not-violate-mans-constitutional-rights-coa-affirms.

11. Jules Gill-Peterson describes trans misogyny using a parallel ideological formation. Trans misogyny "*trans-feminizes* its targets without their assent, usually by sexualizing their presumptive femininity as if it were an expression of male aggression." See Jules Gill-Peterson, *A Short History of Trans Misogyny* (New York: Verso, 2024), vii.
12. See Tommy J. Curry, *The Man-Not: Race, Class, Genre, and the Dilemmas of Black Manhood* (Philadelphia, PA: Temple University Press, 2017), 54–55.
13. Carlyle Van Thompson, *Eating the Black Body: Miscegenation as Sexual Consumption in African American Literature and Culture* (New York: Peter Lang, 2006), 24.
14. As David Marriott puts it, following Frantz Fanon, "the problem is that white phobic anxiety about black men takes the form of a fetishistic investment in their sexuality: crudely, being well-hung, the black man must be hung well. In other words, the violated body of the black man comes to be used as a defence against the anxiety, or hatred, that body appears to generate." See David Marriott, *On Black Men* (New York: Columbia University Press, 2000), 12.
15. Maria L. LaGanga, "Idaho Judge Rules Attack on High School Football Player Was 'Not a Rape' or Racist," *Guardian*, February 24, 2017, https://www.theguardian.com/us-news/2017/feb/24/idaho-football-player-rape-case-coat-hanger-light-sentence.
16. Lauren Porter "White Teen Avoids Prison Time for Brutal Coat Hanger Rape of Disabled Black Student," *Essence*, October 26, 2020, https://www.essence.com/news/white-teen-avoids-jail-for-rape-of-black-student.
17. Susan Brownmiller, *Against Our Will: Men, Women, and Rape* (New York: Fawcett Columbine, 1993).
18. Frantz Fanon, *Black Skin, White Masks*, trans. Richard Philcox (New York: Grove Press, 2008), see especially 133–55. See also Curry, *Man-Not*, 143–52.
19. Rotten Tomatoes Coming Soon, "Hit and Run Official Trailer #1 (2012) Bradley Cooper, Kristen Bell Movie HD," YouTube, May 15, 2012, https://www.youtube.com/watch?v=6nZlXB5okeo.
20. Aliyyah I. Abdur-Rahman, *Against the Closet: Black Political Longing and the Ethics of Race* (Durham, NC: Duke University Press, 2012), 5.

21. Jacinda Read, *The New Avengers: Feminism, Femininity, and the Rape-Revenge Cycle* (Manchester: Manchester University Press, 2000), 25.
22. In *Tendencies*, Eve Sedgwick argues that unspoken knowledge about gay lives and gay sex practices formed a culture of "knowingness," a lore that served to offer sophistication but plausible deniability to respectable people: "Our culture as a whole might be said to vibrate to the tense cord of 'knowingness.' Its epistemological economy depends not on a reserve force of labor, but on a reserve force of information always maintained in readiness to be presumed upon—through jokey allusion, through the semiotic paraphernalia of 'sophistication'—and yet poised also in equal readiness to be disappeared at any moment, leaving a suppositionally virginal surface, unsullied by any admitted knowledge, whose purity may be pornographically understood to be violated and violated and violated yet again each time anew, by always the same information in fact possessed and exploited from the start." One could modify Sedgwick only marginally to read an argument about our culture's fascination with "knowledge" about male/male rape and its coincidence with the disavowal of that knowledge. See Eve Kosofsky Sedgwick, *Tendencies* (Durham, NC: Duke University Press, 1993), 222.
23. My use of *poetics* is indebted to studies of violence in the field of anthropology, especially. See Allen Feldman, *Formations of Violence: The Narrative of the Body and Political Terror in Northern Ireland* (Chicago: University of Chicago Press, 1991); and Neil L. Whitehead, *Dark Shamans: Kanaimà and the Poetics of Violent Death* (Durham, NC: Duke University Press, 2002).
24. Amalendu Misra, *The Landscape of Silence: Sexual Violence against Men in War* (London: Hurst & Company, 2015). See especially 39–43, 67, 70, 100–101, and Misra's defense of this method on 43.
25. Ann J. Cahill, *Rethinking Rape* (Ithaca, NY: Cornell University Press, 2001), 124.
26. This is basic to Brownmiller's work but legible in the work of most major scholars of sexual violence. Their attention is, justifiably, turned toward women as the victims of rape.
27. My list of fourteen nodes of discussion attendant to male/male rape rhetoric is indebted to a similar list in *Tendencies*. See Sedgwick, *Tendencies*, 6.
28. See Phillip Brian Harper, *Are We Not Men? Masculine Anxiety and the Problem of African-American Identity* (New York: Oxford University Press, 1996), 171.
29. Lynn A. Higgins and Brenda R. Silver, "Introduction: Rereading Rape," in *Rape and Representation*, ed. Lynn A. Higgins and Brenda R. Silver (New York: Columbia University Press, 1991), 3.
30. Brownmiller, *Against*, 13–14.
31. Catherine A. MacKinnon, *Toward a Feminist Theory of the State* (Cambridge, MA: Harvard University Press, 1989), 173.
32. MacKinnon, *Toward*, 173; emphasis added.
33. MacKinnon, *Toward*, 173.
34. Cahill, *Rethinking*, 33.
35. MacKinnon puts it this way: "To be rap*able*, a position which is social, not biological, defines what a woman is." Catharine A. MacKinnon, "Feminism, Marxism, Method, and the State: Toward Feminist Jurisprudence," *Signs* 8, no. 4 (1983): 651; emphasis in original.
36. Klaus Theweleit, *Male Fantasies Volume 1: Women, Floods, Bodies, History*, trans. Stephen Conway (Minneapolis: University of Minnesota Press, 1987), 221–22.

37. Abdur-Rahman, *Against the Closet*, 49.
38. Thomas A. Foster, *Rethinking Rufus: Sexual Violations of Enslaved Men* (Athens: University of Georgia Press, 2019), 7.
39. Judith Butler, *Gender Trouble: Feminism and the Subversion of Identity*, 2nd ed. (New York: Routledge, 1999), 32.
40. Butler, *Gender Trouble*, 33. J. L. Austin theorized the term *performative* in a series of lectures at Harvard University called the William James Lectures published as *How to Do Things with Words* (Cambridge, MA: Harvard University Press, 1962). For a discussion of the wide range of uses of the term in theater and performance studies, see Aaron C. Thomas, "Infelicities," *Journal of Dramatic Theory and Criticism* 35, no. 2 (2021): 13–25.
41. Phillip Brian Harper reminds us of "the fundamentally simulacral nature of 'manhood,' which consists in the never-perfect approximation to an imagined standard that is no less exacting for all its illusory character." See Harper, *Are We Not Men?*, 185.
42. Judith Butler, *Bodies That Matter: On the Discursive Limits of "Sex"* (New York: Routledge, 1993), 225.
43. Butler, *Bodies That Matter*, 225; emphasis in original.
44. Judith Butler, *Frames of War: When Is Life Grievable?* (New York: Verso, 2010), 93.
45. Henri Alleg, in his memoir *The Question*, describes his own French torturers in late 1950s Algeria as proudly identifying with the Gestapo of the Second World War. See Henri Alleg, *The Question*, trans. John Calder (Lincoln: University of Nebraska Press, 2006), 47. In an earlier essay, I put it this way: "Violence is . . . always already the context in which violence is committed." See Aaron C. Thomas, "Truth and Translation at the Heart of Violence," *Theater* 49, no. 2 (2019): 60.
46. Jasbir K. Puar, *Terrorist Assemblages: Homonationalism in Queer Times* (Durham, NC: Duke University Press, 2007), 100.
47. See also Lynda E. Boose, "Crossing the River Drina: Bosnian Rape Camps, Turkish Impalement, and Serb Cultural Memory," *Signs* 28, no.1 (2002): 71–96.
48. K. J. Dover, *Greek Homosexuality*, 2nd ed. (Cambridge, MA: Harvard University Press, 1989), 105.
49. Joshua S. Goldstein, *War and Gender: How Gender Shapes the War System and Vice Versa* (Cambridge: Cambridge University Press, 2001), 359.
50. See Élise Féron, *Wartime Sexual Violence against Men: Masculinities and Power in Conflict Zones* (Lanham, MD: Rowman & Littlefield, 2018), especially 82; and Misra, *Landscape of Silence*, 75–105.
51. Leo Bersani, "Is the Rectum a Grave?" *October* 43 (1987): 212; emphasis in original. Bersani cites Michel Foucault, *The Use of Pleasure—Volume 2 of The History of Sexuality*, trans. Robert Hurley (New York: Vintage, 1990), 78–93.
52. Bersani continues this discussion in *Homos* (Cambridge, MA: Harvard University Press, 1995), see especially 105–6.
53. Michael Moon, "A Small Boy and Others: Sexual Disorientation in Henry James, Kenneth Anger, and David Lynch," in *Comparative American Identities: Race, Sex, and Nationality in the Modern Text*, ed. Hortense J. Spillers (New York: Routledge, 1991), 147.
54. Jane Bennett, *Vibrant Matter: A Political Ecology of Things* (Durham, NC: Duke University Press, 2010), 49. See also Mikhail Bakhtin, *Rabelais and His World*, trans. Hélène Iswolsky (Bloomington: Indiana University Press, 1984), 278–302.
55. Butler, *Frames of War*, 52.

56. Guy Hocquenghem, *Homosexual Desire*, trans. by Daniella Dangoor (Durham, NC: Duke University Press, 1993), 96. Hocquenghem is indebted to *Anti-Oedipus* for this idea: Deleuze and Guattari describe the anus as the model for the separation and isolation of all of the organs. For Deleuze and Guattari, "The first organ to suffer privatization, removal from the social field, was the anus." Removal from the social field here means that in "our modern societies," because we have "undertaken a vast privatization of the organs," we find it difficult to understand the body as a "*series* which determines connections, disjunctions, and conjunctions of organs." Anality, for Deleuze and Guattari, is the model for civilization itself and for the individualization that is constitutive of our societies. See Gilles Deleuze and Félix Guattari, *Anti-Oedipus: Capitalism and Schizophrenia*, trans. Robert Hurley, Mark Seem, and Helen R. Lane (Minneapolis: University of Minnesota Press, 1987), 142–43.
57. Eve Kosofsky Sedgwick and Michael Moon, "Divinity: A Dossier, a Performance Piece, a Little-Understood Emotion," in *Tendencies* by Eve Kosofsky Sedgwick (Durham, NC: Duke University Press, 1993), 246–47.
58. Klaus Theweleit, *Male Fantasies Volume 2: Male Bodies—Psychoanalyzing the White Terror*, trans. Erica Carter and Chris Turner (Minneapolis: University of Minnesota Press, 1989), 274.
59. Theweleit, *Male Fantasies Volume 2*, 305; emphasis added.
60. Butler, *Frames of War*, 90–91.
61. Robert McRuer, *Crip Theory: Cultural Signs of Queerness and Disability* (New York: New York University Press, 2006), 9.
62. McRuer, *Crip Theory*, 19.
63. Jesse Sheidlower, ed., *The F Word*, 2nd ed. (New York: Random House, 1999), 124–25. Words such as *faggot, punk, bitch, cocksucker, whore, slut, cunt, slag*, etc. (the list is long) that describe the receptive partner in any penetrative sexual relation have retained their power because of an always implicit rendering of the penetrated person as dirty, valueless, or having lost something.
64. Philip J. Kaplan, *F'd Companies: Spectacular Dot-com Flameouts* (New York: Simon & Schuster, 2002). Gingrich is quoted in Ceci Connolly and John Mintz, "For Cigarette Industry, a Future without GOP Support," *Washington Post*, March 29, 1998.
65. Bersani and Foucault's examples are from ancient Greece and my own are from the United States in the twentieth and twenty-first centuries, but we might also note in passing the continuing power of the mythos of *Malintzin / la Malinche / la chingada* in post-Columbian Meso-American culture, as well as the stigma of the penetrated man in Islamic traditions. See Gloria Anzaldúa, *Borderlands/La Frontera: The New Mestiza*, 3rd ed. (San Francisco, CA: Aunt Lute Books, 2007), 37–45, and Brian Whitaker, *Unspeakable Love: Gay and Lesbian Life in the Middle East* (Berkeley: University of California Press, 2006), particularly chapter 4.
66. Darieck Scott, *Extravagant Abjection: Blackness, Power, and Sexuality in the African American Imagination* (New York: New York University Press, 2010), 158–60.
67. In *Space, Time, and Perversion*, Elizabeth Grosz describes our typical model for sexuality as a hydraulic one, meaning that when we conceptualize sex, we do so primarily using ideas like release or ejaculation. For Grosz, "The fantasy that binds sex to death so intimately is the fantasy of a hydraulic sexuality, a biologically regulated need or instinct, a compulsion, urge, or mode of physical release (the sneeze provides an analogue).

The apparently urgent and compulsive nature of sexual drives is implicit in the claim made by many men who rape, those who frequent prostitutes, and those prostitutes who describe themselves as 'health workers,' insofar as they justify their roles in terms of maintaining the 'health' of their clients." Explanations for rape are frequently rooted in this hydraulic model of sexuality, privileging compulsion and release over pleasure. See Elizabeth Grosz, *Space, Time, and Perversion: Essays on the Politics of Bodies* (New York: Routledge, 1995), 204.
68. Susan J. Brison, *Aftermath: Violence and the Remaking of a Self* (Princeton, NJ: Princeton University Press, 2002), 86. Brison cites Marianne Hirsch, *Family Frames: Photography, Narrative, and Postmemory* (Cambridge, MA: Harvard University Press, 1997).
69. This idea is also central to Cahill's intervention in *Rethinking Rape*. See Cahill, *Rethinking Rape*, 10, 96, 126.
70. Nicola Gavey, *Just Sex? The Cultural Scaffolding of Rape* (London: Routledge, 2005), 92–93.
71. Danielle Sered quoted by Mariame Kaba, *We Do This 'til We Free Us: Abolitionist Organizing and Transforming Justice* by Mariame Kaba (Chicago: Haymarket, 2021), 146.
72. Sharon Marcus, "Fighting Bodies, Fighting Words," *Feminists Theorize the Political*, ed. Judith Butler and Joan W. Scott (London: Routledge, 1992), 391.
73. See Margaret Mitchell, *Gone with the Wind* (New York: Macmillan, 1936), 787–95.
74. Eve Kosofsky Sedgwick, *Between Men: English Literature and Male Homosocial Desire* (New York: Columbia University Press, 1985), 10; emphasis in original. See also Marjorie Garber's discussion of an interracial rape which turns out to be a "legitimized" intraracial seduction in *The Sheik* (1921) in *Vested Interests: Crossed Dressing and Cultural Anxiety* (New York: Routledge, 1992), 310.
75. Sabine Sielke, *Reading Rape: The Rhetoric of Sexual Violence in American Literature and Culture, 1790–1990* (Princeton, NJ: Princeton University Press, 2002), 2.
76. Sielke, *Reading Rape*, 2–3.
77. Michael Savage quoted in Zachary Aranow, "Savage: 'The Children's Minds Are Being Raped by the Homosexual Mafia,'" *Media Matters for America*, June 18, 2008, https://www.mediamatters.org/michael-savage/savage-childrens-minds-are-being-raped-homosexual-mafia.
78. David Wild, "Quentin Tarantino: The Madman of Movie Mayhem," *Rolling Stone*, November 3, 1994, http://www.rollingstone.com/movies/news/quentin-tarantino-the-madman-of-movie-mayhem-19941103.
79. Jeremy Diamond, "Trump: 'We Can't Continue to Allow China to Rape Our Country,'" *CNN*, May 2, 2016, https://www.cnn.com/2016/05/01/politics/donald-trump-china-rape/index.html.
80. Moni Basu, "U.S. Broadens Archaic Definition of Rape," *CNN*, January 6, 2012, http://www.cnn.com/2012/01/06/justice/rape-definition-revised/index.html. See also Cahill's definition in *Rethinking Rape*, 11.
81. See Pamela Haag, *Consent: Sexual Rights and the Transformation of Liberalism* (Ithaca, NY: Cornell University Press, 1999), xvii–xviii. For more on consent and its problematics, see Carole Pateman, *The Sexual Contract* (Palo Alto, CA: Stanford University Press, 1988); Saidiya V. Hartman, *Scenes of Subjection: Terror, Slavery, and Self-making in Nineteenth-Century America* (New York: Oxford University Press, 1997); Joseph J. Fischel, *Sex and Harm in the Age of Consent* (Minneapolis: University of Minnesota Press, 2016); and Avgi Saketopoulou, *Sexuality Beyond Consent: Risk, Race, Traumatophilia* (New York: New York University Press, 2023).

82. This is one of the conclusions of Élise Féron's study. See Féron, *Wartime Sexual Violence*, 172-73.
83. See E. M. Forster, "The Torque," in *The Life to Come and Other Stories*, ed. Oliver Stallybrass (New York: Norton, 1987), 151-65; T. E. Lawrence, *Seven Pillars of Wisdom: A Triumph* (London: Jonathan Cape, 1935), 441-47; Ian McGuire, *The North Water* (New York: Henry Holt, 2016); Howard Brenton, *The Romans in Britain*, in *Brenton Plays: 2* (London: Methuen, 1989) 1-95; Anthony Neilson, *Penetrator*, in *Neilson Plays: 1* (New York: Methuen Drama, 1998), 59-119; Sarah Kane, *Blasted*, in *Kane: Complete Plays* (London: Methuen Drama, 2001), 1-61; Mark Ravenhill, *Shopping and Fucking*, in *Ravenhill Plays: 1* (New York: Methuen Drama, 2001), 1-91.
84. Kenneth Cook, *Wake in Fright* (Melbourne: Text Classics, 2013); Diana Gabaldon, *Outlander* (New York: Dell, 1992); Dennis Cooper, *Frisk* (New York: Grove Weidenfeld, 1991).

CHAPTER 1

Epigraph. Caleb Smith, *The Prison and the American Imagination* (New Haven, CT: Yale University Press, 2009), 199.
1. John Hofsess, "Fortune and Men's Eyes—A Report from the Set in a Quebec City Prison," *Maclean's* 83, no. 12 (1970): 81.
2. Harper, *Are We Not Men?*, 171.
3. David Struckman-Johnson, Cindy Struckman-Johnson, et al., "A Pre-PREA Survey of Inmate and Correctional Staff Opinions on How to Prevent Prison Sexual Assault," *Prison Journal* 93, no. 4 (2013): 430. The Struckman-Johnsons are leading voices in prison-rape prevention, and Cindy Struckman-Johnson was a member of the National Prison Rape Elimination Commission in the United States established by the *Prison Rape Elimination Act* of 2003.
4. *Fortune* is a Canadian play. I use the term *American* to describe both the US and Canada. When I mean only the United States, I use the adjective *US American*.
5. Joseph F. Fishman, *Sex in Prison: Revealing Sex Conditions in American Prisons* (New York: National Library Press, 1934), 18.
6. Fishman, *Sex in Prison*, 85-90.
7. Alexander Berkman, *Memoirs of a Prison Anarchist* (New York: Mother Earth Publishing Association, 1912), 437-40.
8. Fishman, *Sex in Prison*, 98-99.
9. Alan J. Davis, "Sexual Assaults in the Philadelphia Prison System and Sheriff's Vans," *Trans-Action [Society]* 6, no. 2 (1968): 13.
10. Davis, "Sexual Assaults," 13.
11. Davis, "Sexual Assaults," 15.
12. Davis, "Sexual Assaults," 16.
13. Struckman-Johnson and Struckman-Johnson, "Pre-PREA Survey," 18. See Anthony M. Scacco, *Rape in Prison* (Springfield, IL: C. C. Thomas, 1975); Daniel Lockwood, *Prison Sexual Violence* (New York: Elsevier, 1980); William F. Pinar, *The Gender of Racial Politics and Violence in America: Lynching, Prison Rape, and the Crisis of Masculinity* (New York: Peter Lang, 2001).
14. Michelle Alexander, *The New Jim Crow: Mass Incarceration in the Age of Colorblindness*, rev. ed. (New York: New Press, 2012), 40-58.
15. Curry, *Man-Not*, 92.

16. Regina Kunzel, *Criminal Intimacy: Prison and the Uneven History of Modern American Sexuality* (Chicago: University of Chicago Press, 2008), 189.
17. Kunzel, *Criminal Intimacy*, 150–51.
18. The Sexual Offences Act 1967 decriminalized homosexual sex between men (homosexual sex between women was not illegal) in only England and Wales. Scotland would decriminalize homosexual sex in 1980, and Northern Ireland would follow suit in 1982. Homosexuality was decriminalized in Canada as a part of sweeping changes to the criminal code passed with the Criminal Law Amendment Act on May 14, 1969. Homosexuality in the United States was not decriminalized by the legislature but by a finding of the Supreme Court in the case *Lawrence v. Texas* in June 2003. Although there were no changes to US American law due to the Stonewall Riots, as an event signaling upheaval in the United States vis-à-vis its gay population they are difficult to overestimate.
19. John Herbert, *Fortune and Men's Eyes* (New York: Grove Press, 1967), 9.
20. Alexander Paterson, introduction to *"Now Barabbas . . .,"* by William Douglas Home (London: Longmans, Green & Co., 1947), viii.
21. Herbert, *Fortune*, 8.
22. Herbert, *Fortune*, 12.
23. Herbert, *Fortune*, 11.
24. Herbert, *Fortune*, 11.
25. George Chauncey, *Gay New York: Gender, Urban Culture, and the Making of the Gay Male World 1890–1940* (New York: Basic Books, 1994), 286–90; emphasis in original.
26. David M. Halperin, *How to Be Gay* (Cambridge, MA: Harvard University Press, 2012), 207.
27. Herbert, *Fortune*, 21.
28. Herbert, *Fortune*, 22.
29. Herbert, *Fortune*, 23.
30. Herbert, *Fortune*, 35–36.
31. Herbert, *Fortune*, 50, 53.
32. Herbert, *Fortune*, 70.
33. Herbert, *Fortune*, 70–71.
34. The film differs here. In the film, Mona is also raped by these men on the outside. In the play, rape appears to be restricted only to the world of the prison.
35. Herbert, *Fortune*, 89.
36. Herbert, *Fortune*, 96.
37. David Rothenberg, *Fortune in My Eyes: A Memoir of Broadway Glamour, Social Justice, and Political Passion* (Milwaukee, WI: Applause Theatre & Cinema Books, 2012), 50–52.
38. The role of Mona was designed by Herbert to be autobiographical. See Hofsess, "Fortune," 81. Robert Christian would notably go on to play the transfeminine character Ralph Agee in Norman Jewison's 1979 film *. . . And Justice for All*. He also performed for a year (1982) on the NBC soap opera *Another World*. He died of complications related to AIDS during the early years of the epidemic in 1983.
39. Rothenberg, *Fortune in My Eyes*, 61–62.
40. Sylvan Fox, "2 Ex-convicts, Onstage, Tell of 'Living Hell,'" *New York Times*, July 13, 1967, 29.
41. Gertrude Samuels, "A New Lobby—Ex-Cons," *New York Times*, October 19, 1969, SM36.
42. Caoimhe McAvinchey, *Theatre & Prison* (London: Palgrave Macmillan, 2011), 50.
43. Neil Carson, "Sexuality and Identity in *Fortune and Men's Eyes*," *Twentieth Century Literature* 18, no. 3 (1972): 207–8.

44. See also Linda Charlton, "The Terrifying Homosexual World of the Jail System," *New York Times*, April 25, 1971, 40; and David Rothenberg, "As If Imprisonment Itself Is Not Horrendous Enough . . . ," *New York Times*, January 29, 1977, 19.
45. Dan Sullivan, "A Distressing *Fortune and Men's Eyes*," *New York Times*, February 24, 1967, 29. Mario Montez was born René Rivera and was one of Andy Warhol's stars, also working with Charles Ludlam and Jack Smith in the 1960s and '70s. See Laurence Senelick, *The Changing Room: Sex, Drag and Theatre* (New York: Routledge, 2000), 423.
46. Edith Oliver, reviews of *People Is the Thing That the World Is Fullest Of*, *The Rimers of Eldritch*, and *Fortune and Men's Eyes*, *New Yorker*, March 4, 1967, 134. The *Village Voice* also saw the play as sentimental but found it more effective than Oliver and Sullivan did. See Michael Smith, reviews of *Fortune and Men's Eyes*, *MacBIRD!*, *People Is the Thing That the World Is Fullest Of*, and *June Bug Graduates Tonight*, *Village Voice*, March 2, 1967, 21–24.
47. Rosalyn Regelson, "Up the Camp Staircase," *New York Times*, March 3, 1968, D14.
48. Ronald Forsythe, "Why Can't 'We' Live Happily Ever After, Too?" *New York Times*, February 23, 1969, D1; Margaret Harford, "Mineo's Star on Rise Again as Stage Director," *Los Angeles Times*, January 2, 1969, F1. Note that Harford is not talking about Mineo's production here but the play itself. Mineo's production had yet to open.
49. Addison Verrill, review of *Fortune and Men's Eyes*, *Variety*, June 19, 1971, 17. Mart Crowley's *The Boys in the Band* (1968) is widely considered the first gay hit. It ran off-Broadway for more than one thousand performances. It was made into a film twice, directed by William Friedkin in 1970 and by Ryan Murphy in 2020.
50. Charles Marowitz, *Burnt Bridges: A Souvenir of the Swinging Sixties and Beyond* (London: Hodder & Stoughton, 1990), 116.
51. Rich., review of *Fortune and Men's Eyes*, *Variety*, November 13, 1968, 153. (Reviewers in *Variety* were, at this time, designated by four-letter appellations only.)
52. Michael Gregg Michaud, *Sal Mineo: A Biography* (New York: Crown Archetype, 2010), 259; emphasis in original.
53. Sullivan, "Three Plays Examine Dark Side of the Gay Life," *Los Angeles Times*, March 30, 1969, T32.
54. Bill Edwards, review of *Fortune and Men's Eyes*, *Daily Variety*, January 13, 1969, 10.
55. See Harford, "Mineo's Star," F9, Michaud, *Sal Mineo*, 255–78, and H. Paul Jeffers, *Sal Mineo: His Life, Murder, and Mystery* (New York: Carroll & Graf, 2000), 131–43.
56. Fredric L. Milstein, "*Fortune* Opens at Coronet," *Los Angeles Times*, January 11, 1969, B7.
57. Sal Mineo quoted in Michaud, *Sal Mineo*, 261.
58. Michaud, *Sal Mineo*, 262.
59. Jeffers, *Sal Mineo*, 137; Sullivan, "Three Plays," T32.
60. Joe Bonelli quoted in Jeffers, *Sal Mineo*, 140.
61. Clive Barnes, "Question Marks at Stage 73," *New York Times*, October 23, 1969, 55.
62. David De Porte, review of *Fortune and Men's Eyes*, *Village Voice*, November 6, 1969, 45. The reference to 42nd Street may be obscure in the twenty-first century. In 1969 the term was expected to signify sex work.
63. Richard Hummler, review of *Fortune and Men's Eyes*, *Variety*, October 29, 1969, 70.
64. Sandra Schmidt, "Author Disavows *Fortune* Version," *Los Angeles Times*, October 25, 1969, B8.
65. John Herbert, "*Men's Eyes* Playwright Deplores Sex Emphasis in Sal Mineo Staging," *Variety*, October 8, 1969, 66–68.
66. Barnes, "Question Marks," 55; Hummler, review of *Fortune*, 70; Sandra Schmidt, "Author Disavows," B8.

67. Jeffers, *Sal Mineo*, 142.
68. De Porte, review of *Fortune*, 45.
69. This was true in Istanbul as well. See Magdalena J. Zaborowska, *James Baldwin's Turkish Decade: Erotics of Exile* (Durham, NC: Duke University Press, 2009), 183–84.
70. Cluchey's play was written as a part of the San Quentin Drama Workshop. It had its first reading in 1965 in the prison itself. The play premiered in December of 1965 as part of the season of the San Francisco Actor's Workshop, which famously performed Beckett's *Waiting for Godot* for San Quentin's prisoners. It was directed by Kenneth Kitch. It was not widely known at the time, but it also played at Arena Stage in 1969 in a production directed by Kitch. *Short Eyes* premiered in 1974 at the Theatre of the Riverside Church, moving to the Vivian Beaumont Theatre at Lincoln Center in New York City as a part of Joseph Papp's New York Shakespeare Festival in May of that year. It was directed by Marvin Felix Camillo. The 1977 film version of *Short Eyes* was made available in several formats following a renewed interest in Piñero, about whom a biographical film was made in 2001 starring Benjamin Bratt.
71. See John Galsworthy, *Justice: A Tragedy in Four Acts* (New York: Charles Scribner's Sons, 1910), especially 81–84; Martin Flavin, *The Criminal Code: A Drama in Prologue and Three Acts*, in *The Best Plays of 1929–30 and the Year Book of the Drama in America*, ed. Burns Mantle (New York: Dodd Mead, 1934), 71–107; Albert Bein, *Little Ol' Boy: A Play in Three Acts* (New York: Samuel French, 1935); Tennessee Williams, *Not about Nightingales*, in *Plays 1937–1955*, ed. Mel Gussow and Kenneth Holditch (New York: Library of America, 2000), 97–188; and William Douglas Home, *"Now Barabbas . . ."* (London: Longmans, Green & Co., 1947).
72. This pattern holds for prison dramas in the cinema, as well. Consider, for example, Wallace Beery's doomed character in George W. Hill's 1930 film *The Big House* or the nineteen-year-old naïf-cum-criminal played by Eleanor Parker in John Cromwell's *Caged* (1950).
73. Mariame Kaba and Kelly Hayes, "A Jailbreak of the Imagination: Seeing Prisons for What They Are and Demanding Transformation," in *We Do This 'til We Free Us: Abolitionist Organizing and Transforming Justice*, by Mariame Kaba (Chicago: Haymarket, 2021), 20.
74. Peter Dickinson, *Screening Gender, Framing Genre: Canadian Literature into Film* (Toronto: University of Toronto Press, 2007), 107. Dickinson further cites Jerry Wasserman, "Introduction," *Modern Canadian Plays*, rev. ed. (Vancouver: Talonbooks, 1986), 9–23.
75. Alan Sinfield, *Out on Stage: Lesbian and Gay Theatre in the Twentieth Century* (New Haven: Yale University Press, 1999), 124. Further, *Out on Stage* places *Fortune* on a historical timeline with the prison dramas *Little Ol' Boy*, *"Now Barabbas . . . ,"* and Jean Genet's *Deathwatch (Haute Surveillance)*, plays that include queer characters but do not include sexual violence. *"Now Barabbas . . . ,"* for example, includes the suggestion of sex between prisoners, but the play only describes homosexual desire and does not characterize that desire as violent. *Not about Nightingales* includes a prison queen, but it is unclear why Sinfield includes *Little Ol' Boy* in his discussion. The boys in Bein's play exhibit no queerness (or indeed any sexual desires at all), and the play is a prison-reform play like *Justice* or *The Criminal Code*, not one that is primarily a document of prison life like *Short Eyes* or *The Cage*. Because Sinfield's reading figures *Fortune* as a kind of thematic heir to these other three plays, he ignores the rape that is central to the action of *Fortune*. See Jean Genet, *Deathwatch*, in *The Maids and Deathwatch: Two Plays*, trans. Bernard Frechtman, (New York: Grove Press, 1954), 101–63.

76. Anton Wagner's discussion of Canadian critics' responses to the play is especially telling. See *Establishing Our Boundaries: English-Canadian Theatre Criticism* (Toronto: University of Toronto Press, 1999), 38–39.
77. Martin Esslin, "Nudity: Barely the Beginning?" *New York Times*, December 15, 1968, D18; Fox, "2 Ex-convicts," 29.
78. Dan Sullivan, "Three Plays," T32; Regelson, "Up the Camp," D14.
79. Clinton T. Duffy quoted in Samuels, "New Lobby," 46.
80. Herbert, *Fortune*, 89.
81. Kunzel, *Criminal Intimacy*, 153.
82. Miguel Piñero, *Short Eyes* (New York: Hill and Wang, 1975), 65–69.
83. Rick Cluchey, *The Cage: A Play in One Act* (San Francisco, CA: Barbwire Press, 1970), see especially 18–22.
84. Kunzel, *Criminal Intimacy*, 6.
85. Regelson, "Up the Camp," D14.
86. Human Rights Watch, *No Escape: Male Rape in U.S. Prisons* (New York: Human Rights Watch, 2001), 3. Human Rights Watch does not credit her, but this citation is a word-for-word direct quotation from Joanne Mariner's "Body and Soul: The Trauma of Prison Rape" in *Building Violence: How America's Rush to Incarcerate Creates More Violence*, ed. John P. May (Thousand Oaks, CA: SAGE Publications, 2000), 125–31.
87. Peter Wade, "Crowd Cheers and Laughs When Trump Threatens Journalists with Prison Rape," *Rolling Stone*, October 23, 2022, https://www.rollingstone.com/politics/politics-news/trump-threatens-journalists-prison-rape-1234616603.

CHAPTER 2

1. Robert F. Kiernan, *Gore Vidal* (New York: Frederick Ungar, 1982), 8.
2. Gore Vidal, "An Afterword," in *The City and the Pillar Revised* (New York: Signet, 1965), 157. The original novel is divided into two sections: "The City" and "The Pillar of Salt"; *City Revised* has no divisions.
3. Gore Vidal, *The City and the Pillar* (New York: E. P. Dutton, 1948), 306.
4. Gore Vidal, *Palimpsest: A Memoir* (New York: Random House, 1995), 190. I address Vidal's use of *same-sexualists* later in this chapter.
5. Byrne R. S. Fone, *The Columbia Anthology of Gay Literature: Readings from Western Antiquity to the Present Day* (New York Columbia University Press, 1998), 690–91.
6. See Vidal, *Palimpsest*, 189.
7. See Ray Lewis White, *Gore Vidal* (New York: Twayne, 1968), 56–57; Claude J. Summers, *Gay Fictions: Wilde to Stonewall: Studies in a Male Homosexual Literary Tradition* (New York: Continuum, 1990), 127; Stephen Adams, *The Homosexual as Hero in Contemporary Fiction* (London: Vision, 1980), 24; Kiernan, *Gore Vidal*, 38; Vidal, *Palimpsest*, 152.
8. For discussions of the prose style see Summers, *Gay Fictions*, 116; and White, *Gore Vidal*, 56.
9. Richard McLaughlin, "Precarious Status," *Saturday Review of Literature*, January 10, 1948, 14.
10. McLaughlin, "Precarious Status," 14.
11. Gore Vidal, *The City and the Pillar Revised, with a New Preface by the Author and Seven Early Stories* (New York: Random House, 1995), 66.
12. Angela Fratarrola, "Frustration and Silence in Gore Vidal's *The City and the Pillar*," *Literature and Homosexuality*, ed. Michael J. Meyer (Amsterdam: Rodopi, 2000), 35.

13. Dennis Altman, *Gore Vidal's America* (Cambridge, MA: Polity Press, 2005), 128–29.
14. Michel Foucault, *The History of Sexuality—Volume 1: An Introduction*, trans. Robert Hurley (New York: Vintage, 1990), 43.
15. See also Nikolai Endres, "The Pillaged Pillar: *Hubris* and *Polis* in Gore Vidal's *The City and the Pillar*," *Classical and Modern Literature* 24, no. 2 (2004): 50.
16. Harry Thomas, "'Immaculate Manhood': *The City and the Pillar*, *Giovanni's Room*, and the Straight-Acting Gay Man," *Twentieth-Century Literature* 59, no. 4 (2013): 603. See Vidal, *City and the Pillar Revised*, 66.
17. White, *Gore Vidal*, 56.
18. Vidal's interest in antiquity is well documented; see Quentin J. Broughall, *Gore Vidal and Antiquity: Sex, Politics and Religion* (London: Routledge, 2023).
19. This sequence is equally short in the original, see Vidal, *City and the Pillar*, 306–7.
20. Vidal, *City and the Pillar Revised*, 203.
21. See Augustine, *The City of God against the Pagans*, vol. 1, trans. George E. McCracken (Cambridge, MA: Harvard University Press, 1957): 16.2. "[If] a will remains unshaken and steadfast, no matter what anyone else does with the body, . . . no blame attaches to the one who suffers it. But since it is not only the occasion of pain, but also the occasion of lust that can be inflicted on another's body by force, in the latter case, though shamefastness, to which a superlatively steadfast mind holds fast, is not thrust out [*excutit*], yet shame is thrust in [*incutit*], shame for fear that the mind too may be thought to have consented to an act that could perhaps not have taken place without some carnal pleasure."
22. Vidal, *City and the Pillar Revised*, 203.
23. Vidal, *City and the Pillar Revised*, 202.
24. Vidal, *City and the Pillar Revised*, 126. The original version mentions neither rape nor sex; it reads "For the first time in months Jim felt the hot, almost painful, sensation in his stomach, the burning that must be released." See Vidal, *City and the Pillar*, 189.
25. In his 1965 afterword he says, "there is of course no such thing as a homosexual. Despite current usage, the word is an adjective describing a sexual action, not a noun describing a recognizable type." See Vidal, "An Afterword," 155.
26. Fredric Jameson, "The Great American Hunter, or, Ideological Content in the Novel," *College English* 34, no. 2 (1972): 186; Anthony Thwaite, "Out of Bondage," *New Statesman*, September 11, 1970, 310.
27. Dwight Garner, "*Deliverance*: A Dark Heart Still Beating," *New York Times*, August 25, 2010, C1.
28. Henry Hart, *James Dickey: The World as a Lie* (New York: Picador, 2000), 487.
29. Pamela E. Barnett, *Dangerous Desire: Literature of Sexual Freedom and Sexual Violence since the Sixties* (New York: Routledge, 2004), 59; Jennie Lightweis-Goff, "'How Willing to Let Anything Be Done': James Dickey's Feminist Praxis," in *The Way We Read James Dickey*, ed. Willam B. Thesing and Theda Wrede (Columbia: University of South Carolina Press, 2009), 239.
30. J. W. Williamson, *Hillbillyland: What the Movies Did to the Mountains and What the Mountains Did to the Movies* (Chapel Hill: University of North Carolina Press, 1995), 291.
31. As Lightweis-Goff argues, "Though [*Deliverance*] has provoked four decades of laughter, that laughter does not reside within the text." Lightweis-Goff, "How Willing," 248; emphasis in original.
32. Even a text like Sally Robinson's *Marked Men: White Masculinity in Crisis* (New York: Columbia University Press, 2000), which aims to treat the novel and the film separately,

cannot help but place the two next to one another, doing so with such frequency that when reading her analysis, it is difficult to keep the film and the novel distinct.
33. James Dickey, *Deliverance* (New York: Dell, 1970), 191.
34. Dickey, *Deliverance*, 275-76.
35. See Ronald Baughman, *Understanding James Dickey* (Columbia: University of South Carolina Press, 1985), 109; Douglas Keesey, "James Dickey and the Macho Persona," in *Critical Essays on James Dickey*, ed. Robert Kirschten (New York: G. K. Hall, 1994), 205; Barnett, *Dangerous Desire*, 36; Joyce M. Pair, "Measuring the Fictive Motion: War in *Deliverance, Alnilam*, and *To the White Sea*," *Texas Review* 17, no. 3-4 (1996): 55-92.
36. See Casey Howard Clabough, *Elements: The Novels of James Dickey* (Macon, GA: Mercer University Press, 2002), 38; Jameson, "Great American Hunter," 186; Ed Madden, "The Buggering Hillbilly and the Buddy Movie: Male Sexuality in *Deliverance*," in Thesing and Wrede, eds., *The Way We Read James Dickey*, 199-200.
37. For discussions of nature and civilization in *Deliverance* see Cherry Levin, "Adherence to Propp: James Dickey's *Deliverance* in Novel and Film," in Thesing and Wrede, eds., *The Way We Read James Dickey*, 83; Theda Wrede, "Nature and Gender in James Dickey's *Deliverance*: An Ecofeminist Reading," in Thesing and Wrede, eds., *The Way We Read James Dickey*, 177; Allison Graham, *Framing the South: Hollywood, Television, and Race during the Civil Rights Struggle* (Baltimore, MD: Johns Hopkins University Press, 2001), 24; Scott Slovic, "Visceral Faulkner: Fiction and the Tug of the Organic World," in *Faulkner and the Ecology of the South*, ed. Joseph R. Urgo and Ann J. Abadie (Jackson: University Press of Mississippi, 2005), 128.
38. See Baughman, *Understanding James Dickey*, 117; and Richard J. Calhoun and Robert W. Hill, *James Dickey* (Boston: Twayne, 1983), 115.
39. Dickey, *Deliverance*, 144-45.
40. Dickey, *Deliverance*, 161, 176.
41. Dickey, *Deliverance*, 208.
42. Calhoun and Hill, *James Dickey*, 109; Wrede, "Nature and Gender," 182.
43. Barnett, *Dangerous Desire*, 47.
44. Dickey, *Deliverance*, 73.
45. Dickey, *Deliverance*, 80. Note that the current enters into Ed without penetration here, possessing him or empowering him in a nongendered way.
46. Dickey, *Deliverance*, 80-81.
47. Ed explicitly describes the river without gendering it. See Dickey, *Deliverance*, 72.
48. Pair, "Measuring the Fictive Motion," 62.
49. See Michael S. Kimmel, *Manhood in America: A Cultural History*, 2nd ed. (Oxford: Oxford University Press, 2006), 45-46.
50. Dickey, *Deliverance*, 69.
51. *Il existe à la base de la vie humaine, un principe d'insuffisance*. Dickey, *Deliverance*, v. For the translation see Georges Bataille, *Inner Experience*, trans. Stuart Kendall (Albany: State University of New York Press, 2014), 85.
52. James Dickey, quoted in Hart, *James Dickey*, 473. It is worth noting, here, that Dickey uses the phrase "penetration *to*"—rape doesn't figure in this phrase at all. Rodger Cunningham, too, has noted that "*Deliverance* has the structure of a rite of passage to adulthood." See Cunningham, *Apples on the Flood: The Southern Mountain Experience* (Knoxville: University of Tennessee Press, 1987), 130.
53. Dickey, *Deliverance*, 119-21.

54. Dickey, *Deliverance*, 108.
55. Dickey, *Deliverance*, 112; Jean Améry, *At the Mind's Limits: Compilations by a Survivor of Auschwitz and Its Realities*, trans. Sidney Rosenfeld and Stella P. Rosenfeld (Bloomington: Indiana University Press, 1984), 27.
56. Dickey, *Deliverance*, 113.
57. Dickey, *Deliverance*, 114.
58. Dickey, *Deliverance*, 119.
59. Dickey, *Deliverance*, 128.
60. Barnett, *Dangerous Desire*, 45-6.
61. Instead, at the end of *Deliverance*, Ed describes Bobby as "dead weight," an appellation he has used much earlier in the novel. See Dickey, *Deliverance*, 276.
62. Barnett, *Dangerous Desire*, 36.
63. Madden, "Buggering Hillbilly," 202.
64. Dickey, *Deliverance*, 22. See also Peggy Goodman Endel, "Dickey, Dante, and the Demonic: Reassessing *Deliverance*," *American Literature* 60, no. 4 (1988): 611-24. I noted earlier that he describes the river entering his rectum, translating this penetration as pleasure, but Ed also meditates on the possibility of being physically entered by a man and does so without apparent disgust. Staring at the man he has finally killed, Ed tells us that "If Lewis had not shot his companion, he and I would have made a kind of love, painful and terrifying to me, in some dreadful way pleasurable to him, but we would have been together in the flesh, there on the floor of the woods." See Dickey, *Deliverance*, 180.
65. See Barnett, *Dangerous Desire*; Williamson, *Hillbillyland*; Pair, "Measuring the Fictive Motion"; Wrede, "Nature and Gender"; and especially John M. Clum, *"He's All Man": Learning Masculinity, Gayness, and Love from American Movies* (London: Palgrave Macmillan 2002).
66. Hart, *James Dickey*, 90.
67. James Dickey quoted in Hart, *James Dickey*, 470.
68. John Boorman, *Adventures of a Suburban Boy* (London: Faber and Faber, 2003), 202.
69. Barnett, *Dangerous Desire*, 57; Pair, "Measuring the Fictive Motion," 62.
70. Dickey, *Deliverance*, 268.
71. Dickey, *Deliverance*, 36.
72. Scott, *Extravagant Objection*, 9.
73. José Esteban Muñoz, *Disidentifications: Queers of Color and the Performance of Politics* (Minneapolis: University of Minnesota Press, 1999), 58.
74. Barnett, *Dangerous Desire*, 46.
75. See Zaborowska, *Baldwin's Turkish Decade*, 141-95. The title in Turkish is a play on words, referencing a longer idiom meaning something akin to "nobody loves you when you're down and out." The implication in the Turkish title is that the person will have a friend after all and will not find himself in a position to "all alone beweep my outcast state."
76. Melinda Plastas and Eve Allegra Raimon, "Brutality and Brotherhood: James Baldwin and Prison Sexuality," *African American Review* 46, no. 4 (2013): 687.
77. Plastas and Raimon, "Brutality and Brotherhood," 688.
78. In *Train*, Baldwin has Caleb Proudhammer, in a discussion explicitly about masculinity, declare both his potential openness to having sex with a man and his absolute refusal to suffer rape. See James Baldwin, *Tell Me How Long the Train's Been Gone*, in *James Baldwin: Later Novels*, ed. Darryl Pinckney (New York: Library of America, 2015), 178.
79. Zaborowska, *Baldwin's Turkish Decade*, 170-73.

80. Zaborowska, *Baldwin's Turkish Decade*, 180.
81. While Baldwin's thinking was obviously informed by the play, it is likely that James Dickey, too, took note of *Fortune*. According to Dickey's biographer, he "considered using a title for the novel—*Trouble Deaf Heaven*—suggested by [Lester] Mansfield. The phrase fit the existentialist conviction that heaven was 'deaf' to human misery because it and God did not exist." The phrase "trouble deaf heaven" is from Shakespeare's Sonnet 29, which begins: "When in disgrace with fortune and men's eyes." See Hart, *James Dickey*, 174.
82. Patrick Elliot Alexander, *From Slave Ship to Supermax: Mass Incarceration, Prisoner Abuse, and the New Neo-Slave Novel* (Philadelphia, PA: Temple University Press, 2018), 31.
83. Ernest L. Gibson III, *Salvific Manhood: James Baldwin's Novelization of Male Intimacy* (Lincoln: University of Nebraska Press), 99–123, especially 117.
84. Marriott, *On Black Men*, 15-21
85. Marlon B. Ross, "Race, Rape, Castration: Feminist Theories of Sexual Violence and Masculine Strategies of Black Protest," in *Masculinity Studies and Feminist Theory: New Directions*, ed. Judith Kegan Gardiner (New York: Columbia University Press, 2002), 327.
86. For Baldwin's fears see James Baldwin, "Freaks and the American Ideal of Manhood," in *James Baldwin: Collected Essays*, ed. Toni Morrison (New York: Library of America, 1998), 814-29; and *No Name in the Street*, in Morrison, ed., *James Baldwin*, 390. For *Lawrence of Arabia*, see James Baldwin, "The Devil Finds Work," in Morrison, ed., *James Baldwin*, 532-41. Baldwin's reading of the violence in *Lawrence* is intriguing because it makes clear what is decidedly unclear in *Seven Pillars of Wisdom* and even less clear in David Lean's film. There was, however, a notable play about Lawrence produced at London's Haymarket Theatre in May 1960, and the sexual violence is much more clearly articulated in that, though still decidedly offstage. See Terence Rattigan, *Ross: A Dramatic Portrait* (London: Hamish Hamilton, 1960), 82–90.
87. Barry Jenkins's sumptuous, award-winning film version of *Beale Street* completely elides male/male rape as a topic.
88. Herbert R. Lottman, "It's Hard to Be James Baldwin," *Intellectual Digest* 2 (July 1972), 68.
89. Baldwin had originally envisioned the false charged to be stealing a television set. See Lottman, "It's Hard to Be," 68.
90. James Baldwin, *If Beale Street Could Talk*, in *James Baldwin: Later Novels*, ed. Darryl Pinckney (New York: Library of America, 2015) 505; emphasis in original.
91. Curry, *Man-Not*, 28.
92. Curry, *Man-Not*, 92.
93. Baldwin, *Beale Street*, 506.
94. Baldwin, *Beale Street*, 437.
95. Baldwin, *Beale Street*, 442-43.
96. Baldwin, *Beale Street*, 440.
97. Baldwin, *Beale Street*, 445.
98. Baldwin, *Beale Street*, 492.
99. Gibson, *Salvific Manhood*, 173.
100. Trudier Harris, "The Eye as Weapon in *If Beale Street Could Talk*," *MELUS* 5, no. 3 (1978): 59.
101. Baldwin, *Beale Street*, 490; emphasis in original.
102. Aaron Ngozi Oforlea, *James Baldwin, Toni Morrison, and the Rhetorics of Black Male Subjectivity* (Columbus: Ohio State University Press, 2017), 178–79.
103. Baldwin, *Beale Street*, 443.

104. Baldwin, *Beale Street*, 444.
105. Baldwin, *Beale Street*, 373.
106. See especially Baldwin, *Beale Street*, 440.
107. Baldwin notes this day as Columbus Day, October 12, 1973, which is also Yom Kippur, the Day of Atonement; new worlds are everywhere in this schema.
108. Baldwin, *Beale Street*, 509.
109. Baldwin, *Beale Street*, 442.
110. See Edward Margolies and Michel Fabre, *The Several Lives of Chester Himes* (Jackson: University Press of Mississippi, 1997), 31; Lawrence P. Jackson, *Chester B. Himes: A Biography* (New York: Norton, 2017), 105, 108.
111. Thomas Alan Dichter, "'An Extreme Sense of Protest against Everything': Chester Himes's Prison Novel," *American Literature* 90, no. 1 (2018): 112.
112. Jimmy Monroe is white, despite the novel's autobiographical character. For discussion of this topic, see Chester Himes, *The Quality of Hurt: The Autobiography of Chester Himes—Volume 1* (New York: Doubleday, 1972), 117; Dennis Childs, *Slaves of the State: Black Incarceration from the Chain Gang to the Penitentiary* (Minneapolis: University of Minnesota Press, 2015), 148–54; and Clare Rolens, "Write like a Man: Chester Himes and the Criminal Text Beyond Bars," *Callaloo* 37, no. 2 (2014): 443–46.
113. Rolens, "Write like a Man," 432.
114. See Chester Himes, *Cast the First Stone* (New York: Signet, 1972), 141.
115. See Mitchel P. Roth, *Fire in the Big House: America's Deadliest Prison Disaster* (Athens: Ohio University Press, 2019), especially 1–37.
116. Rolens, "Write like a Man," 434.
117. Childs, *Slaves of the State*, 169.
118. Childs, *Slaves of the State*, 167.
119. Chester Himes, *Yesterday Will Make You Cry* (New York: Norton, 1998), 315. Jimmy's jealousy is omitted in *Cast*. See Himes, *Cast*, 258.
120. Himes, *Yesterday*, 316. Rico's sexual pleasure is omitted in *Cast*. See Himes, *Cast*, 259.
121. Himes, *Yesterday*, 317. Cf. Himes, *Cast*, 260.
122. Earlier in the novel, Jimmy refuses to take the passive position in sex with Lively, despite being in love with him. See Himes, *Yesterday*, 200–201. This passage does not appear in *Cast*.
123. Himes, *Yesterday*, 119. This passage does not appear in *Cast*.
124. Himes, *Yesterday*, 124. This passage does not appear in *Cast*.
125. Himes, *Yesterday*, 311. The same passage in *Cast* omits "sissy." See Himes, *Cast*, 256.
126. This is true of the sexuality he finds in prison as well as the gambling and other so-called vices. See Himes, *Quality*, 61.
127. Margolies and Fabre, *Several Lives*, 34. In *Cast*, the narrative is restricted only to the prison, and the outside world appears very far away. As Robert Lee argues of the earlier version, "The outside world Himes only marginally keeps in view. Jimmy gets letters from his mother. Clothes, cigarettes and food are smuggled in on the prison underground. In the main, however, the prison is its own total world, inverting all normal canons of behavior. The prison hospital becomes a haven of sexual inversion rather than cure; prison reality to Jimmy is unreal; religious liberty is practiced in a guarded church. Love, need, human contact are made over into parasitic, threatening processes." See A. Robert Lee, "Violence Real and Imagined: The World of Chester Himes' Novels," *Negro American Literature Forum* 10, no. 1 (1976): 17.

128. Himes, *Yesterday*, 323. The passage is, predictably, omitted in *Cast*. See Himes, *Cast*, 261.
129. Rolens, "Write like a Man," 437.
130. Himes, *Yesterday*, 356. Cf. Himes, *Cast*, 291.
131. Himes, *Yesterday*, 360. Cf. Himes, *Cast*, 295.

CHAPTER 3

Epigraph. Tony Hoagland, *What Narcissism Means to Me* (Saint Paul, MN: Graywolf Press, 2000), 56.

1. R. Barton Palmer, "Narration, Text, Intertext: The Two Versions of *Deliverance*," in *"Struggling for Wings": The Art of James Dickey*, ed. Robert Kirschten (Columbia: University of South Carolina Press, 1997), 194. Palmer is not alone in his belief that *Deliverance* is the first male/male rape in cinema; see also Levin, "Adherence to Propp," 79.
2. Verrill, review of *Fortune*, 17.
3. Peter Biskind, *Easy Riders, Raging Bulls: How the Sex-Drugs-and-Rock 'n' Roll Generation Saved Hollywood* (New York: Simon & Schuster, 1998), 15.
4. See also Dominic Lennard, R. Barton Palmer, and Murray Pomerance, eds., *The Other Hollywood Renaissance* (Edinburgh: Edinburgh University Press, 2020) and David A. Cook, *Lost Illusions: American Cinema in the Shadow of Watergate and Vietnam, 1970-1979* (New York: Charles Scribner, 2000).
5. Quentin Tarantino, *Cinema Speculation* (New York: HarperCollins, 2022).
6. Stephen Prince, *Classical Film Violence: Designing and Regulating Brutality in Hollywood Cinema, 1930-1968* (New Brunswick, NJ: Rutgers University Press, 2003), 220.
7. For a discussion of the film's editing, see Glenn Frankel, *Shooting Midnight Cowboy: Art, Sex, Loneliness, Liberation, and the Making of a Dark Classic* (New York: Farrar, Straus and Giroux, 2021), 241-46.
8. Charles Champlin, "*Midnight Cowboy* Rides Manhattan's Lower Depths," *Los Angeles Times*, July 27, 1969, P22.
9. Vincent Canby, review of *Midnight Cowboy*, *New York Times*, May 26, 1969, 54.
10. Louise Sweeney, "Hoffman, Voight in Schlesinger Film," *Christian Science Monitor*, June 13, 1969, 4; Gary Arnold, review of *Midnight Cowboy*, *Washington Post*, July 31, 1969, C1ff.
11. Frankel, *Shooting Midnight Cowboy*, 140.
12. James Leo Herlihy, *Midnight Cowboy* (New York: Simon & Schuster, 1965), 89-91.
13. Robert J. Landry, review of *Midnight Cowboy*, *Variety*, May 14, 1969, 6.
14. Frankel, *Shooting Midnight Cowboy*, 140.
15. Boorman, *Adventures of a Suburban Boy*, 181. Boorman's films continued to explore these themes, most explicitly in *Zardoz* (1974) and *The Emerald Forest* (1985).
16. Cunningham, *Apples on the Flood*, 122; Williamson, *Hillbillyland*, 157.
17. Carol J. Clover, *Men, Women, and Chain Saws: Gender in the Modern Horror Film* (Princeton, NJ: Princeton University Press, 1992), 126.
18. David Griffith, *A Good War Is Hard to Find* (Brooklyn, NY: Soft Skull Press, 2006), 77.
19. Stanley Kubrick quoted in Boorman, *Adventures of a Suburban Boy*, 197; Madden, "Buggering Hillbilly," 196.
20. Brownmiller, *Against Her Will*, 304.
21. Prince, *Classical Film Violence*, 88-89.
22. Prince, *Classical Film Violence*, 9.
23. Dickey, *Deliverance*, 114.

24. Brownmiller, *Against Her Will*, 303.
25. Prince, *Classical Film Violence*, 69. Prince cites D. Caroline Blanchard, Barry Graczyk, and Robert J. Blanchard, "Differential Reactions of Men and Women to Realism, Physical Damage, and Emotionality in Violent Films," *Aggressive Behavior* 12, no. 1 (1986): 45–55.
26. Prince, *Classical Film Violence*, 75.
27. All of the porcine imagery was added for the film. It does not appear anywhere in the novel, nor does it appear in Dickey's (unfilmed) screenplay. See James Dickey, *Deliverance* [screenplay] (Carbondale: Southern Illinois University Press, 1982). Many, however, have claimed to have added the "squeal like a pig" language. In the director's commentary on the 2007 DVD release of *Deliverance*, Boorman credits his creative assistant Rospo Pallenberg with the line, saying that "squeal like a pig" was originally intended "to take the place of a more powerful kind of language" in a cleaned-up-for-television version of the movie, "but it was so good that I decided to keep it in the main version." Frank Rickman, who worked on *Deliverance* as the liaison between Boorman and the locals in Rabun County, Georgia, claimed in a 1973 issue of *Foxfire* that squealing like a hog was his addition; see Barbara Taylor and Mary Thomas, "He Shouted Loud, 'Hosanna, Deliverance Will Come,'" *Foxfire* 7, no. 4 (1973): 304. Dickey's biographer and other critics have repeated Rickman's story, but Ned Beatty has also taken credit for the line. At the RiverRun International Film Festival in 2006, Beatty claimed that "the whole 'Squeal Like a Pig' thing . . . came from guess who." Mark Burger reports that "as the audience laughed, [Beatty] theatrically put his head in his hands and silently pointed to himself, before elaborating how director Boorman encouraged him to improvise the scene with his onscreen tormenter"; see Mark Burger, "Beatty Given Master of Cinema Award: Character Actor Is a Veteran of More Than 200 Film and Television Productions," *Winston-Salem [NC] Journal*, March 19, 2006, B1. If Beatty's tale appears improbable, Boorman's and Rickman's stories are equally specious. As I have demonstrated, the pig references last throughout the entire sequence, including extremely specific choreography and three unique pieces of text. Further, the extended sequence of squeals and their repetition is integral to the way Boorman presents the moment of Bobby's violent penetration. The porcine imagery is part of the very structure of the sequence and cannot be explained away as a simple linguistic invention necessitated by television censorship.
28. Cunningham, *Apples on the Flood*, 125.
29. Carol Mason, "The Hillbilly Defense: Culturally Mediating U.S. Terror at Home and Abroad," *NWSA Journal* 17, no. 3 (2005): 52.
30. Mel Y. Chen, *Animacies: Biopolitics, Racial Mattering, and Queer Affect* (Durham, NC: Duke University Press, 2012), 102–15.
31. Graham, *Framing the South*, 182.
32. Clover, *Men, Women, and Chain Saws*, 131.
33. Clover's chief example is Meir Zarchi's *I Spit on Your Grave* (1978), see 114–65.
34. Kevin Kelly, "*Godspell, Scarecrow*—New Films," *Boston Globe*, April 13, 1973, 31.
35. Rex Reed, "Sensitive Bums; Lead Balloon; Mairzy Doats," *[NY] Daily News*, April 13, 1973, 80. The child is not an infant. This is an error in Reed's description.
36. Kelly, "*Godspell, Scarecrow*," 31.
37. Perry Stewart, "Huzzahs for Hackman," *Fort Worth Star-Telegram*, June 21, 1973, 8-B.
38. See also R. Barton Palmer, "Jerry Schatzberg's Downfall Portraits: His Cinema of Loneliness," in *The Other Hollywood Renaissance*, ed. Dominic Lennard, R. Barton Palmer, and Murray Pomerance (Edinburgh: University of Edinburgh Press, 2020), 308–28.

39. Peter Bradshaw, review of *Scarecrow*, *Guardian*, April 25, 2013, https://www.theguardian.com/film/2013/apr/25/scarecrow-review.
40. Charles Champlin, "The Odyssey of a Couple of Oddballs," *Los Angeles Times*, April 4, 1973, C1.
41. Gene Siskel, review of *Scarecrow*, *Chicago Tribune*, June 27, 1973, 52; John Huddy, "*Scarecrow* Is Warm, Funny, Human: Takes over Where *Midnight Cowboy*, *Easy Rider* Left Off," *Miami Herald*, June 26, 1973, 10C; Roger Ebert, review of *Scarecrow*, RogerEbert.com, April 12, 1973, https://www.rogerebert.com/reviews/scarecrow-1973.
42. Aljean Harmetz, "Boy Meets Boy—or, Where the Girls Aren't," *New York Times*, January 20, 1974, B1.
43. Harmetz, "Boy Meets Boy," B11.
44. Stephen Farber, "Just a Locker Room Fantasy?" *New York Times*, May 13, 1973, D13.
45. Farber, "Just a Locker Room," D13.
46. Sedgwick, *Between Men*, 3.
47. For Robin Wood this is one of the key features of the '70s buddy film. See Robin Wood, *Hollywood from Vietnam to Reagan . . . and Beyond*, 2nd ed. (New York: Columbia University Press), 203.
48. Kaja Silverman, *Male Subjectivity at the Margins* (New York: Routledge, 1992), 55.
49. "Bearly Men," *Married with Children*, season 10, episode 12, original air date December 3, 1995, written by Russell Marcus, directed by Gerry Cohen.
50. "The Juggs Have Left the Building," *Married with Children*, season 11, episode 7, original air date December 1, 1996, written by Vince Cheung and Ben Montanio, directed by Gerry Cohen.
51. "The Last Man on Earth," *In Living Color*, season 3, episode 23, original air date March 29, 1992, directed by Terri McCoy.
52. Sigmund Freud, *Jokes and Their Relation to the Unconscious*, standard ed., trans. James Strachey (New York: Norton, 1960), 243–44; emphasis added.
53. Freud, *Jokes*, 250.
54. Silverman, *Male Subjectivity*, 64.

CHAPTER 4

Epigraph. Clover, *Men, Women, and Chain Saws*, 154.
1. Manohla Dargis, "Pulp Instincts," *Sight and Sound* 4, no. 5 (1994): 9.
2. Joe Wlodarz, "Rape Fantasies: Hollywood and Homophobia," in *Masculinity: Bodies, Movies, Culture*, ed. Peter Lehman (New York: Routledge, 2001), 68.
3. As a gauge of these movies' popularity, one might note that both of their screenplays have been published (this is true of none of the other films in this chapter), and both are consistently ranked as among the top ten films of all time by users of the Internet Movie Database, the popular website where *Shawshank* has held the number one slot since 2008 and *Pulp Fiction* remains in the top ten. See "IMDb Top 250," Internet Movie Database, accessed June 19, 2025, http://www.imdb.com/chart/top.
4. Mark Browning, *Stephen King on the Big Screen* (Bristol: Intellect, 2009), 149.
5. Fredric Jameson, *Postmodernism, or, The Cultural Logic of Late Capitalism* (Durham, NC: Duke University Press, 1991), 20–21.
6. Linda Williams, "Film Bodies: Gender, Genre, and Excess," *Film Quarterly* 44, no. 4 (1991): 3.

7. I take seriously Steven Shaviro's dictum that "The alternative between presence and mediation, or phenomenological immediacy and linguistic deferral, is . . . a false one: experience is *at once* textualized (or opened to the play of negations and differences) and anchored in a living present. Signification and presence are two coexistent dimensions of perceptual 'truth.'" Steven Shaviro, *The Cinematic Body* (Minneapolis: University of Minnesota Press, 1993), 27–28.
8. Eve Kosofsky Sedgwick, *Touching Feeling: Affect, Pedagogy, Performativity* (Durham, NC: Duke University Press, 2003), 32.
9. Sedgwick, *Touching Feeling*, 36.
10. Sedgwick, *Touching Feeling*, 37; emphasis in original.
11. Tomkins' affects are Interest-Excitement, Enjoyment-Joy, Anger, Fear-Terror, Surprise-Startle, Distress-Anguish, Shame-Humiliation, Disgust, and Contempt-Dismell. Silvan Tomkins, *Shame and Its Sisters: A Silvan Tomkins Reader*, ed. Eve Kosofsky Sedgwick and Adam Frank (Durham, NC: Duke University Press, 1995).
12. Tomkins, *Shame and Its Sisters*, 134.
13. Tomkins, *Shame and Its Sisters*, 136.
14. Sedgwick, *Touching Feeling*, 36.
15. Douglas Crimp, "Mario Montez, For Shame," in *Gay Shame*, ed. David M. Halperin and Valerie Traub (Chicago: University of Chicago Press, 2008), 71.
16. Scott, *Extravagant Abjection*, 102. See James Weldon Johnson, *The Autobiography of an Ex-Colored Man* (Boston, MA: Sherman, French & Company, 1912), 182–85.
17. Konrad Szczesniak, "Stigma," in *Encyclopedia of Rape*, ed. Merril D. Smith (Westport, CT: Greenwood Press, 2004), 243.
18. Bernard Williams points out that shame "is straightforwardly connected with nakedness, particularly in sexual connotations. The word *aidoia*, a derivative of *aidōs* 'shame,' is a standard Greek word for the genitals, and similar terms are found in other languages. The reaction is to cover oneself or to hide, and people naturally take steps to avoid the situations that call for it. . . . When the gods went to laugh at the spectacle of Aphrodite and Ares caught inextricably *in flagrante delicto* by Hephaistus's nets, the goddesses stayed at home, *aidōi*, 'from shame.'" Shame can be, then, a direct response to the exposure of an area of the body considered private; for the Greeks, this is the genitals engaged in sexual conduct. See Bernard Williams, *Shame and Necessity* (Berkeley: University of California Press, 1993), 78.
19. See, again, Augustine, *City of God*, 1:16.2.
20. Scarce, *Male on Male Rape*, 19.
21. Heather Schmidt, "Male Rape," in *Encyclopedia of Rape*, ed. Merril D. Smith, (Westport, CT: Greenwood Press, 2004), 121–22.
22. Elaine Scarry, *The Body in Pain: The Making and Unmaking of the World* (New York: Oxford University Press, 1985), 14.
23. The entirety of this sequence, "The Gold Watch," is prefaced with a story delivered by Christopher Walken as Captain Koons in which he tells a young Butch that both he and his father hid the watch in their anal cavities while prisoners of war in Vietnam. For discussion of this scene's relation to anal shame and homosociality, see Fred Botting and Scott Wilson, *The Tarantinian Ethics* (London: SAGE Publications, 2001), 13–25.
24. Is a foot massage sex? *Pulp Fiction*'s interest in women's feet has also been noticed by scholars (see Botting and Wilson, *Tarantinian Ethics*, 25–31), but probably not as much as it ought to have been. In addition to the fact that Mia constantly has her shoes off, Esmer-

alda also drives her taxicab with bare feet, and Fabienne's feet are bare for the majority of her scenes in the film. The idea of a filmic economy of women's feet, indeed, might work better to describe *Pulp Fiction* than explanations that privilege the phallus or the anus.
25. Quentin Tarantino, *Pulp Fiction: A Quentin Tarantino Screenplay* (New York: Hyperion, 1994), 119.
26. Tarantino, *Pulp Fiction*, 131.
27. Randall E. Auxier calls it "a rerun of the rape of Ned Beatty," and Gary Groth says that "[Butch] and Marsellus's predicament at the hands of the rednecks is straight out of *Deliverance*." See Auxier, "Vinnie's Very Bad Day: Twisting the Tale of Time in Pulp Fiction," *Quentin Tarantino and Philosophy: How to Philosophize with a Pair of Pliers and a Blowtorch*, ed. Richard Greene and K. Silem Mohammad (Chicago: Open Court, 2007), 139; and Gary Groth, "A Dream of Perfect Reception: The Movies of Quentin Tarantino," *Commodify Your Dissent: Salvos from The Baffler*, ed. Thomas Frank and Matt Weiland (New York: Norton, 1997), 188.
28. See Henry A. Giroux, *Fugitive Cultures: Race, Violence, and Youth* (London: Routledge, 1996), 78; and Stephen Paul Miller, *The Seventies Now: Culture as Surveillance* (Durham, NC: Duke University Press, 1999), 67.
29. Joseph Natoli, *Speeding to the Millennium: Film & Culture, 1993-1995* (Albany: State University of New York Press, 1998), 267. For David Bell, the reference to "hillbillies" doesn't indicate homosexual desire in the rapists so much as it indicates a sexual obsession with rural erotics on the part of the viewer, as his discussion of the eroticization of "white trash" in heterosexual pornography reminds us. Rural bodies are represented as "vulgar, embarrassing, Rabelaisian," and country men are represented as sexually naive or rendered perverse through the mobilization of a hierarchy of animacy. This is essential to *Pulp Fiction*, of course, because the film is articulating a new cool. Zed and Maynard are characters who are fundamentally not cool, and these characters (like Brett and Flock of Seagulls earlier in the movie) will die. See Bell, "Eroticizing the Rural," in *De-centring Sexualities: Politics and Representations beyond the Metropolis*, ed. Richard Phillips, Diane Watt, and David Shuttleton (London: Routledge, 2000), 90.
30. Jim Smith, *Tarantino* (London: Virgin Books, 2005), 101.
31. Travis Anderson, "Unleashing Nietzsche on the Tragic Infrastructure of Tarantino's *Reservoir Dogs*," in *Quentin Tarantino and Philosophy: How to Philosophize with a Pair of Pliers and a Blowtorch*, ed. Richard Greene and K. Silem Mohammad (Chicago: Open Court, 2007), 24.
32. Tarantino, *Pulp Fiction*, 125. Following Tarantino's constant references to New Hollywood cinema, The Gimp seems to me to be a direct citation of William Friedkin's *Cruising* (1980). The Gimp has also become an iconic reference for jokes about male/male rape akin to "squeal like a pig" or "Dueling Banjos." In Evan Goldberg and Seth Rogan's raunchy buddy comedy *This Is the End* (2013), for example, male/male rape is both a running theme and a running joke. At one point near the film's end, Channing Tatum's character appears chained up next to Danny McBride's character in an obvious reference to the rape sequence in *Pulp Fiction*.
33. See Allan Campbell, "'Fuck Boy Meets Girl': Heterosexual Aspirations and Masculine Interests in the World of Quentin Tarantino," in *Hetero: Queering Representations of Straightness*, ed. Sean Griffin (Albany: State University of New York Press, 2009), 216; Marsha Kinder, "Violence American Style: the Narrative Orchestrations of Violent Attractions," in *Violence and American Cinema*, ed. J. David Slocum (New York:

Routledge, 2001), 84; bell hooks, *Reel to Real: Race, Sex, and Class at the Movies* (New York: Routledge, 1996), 49.

34. Devon Jackson, "Quentin Tarantino's Negro Problem—and Hollywood's," *Village Voice* 40, no. 13 (March 28, 1995): 40.
35. Tarantino, *Pulp Fiction*, 126. The children's rhyme is in the script. The racist slur is not.
36. Curry, *The Man-Not*, 35.
37. Curry, *The Man-Not*, 145.
38. Curry, *The Man-Not*, 146. See also Vincent Woodard, *The Delectable Negro: Human Consumption and Homoeroticism within U.S. Slave Culture* (New York: New York University Press, 2014), and Sharon Patricia Holland, *The Erotic Life of Racism* (Durham, NC: Duke University Press, 2012).
39. As should be obvious from Marsellus's response here, there is no reason to believe, as Samuel Kimball does, that "the violation of Marsellus is the most abject humiliation that can befall a heterosexual male in this movie." See A. Samuel Kimball, "'Bad-Ass Dudes' in *Pulp Fiction*: Homophobia and the Counterphobic Idealization of Women," *Quarterly Review of Film and Video* 16, no. 2 (1997): 179. For a man, castration by gunshot is obviously still a much worse fate and one that fascinates Tarantino: in *True Romance*, Clarence (Christian Slater) shoots Drexl (Gary Oldman) in the genitals, and Tarantino will repeat this gesture in *The Hateful Eight* (2015), in which a mysterious man under the floorboards shoots Warren (Samuel L. Jackson) in the genitals after we watch him orally rape a young man (Craig Stark).
40. Tarantino, *Pulp Fiction*, 130–31.
41. Tarantino, *Pulp Fiction*, 131.
42. Tarantino, *Pulp Fiction*, 131.
43. There is a poetry to this, too. Early on in *Pulp Fiction*, Jules points a gun at Brett and asks him if Marsellus "look[s] like a bitch," a question he follows with: "Then why did you try to fuck 'im like a bitch?!" See Tarantino, *Pulp Fiction*, 32. The complete absurdity and impossibility of someone "fucking Marsellus Wallace like a bitch" is linked in this scene to *what happens when someone attempts to do just that*, as Jules and Vincent proceed to kill everyone in the apartment except Marvin, who will be killed later as Jules and Vincent drive around in Toluca Lake.
44. Mark Kermode, *The Shawshank Redemption* (London: British Film Institute, 2003), 21–23.
45. Kermode, *Shawshank*, 26.
46. My attention was drawn to a number of these films by Oliver Noble, "Why Is Prison Rape Hollywood's Solution to Violent Crime? (Video)," *HuffPost*, April 23, 2014, https://www.huffpost.com/entry/american-justice-prison-rape-n_5154880.
47. Frank Darabont, *The Shawshank Redemption: The Shooting Script* (New York: Newmarket Press, 1996), 17.
48. Darabont, *Shawshank*, 21. I quote directly from the film, but I will cite the scene's location in the published script, although it differs considerably.
49. Darabont, *Shawshank*, 23.
50. Browning, *Stephen King*, 153.
51. Kermode, *Shawshank*, 25. Kermode quotes Darabont, *Shawshank*, 28.
52. Kermode, *Shawshank*, 85–86. Browning also thinks the film overdoes its sentimentality, referring to "the bumper-sticker quality to the gnomic utterances that start to stack up towards the end of the film." See Browning, *Stephen King*, 158.
53. Browning, *Stephen King*, 152.

54. Michelle Brown, *The Culture of Punishment: Prison, Society, and Spectacle* (New York: New York University Press, 2009), 61.
55. Darabont, *Shawshank*, 142. The cut scene is on 29.
56. Darabont, *Shawshank*, 24.
57. Darabont, *Shawshank*, 24.
58. Darabont, *Shawshank*, 39–40. See Tony Magistrale, "Redemption through the Feminine in *The Shawshank Redemption*, or, Why Rita Hayworth's Name Belongs in the Title," *The Films of Stephen King: From Carrie to Secret Window*, ed. Tony Magistrale (London: Palgrave Macmillan, 2008), 105.
59. See Stephen King, "Rita Hayworth and Shawshank Redemption," in *Different Seasons* (New York: Viking Press, 1982), 23.
60. Kermode tells us that "although the novella includes this assaul[t] and its permanently disabling effect on Bogs, a slight rearrangement of King's chronology allows Darabont to attribute Bogs' demise to Haley's protection of his new investment, a twisting of the source[,] which situates the rooftop showdown a year or so *after* Bogs' beating." See Kermode, *Shawshank*, 43.
61. Darabont, *Shawshank*, 144.
62. Magistrale, "Redemption through the Feminine," 105.
63. In fact, Darabont makes Andy more innocent than his source does. In King's novella, Red tells us clearly that Andy and the capital at his command are responsible for Bogs's demise: "My guess is that, if Bogs was done, it cost someone a serious piece of change—fifteen bucks, we'll say, for the turnkey, and two or three apiece for each of the lump-up guys. I'm not saying it was Andy Dufresne, but I do know that he brought in five hundred dollars when he came, and he was a banker in the straight world—a man who understands better than the rest of us the ways in which money can become power." Darabont, *Shawshank*, 24–25.
64. Claire O'Neill, "The Photo That Changed the Face of AIDS," NPR.org, December 1, 2011, https://www.npr.org/sections/pictureshow/2011/12/01/142998189/the-photo-that-changed-the-face-of-aids.
65. Michael Davidson, "Phantom Limbs: Film Noir and the Disabled Body," *GLQ: A Journal of Lesbian and Gay Studies* 9, no. 1–2 (2003): 57–77.
66. Michelle C. Velasquez-Potts, "Regulatory Sites: Management, Confinement and HIV/AIDS," in *Captive Genders: Trans Embodiment and the Prison Industrial Complex*, 2nd ed., ed. Eric A. Stanley and Nat Smith (Chico, CA: AK Press, 2015), 123.
67. In Conroy's novel, although the men are escaped prisoners, Callenwolde is actually the name of one of the rapists, and the men are killed not by Tom's brother but by Caesar, the Wingos' pet tiger. See Pat Conroy, *The Prince of Tides* (Boston, MA: Houghton Mifflin, 1986), 410–19.
68. In his perceptive essay on *Sleepers*, Joe Wlodarz points out the film's insistent eroticization of these boys—I've tried to capture some of that here, as well—before the film disavows any sexual interest in them in act 2. See Wlodarz, "Rape Fantasies."
69. To be fair to Levinson's screenplay, Carcaterra's original memoir-novel is very heavy on homespun wisdom ("One of the earliest lessons learned in Hell's Kitchen was that death was the only thing in life that came easy"), metaphysical harbingers of doom ("In the short distance behind us, a guard's whistle blew. Overhead, rain clouds gathered, darkening the skies, hiding the sun in their mist"), and intentionally contentless cliffhangers ("The four of us had been locked inside the walls of Wilkinson long enough to expect

nothing but the unimaginable"). See Lorenzo Carcaterra, *Sleepers* (New York: Ballantine, 1995), 136, 246, 190.
70. Wlodarz, "Rape Fantasies," 72.
71. James Kincaid, *Erotic Innocence: The Culture of Child Molesting* (Durham, NC: Duke University Press, 1998), 189.
72. In this way the film reflects the fact that the Zoot Suit Riots were not attacks by Mexican Americans; they were attacks by United States military servicemen—sailors and marines—on persons perceived to be Mexican American.
73. This second rape sequence also introduces the idea of anal penetration by a sharp object, as the rapist threatens that he will sodomize Santana with the knife if he doesn't keep quiet.
74. Frederick Luis Aldama, "Penalizing Chicano/a Bodies in Edward J. Olmos's *American Me*," in *Decolonial Voices: Chicana and Chicano Cultural Studies in the 21st Century*, ed. Arturo J. Aldama and Naomi H. Quiñonez (Bloomington: Indiana University Press, 2002), 80.
75. Aldama, "Penalizing Chicano/a Bodies," 80.
76. Aldama, "Penalizing Chicano/a Bodies," 91.
77. Rosa-Linda Fregoso, *The Bronze Screen: Chicana and Chicano Film Culture* (Minneapolis: University of Minnesota Press, 1993), 123.
78. Fregoso, *Bronze Screen*, 126.
79. Manohla Dargis, "Skin Deep," *LA Weekly*, October 28, 1998, https://www.laweekly.com/skin-deep.
80. Janet Maslin, "The Darkest Chambers of a Nation's Soul," *New York Times*, October 28, 1998, E1.
81. Dargis, "Skin Deep."
82. Crimp, "Mario Montez," 73.
83. My argument here is slightly different from the one Carolyn Dinshaw offers in *Getting Medieval*. She argues that Marsellus's "getting medieval" is an attempt to ward off fears of a "condition of inessentiality, the basic condition of the impossibility of essential being." Focusing on audience's affective responses, as I am, I see the violence as a way of channeling the very specific affective experience of shame into something masculinity can bear. See Carolyn Dinshaw, *Getting Medieval: Sexualities and Communities, Pre- and Post-Modern* (Durham, NC: Duke University Press, 1999), 187.
84. Sedgwick, *Touching Feeling*, 63; emphasis in original.
85. In terms of directorial identification, it is perhaps worth remarking that, according to Ving Rhames, Tarantino himself acted as Zed's stand-in, writhing on the ground in the scene "right after where I shoot the guy in the groin. The actor wasn't there, and Quentin was lying on the ground under the camera, acting as if he was that character. I had to say, look, cut. Uh, Quentin, don't do that, you're destroying my concentration." See Jami Bernard, *Quentin Tarantino: The Man and His Movies* (New York: Harper Collins, 1995), 207–8.
86. We see images of the male/male rape-revenge trope from the 1990s put to use after the September 11 attacks in 2001. Jasbir Puar and Amit Rai report a group of extraordinary homophobic, transphobic, misogynist, white-supremacist images and slogans promoting US nationalism following the attacks. I see in these images a recirculation of 1990s cinematic revenge plots: as the hardbody becomes vulnerable to violence, revenge becomes all the more necessary; as elements of gay subjectivity are welcomed into the national imaginary, heteronormativity must violently reassert itself. See Jasbir K. Puar

and Amit S. Rai, "Monster, Terrorist, Fag: The War on Terrorism and the Production of Docile Patriots," *Social Text* 20, no. 3 (2002): 126–27.

CHAPTER 5

Epigraph. *Network*, 1976, Sidney Lumet, director.
1. This does not happen in every one of these narratives, but it is the most common outcome.
2. Mark Simpson, "Two Men in a Prison Cell. The Guard's Nowhere to Be Seen. Shouldn't They Be Having It Off?" *Guardian*, December 3, 1998, 10.
3. "Mum," *The Shield*, season 3, episode 5, original air date April 6, 2004, written by Kurt Sutter and Shawn Ryan, directed by Nick Gomez; "That's My Dog," *Six Feet Under*, season 4, episode 5, original air date July 18, 2004, written by Scott Buck, directed by Alan Poul. For a thoughtful discussion of this episode see Emily Nussbaum, "Captive Audience," *New York Magazine*, August 9, 2004, https://nymag.com/nymetro/arts/tv/reviews/9579/.
4. RDLwebcam212, "General Hospital Michael Corinthos Prison Rape Storyline," YouTube, July 30, 2010, https://www.youtube.com/watch?v=Nm_vmVT_hPU.
5. See Michael Logan, "*General Hospital*'s Michael Reveals He Was Raped," *TV Guide*, January 27, 2011, http://www.tvguide.com/news/general-hospitals-michael-1028422/.
6. See Todd S. Purdum, "St. Paul's Before and After the Owen Labrie Rape Trial," *Vanity Fair*, March 1, 2016, www.vanityfair.com/news/2016/03/st-pauls-owen-labrie-rape-trial; and Benjamin Wallace, "How St. George's Atonement for Its Sex-Abuse Scandals Turned Ugly," *Vanity Fair*, July 8, 2016, http://www.vanityfair.com/news/2016/07/st-georges-sex-abuse-scandals.
7. Brian Moylan, "American Crime: The First Must-Watch TV Show of 2016," *Guardian*, January 6, 2016, https://www.theguardian.com/tv-and-radio/2016/jan/06/american-crime-second-season-must-watch-tv-2016; Robert Bianco, "Critic's Corner," *USA Today*, March 9, 2016, 6D.
8. Lisa M. Cuklanz, *Rape on Prime Time: Television, Masculinity, and Sexual Violence* (Philadelphia: University of Pennsylvania Press, 2000), 62.
9. Consent, in other words, is never at issue in episodes that use this basic pattern. Cuklanz, *Rape on Prime Time*, 94.
10. "Violation," *Cagney & Lacey*, season 4, episode 21, original air date March 18, 1985, written by Les Carter, directed by Allen Baron.
11. "Cheek to Cheek," *St. Elsewhere*, season 4, episode 21, original air date March 12, 1986, teleplay by Eric Overmyer, story by John Masius and Tom Fontana, directed by Helaine Head.
12. *The Rape of Richard Beck* was released on home video as *Deadly Justice*, a generic title designed to obscure the film's subject matter and that makes no sense whatsoever when one considers that none of the film's characters is killed. The film's original air date was May 27, 1985.
13. Cuklanz, *Rape on Prime Time*, 36–40.
14. Cuklanz's book cites an even earlier episode dealing with male/male rape—from the 1978–1979 series *Kaz*. The plot of this episode involves a murder trial where a man named David Faraday (Sam Groom) has strangled his colleague Charlie Briggs after an argument. Witnesses testify to the argument, but the subject matter of the fight is unclear, and the client will not be honest with his attorneys. The defendant behaves strangely, continually threatening to discharge his attorneys and hiding information from them.

Whom David Faraday is protecting is revealed when the show's protagonist locates the younger Faraday brother, a college dropout named Carl (Richard Stanley). Carl had been working for David's firm and had become close with David's colleague Briggs, the murdered man. "I am the person they were fighting about," Carl tells the lawyers, and he also tells them that he is unsure about his sexuality—that he thinks he might be homosexual. What actually happened with Briggs remains unclear. Or rather, it is clear that Briggs and Carl Faraday had a sexual encounter ("I'd never had an experience like that," Carl says) but that afterward Carl was crying and scared. Whether he was scared that he is a homosexual or scared because he has been raped, however, is unstated. No one in the episode mentions the word *rape*; the only word used is *seduction*. After Carl confesses to the attorneys, they agree to have Carl testify that he was "seduced" by Charlie—which is true—and they trust that the jury will then agree to their version of events, which is that David didn't murder Charlie, although, of course, he did. The idea is to put the victim on trial and have the jury acquit because the victim deserved to be murdered. It works. The important thing to note here, is that at no point does *Kaz* represent what happened as if it is rape. Rather, what the show represents is *homosexuality as equivalent to rape* along the lines of the early discussions of *Fortune and Men's Eyes* that I described in Chapter 1. In this episode of *Kaz*, David Faraday is justified in murdering his business partner because he seduced his younger, sensitive, college-age brother and somehow simultaneously confirmed the young man's homosexuality. "A Case of Murder," *Kaz*, season 1, episode 12, original air date January 17, 1979, written by Michael Genelin, directed by Don Medford. In her discussion, Cuklanz misreads this episode entirely, but it is likely that she only read the script and didn't see the episode; the two may have differed significantly. See Cuklanz, *Rape on Prime Time*, 132-33.

15. Interested parties may consult the *Oz* wiki (http://oztv.wikia.com), which aims to document every character on the show, as well as deaths, criminal activities, and storylines.
16. For critics and promoters who describe the show as real, see Bill Yousman, *Prime Time Prisons on U.S. TV: Representation of Incarceration* (New York: Peter Lang, 2009), 142-43, and Lara Stemple, "HBO's *Oz* and the Fight against Prisoner Rape: Chronicles from the Front Line," in *Third Wave Feminism and Television: Jane Puts It in a Box*, ed. Merri Lisa Johnson (New York: I. B. Tauris, 2007), 166-67.
17. Yousman, *Prime Time Prisons*, 144.
18. Yousman, *Prime Time Prisons*, 145.
19. Stemple, "HBO's *Oz*," 167.
20. "The Routine," *Oz*, season 1, episode 1, original air date July 12, 1997, written by Tom Fontana, directed by Darnell Martin.
21. "God's Chillin'," *Oz*, season 1, episode 3, original air date July 21, 1997, written by Tom Fontana, directed by Jean de Segonzac; "Straight Life," *Oz*, season 1, episode 5, original air date August 4, 1997, written by Tom Fontana, directed by Leslie Libman & Larry Williams; "To Your Health," *Oz*, season 1, episode 6, original air date August 11, 1997, written by Tom Fontana, directed by Alan Taylor.
22. "Visits, Conjugal and Otherwise," *Oz*, season 1, episode 2, original air date July 14, 1997, written by Tom Fontana, directed by Nick Gomez.
23. Although prisoners in the real world have over a dozen terms with various nuances for passive homosexual partners, *prag* appears nowhere in the exhaustive "Lexicon of Prison Sexuality and Homosexual Sex" that appears as an appendix to Mark S. Fleisher

and Jessie L. Krienert's *The Myth of Prison Rape: Sexual Culture in American Prisons* (Lanham, MD: Rowman & Littlefield, 2009).
24. "Straight Life."
25. "Plan B," *Oz*, season 1, episode 7, original air date August 18, 1997, written by Tom Fontana, directed by Darnell Martin.
26. "Animal Farm," *Oz*, season 2, episode 7, original air date August 24, 1998, story by Tom Fontana, teleplay by Tom Fontana and Debbie Sarjeant, directed by Mary Harron. Fontana spells *O'Reily* with only a single *l*. It looks strange, but this is the correct spelling.
27. The single exception is "Gray Matter," *Oz*, season 4, episode 5, original air date August 9, 2000, written by Tom Fontana, directed by Brian Cox. An unnamed Black man rapes another unnamed Black man in a brief scene. Neither man appears in the series again.
28. "Strange Bedfellows," *Oz*, season 2, episode 6, original air date August 17, 1998, written by Tom Fontana, directed by Alan Taylor.
29. "Laws of Gravity," *Oz*, season 5, episode 2, original air date January 13, 2002, written by Tom Fontana and Sean Whitesell, directed by Rob Morrow.
30. "Dream a Little Dream of Me," *Oz*, season 5, episode 3, original air date January 20, 2002, written by Tom Fontana and Sean Whitesell, directed by Adam Bernstein.
31. "Variety," *Oz*, season 5, episode 6, original air date February 10, 2002, written by Tom Fontana and Bradford Winters, directed by Roger Rees.
32. Stemple, "HBO's *Oz*," 183.
33. This show is outrageous. "The Tip," *Oz*, season 2, episode 1, original air date July 11, 1998, written by Tom Fontana, directed by Nick Gomez. This sequence harks back to Andy Dufresne's threat to Bogs in *Shawshank*.
34. "Napoleon's Boney Parts," *Oz*, season 3, episode 2, original air date July 21, 1999, written by Tom Fontana, directed by Matt Dillon.
35. "Next Stop: Valhalla," *Oz*, season 5, episode 4, original air date January 27, 2002, written by Tom Fontana and Sunil Nayar, directed by J. Miller Tobin.
36. "Impotence," *Oz*, season 5, episode 8, original air date February 24, 2002, written by Tom Fontana, directed by Alex Zakrzewski.
37. "See No Evil, Hear No Evil, Smell No Evil," *Oz*, season 6, episode 2, original air date January 12, 2003, written by Tom Fontana and Sunil Nayar, directed by Marc Klasfield.
38. "4giveness," *Oz*, season 6, episode 5, original air date February 2, 2003, written by Tom Fontana and Bradford Winters, directed by John Henry Davis.
39. "A Day in the Death . . . ," *Oz*, season 6, episode 6, original air date February 9, 2003, written by Tom Fontana, Sunil Nayar, and Bradford Winters, directed by Daniel Loflin.
40. Stemple, "HBO's *Oz*," 182–83.
41. Fleisher and Krienert, *Myth of Prison Rape*.
42. Ellen Rooney, "'A Little More than Persuading': Tess and the Subject of Sexual Violence," in *Rape and Representation*, ed. Lynn A. Higgins and Brenda R. Silver (New York: Columbia University Press, 1991), 92.
43. Joe Wlodarz, "Maximum Insecurity: Genre Trouble and Closet Erotics in and out of HBO's *Oz*," *Camera Obscura* 20, no. 1 (2005): 58–105. In her book *Male Rape: The Emergence of a Social and Legal Issue*, for example, Noreen Abdullah-Khan charts the rise in research aimed at studying trauma experienced by male/male rape victims in the late 1990s. See Abdullah-Khan, *Male Rape*, 36–38.
44. Schmidt, "Male Rape," 121.

45. This exasperation is widespread in the literature. See, for example, Misra, *Landscape of Silence*, 174–76.
46. Foucault, *History of Sexuality—Volume 1*, 60.
47. Foucault, *History of Sexuality—Volume 1*, 60; Michel Foucault, *Abnormal: Lectures at the Collège de France, 1974–1975*, trans. Graham Burchell (New York: Picador, 2003), 185.
48. Foucault, *Abnormal*, 186.
49. Christopher Grobe, *The Art of Confession: The Performance of Self from Robert Lowell to Reality TV* (New York: New York University Press, 2017), 198.
50. "Season Two: Episode One," *American Crime*, original air date January 6, 2016, written and directed by John Ridley.
51. "Season Two: Episode Three," *American Crime*, original air date January 20, 2016, written by Sonay Hoffman, directed by Gregg Araki.
52. "Season Two: Episode Two," *American Crime*, original air date January 13, 2016, written by Ernie Pandish, directed by Clement Virgo.
53. "Season Two: Episode Four," *American Crime*, original air date January 27, 2016, written by Kirk A. Moore, directed by Julie Hébert. Kevin Kantor (see Chapter 6) appears in this episode performing a poem.
54. Foucault, *History of Sexuality—Volume 1*, 43.
55. Michel Foucault, *Discipline and Punish: The Birth of the Prison*, trans. Alan Sheridan (New York: Vintage, 1995), 251.
56. Foucault, *Discipline and Punish*, 252.
57. The young men's whiteness makes this easier. In a popular culture in which gayness is portrayed as overwhelmingly white, it is much easier to understand young white men as "gay" than it is to understand young men of color this way. *American Crime*'s second season—unlike its first season—attempts to side-step questions of race and analyze questions of class in the US instead. Both Taylor's and Eric's families are white. The captain of Leyland's basketball team is Black, but their family—unlike Taylor's—is quite wealthy, and the captain is involved in the rape only insofar as he throws the party and lectures the team about masculinity.
58. Lynn A. Higgins, "Screen/Memory: Rape and Its Alibis in *Last Year at Marienbad*," in *Rape and Representation*, ed. Lynn A. Higgins and Brenda R. Silver (New York: Columbia University Press, 1991), 307; emphasis in original.
59. Higgins, "Screen/Memory," 307.
60. See Michael Cobb, *God Hates Fags: The Rhetoric of Religious Violence* (New York: New York University Press, 2006), 1–2.
61. Phil Gast and Tessa Carletta, "Season Called Off for Tennessee Boys' Basketball Team after Rape Charges," CNN, January 6, 2016, http://www.cnn.com/2016/01/06/us/tennessee-high-school-team-assault/index.html.
62. Stephen Young, "Ellis County Firefighters Sexually Assaulted Trainee with Chorizo, Rangers Allege," *Dallas Observer*, April 7, 2015, http://www.dallasobserver.com/news/ellis-county-firefighters-sexually-assaulted-trainee-with-chorizo-rangers-allege-7137733.
63. Stephen Young, "Seven Ellis County Volunteer Firefighters Indicted in Chorizo Sex Assault Case," *Dallas Observer*, September 10, 2015, http://www.dallasobserver.com/news/seven-ellis-county-volunteer-firefighters-indicted-in-chorizo-sex-assault-case-7572560.
64. Moon, "Small Boy," 142.
65. "Season Two: Episode Six," *American Crime*, original air date February 10, 2016, written by Stacy A. Littlejohn, directed by Jessica Yu.

66. "Season Two: Episode Ten," *American Crime*, original air date March 9, 2016, written by Diana Son, directed by Nicole Kassell.
67. A further example of the importance of confession in male/male rape narratives on television in this period is a 2018 episode of *RuPaul's Drag Race* in which a contestant talks on the mainstage about having been raped. See "Drag Con Panel Extravaganza," *RuPaul's Drag Race*, season 10, episode 6, original air date April 26, 2018. Reality television, as Christopher Grobe has argued, lends itself to the confessional mode. But the enduring power of the confessional mode for male/male rape narratives can also be seen in *Thirteen Reasons Why*, in which there are several narratives of male/male rape, and young people are continually enjoined to testify about rape and other secrets. Male/male rape in the series is primarily driven by the closeted homosexual Monty (Timothy Granaderos), who rapes the shy student Tyler (Devin Druid) at the end of season 2. Numerous episodes in seasons 3 and 4 follow Tyler's various confessions to different people about the sexual violence he experienced. See "Bye," *Thirteen Reasons Why*, season 2, episode 13, original air date May 18, 2018, written by Brian Yorkey, directed by Kyle Patrick Alvarez; "In High School, Even on a Good Day, It's Hard to Tell Who's on Your Side," *Thirteen Reasons Why*, season 3, episode 8, original air date August 23, 2019, written by Felischa Marye, directed by Kevin Dowling; "There Are a Few Things I Haven't Told You," *Thirteen Reasons Why*, season 3, episode 11, original air date August 23, 2019, written by Helen Shang, directed by Kevin Dowling.
68. Conley's memoir appeared at a peak moment in this national conversation. See "Conversion 'Therapy' Laws," Movement Advancement Project, accessed 8 July 2024, https://www.lgbtmap.org/equality-maps/conversion_therapy.
69. Noe Kamelamela, review of *Boy Erased*, Edge Media Network, May 11, 2016, https://www.edgemedianetwork.com/story/196373.
70. Garrard Conley, *Boy Erased: A Memoir of Identity, Faith, and Family* (New York: Riverhead Books, 2016), 113.
71. Conley, *Boy Erased*, 134.
72. Incidentally, this isn't how Joel Edgerton's 2018 film adaptation of the memoir works at all. In the movie's narrative, the rape (the specifics of which are significantly altered) functions much more as a plot point—a large-scale betrayal of Christian values that turn out to be sexually violent rather than salvific.
73. Jonathan Parks-Ramage, *Yes, Daddy* (Boston: Houghton Mifflin Harcourt, 2021), 232.
74. Parks-Ramage, *Yes, Daddy*, 239.
75. Parks-Ramage, *Yes, Daddy*, 241–42.
76. Parks-Ramage, *Yes, Daddy*, 235.
77. Michaela Coel quoted in Anne McElvoy, "Michaela Coel: 'Like Arabella, I Realised My Life Was About to Change for Ever,'" *Guardian*, July 10, 2020, https://www.theguardian.com/tv-and-radio/2020/jul/10/michaela-coel-i-may-destroy-you-bbc-arabella-assault-racism.
78. One of the central ideas in the series is that there is no such thing as a perfect victim. This is one of the basic tenets of abolitionist organizing. See Mariame Kaba and Brit Schulte, "Not a Cardboard Cutout: Cyntoia Brown and the Framing of a Victim," in *We Do This 'til We Free Us: Abolitionist Organizing and Transforming Justice*, by Mariame Kaba (Chicago: Haymarket, 2021), 35–40.
79. "That Was Fun," episode 4, *I May Destroy You*, original US air date June 29, 2020, written by Michaela Coel, directed by Sam Miller and Michaela Coel.
80. ". . . It Just Came Up," *I May Destroy You*, episode 5, original US air date July 6, 2020, written by Michaela Coel, directed by Sam Miller and Michaela Coel.

81. "The Alliance," *I May Destroy You*, episode 6, original US air date July 13, 2020, written by Michaela Coel, directed by Sam Miller and Michaela Coel.
82. See also Sam Eckmann, "Paapa Essiedu (*I May Destroy You*) on Kwame's Trauma: 'I Really Liked the Idea of What Can Be Said with the Unsaid,'" *Gold Derby*, May 28, 2021, https://www.goldderby.com/feature/paapa-essiedu-i-may-destroy-you-hbo-video-interview-1204272813.
83. "Happy Animals," *I May Destroy You*, episode 7, original US air date July 20, 2020, written by Michaela Coel, directed by Sam Miller and Michaela Coel.
84. "Ego Death," *I May Destroy You*, episode 12, original US air date August 24, 2020, written by Michaela Coel, directed by Sam Miller and Michaela Coel.
85. Michaela Coel quoted in E. Alex Jung, "How Michaela Coel Wrote *I May Destroy You*'s Dreamlike Ending," *Vulture*, August 24, 2020, https://www.vulture.com/2020/08/i-may-destroy-you-ending-explained-michaela-coel.html.
86. See Kaba, *We Do This*, and also Mariame Kaba and Andrea J. Ritchie, *No More Police. A Case for Abolition*, (New York: New Press, 2022).
87. Richard Gadd, *Baby Reindeer* (London: Bloomsbury, 2019). *Monkey See Monkey Do* has not been published, but there are a few clips available on TikTok and other social media.
88. Joy Press, "The *Baby Reindeer* Dilemma: When 'True Story' TV Shows Go Too Far," *Vanity Fair*, May 24, 2024, https://www.vanityfair.com/hollywood/story/baby-reindeer-tv-shows-based-on-true-stories-legal-trouble.
89. "Episode 1," *Baby Reindeer*, original air date April 11, 2024, written by Richard Gadd, directed by Weronika Tofilska.
90. "Episode 2," *Baby Reindeer*, original air date April 11, 2024, written by Richard Gadd, directed by Weronika Tofilska.
91. "Episode 4," *Baby Reindeer*, original air date April 11, 2024, written by Richard Gadd, directed by Weronika Tofilska.
92. "Episode 6," *Baby Reindeer*, original air date April 11, 2024, written by Richard Gadd, directed by Josephine Bornebusch.
93. "Episode 7," *Baby Reindeer*, original air date April 11, 2024, written by Richard Gadd, directed by Josephine Bornebusch.
94. In a review of the series for NPR, Glen Weldon objects to *Baby Reindeer*'s depiction of queerness, arguing that "Purely for dramatic purposes, *Baby Reindeer* implies that Donny's sexuality conforms to the laws of cause (the abuse) and effect (queerness). Worse, it does so in a way that seems specifically designed to reassure those audiences who believe queerness is something that happens to people, something that can be triggered from the outside." I am unconvinced by his argument, not only because Weldon assumes the existence of queerness as essential rather than thinking about sexuality as "a journey," as Donny calls it, but also because the show is explicitly critical of heteronormativity at every turn. Certainly, the show explores the possibility that Donny never had homosexual desires before he was raped, but *Baby Reindeer* does not frame queerness as harmful or negative. Indeed, Teri, the show's trans character, is *Baby Reindeer*'s most reasonable, balanced voice. See Glen Weldon, "Netflix's *Baby Reindeer*: A Dark, Haunting Story Bungles Its Depiction of Queerness," NPR, April 25, 2024, https://www.npr.org/2024/04/25/1247130712/baby-reindeer-review-netflix; see also Mey Rude, "Deer Nava," *Out*, July/August 2024, 12.

CHAPTER 6

Epigraph. Lady Gaga, "Til It Happens to You," written by Diane Warren and Lady Gaga, *Til It Happens to You* (Santa Monica: Interscope, 2015). Gaga and Warren spell *till* without its customary second *l*.

1. Brownmiller, *Against Her Will*, 7.
2. Ann Cahill and Susan Brison also both answer this question on the first pages of their books. See Cahill, *Rethinking Rape*, 1; Brison, *Aftermath*, ix.
3. McRuer, *Crip Theory*, 75–76.
4. Thompson, *Eating the Black Body*, 164.
5. See Misra, *Landscape of Silence*, 71, 101, 180–83.
6. See Scott, *Extravagant Objection*, 153–71. I am deeply indebted to Scott's thinking on this topic.
7. Féron, *Wartime Sexual Violence*, 38.
8. Thompson, *Eating the Black Body*, 161; Misra, *Landscape of Silence*, 169.
9. See Robert Alexander Innes and Kim Anderson, eds. *Indigenous Men and Masculinities: Legacies, Identities, Regeneration* (Winnipeg: University of Manitoba Press, 2015). See also Curry, *Man-Not*, 145, 214.
10. ClayArts Vegas, "Sweet and Slippery Slope 2016," *YouTube*, May 7, 2016, https://youtu.be/iv1m3P1qHXI.
11. Benjamin Peterson, personal interview, July 24, 2016.
12. Peterson, personal interview.
13. Robin Bernstein, *Racial Innocence: Performing American Childhood from Slavery to Civil Rights* (New York: New York University Press, 2011), 73.
14. I asked Peterson about violet glaze, and he responded by noting his commitment to keeping open possible readings of violation: "I remember thinking about violet and deciding it would be distinctively queer and maybe read too specifically as a queer object, and imply anal sex, possibly denying other readings of violence."
15. Button Poetry, "Kevin Kantor 'People You May Know' (CUPSI 2015 Finals)," YouTube, April 5, 2015, https://www.youtube.com/watch?v=LoyfunmYIpU.
16. Kevin Kantor, "People You May Know," *Endowing Vegetables with Too Much Meaning* (Seattle: CreateSpace Independent Publishing, 2015), 30.
17. Bill Leff and Wendy Snyder, "Kevin Kantor Was One of the Sexual Assault Survivors on Stage with Lady Gaga at the Oscars," WGNRadio, March 1, 2016, http://wgnradio.com/2016/03/01/kevin-kantor-was-one-of-the-sexual-assault-survivors-on-stage-with-lady-gaga-at-the-oscars.
18. Kerry Lengel, "How a Transgender Character Changed When a Trans Actor was Hired for the Role," *Arizona Republic*, May 9, 2019, https://www.azcentral.com/story/entertainment/arts/2019/05/09/transgender-actor-helped-rewrite-role-things-know-true-arizona-theatre-company/1138678001.
19. One of the stories in *The Hunting Ground* involves a cover-up at my own institution, Florida State University.
20. Rousse Arielle, "Beyond the Binaries: Exclusive Dichotomies in the Anti-Sexual Violence Movement," in *Queering Sexual Violence: Radical Voices from with the Anti-Violence Movement*, ed. Jennifer Patterson (Riverdale, NY: Riverdale Avenue Books, 2016), 46–47.

Bibliography

Abdullah-Khan, Noreen. *Male Rape: The Emergence of a Social and Legal Issue*. London: Palgrave Macmillan, 2008.
Abdur-Rahman, Aliyyah I. *Against the Closet: Black Political Longing and the Ethics of Race*. Durham, NC: Duke University Press, 2012.
Adams, Stephen. *The Homosexual as Hero in Contemporary Fiction*. London: Vision, 1980.
Aldama, Frederick Luis. "Penalizing Chicano/a Bodies in Edward J. Olmos's *American Me*." In *Decolonial Voices: Chicana and Chicano Cultural Studies in the 21st Century*, edited by Arturo J. Aldama and Naomi H. Quiñonez, 78–97. Bloomington: Indiana University Press, 2002.
Alexander, Michelle. *The New Jim Crow: Mass Incarceration in the Age of Colorblindness*. Rev. ed. New York: New Press, 2012.
Alexander, Patrick Elliot. *From Slave Ship to Supermax: Mass Incarceration, Prisoner Abuse, and the New Neo-Slave Novel*. Philadelphia, PA: Temple University Press, 2018.
Alleg, Henri. *The Question*. Translated by John Calder. Lincoln: University of Nebraska Press, 2006.
Altman, Dennis. *Gore Vidal's America*. Cambridge, MA: Polity Press, 2005.
Améry, Jean. *At the Mind's Limits: Compilations by a Survivor of Auschwitz and Its Realities*. Translated by Sidney Rosenfeld and Stella P. Rosenfeld. Bloomington: Indiana University Press, 1984.
Anderson, Travis. "Unleashing Nietzsche on the Tragic Infrastructure of Tarantino's *Reservoir Dogs*." In *Quentin Tarantino and Philosophy: How to Philosophize with a Pair of Pliers and a Blowtorch*, edited by Richard Greene and K. Silem Mohammad, 21–39. Chicago: Open Court, 2007.
Anzaldúa, Gloria. *Borderlands/La Frontera: The New Mestiza*. 3rd ed. San Francisco: Aunt Lute Books, 2007.
Arielle, Rousse. "Beyond the Binaries: Exclusive Dichotomies in the Anti-Sexual Violence Movement." In *Queering Sexual Violence: Radical Voices from with the Anti-Violence Movement*, edited by Jennifer Patterson, 39–47. Riverdale, NY: Riverdale Avenue Books, 2016.
Augustine. *The City of God against the Pagans*. Vol. 1. Translated by George E. McCracken. Cambridge, MA: Harvard University Press, 1957.
Austin, J. L. *How to Do Things with Words*. Cambridge, MA: Harvard University Press, 1962.
Auxier, Randall E. "Vinnie's Very Bad Day: Twisting the Tale of Time in *Pulp Fiction*." In *Quentin Tarantino and Philosophy: How to Philosophize with a Pair of Pliers and a

Blowtorch, edited by Richard Greene and K. Silem Mohammad, 123–40. Chicago: Open Court, 2007.

Bakhtin, Mikhail. *Rabelais and His World*. Translated by Hélène Iswolsky. Bloomington: Indiana University Press, 1984.

Baldwin, James. "The Devil Finds Work." In *James Baldwin: Collected Essays*, edited by Toni Morrison, 477–572. New York: Library of America, 1998.

———. "Freaks and the American Ideal of Manhood." In *James Baldwin: Collected Essays*, edited by Toni Morrison, 814–29. New York: Library of America, 1998.

———. *If Beale Street Could Talk*. In *James Baldwin: Later Novels*, edited by Darryl Pinckney, 363–509. New York: Library of America, 2015.

———. *No Name in the Street*. In *James Baldwin: Collected Essays*, edited by Toni Morrison, 349–475. New York: Library of America, 1998.

———. *Tell Me How Long the Train's Been Gone*. In *James Baldwin: Later Novels*, edited by Darryl Pinckney, 1–362. New York: Library of America, 2015.

Barnett, Pamela E. *Dangerous Desire: Literature of Sexual Freedom and Sexual Violence since the Sixties*. New York: Routledge, 2004.

Bataille, Georges. *Inner Experience*. Translated by Stuart Kendall. Albany: State University of New York Press, 2014.

Baughman, Ronald. *Understanding James Dickey*. Columbia: University of South Carolina Press, 1985.

Bein, Albert. *Little Ol' Boy: A Play in Three Acts*. New York: Samuel French, 1935.

Bell, David. "Eroticizing the Rural." In *De-centring Sexualities: Politics and Representations beyond the Metropolis*, edited by Richard Phillips, Diane Watt, and David Shuttleton, 83–101. London: Routledge, 2000.

Bennett, Jane. *Vibrant Matter: A Political Ecology of Things*. Durham, NC: Duke University Press, 2010.

Berkman, Alexander. *Memoirs of a Prison Anarchist*. New York: Mother Earth Publishing Association, 1912.

Bernard, Jami. *Quentin Tarantino: The Man and His Movies*. New York: Harper Collins, 1995.

Bernstein, Robin. *Racial Innocence: Performing American Childhood from Slavery to Civil Rights*. New York: New York University Press, 2011.

Bersani, Leo. *Homos*. Cambridge, MA: Harvard University Press, 1995.

———. "Is the Rectum a Grave?" *October* 43 (1987): 197–222.

Biskind, Peter. *Easy Riders, Raging Bulls: How the Sex-Drugs-and-Rock 'n' Roll Generation Saved Hollywood*. New York: Simon & Schuster, 1998.

Blanchard, D. Caroline, Barry Graczyk, and Robert J. Blanchard. "Differential Reactions of Men and Women to Realism, Physical Damage, and Emotionality in Violent Films." *Aggressive Behavior* 12, no. 1 (1986): 45–55.

Boorman, John. *Adventures of a Suburban Boy*. London: Faber and Faber, 2003.

Boose, Lynda E. "Crossing the River Drina: Bosnian Rape Camps, Turkish Impalement, and Serb Cultural Memory." *Signs* 28, no. 1 (2002): 71–96.

Botting, Fred, and Scott Wilson. *The Tarantinian Ethics*. London: SAGE Publications, 2001.

Brenton, Howard. *The Romans in Britain*. In *Plays: 2*. London: Methuen, 1989.

Brison, Susan. *Aftermath: Violence and the Remaking of a Self*. Princeton, NJ: Princeton University Press, 2002.

Broughall, Quentin J. *Gore Vidal and Antiquity: Sex, Politics and Religion*. London: Routledge, 2023.

Brown, Michelle. *The Culture of Punishment: Prison, Society, and Spectacle.* New York: New York University Press, 2009.
Browning, Mark. *Stephen King on the Big Screen.* Bristol: Intellect, 2009.
Brownmiller, Susan. *Against Our Will: Men, Women and Rape.* New York: Fawcett Columbine, 1993.
Butler, Judith. *Bodies That Matter: On the Discursive Limits of "Sex."* New York: Routledge, 1993.
———. *Frames of War: When Is Life Grievable?* New York: Verso, 2010.
———. *Gender Trouble: Feminism and the Subversion of Identity.* 2nd ed. New York: Routledge, 1999.
Cahill, Ann J. *Rethinking Rape.* Ithaca, NY: Cornell University Press, 2001.
Calhoun, Richard J., and Robert W. Hill. *James Dickey.* Boston: Twayne, 1983.
Campbell, Allan. "'Fuck Boy Meets Girl': Heterosexual Aspirations and Masculine Interests in the World of Quentin Tarantino." In *Hetero: Queering Representations of Straightness*, edited by Sean Griffin, 209–25. Albany: State University of New York Press, 2009.
Carcaterra, Lorenzo. *Sleepers.* New York: Ballantine, 1995.
Carson, Neil. "Sexuality and Identity in *Fortune and Men's Eyes.*" *Twentieth Century Literature* 18, no. 3 (1972): 207–18.
Chauncey, George. *Gay New York: Gender, Urban Culture, and the Making of the Gay Male World 1890–1940.* New York: Basic Books, 1994.
Chen, Mel Y. *Animacies: Biopolitics, Racial Mattering, and Queer Affect.* Durham, NC: Duke University Press, 2012.
Childs, Dennis. *Slaves of the State: Black Incarceration from the Chain Gang to the Penitentiary.* Minneapolis: University of Minnesota Press, 2015.
Clabough, Casey Howard. *Elements: The Novels of James Dickey.* Macon, GA: Mercer University Press, 2002.
Clover, Carol J. *Men, Women, and Chain Saws: Gender in the Modern Horror Film.* Princeton, NJ: Princeton University Press, 1992.
Cluchey, Rick. *The Cage: A Play in One Act.* San Francisco, CA: Barbwire Press, 1970.
Clum, John M. *"He's All Man": Learning Masculinity, Gayness, and Love from American Movies.* London: Palgrave Macmillan, 2002.
Cobb, Michael. *God Hates Fags: The Rhetoric of Religious Violence.* New York: New York University Press, 2006.
Conley, Garrard. *Boy Erased: A Memoir of Identity, Faith, and Family.* New York: Riverhead Books, 2016.
Conroy, Pat. *The Prince of Tides.* Boston, MA: Houghton Mifflin, 1986.
Cook, David A. *Lost Illusions: American Cinema in the Shadow of Watergate and Vietnam, 1970–1979.* New York: Charles Scribner, 2000.
Cook, Kenneth. *Wake in Fright.* Melbourne: Text Classics, 2013.
Cooper, Dennis. *Frisk.* New York: Grove Weidenfeld, 1991.
Crimp, Douglas. "Mario Montez, for Shame." In *Gay Shame*, edited by David M. Halperin and Valerie Traub, 63–75. Chicago: University of Chicago Press, 2008.
Cuklanz, Lisa M. *Rape on Prime Time: Television, Masculinity, and Sexual Violence.* Philadelphia: University of Pennsylvania Press, 2000.
Cunningham, Rodger. *Apples on the Flood: The Southern Mountain Experience.* Knoxville: University of Tennessee Press, 1987.
Curry, Tommy J. *The Man-Not: Race, Class, Genre, and the Dilemmas of Black Manhood.* Philadelphia, PA: Temple University Press, 2017.

Darabont, Frank. *The Shawshank Redemption: The Shooting Script*. New York: Newmarket Press, 1996.
Davidson, Michael. "Phantom Limbs: Film Noir and the Disabled Body." *GLQ: a Journal of Lesbian and Gay Studies* 9, no. 1–2 (2003): 57–77.
Davis, Alan J. "Sexual Assaults in the Philadelphia Prison System and Sheriff's Vans." *Trans-Action [Society]* 6, no. 2 (1968): 8–17.
Deleuze, Gilles and Félix Guattari. *Anti-Oedipus: Capitalism and Schizophrenia*. Translated by Robert Hurley, Mark Seem, and Helen R. Lane. Minneapolis: University of Minnesota Press, 1987.
Dichter, Thomas Alan. "'An Extreme Sense of Protest against Everything': Chester Himes's Prison Novel." *American Literature* 90, no. 1 (2018): 111–40.
Dickey, James. *Deliverance* [novel]. New York: Dell, 1970.
———. *Deliverance* [screenplay]. Carbondale: Southern Illinois University Press, 1982.
Dickinson, Peter. *Screening Gender, Framing Genre: Canadian Literature into Film*. Toronto: University of Toronto Press, 2007.
Dinshaw, Carolyn. *Getting Medieval: Sexualities and Communities, Pre- and Post-modern*. Durham, NC: Duke University Press, 1999.
Douglas Home, William. *"Now Barabbas . . ."* London: Longmans, Green, 1947.
Dover, K. J. *Greek Homosexuality*. 2nd ed. Cambridge, MA: University of Harvard Press, 1989.
Endel, Peggy Goodman. "Dickey, Dante, and the Demonic: Reassessing *Deliverance*." *American Literature* 60, no. 4 (1988): 611–24.
Endres, Nikolai. "The Pillaged Pillar: *Hubris* and *Polis* in Gore Vidal's *The City and the Pillar*." *Classical and Modern Literature* 24, no. 2 (2004): 47–78.
Fanon, Frantz. *Black Skin, White Masks*. Translated by Richard Philcox. New York: Grove Press, 2008.
Feldman, Allen. *Formations of Violence: The Narrative of the Body and Political Terror in Northern Ireland*. Chicago: University of Chicago Press, 1991.
Féron, Élise. *Wartime Sexual Violence against Men: Masculinities and Power in Conflict Zones*. Lanham, MD: Rowman & Littlefield, 2018.
Fischel, Joseph J. *Sex and Harm in the Age of Consent*. Minneapolis: University of Minnesota Press, 2016.
Fishman, Joseph F. *Sex in Prison: Revealing Sex Conditions in American Prisons*. New York: National Library Press, 1934.
Flavin, Martin. *The Criminal Code: A Drama in Prologue and Three Acts*. In *The Best Plays of 1929–1930 and the Year Book of the Drama in America*, edited by Burns Mantle, 71–107. New York: Dodd Mead, 1934.
Fleisher, Mark S., and Jessie L. Krienert. *The Myth of Prison Rape: Sexual Culture in American Prisons*. Lanham, MD: Rowman & Littlefield, 2009.
Fone, Byrne R. S., ed. *The Columbia Anthology of Gay Literature: Readings from Western Antiquity to the Present Day*. New York Columbia University Press, 1998.
Forster, E. M. "The Torque." In *The Life to Come and Other Stories*, edited by Oliver Stallybrass, 151–65. New York: Norton, 1987.
Foster, Thomas A. *Rethinking Rufus: Sexual Violations of Enslaved Men*. Athens: University of Georgia Press, 2019.
Foucault, Michel. *Abnormal: Lectures at the Collège de France, 1974–1975*. Translated by Graham Burchell. New York: Picador, 2003.

———. *Discipline and Punish: The Birth of the Prison*. Translated by Alan Sheridan. New York: Vintage, 1995.

———. *The History of Sexuality—Volume 1: An Introduction*. Translated by Robert Hurley. New York: Vintage, 1990.

———. *The Use of Pleasure—Volume 2 of the History of Sexuality*. Translated by Robert Hurley. New York: Vintage, 1990.

Frankel, Glenn. *Shooting Midnight Cowboy: Art, Sex, Loneliness, Liberation, and the Making of a Dark Classic*. New York: Farrar, Straus and Giroux, 2021.

Fratarrola, Angela. "Frustration and Silence in Gore Vidal's *The City and the Pillar*." In *Literature and Homosexuality*, edited by Michael J. Meyer, 35–54. Amsterdam: Rodopi, 2000.

Fregoso, Rosa Linda. *The Bronze Screen: Chicana and Chicano Film Culture*. Minneapolis: University of Minnesota Press, 1993.

Freud, Sigmund. *Jokes and Their Relation to the Unconscious*. Standard ed. Translated by James Strachey. New York: Norton, 1960.

Gabaldon, Diana. *Outlander*. New York: Dell, 1992.

Gadd, Richard. *Baby Reindeer*. London: Bloomsbury, 2019.

Galsworthy, John. *Justice: A Tragedy in Four Acts*. New York: Charles Scribner's Sons, 1910.

Garber, Marjorie. *Vested Interests: Crossed Dressing and Cultural Anxiety*. New York: Routledge, 1992.

Gavey, Nicola. *Just Sex? The Cultural Scaffolding of Rape*. London: Routledge, 2005.

Genet, Jean. *Deathwatch*. In *The Maids and Deathwatch: Two Plays*, translated by Bernard Frechtman, 101–63. New York: Grove Press, 1954.

Gibson, Ernest L., III. *Salvific Manhood: James Baldwin's Novelization of Male Intimacy*. Lincoln: University of Nebraska Press.

Gill-Peterson, Jules. *A Short History of Trans Misogyny*. New York: Verso, 2024.

Giroux, Henry A. *Fugitive Cultures: Race, Violence, and Youth*. London: Routledge, 1996.

Goldstein, Joshua S. *War and Gender: How Gender Shapes the War System and Vice Versa*. Cambridge: Cambridge University Press, 2001.

Graham, Allison. *Framing the South: Hollywood, Television, and Race during the Civil Rights Struggle*. Baltimore, MD: Johns Hopkins University Press, 2001.

Griffith, David. *A Good War Is Hard to Find*. Brooklyn: Soft Skull Press, 2006.

Grobe, Christopher. *The Art of Confession: The Performance of Self from Robert Lowell to Reality TV*. New York: New York University Press, 2017.

Grosz, Elizabeth. *Space, Time, and Perversion: Essays on the Politics of Bodies*. New York: Routledge, 1995.

Groth, Gary. "A Dream of Perfect Reception: The Movies of Quentin Tarantino." In *Commodify Your Dissent: Salvos from The Baffler*, edited by Thomas Frank and Matt Weiland, 183–93. New York: Norton, 1997.

Haag, Pamela. *Consent: Sexual Rights and the Transformation of Liberalism*. Ithaca, NY: Cornell University Press, 1999.

Halperin, David M. *How to Be Gay*. Cambridge, MA: Harvard University Press, 2012.

Harper, Phillip Brian. *Are We Not Men? Masculine Anxiety and the Problem of African-American Identity*. New York: Oxford University Press, 1996.

Harris, Trudier. "The Eye as Weapon in *If Beale Street Could Talk*." *MELUS* 5, no. 3 (1978): 54–66.

Hart, Henry. *James Dickey: The World as a Lie*. New York: Picador, 2000.

Hartman, Saidiya V. *Scenes of Subjection: Terror, Slavery, and Self-Making in Nineteenth-Century America*. New York: Oxford University Press, 1997.
Herbert, John. *Fortune and Men's Eyes*. New York: Grove Press, 1967.
Herlihy, James Leo. *Midnight Cowboy*. New York: Simon & Schuster, 1965.
Higgins, Lynn A. "Screen/Memory: Rape and Its Alibis in *Last Year at Marienbad*." In *Rape and Representation*, edited by Lynn A. Higgins and Brenda R. Silver, 303–21. New York: Columbia University Press, 1991.
Higgins, Lynn A., and Brenda R. Silver. "Introduction: Rereading Rape." In *Rape and Representation*, edited by Lynn A. Higgins and Brenda R. Silver, 1–11. New York: Columbia University Press, 1991.
Himes, Chester. *Cast the First Stone*. New York: Signet, 1972.
———. *The Quality of Hurt: The Autobiography of Chester Himes—Volume 1*. New York: Doubleday, 1972.
———. *Yesterday Will Make You Cry*. New York: Norton, 1998.
Hirsch, Marianne. *Family Frames: Photography, Narrative, and Postmemory*. Cambridge, MA: Harvard University Press, 1997.
Hoagland, Tony. *What Narcissism Means to Me*. Saint Paul, MN: Graywolf Press, 2000.
Hocquenghem, Guy. *Homosexual Desire*. Translated by Daniella Dangoor. Durham, NC: Duke University Press, 1993.
Holland, Sharon Patricia. *The Erotic Life of Racism*. Durham, NC: Duke University Press, 2012.
hooks, bell. *Reel to Real: Race, Sex, and Class at the Movies*. New York: Routledge, 1996.
Human Rights Watch. *No Escape: Male Rape in U.S. Prisons*. New York: Human Rights Watch, 2001.
Innes, Robert Alexander, and Kim Anderson, eds. *Indigenous Men and Masculinities: Legacies, Identities, Regeneration*. Winnipeg: University of Manitoba Press, 2015.
Jackson, Lawrence P. *Chester B. Himes: A Biography*. New York: Norton, 2017.
Jameson, Fredric. "The Great American Hunter, or, Ideological Content in the Novel." *College English* 34, no. 2 (1972): 180–97.
———. *Postmodernism, or, The Cultural Logic of Late Capitalism*. Durham, NC: Duke University Press, 1991.
Jeffers, H. Paul. *Sal Mineo: His Life, Murder, and Mystery*. New York: Carroll & Graf, 2000.
Johnson, James Weldon. *The Autobiography of an Ex-Colored Man*. Boston: Sherman, French & Company, 1912.
Kaba, Mariame. *We Do This 'til We Free Us: Abolitionist Organizing and Transforming Justice*. Chicago: Haymarket, 2021.
Kaba, Mariame, and Andrea J. Ritchie. *No More Police: A Case for Abolition*. New York: New Press, 2022.
Kaba, Mariame, and Brit Schulte. "Not a Cardboard Cutout: Cyntoia Brown and the Framing of a Victim." In *We Do This 'til We Free Us: Abolitionist Organizing and Transforming Justice*, by Mariame Kaba, 35–40. Chicago: Haymarket, 2021.
Kaba, Mariame and Kelly Hayes. "A Jailbreak of the Imagination: Seeing Prisons for What They Are and Demanding Transformation." In *We Do This 'til We Free Us: Abolitionist Organizing and Transforming Justice*, by Mariame Kaba, 18–25. Chicago: Haymarket, 2021.
Kane, Sarah. *Blasted*. In *Kane: Complete Plays*, 1–61. London: Methuen Drama, 2001.
Kantor, Kevin. "People You May Know." In *Endowing Vegetables with Too Much Meaning*, 28–30. Seattle, MA: CreateSpace Independent Publishing, 2015.

Kaplan, Philip J. *F'd Companies: Spectacular Dot-com Flameouts*. New York: Simon & Schuster, 2002.
Keesey, Douglas. "James Dickey and the Macho Persona." In *Critical Essays on James Dickey*, edited by Robert Kirschten, 201–10. New York: G. K. Hall, 1994.
Keith, Toby. "Courtesy of the Red, White, & Blue (The Angry American)." *Unleashed*. Nashville, TN: DreamWorks Records, 2002.
Kermode, Mark. *The Shawshank Redemption*. London: British Film Institute, 2003.
Kiernan, Robert F. *Gore Vidal*. New York: Frederick Ungar, 1982.
Kimball, A. Samuel. "'Bad-Ass Dudes' in *Pulp Fiction*: Homophobia and the Counterphobic Idealization of Women." *Quarterly Review of Film and Video* 16, no. 2 (1997): 171–92.
Kimmel, Michael S. *Manhood in America: A Cultural History*. 2nd ed. Oxford: Oxford University Press, 2006.
Kincaid, James. *Erotic Innocence: The Culture of Child Molesting*. Durham, NC: Duke University Press, 1998.
Kinder, Marsha. "Violence American Style: The Narrative Orchestrations of Violent Attractions." In *Violence and American Cinema*, edited by J. David Slocum, 63–100. New York: Routledge, 2001.
King, Stephen. "Rita Hayworth and Shawshank Redemption." In *Different Seasons*, 1–101. New York: Viking Press, 1982.
Kunzel, Regina. *Criminal Intimacy: Prison and the Uneven History of Modern American Sexuality*. Chicago: University of Chicago Press, 2008.
Lawrence, T. E. *Seven Pillars of Wisdom: A Triumph*. London: Jonathan Cape, 1935.
Lee, A. Robert. "Violence Real and Imagined: The World of Chester Himes' Novels." *Negro American Literature Forum* 10, no. 1 (1976): 13–22.
Lennard, Dominic, R. Barton Palmer, and Murray Pomerance, eds. *The Other Hollywood Renaissance*. Edinburgh: Edinburgh University Press, 2020.
Levin, Cherry. "Adherence to Propp: James Dickey's *Deliverance* in Novel and Film." In Thesing and Wrede, eds., *The Way We Read James Dickey*, 76–87.
Lightweis-Goff, Jennie. "'How Willing to Let Anything Be Done': James Dickey's Feminist Praxis." In Thesing and Wrede, eds., *The Way We Read James Dickey*, 239–51.
Lockwood, Daniel. *Prison Sexual Violence*. New York: Elsevier, 1980.
MacKinnon, Catharine A. "Feminism, Marxism, Method, and the State: Toward Feminist Jurisprudence." *Signs* 8, no. 4 (1983): 635–58.
———. *Toward a Feminist Theory of the State*. Cambridge, MA: Harvard University Press, 1989.
Madden, Ed. "The Buggering Hillbilly and the Buddy Movie: Male Sexuality in *Deliverance*." In Thesing and Wrede, eds., *The Way We Read James Dickey*, 195–209.
Magistrale, Tony. "Redemption through the Feminine in *The Shawshank Redemption*; or, Why Rita Hayworth's Name Belongs in the Title." In *The Films of Stephen King: From Carrie to Secret Window*, edited by Tony Magistrale, 101–13. London: Palgrave Macmillan, 2008.
Marowitz, Charles. *Burnt Bridges: A Souvenir of the Swinging Sixties and Beyond*. London: Hodder & Stoughton, 1990.
Marcus, Sharon. "Fighting Bodies, Fighting Words." In *Feminists Theorize the Political*, edited by Judith Butler and Joan W. Scott, 385–403. London: Routledge, 1992.
Margolies, Edward, and Michel Fabre. *The Several Lives of Chester Himes*. Jackson: University Press of Mississippi, 1997.

Mariner, Joanne. "Body and Soul: The Trauma of Prison Rape." In *Building Violence: How America's Rush to Incarcerate Creates More Violence*, edited by John P. May, 125-31. Thousand Oaks, CA: SAGE Publications, 2000.
Marriott, David. *On Black Men*. New York: Columbia University Press, 2000.
Mason, Carol. "The Hillbilly Defense: Culturally Mediating U.S. Terror at Home and Abroad." *NWSA Journal* 17, no. 3 (2005): 39-63.
McAvinchey, Caoimhe. *Theatre & Prison*. London: Palgrave Macmillan, 2011.
McGuire, Ian. *The North Water*. New York: Henry Holt, 2016.
McRuer, Robert. *Crip Theory: Cultural Signs of Queerness and Disability*. New York: New York University Press, 2006.
Michaud, Michael Gregg. *Sal Mineo: A Biography*. New York: Crown Archetype, 2010.
Miller, Stephen Paul. *The Seventies Now: Culture as Surveillance*. Durham, NC: Duke University Press, 1999.
Misra, Amalendu. *The Landscape of Silence: Sexual Violence against Men in War*. London: Hurst & Company, 2015.
Mitchell, Margaret. *Gone with the Wind*. New York: Macmillan, 1936.
Moon, Michael. "A Small Boy and Others: Sexual Disorientation in Henry James, Kenneth Anger, and David Lynch." In *Comparative American Identities: Race, Sex, and Nationality in the Modern Text*, edited by Hortense J. Spillers, 141-56. New York: Routledge, 1991.
Muñoz, José Esteban. *Disidentifications: Queers of Color and the Performance of Politics*. Minneapolis: University of Minnesota Press, 1999.
Natoli, Joseph. *Speeding to the Millennium: Film & Culture, 1993-1995*. Albany: State University of New York Press, 1998.
Neilson, Anthony. *Penetrator*. In *Neilson Plays: 1*, 59-119. New York: Methuen Drama, 1998.
Oforlea, Aaron Ngozi. *James Baldwin, Toni Morrison, and the Rhetorics of Black Male Subjectivity*. Columbus: Ohio State University Press, 2017.
Pair, Joyce M. "Measuring the Fictive Motion: War in *Deliverance*, *Alnilam*, and *To the White Sea*." *Texas Review* 17, no. 3-4 (1996): 55-92.
Palmer, R. Barton. "Jerry Schatzberg's Downfall Portraits: His Cinema of Loneliness." In *The Other Hollywood Renaissance*, edited by Dominic Lennard, R. Barton Palmer, and Murray Pomerance, 308-28. Edinburgh: University of Edinburgh Press, 2020.
———. "Narration, Text, Intertext: The Two Versions of *Deliverance*." In *"Struggling for Wings": The Art of James Dickey*, edited by Robert Kirschten, 194-203. Columbia: University of South Carolina Press, 1997.
Parks-Ramage, Jonathan. *Yes, Daddy*. Boston: Houghton Mifflin Harcourt, 2021.
Pateman, Carole. *The Sexual Contract*. Palo Alto, CA: Stanford University Press, 1988.
Paterson, Alexander. Introduction to *"Now Barabbas . . . ,"* by William Douglas Home. London: Longmans, Green & Co., 1947.
Pinar, William F. *The Gender of Racial Politics and Violence in America: Lynching, Prison Rape, and the Crisis of Masculinity*. New York: Peter Lang, 2001.
Piñero, Miguel. *Short Eyes*. New York: Hill and Wang, 1975.
Plastas, Melinda, and Eve Allegra Raimon. "Brutality and Brotherhood: James Baldwin and Prison Sexuality." *African American Review* 46, no. 4 (2013): 687-99.
Prince, Stephen. *Classical Film Violence: Designing and Regulating Brutality in Hollywood Cinema, 1930-1968*. New Brunswick, NJ: Rutgers University Press, 2003.
Puar, Jasbir K. *Terrorist Assemblages: Homonationalism in Queer Times*. Durham, NC: Duke University Press, 2007.

Puar, Jasbir K., and Amit S. Rai. "Monster, Terrorist, Fag: The War on Terrorism and the Production of Docile Patriots." *Social Text* 20, no. 3 (2002): 117–48.

Rattigan, Terence. *Ross: A Dramatic Portrait*. London: Hamish Hamilton, 1960.

Ravenhill, Mark. *Shopping and Fucking*. In *Ravenhill Plays: 1*, 1–91. New York: Methuen Drama, 2001.

Read, Jacinda. *The New Avengers: Feminism, Femininity, and the Rape-revenge Cycle*. Manchester: Manchester University Press, 2000.

Robinson, Sally. *Marked Men: White Masculinity in Crisis*. New York: Columbia University Press, 2000.

Rolens, Clare. "Write like a Man: Chester Himes and the Criminal Text Beyond Bars." *Callaloo* 37, no. 2 (2014): 432–51.

Rooney, Ellen. "'A Little More than Persuading': Tess and the Subject of Sexual Violence." In *Rape and Representation*, edited by Lynn A. Higgins and Brenda R. Silver, 87–114. New York: Columbia University Press, 1991.

Ross, Marlon B. "Race, Rape, Castration: Feminist Theories of Sexual Violence and Masculine Strategies of Black Protest." In *Masculinity Studies and Feminist Theory: New Directions*, edited by Judith Kegan Gardiner, 305–43. New York: Columbia University Press, 2002.

Roth, Mitchel P. *Fire in the Big House: America's Deadliest Prison Disaster*. Athens: Ohio University Press, 2019.

Rothenberg, David. *Fortune in My Eyes: A Memoir of Broadway Glamour, Social Justice, and Political Passion*. Milwaukee: Applause Theatre & Cinema Books, 2012.

Said, Edward. *Orientalism*. New York: Vintage Books, 1979.

Saketopoulou, Avgi. *Sexuality Beyond Consent: Risk, Race, Traumatophilia*. New York: New York University Press, 2023.

Scacco, Anthony M. *Rape in Prison*. Springfield, IL: C. C. Thomas, 1975.

Scarce, Michael. *Male on Male Rape: The Hidden Toll of Stigma and Shame*. New York: Insight Books, 1997.

Scarry, Elaine. *The Body in Pain: The Making and Unmaking of the World*. New York: Oxford University Press, 1985.

Schmidt, Heather. "Male Rape." In *Encyclopedia of Rape*, edited by Merril D. Smith, 121–22. Westport, CT: Greenwood Press, 2004.

Scott, Darieck. *Extravagant Abjection: Blackness, Power, and Sexuality in the African American Imagination*. New York: New York University Press, 2010.

Sedgwick, Eve Kosofsky. *Between Men: English Literature and Male Homosocial Desire*. New York: Columbia University Press, 1985.

———. *Tendencies*. Durham, NC: Duke University Press, 1993.

———. *Touching Feeling: Affect, Pedagogy, Performativity*. Durham, NC: Duke University Press, 2003.

Sedgwick, Eve Kosofsky, and Michael Moon. "Divinity: A Dossier, a Performance Piece, a Little-Understood Emotion." In *Tendencies*, by Eve Kosofsky Sedgwick, 215–51. Durham, NC: Duke University Press, 1993.

Senelick, Laurence. *The Changing Room: Sex, Drag and Theatre*. New York: Routledge, 2000.

Shaviro, Steven. *The Cinematic Body*. Minneapolis: University of Minnesota Press, 1993.

Sheidlower, Jesse, ed. *The F Word*. 2nd ed. New York: Random House, 1999.

Sielke, Sabine. *Reading Rape: The Rhetoric of Sexual Violence in American Literature and Culture, 1790–1990*. Princeton, NJ: Princeton University Press, 2002.

Silverman, Kaja. *Male Subjectivity at the Margins*. New York: Routledge, 1992.
Sinfield, Alan. *Out on Stage: Lesbian and Gay Theatre in the Twentieth Century*. New Haven, CT: Yale University Press, 1999.
Slovic, Scott. "Visceral Faulkner: Fiction and the Tug of the Organic World." In *Faulkner and the Ecology of the South*, edited by Joseph R. Urgo and Ann J. Abadie, 115–32. Jackson: University Press of Mississippi, 2005.
Smith, Caleb. *The Prison and the American Imagination*. New Haven, CT: Yale University Press, 2009.
Smith, Jim. *Tarantino*. London: Virgin Books, 2005.
Stemple, Lara. "HBO's *Oz* and the Fight against Prisoner Rape: Chronicles from the Front Line." In *Third Wave Feminism and Television: Jane Puts It in a Box*, edited by Merri Lisa Johnson, 166–88. New York: I. B. Tauris, 2007.
Struckman-Johnson, David, Cindy Struckman-Johnson, et al. "A Pre-PREA Survey of Inmate and Correctional Staff Opinions on How to Prevent Prison Sexual Assault." *Prison Journal* 93, no. 4 (2013): 429–52.
Summers, Claude J. *Gay Fictions: Wilde to Stonewall: Studies in a Male Homosexual Literary Tradition*. New York: Continuum, 1990.
Szczesniak, Konrad. "Stigma." In *Encyclopedia of Rape*, edited by Merril D. Smith, 243. Westport, CT: Greenwood Press, 2004.
Tarantino, Quentin. *Cinema Speculation*. New York: HarperCollins, 2022.
———. *Pulp Fiction: A Quentin Tarantino Screenplay*. New York: Hyperion, 1994.
Taylor, Barbara, and Mary Thomas. "He Shouted Loud, 'Hosanna, Deliverance Will Come.'" *Foxfire* 7, no. 4 (1973): 304.
Thesing, Willam B., and Theda Wrede, eds. *The Way We Read James Dickey*. Columbia: University of South Carolina Press, 2009.
Theweleit, Klaus. *Male Fantasies Volume 1: Women, Floods, Bodies, History*. Translated by Stephen Conway. Minneapolis: University of Minnesota Press, 1987.
———. *Male Fantasies Volume 2: Male Bodies—Psychoanalyzing the White Terror*. Translated by Erica Carter and Chris Turner. Minneapolis: University of Minnesota Press, 1989.
Thomas, Aaron C. "Infelicities." *Journal of Dramatic Theory and Criticism* 35, no. 2 (2021): 13–25.
———. "Truth and Translation at the Heart of Violence," *Theater* 49, no. 2 (2019): 48–61.
Thomas, Harry. "'Immaculate Manhood': *The City and the Pillar*, *Giovanni's Room*, and the Straight-Acting Gay Man." *Twentieth-Century Literature* 59, no. 4 (2013): 596–618.
Thompson, Carlyle Van. *Eating the Black Body: Miscegenation as Sexual Consumption in African American Literature and Culture*. New York: Peter Lang, 2006.
Tomkins, Silvan. *Shame and Its Sisters: A Silvan Tomkins Reader*. Edited by Eve Kosofsky Sedgwick and Adam Frank. Durham, NC: Duke University Press, 1995.
Velasquez-Potts, Michelle C. "Regulatory Sites: Management, Confinement and HIV/AIDS." In *Captive Genders: Trans Embodiment and the Prison Industrial Complex*, 2nd ed., edited by Eric A. Stanley and Nat Smith, 119–32. Chico, CA: AK Press, 2015.
Vidal, Gore. "An Afterword." In *The City and the Pillar Revised*, 155–58. New York: Signet, 1965.
———. *The City and the Pillar*. New York: E. P. Dutton, 1948.
———. *The City and the Pillar Revised, with a New Preface by the Author and Seven Early Stories*. New York: Random House, 1995.
———. *Palimpsest: A Memoir*. New York: Random House, 1995.

Wagner, Anton. *Establishing Our Boundaries: English-Canadian Theatre Criticism.* Toronto: University of Toronto Press, 1999.
Wasserman, Jerry. Introduction to *Modern Canadian Plays.* Rev. ed. Vancouver: Talonbooks, 1986.
Whitaker, Brian. *Unspeakable Love: Gay and Lesbian Life in the Middle East.* Berkeley: University of California Press, 2006.
White, Ray Lewis. *Gore Vidal.* New York: Twayne, 1968.
Whitehead, Neil L. *Dark Shamans: Kanaimà and the Poetics of Violent Death.* Durham, NC: Duke University Press, 2002.
Williams, Bernard. *Shame and Necessity.* Berkeley: University of California Press, 1993.
Williams, Linda. "Film Bodies: Gender, Genre, and Excess." *Film Quarterly* 44, no. 4 (1991): 2–13.
Williams, Tennessee. *Not about Nightingales.* In *Plays 1937–1955,* edited by Mel Gussow and Kenneth Holditch, 97–188. New York: Library of America, 2000.
Williamson, J. W. *Hillbillyland: What the Movies Did to the Mountains and What the Mountains Did to the Movies.* Chapel Hill: University of North Carolina Press, 1995.
Wlodarz, Joe. "Maximum Insecurity: Genre Trouble and Closet Erotics in and out of HBO's *Oz.*" *Camera Obscura* 20, no. 1 (2005): 58–105.
———. "Rape Fantasies: Hollywood and Homophobia." In *Masculinity: Bodies, Movies, Culture,* edited by Peter Lehman, 67–80. New York: Routledge, 2001.
Wood, Robin. *Hollywood from Vietnam to Reagan . . . and Beyond.* 2nd ed. New York: Columbia University Press.
Woodard, Vincent. *The Delectable Negro: Human Consumption and Homoeroticism within U.S. Slave Culture.* New York: New York University Press, 2014.
Wrede, Theda. "Nature and Gender in James Dickey's *Deliverance*: An Ecofeminist Reading." In Thesing and Wrede, eds., *The Way We Read James Dickey,* 177–93.
Yousman, Bill. *Prime Time Prisons on U.S. TV: Representation of Incarceration.* New York: Peter Lang, 2009.
Zaborowska, Magdalena J. *James Baldwin's Turkish Decade: Erotics of Exile.* Durham, NC: Duke University Press, 2009.

LIST OF FILMS AND TELEVISION EPISODES REFERENCED

American Crime. "Season Two: Episode Four." Julie Hébert, director. Kirk A. Moore, screenwriter. January 27, 2016.
———. "Season Two: Episode One." John Ridley, director and screenwriter. January 6, 2016.
———. "Season Two: Episode Six." Jessica Yu, director. Stacy A. Littlejohn, screenwriter. February 10, 2016.
———. "Season Two: Episode Ten." Nicole Kassell, director. Diana Son, screenwriter. March 9, 2016.
———. "Season Two: Episode Three." Gregg Araki, director. Sonay Hoffman, screenwriter. January 20, 2016.
———. "Season Two: Episode Two." Clement Virgo, director. Ernie Pandish, screenwriter. January 13, 2016.
American History X. 1998. Tony Kaye, director.
American Me. 1992. Edward James Olmos, director.

. . . *And Justice for All.* 1979. Norman Jewison, director.
Animal Factory. 2000. Steve Buscemi, director.
Avalon. 1990. Barry Levinson, director.
Baby Reindeer. "Episode 4." Weronika Tofilska, director. Richard Gadd, screenwriter. April 11, 2024.
———. "Episode 1." Weronika Tofilska, director. Richard Gadd, screenwriter. April 11, 2024.
———. "Episode 7." Josephine Bornebusch, director. Richard Gadd, screenwriter. April 11, 2024.
———. "Episode 6." Josephine Bornebusch, director. Richard Gadd, screenwriter. April 11, 2024.
———. "Episode 2." Weronika Tofilska, director. Richard Gadd, screenwriter. April 11, 2024.
Beyond the Walls. 1984. Uri Barbash, director.
The Big House. 1930. George Roy Hill, director.
Big Stan. 2007. Rob Schneider, director.
Birdman of Alcatraz. 1962. John Frankenheimer, director.
Boom Town. 1940. Jack Conway, director.
Boy Erased. 2018. Joel Edgerton, director.
The Boys in the Band. 1970. William Friedkin, director.
The Boys in the Band. 2020. Ryan Murphy, director.
The Brutalist. 2024. Brady Corbet, director.
Butch Cassidy and the Sundance Kid. 1969. George Roy Hill, director.
The Butterfly Effect. 2004. Eric Bress and J. Mackye Gruber, directors.
Caged. 1950. John Cromwell, director.
Cagney & Lacey. "Violation." Allen Baron, director. Les Carter, screenwriter. Season 4, episode 21. March 18, 1985.
The Client. 1994. Joel Schumacher, director.
A Clockwork Orange. 1971. Stanley Kubrick, director.
Closet Monster. 2015. Stephen Dunn, director.
Come Back Charleston Blue. 1972. Mark Warren, director.
Cotton Comes to Harlem. 1970. Ossie Davis, director.
Cruising. 1980. William Friedkin, director.
Dazed and Confused. 1994. Richard Linklater, director.
Deadly Justice [*The Rape of Richard Beck*]. 1985. Karen Arthur, director.
Death Becomes Her. 1992. Robert Zemeckis, director.
Death Wish. 1974. Michael Winner, director.
Deliverance. 1972. John Boorman, director.
Diner. 1982. Barry Levinson, director.
Easy Rider. 1969. Dennis Hopper, director.
The Emerald Forest. 1985. John Boorman, director.
Felon. 2008. Ric Roman Waugh, director.
Forrest Gump. 1994. Robert Zemeckis, director.
Fortune and Men's Eyes. 1971. Harvey Hart, director.
The Great Escape. 1963. John Sturges, director.
Hard to Kill. 1990. Bruce Malmuth, director.
Harold & Kumar Escape from Guantanamo Bay. 2008. Jon Hurwitz and Hayden Schlossberg, directors.
The Hateful Eight. 2015. Quentin Tarantino, director.

The Hills Have Eyes. 1977. Wes Craven, director.
Hit & Run. 2012. David Palmer and Dax Shepard, directors.
The Hunting Ground. 2015. Kirby Dick, director.
Husbands. 1970. John Cassavetes, director.
I Love You Phillip Morris. 2009. Glenn Ficarra and John Requa, directors.
I May Destroy You. "The Alliance." Sam Miller and Michaela Coel, directors. Michaela Coel, screenwriter. Episode 6. June 13, 2020.
———. "Ego Death." Sam Miller and Michaela Coel, directors. Michaela Coel, screenwriter. Episode 12. August 24, 2020.
———. "Happy Animals." Sam Miller and Michaela Coel, directors. Michaela Coel, screenwriter. Episode 7. July 20, 2020.
———. ". . . It Just Came Up." Sam Miller and Michaela Coel, directors. Michaela Coel, screenwriter. Episode 5. July 6, 2020.
———. "That Was Fun." Sam Miller and Michaela Coel, directors. Michaela Coel, screenwriter. Episode 4. June 29, 2020.
I Spit on Your Grave. 1978. Meir Zarchi, director.
If Beale Street Could Talk. 2018. Barry Jenkins, director.
I'll Sleep When I'm Dead. 2003. Mike Hodges, director.
In Living Color. "The Last Man on Earth." Terri McCoy, director. Season 3, episode 23. March 29, 1992.
In the Heat of the Night. 1967. Norman Jewison, director.
In Too Deep. 1999. Michael Rymer, director.
An Innocent Man. 1989. Peter Yates, director.
Jaws. 1975. Steven Spielberg, director.
The Jewel in the Crown. "Incidents at a Wedding." Christopher Morahan, director. Ken Taylor, screenwriter. Episode 4. January 24, 1984.
———. "Questions of Loyalty." Christopher Morahan, director. Ken Taylor, screenwriter. Episode 3. January 17, 1984.
Kaz. "A Case of Murder" ["A Day in Court"]. Don Medford, director. Michael Genelin, screenwriter. Season 1, episode 12. January 17, 1979.
King of New York. 1990. Abel Ferrara, director.
Kinjite: Forbidden Subjects. 1989. J. Lee Thompson, director.
Lawrence of Arabia. 1962. David Lean, director.
Let's Go to Prison. 2006. Bob Odenkirk, director.
Lockdown. 2000. John Luessenhop, director.
Longtime Companion. 1989. Norman René, director.
Married with Children. "Bearly Men." Gerry Cohen, director. Russell Marcus, screenwriter. Season 10, episode 12. December 3, 1995.
———. "The Juggs Have Left the Building." Gerry Cohen, director. Vince Cheung and Ben Montanio, screenwriters. Season 11, episode 7. December 1, 1996.
Memento. 2000. Christoper Nolan, director.
Midnight Cowboy. 1969. John Schlesinger, director.
The Mudge Boy. 2003. Michael Burke, director.
Murphy's Law. 1986. J. Lee Thompson, director.
Mysterious Skin. 2004. Gregg Araki, director.
The Natural. 1984. Barry Levinson, director.
Natural Born Killers. 1994. Oliver Stone, director.

Network. 1976. Sidney Lumet, director.
Of Mice and Men. 1939. Lewis Milestone, director.
Outrage. 1950. Ida Lupino, director.
Oz. "Animal Farm." Mary Harron, director. Tom Fontana and Debbie Sarjeant, screenwriters. Season 2, episode 7. August 24, 1998.
———. "A Day in the Death . . ." Daniel Loflin, director. Tom Fontana, Sunil Nayar, and Bradford Winters, screenwriters. Season 6, episode 6. February 9, 2003.
———. "Dream a Little Dream of Me." Adam Bernstein, director. Tom Fontana and Sean Whitesell, screenwriters. Season 5, episode 3. January 20, 2002.
———. "4giveness." John Henry Davis, director. Tom Fontana and Bradford Winters, screenwriters. Season 6, episode 5. February 2, 2003.
———. "God's Chillin'." Jean de Segonzac, director. Tom Fontana, screenwriter. Season 1, episode 3. July 21, 1997.
———. "Gray Matter." Brian Cox, director. Tom Fontana, screenwriter. Season 4, episode 5. August 9, 2000.
———. "Impotence." Alex Zakrzewski, director. Tom Fontana, screenwriter. Season 5, episode 8. February 24, 2002.
———. "Laws of Gravity." Rob Morrow, director. Tom Fontana and Sean Whitesell, screenwriters. Season 5, episode 2. January 13, 2002.
———. "Napoleon's Boney Parts." Matt Dillon, director. Tom Fontana, screenwriter. Season 3, episode 2. July 21, 1999.
———. "Next Stop: Valhalla." J. Miller Tobin, director. Tom Fontana and Sunil Nayar, screenwriters. Season 5, episode 4. January 27, 2002.
———. "Plan B." Darnell Martin, director. Tom Fontana, screenwriter. Season 1, episode 7. August 18, 1997.
———. "The Routine." Darnell Martin, director. Tom Fontana, screenwriter. Season 1, episode 1. July 12, 1997.
———. "See No Evil, Hear No Evil, Smell No Evil." Marc Klasfield, director. Tom Fontana and Sunil Nayar, screenwriters. Season 6, episode 2. January 12, 2003.
———. "Straight Life." Leslie Libman and Larry Williams, directors. Tom Fontana, screenwriter. Season 1, episode 5. August 4, 1997.
———. "Strange Bedfellows." Alan Taylor, director. Tom Fontana, screenwriter. Season 2, episode 6. August 17, 1998.
———. "The Tip." Nick Gomez, director. Tom Fontana, screenwriter. Season 2, episode 1. July 11, 1998.
———. "To Your Health." Alan Taylor, director. Tom Fontana, screenwriter. Season 1, episode 6. August 11, 1997.
———. "Variety." Roger Rees, director. Tom Fontana and Bradford Winters, screenwriters. Season 5, episode 6. February 10, 2002.
———. "Visits, Conjugal and Otherwise." Nick Gomez, director. Tom Fontana, screenwriter. Season 1, episode 2. July 14, 1997.
Philadelphia. 1993. Jonathan Demme, director.
Piñero. 2001. Leon Ichaso, director.
The Prince of Tides. 1991. Barbra Streisand, director.
The Principal. 1987. Christopher Cain, director.
The Professionals. 1966. Richard Brooks, director.
Pulp Fiction. 1994. Quentin Tarantino, director.

The Rape of Richard Beck. 1985. Karen Arthur, director.
Reservoir Dogs. 1992. Quentin Tarantino, director.
The Return. 2024. Uberto Pasolini, director.
RuPaul's Drag Race. "Drag Con Panel Extravaganza." Season 10, episode 6. April 26, 2018.
Scarecrow. 1973. Jerry Schatzberg, director.
Screen Test #2. 1965. Andy Warhol, director.
Scum. 1979. Alan Clarke, director.
South Park. "Imaginationland Episode I." Trey Parker, director and screenwriter. Season 11, episode 10. October 17, 2007.
———. "Imaginationland Episode II." Trey Parker, director and screenwriter. Season 11, episode 11. October 24, 2007.
———. "Imaginationland Episode III." Trey Parker, director and screenwriter. Season 11, episode 12. October 31, 2007.
The Shawshank Redemption. 1994. Frank Darabont, director.
The Shield. "Mum." Nick Gomez, director. Kurt Sutter and Shawn Ryan, screenwriters. Season 3, episode 5. 6 April 2004.
Short Eyes. 1977. Robert M. Young, director.
Shrek Forever After. 2010. Mike Mitchell, director.
Six Feet Under. "That's My Dog." Alan Poul, director. Scott Buck, screenwriter. Season 4, episode 5. July 18, 2004.
Sleepers. 1996. Barry Levinson, director.
Snowtown [*The Snowtown Murders*]. 2011. Justin Kurzel, director.
St. Elsewhere. "Cheek to Cheek." Helaine Head, director. Eric Overmyer, John Masius, and Tom Fontana, screenwriters. Season 4, episode 21. March 12, 1986.
A Streetcar Named Desire. 1951. Elia Kazan, director.
The Ten. 2007. David Wain, director.
The Texas Chain Saw Massacre. 1974. Tobe Hooper, director.
Thirteen Reasons Why. "Bye." Kyle Patrick Alvarez, director. Brian Yorkey, screenwriter. Season 2, episode 13. May 18, 2018.
———. "In High School, Even on a Good Day, It's Hard to Tell Who's on Your Side." Kevin Dowling, director. Felischa Marye, screenwriter. Season 3, episode 8. August 23, 2019.
———. "There Are a Few Things I Haven't Told You." Kevin Dowling, director. Helen Shang, screenwriter. Season 3, episode 11. August 23, 2019.
This Is the End. 2013. Evan Goldberg and Seth Rogan, directors.
True Romance. 1993. Tony Scott, director.
Turned Out: Sexual Assault behind Bars. 2004. Jonathan Schwartz, director.
Twentynine Palms. 2003. Bruno Dumont, director.
Un Zoo la Nuit. 1987. Jean-Claude Lauzon, director.
Zardoz. 1974. John Boorman, director.

Index

Page numbers in *italic* refer to figures.

ableism, 3, 21, 129, 140, 149, 209–11, 217
Abu Ghraib, 2, 17–18
Adventures of Priscilla, Queen of the Desert, The, 66
Affleck, Ben, 127
AIDS. *See* HIV/AIDS
Ajewole, Samson, 201
Akinnuoye-Agbaje, Adewale, 179
Ali, Mahershala, 66
American Crime, 31, 170–71, 199, 205, 214
   and confession, 188–93, 198, 216
   and masculinity, 193–97
   and the procedural, 189
American History X, 30, 99, 131, 163–67, 178
American Me, 30, 131, 132, 150, 159–63, 166, 167
ancient Greece, 18–19, 64, 198, 223n65, 238n18
. . . And Justice for All, 226n38
Animal Factory, 168
Another Country (Baldwin), 83
Another World, 226n38
Araki, Gregg, 28
Arena Stage, 228n70
Arnold, Tom, 8
Arthur, Karen, 173
Attica Correctional Facility, 38, 84, 172–73
Augustine, 65, 230n21
Avalon, 154
Aztecs, 18, 223n65

Baby Reindeer, 31, 171, 197, 203–6
Bacon, Kevin, 154–57
Baldwin, James, 233n86
   and *Another Country*, 83
   and *Düşenin Dostu*, 81–82
   and erotics of violence, 7, 83, 140
   and *If Beale Street Could Talk*, 30, 59–60, 83–90, 91, 95, 233n89, 234n107
   and *Tell Me How Long the Train's Been Gone*, 232n78
Baptist church, 193, 197–98. *See also* Christianity
Barbash, Uri, 28
BDSM, 138
Beach Boys, 154
Beatty, Ned, 107, 109–15, *110*, *113*, *114*, 236n27, 239n27
Beckett, Samuel, 228n70
Bein, Albert, 50, 228n75
Bell, Kristen, 8, 10
Berkman, Alexander, 35
Beyond the Walls, 28
Big House, The, 228n72
Big Stan, 168–69
Birdman of Alcatraz, 146
Bonds, De'Aundre, 168
Boom Town, 124
Boorman, John, 30, 68–69, 96, 108–15, 236n27
   correspondence with James Dickey, 76, 79
   and nature, 106–7, 116, 235n15

267

Boorman, John (cont'd.)
  and *Pulp Fiction*, 137–38, 166
Boy Erased (Conley), 31, 171, 197–99, 200, 205
  film adaptation, 28, 247n72
Boys in the Band, The, 227n49
Bratt, Benjamin, 228n70
Brenton, Howard, 28
Bridges, Beau, 8
brokenness, 209–11. *See also* ableism; disability; revenge; torture
Bronson, Charles, 144
Brooks, Avery, 164
Brown, Clancy, 144, 148
Brownmiller, Susan, 7, 15–17, 107, 109, 207–9, 221n26
Brutalist, The, 28
buddy film, 30, 123–26, 168–69
Butch Cassidy and the Sundance Kid, 124
Butterfly Effect, The, 57, 168

Cage, The (Cluchey), 29, 50, 54–57, 228n75
Caged, 228n72
Cagney & Lacey, 172–74, 178, 196
Camillo, Marvin Felix, 228n70
Cannes Film Festival, 123, 167
Cast the First Stone (Himes), 59, 90–91, 234nn119–27, 235nn128–31
castration, 4, 27143, 163, 240n39
Catholic church, 159, 187, 205. *See also* Christianity
celibacy, 199–200
Chenoweth, Kristin, 8
child rape, 25, 150–55, 159, 162, 184
Christian, Robert, 44, 226n38
Christianity, 31, 159, 193, 198–200, 205, 247n72
Clarke, Alan, 28
Client, The, 154
Clockwork Orange, A, 107
Close, Eric, 159
Closet Monster, 28
Cluchey, Rick, 29, 50, 54–57, 228n75
Coel, Michaela, 31, 171, 200–203, 206
Come Back Charleston Blue, 90
confession, 12, 31, 171, 207–8 216
  and television, 184, 186–93, 196–205, 247n67

Conley, Garrard, 31, 171, 197–98, 247n68
Conroy, Pat, 241n67
consent, 26–27, 185–86, 200–202, 224n81, 230n21, 243n9
conversion therapy, 171, 197, 199, 247n68
Cooper, Bradley, 8–9
Cooper, Clarence, 44
Cooper, Dennis, 28
Cooper, James Fenimore, 75
Cotton Comes to Harlem, 90
Coward, Cowboy, 109, *111*, *112*, *114*
Crenna, Richard, 173
Criminal Code, The, 50, 228n75
Cromwell, John, 228n72
Crowley, Mart, 227n49
Crudup, Billy, 155, *158*
Cruising, 239n32

Darabont, Frank, 131, 143, 145–48, 241n60, 241n63
Davis, Alan J., 34–36, 37–38, 178
Dazed and Confused, 127
De Niro, Robert, 155
Deadly Justice. *See Rape of Richard Beck, The*
Death Becomes Her, 144
Death Wish, 139
Deathtrap (Levin), 57
Deathwatch (Genet), 228n75
Deliverance (Dickey), 29, 59–60, 71, 90, 92–93
  Baldwin's use of title, 86, 89
  differences between novel and film, 30, 68–70, 109
  film adaptation, 96–98, 115, 116–19, 122–23, 125–26
  and jokes, 127–29, 169
  and masculinity, 75–81, 95, 133, 166, 232n64
  and metaphors, 70, 72–74, 80, 106–8
  pig imagery in film, 109, *110*, 111, 113, 116, 236n27
  referenced by later films, 131, 137–39, *138*, 147, 174, 178–79, 239n27
  see also buddy film; "Dueling Banjos"
Dickey, James, 29, 59–60, 68–70, 72–81, 89, 95, 106, 108–9. *See also Deliverance* (Dickey)
Diner, 154

disability, 5–7, 21, 140, 149, 208, 241n60. *See also* ableism
discourse, defined, 1–3, 23
Donovan, Jeffrey, 156
Douglas Home, William, 39, 50
Duell, Chad, 170
"Dueling Banjos," 69, *70*, 76, 127–29, 239n32
Dunn, Stephen, 28
Düşenin Dostu (Herbert), 81–82, 232n75

Easy Rider, 97, 117
eating, 19, 234n127
Edgerton, Joel, 28, 247n72
Edmond (Mamet), 57
effeminacy, 51, 63, 74, 81. *See also* femininity
Eldard, Ron, 155, *158*
Emerald Forest, The, 235n15
Essiedu, Paapa, 201

Fanon, Frantz, 7, 139, 220n14
Felon, 168
femininity, 13–14, 18, 56, 95, 130, 215, 217
   associations with penetrability, 23
   and *City and the Pillar, The*, 62–64, 66–68
   and *Deliverance*, 72, 74–75, 79–81
   and *Fortune and Men's Eyes*, 39, 41, 44, 82
   and *If Beale Street Could Talk*, 29–30, 87
   and *Oz*, 180, 185
   and *Yesterday Will Make You Cry*, 93
feminism, 7, 11, 15, 23, 24, 173–74
Femme, 66
Fernández, Evelina, 159
fire departments, 2, 194
Fishman, Joseph F., 34–35, 36
Flavin, Martin, 50
Folsom Penitentiary, 159–60
Fontana, Tom, 169, 173, 178, 183, 186, 245n26
Forrest Gump, 131, 137
Forster, E. M., 28, 35
Fortune and Men's Eyes (Herbert), 29, 33–34, 38–44, 66, 225n4, 228n75
   film adaptation, 32–33, 96
   influence on later media, 50–58, 60, 67, 86, 118, 233n81, 243n14
   Istanbul production, 81–82

   London production, 46–47
   premier New York production, 44–46
   Sal Mineo productions, 47–50
Foucault, Michel, 17, 18–19, 63, 187, 192
Fox, Jeremy, 127
Fralick, David Shark, 168
Frankenheimer, John, 146
fraternities, 13, 31
Freeman, Morgan, 144
Freud, Sigmund, 128–29
Friedkin, William, 227n49, 239n32
Front Runner, The (Warren), 57
Furlong, Edward, 163

Gadd, Richard, 31, 171, 203–4, 206
Galsworthy, John, 50
gang rape, 5–6, 32–33, 36, 86
   in *American History X*, 163
   in *American Me*, 159–60
   in *Fortune and Men's Eyes*, 42–43
   in *If Beale Street Could Talk*, 86
   in *Midnight Cowboy*, 98–99, 105
   in *Shawshank Redemption, The*, 143–45, 147
   in *Sleepers*, 154–55
   in *Yes, Daddy*, 199
gender binary, 12, 13, 15, 18, 39, 74, 160
General Hospital, 170
Genet, Jean, 45, 228n75
Gingrich, Newt, 21
Going to Meet the Man (Baldwin), 83
Goldberg, Evan, 239n32
Gómez, Panchito, 159
Gone with the Wind (Mitchell), 24
Goodman-Hill, Tom, 204
Great Escape, The, 146
Greece. *See* ancient Greece
Green Book, 66
Greene, Peter, 137
Grier, David Alan, 127
Grindr, 191–92
Groom, Sam, 243n14

Hackman, Gene, 97, 117, 122, 123–24
Hard to Kill, 144
Harold and Kumar Escape from Guantanamo Bay, 168

Hateful Eight, The, 240n39
Hayworth, Rita, 146
Herbert, John, 29, 32–33, 38–45, 48–57, 82, 91, 226n38
Herlihy, James Leo, 104
Hibbert, Stephen, 138
Hills Have Eyes, The, 117
Himes, Chester, 30, 59–60, 83, 90–95
Hingle, Pat, 174
Hit & Run, 8–11, 33, 169
HIV/AIDS, 149–50, 160
homophobia, 24, 51, 66, 125, 199–200, 201, 209, 242n86
   on *American Crime*, 170, 193, 195
   on *Cagney & Lacey*, 173
   in *Deliverance*, 29, 69–70, 78, 80
homosexuality, alternative concepts, 23, 35–38, 63–64, 83, 192, 230n25
Hooper, Tobe, 138
Howard, John R. K., 5–6, 8
Hudson, Ernie, 179
Huffman, Felicity, 190
Human Rights Watch, 57
Hunting Ground, The, 207, 215, 249n19
Husbands, 124
Hutton, Timothy, 191

I Love You Phillip Morris, 169
I May Destroy You, 31, 171, 197, 200–203, 205–6
I Spit on Your Grave, 236n33
ICE (Immigration and Customs Enforcement), 2, 149, 209
If Beale Street Could Talk (Baldwin), 30, 59–60, 81–90, 93, 95, 140
   film adaptation, 233n87
If He Hollers Let Him Go (Himes), 90
I'll Sleep When I'm Dead, 168
Immigration and Customs Enforcement (ICE), 2, 149, 209
In Living Color, 127
In the Heat of the Night, 117
In Too Deep, 28, 168
Independence of Eddie Rose, The (Yellow Robe), 57
Innocent Man, An, 28

Jackson, Samuel L., 132, 240n39
Jarman, Derek, 12
Jaws, 148
Jenkins, Barry, 233n87
Jessup, Connor, 189
Jewison, Norman, 117, 226n38.
Johnson, James Weldon, 135
jokes about rape, 3, 24, 144, 169, 221n22, 239n32
   as coping mechanism, 30, 127–29
   and *Deliverance*, 69, 76, 127–29
   in *Hit & Run*, 8–11
Just Detention International, 2, 183
Justice (Galsworthy), 50, 228n75

Kane, Sarah, 28
Kantor, Kevin, 31, 211, 213–17
Kaye, Tony, 163–64
Kaz, 243n14
Kelly, Brendan, 183
King, Stephen, 143, 146–47, 241n60, 241n63
King of New York, 144
Kinjite: Forbidden Subjects, 144
kink, 138–39
Kinney, Terry, 156, 177
Kirby, David, 149
Kitch, Kenneth, 228n70
Kubrick, Stanley, 107
Kutcher, Ashton, 168

Lawrence, T. E., 28, 233n86
Lawrence of Arabia, 28, 83, 233n86
Lawrence v. Texas, 226n18
Lean, David, 83, 233n86
Let's Go to Prison, 168
Levin, Ira, 57
Levinson, Barry, 132, 153–59, 241n69
Linklater, Richard, 127
Little Ol' Boy (Bein), 50, 228n75
Lockdown, 168
Loftin, Lennie, 156
London, Jack, 75
London Prison Farm, 90
Lonely Crusade, The (Himes), 90
Longtime Companion, 149
Ludlam, Charles, 227n45

Lupino, Ida, 123
Lynch, Richard, 118, *119*
lynching, 4–5, 84, 135–36, 154

MacKinnon, Catharine, 15–16, 22, 221n35
Malavarca, Eddie, 179
Malintzin, 223n65
Mamet, David, 57
Manhattan Detention Complex, 84, 90
Marowitz, Charles, 46
Maurice (Forster), 35
McBride, Danny, 239n32
McGarry, Pat, 44
McGuire, Ian, 28
McKinney, Bill, 109, *110*, 112, *114*
Medrano, Frank, 144
Memento, 99
metaphors, 11, 14, 21, 24–26
  and *Deliverance*, 70, 72, 74, 76, 78, 80–81, 90
  in film, 98, 106–8, 117, 126, 129
  and *Fortune and Men's Eyes*, 56–57
  and *If Beale Street Could Talk*, 84, 87–88, 90
metonymic displacement, 42, 99–103, 109, 111, 145
Midnight Cowboy, 30, 96–98, 116, 122–23, 127
  influence on later representations, 145, 147, 178
  rape sequence in, 98–105, 108–9, 111, 115, 118–19
  in *Scarecrow* reviews, 122, 123–26
military, 1–2, 10, 18, 67, 124, 195, 209
Mineo, Sal, 46, 47–49
molestation. *See* child rape
Monkey See Monkey Do (Gadd), 203, 204
Monroe, Marilyn, 146
Montez, Mario, 45, 165, 227n45
Moreno, Rita, 176
Morse, David, 173
Motion Picture Association of America, 97
Mudge Boy, The, 168
Murphy, Ryan, 227n49
Murphy's Law, 144
Mysterious Skin, 28

National Prison Rape Elimination Commission, 225n3
Natural, The, 154
Natural Born Killers, 130
Neilson, Anthony, 28
Network, 168
New Hollywood, 30, 97–98, 117, 119, 123, 126, 133
  influence on later films, 130, 239n32
New York Shakespeare Festival, 228n70
Nolte, Nick, 151, *152*
North Water, The (McGuire), 28
Norton, Edward, 163, 165
Not about Nightingales (Williams), 39, 50, 228n75
"*Now Barabbas . . .*" (Douglas Home), 39, 50, 228n75

Of Mice and Men, 124
Ohio State Penitentiary, 90, 92
Oldman, Gary, 240n39
Oleson, Nicholas R.
Opia, Weruche, 201
Ōshima Nagisa, 12
Outrage, 123
Oz, 30–31, 37, 57, 169–71, 173, 174–88, 216

Pacino, Al, 97, 117, *120*, *121*, 122–24,
Palmer, David, 8
Palumbo, John, 180
Papp, Joseph, 228n70
Parker, Alan, 12
Parks-Ramage, Jonathan, 31, 171, 199–200
Patric, Jason, 156, *157*
Peckinpah, Sam, 130
Penn, Arthur, 130
performativity, 17–18, 21, 23, 65, 133–36, 215, 222n40
Perrino, Joe, 154, *154*, 156
Peterson, Benjamin, 31, 211–13, 217
Philadelphia, 149
Philadelphia Prison System, 32–35
Piñero, 228n70
Piñero, Miguel, 29, 50, 54, 57, 228n70
Pitt, Brad, 156, *157*
poetics, 11, 24, 27, 31, 60, 68, 216, 221n23

police
    and Black men, 30, 55, 66, 82–89, 95
    and rape victims, 171, 173, 190–91, 193, 201–3, 214, 216
    and violence, 13, 82–89, 140, 209
Pollari, Joey, 191
pornography, 11, 31, 45, 133, 221n22, 239n29
Prince of Tides, The, 30, 131, 150–53, 157, 162, 166
    differences between novel and film, 241n67
Principal, The, 144
Prison Rape Elimination Act, 2, 225n3
privacy, 20, 135–36, 213, 223n56, 238n18
Production Code, 30, 97–98, 109, 115, 123
Professionals, The, 124
prostitution. *See* sex work
psychoanalysis, 20, 128–29, 171
Pulp Fiction, 25, 30, 130–32, 137–43, 147, 166, 178–79
    and *The Shawshank Redemption*, 143, 145–47, 149–50, 177

Quality of Hurt, The (Himes), 94

race, 3, 5–11, 13–14, 17–18, 24, 30, 34, 60
    and *American Crime*, 246n57
    and *Cagney & Lacey*, 172
    and *Deliverance*, 80, 106, 116–17
    and *Fortune and Men's Eyes*, 33–34, 44, 55
    and *If Beale Street Could Talk*, 83, 88, 90
    and *Oz*, 178
    and prison rape in the 1960s, 36–37
    and *Pulp Fiction*, 137–40
    and *The Shawshank Redemption*, 132, 147, 150
    and *Yesterday Will Make You Cry*, 30
Ralston, Mark, 144, *145*
rape culture, 23, 214–15
Rape of Richard Beck, The, 173–74, 243n12
Rattigan, Terence, 233n86
Ravenhill, Mark, 28
Reagan era, 131
Renfro, Brad, 154, *156*
Reservoir Dogs, 130, 144

Return, The, 28
revenge, 11–13, 25, 30, 130–31, 133, 196, 208–9, 215–17
    and *American History X*, 163–64, 166
    and *American Me*, 162–63, 166
    and *Baby Reindeer*, 206
    and *Deliverance*, 107
    and *Fortune and Men's Eyes*, 43, 51
    and *I May Destroy You*, 202
    and *Oz*, 181, 182, 188
    and *Pulp Fiction*, 137, 141, 143, 150, 177
    and *The Shawshank Redemption*, 148–49, 150, 177
    and *Sleepers*, 153, 156–58
    and *Yes, Daddy*, 200
Reynolds, Burt, 79, 106, *114*
Rhames, Ving, 137, *141*, *142*, 242n85
Rikers Island, 172–73
Robbins, Tim, 143
Rodgers, R. E., 183
Rogan, Seth, 239n32
Romans in Britain, The (Brenton), 28
Ross (Rattigan), 233n86
Rothenberg, David, 43–44
RuPaul's Drag Race, 247n67

Sadler, William, 144
sadomasochism, 138–39, 194–5
Salt, Jennifer, 98
Salt, Waldo, 105
San Francisco Actor's Workshop, 228n70
San Quentin Drama Workshop, 228n70
San Quentin prison, 47, 53, 228n70
Savage, Michael, 25
Savant, Doug, 172
Scarecrow, 30, 97–98, 117–27, 144, 147, 178
Schatzberg, Jerry, 30, 97, 117–18, 123–24
Schlesinger, John, 30, 96, 98–100, 103–5, 109, 111, 124
Screen Test #2, 165
Scum, 28
Seagal, Steven, 144
Seven Pillars of Wisdom (Lawrence), 28, 233n86
sex work, 40, 223–24n67, 227n62
Sexual Offences Act, 1967, 226n18
Shakespeare, William, 233n81

shame, 13–14, 20, 22, 30–31, 35, 41, 165–67, 209–10
   and *American Crime*, 190
   and *American History X*, 163, 165
   and antiquity, 38n18
   and *The City and the Pillar*, 64, 65, 67
   and *Deliverance*, 77, 81
   and *Oz*, 176, 179–80, 188
   and *The Prince of Tides*, 152, 162
   and *Pulp Fiction*, 141–43, 238n23, 242n83
   and *Sleepers*, 158, 162
   and *Vasses*, 213, 217
   and watching movies, 133–36, 168
Shaner, Michael, 159, *161*
Shawshank Redemption, The, 12, 30, 143–50, 167, 177, 179, 183
   as ahistorical, 131–32, 139, 146–47
   and *American Me*, 150, 160, 163
   differences between novel and film, 241n60, 241n63
Sheik, The, 224n74
Shepard, Dax, 8, 10, 11
Shield, The, 170, 184
Short Eyes (Piñero), 29, 50, 54–57, 228n70, 228n75
Shrek Forever After, 127–28
Sierra, Gregory, 172
silence, 1–2, 11, 13, 136, 186–88, 201, 216
   in *The City and the Pillar*, 67
   in *Deliverance*, 80
   in *Fortune and Men's Eyes*, 42
   in 1990s cinema, 142–43, 151–53, 157, 162, 166–67
Simmons, J. K., 176
sissy, 63, 94, 234n125. *See also* effeminacy; femininity
Six Feet Under, 169
Slater, Christian, 240n39
Sleepers, 30, 131–32, 150, 153–59, 162–63, 167, 241n68
Smith, Jack, 227n45
Snowtown Murders, The, 28
South Park, 28, 108
squeal like a pig, 69, 111–13, 115–16, 127–29, 174, 236n27
St. Elsewhere, 173–74, 178
Stacy, Chris, 151, *153*

Stanley, Richard, 243–44n14
Stark, Craig, 240n39
Stoker, Randy, 6–8, 10–11
Stonewall Riots, 38, 48–49, 226n18
Stop Prisoner Rape, 2, 183
Streetcar Named Desire, A, 123
Streisand, Barbra, 108, 151
Sturges, John, 146
Sudduth, Skipp, 179

Tarantino, Quentin, 25, 30, 108, 130–31, 137–41, 166, 240n39, 242n85
   and New Hollywood, 97, 239n32
Tatum, Channing, 239n32
Taylor, Lili, 189
Tell Me How Long the Train's Been Gone (Baldwin), 81–82, 232n78
Ten, The, 168
Tergesen, Lee, 176
Texas Chain Saw Massacre, The, 117
Theatre of the Riverside Church, 228n70
Thirteen Reasons Why, 247n67
This Is the End, 239n32
Tombs, The, 84, 90
torture, 9, 13, 17–18, 20–21, 23, 143, 209, 222n45
Travolta, John, 137
True Romance, 130, 144, 240n39
Trump, Donald, 25, 57–58
Turned Out, 28
Twentynine Palms, 28

Valdez, Luis, 162
Valli, Frankie, 154
Vidal, Gore, 29, 59–67, 75, 230n18, 230n25
Vietnam War, 60, 72, 75
violate, defined, 3–4
violet, 3–4, 213, 249n14
Vivian Beaumont Theatre, 228n70
Voight, Jon, 97, 98, *100*, *102*, *103*, 109, *112*, *114*

Waiting for Godot (Beckett), 228n70
Walken, Christopher, 238n23
Walker, Eamonn, 180
Warhol, Andy, 165, 227n45
Warren, Patricia Nell, 57

Wayans, Damon, 127
Wedding Crashers, 8
Weiss, Peter, 45
Welch, Raquel, 146
Whitaker, Duane, 137, *138*
White, Gary Michael, 118
white supremacist violence, 4–5, 7, 17, 30, 75, 135–36, 139
    and *American History X*, 163–65
    and *American Me*, 159
    and *If Beale Street Could Talk*, 83–88, 95, 140
    and *Oz*, 176, 178–79, 182
Whitmore, James, 146
Williams, Tennessee, 39, 50
Willis, Bruce, 137, 139, *142*
Wingate, Josh, 170
Winters, Dean, 177
Winters, Scott William, 177

women as victims, 12, 15–19, 23, 26–27, 123, 161, 215, 221n26
    on television, 171–74

Yates, Peter, 28
Yearwood, Trey, 151
Yellow Robe, William S., 57
Yes, Daddy (Parks-Ramage), 31, 171, 197, 199–200, 202
Yesterday Will Make You Cry (Himes), 30, 59–60, 90–95. *See also Cast the First Stone* (Himes)

Zarchi, Meir, 236n33
Zardoz, 235n15
Zemeckis, Robert, 131
Zito, Chuck, 180
Zoo la Nuit, Un, 28
Zoot Suit Riots, 159, 242n72

www.ingramcontent.com/pod-product-compliance
Lightning Source LLC
Chambersburg PA
CBHW030530230426
43665CB00010B/832